# ⤳ CATO ⤳
# SUPREME COURT
# REVIEW
## *2007 — 2008*

# ⟨ CATO ⟩
# SUPREME COURT
# REVIEW
## 2 0 0 7 — 2 0 0 8

ROGER PILON
Publisher

ILYA SHAPIRO
Editor in Chief

ROBERT A. LEVY
Associate Editor

TIMOTHY LYNCH
Associate Editor

**CENTER FOR CONSTITUTIONAL STUDIES**

CATO
INSTITUTE
Washington, D.C.

THE CATO SUPREME COURT REVIEW (ISBN 978-1-933995-17-5) is published annually at the close of each Supreme Court term by the Cato Institute, 1000 Massachusetts Ave., N.W., Washington, D.C. 20001-5403.

CORRESPONDENCE. Correspondence regarding subscriptions, changes of address, procurement of back issues, advertising and marketing matters, and so forth, should be addressed to:

Publications Department
The Cato Institute
1000 Massachusetts Ave., N.W.
Washington, D.C. 20001

All other correspondence, including requests to quote or reproduce material, should be addressed to the editor.

CITATIONS: Citation to this volume of the Review should conform to the following style: 2007-2008 Cato Sup. Ct. Rev. (2008).

DISCLAIMER. The views expressed by the authors of the articles are their own and are not attributable to the editor, the editorial board, or the Cato Institute.

INTERNET ADDRESS. Articles from past editions are available to the general public, free of charge, at www.cato.org/pubs/scr.

Printed in the United States of America.

Cato Institute
1000 Massachusetts Ave., N.W.
Washington, D.C. 20001
www.cato.org

# Contents

CONTENTS

FOREWORD

# Is the Court Any Longer Constrained by the Constitution?

*Roger Pilon*

The Cato Institute's Center for Constitutional Studies is pleased to publish this seventh volume of the *Cato Supreme Court Review*, an annual critique of the Court's most important decisions from the term just ended, plus a look at the cases ahead—all from a classical Madisonian perspective, grounded in the nation's first principles, liberty and limited government. We release this volume each year at Cato's annual Constitution Day conference. And each year in this space I discuss briefly a theme that seemed to emerge from the Court's term or from the larger setting in which the term unfolded.

This was the third term of the Roberts Court—the second full term with both Chief Justice John Roberts and Justice Samuel Alito—but still it appears too early to place any clear stamp on its character. At term's end, Court-watchers were quick to note that the Court handed down only 67 merits opinions, the fewest in over half a century. And unlike in the previous term when the Court divided 5–4 in 24 cases, fully one-third of its docket, in this term it divided 5–4 in only 11 cases—although 3 other decisions, absent recusals, would likely have been 5–4. It would seem, therefore, that the Chief Justice was gradually moving the Court toward speaking with one voice, a hope he had expressed during his 2005 Senate confirmation hearings. But when looked at from the other end, that hope receded, for only 20 percent of the cases were decided by a fully unanimous Court (no dissents or concurrences), which contrasts with 25 percent in the previous term, and 45 percent in the term before that. Clearly, the court is still divided. And the divide has deep roots.

At least three of those 5–4 decisions—*Kennedy v. Louisiana, District of Columbia v. Heller,* and *Boumediene v. Bush*—take us to constitutional first principles—to basic questions of political and legal theory and, in particular, to questions about the authority of the Court under that theory. The Court articulated its authority seminally in *Marbury v. Madison*, of course, a unanimous opinion that drew upon ideas that had evolved over years and upon principles that underpinned both the nation's founding and the Constitution itself. At the Founding, the Declaration of Independence had set forth the nation's theory of political legitimacy: that individuals are born free and are endowed with equal rights, including the right to create governments to secure those rights—their "just powers" derived "from the Consent of the Governed." Eleven years later, speaking for "We the People of the United States," the Framers drafted a new constitution that largely reflected that theory of legitimacy. Once ratified through state conventions, the document became the positive law under which the founding generation, their posterity, and those who in time would become Americans would govern themselves—which we've done ever since.

Thus, the Constitution is a compact among Americans—among "We the People of the United States"—reflecting the principles and legal relationships we've ratified—originally, and through amendment—that we believe will best serve the ends set forth in the document's Preamble. More precisely, it sets forth powers that have been granted by the people, vested in particular offices, and then checked and balanced against each other to ensure that they fully serve their ends, but only those ends.

But the positive law established by the Constitution does not enforce itself, of course. In particular, when disagreements arise over the document's rules or over actions taken under them, a disinterested "umpire," as Chief Justice Roberts has put it, must settle those disagreements. Under our written Constitution that role falls ultimately to the Supreme Court. In *Marbury* Chief Justice John Marshall stated that clearly: He held, to put it succinctly, that the Court had jurisdiction to say that, in the matter before it, it had no jurisdiction. Thus, in one fell swoop the Court announced both its power and the limits on its power.

What Marshall was saying more particularly was that pursuant to the "Judicial Power" the people had vested in the Supreme Court under Article III, it was the duty of the Court "to say what the law is," as Alexander Hamilton had explained in *Federalist* No. 78; but that in exercising that jurisdiction the Court had looked again at the constitutional text and found that it lacked jurisdiction over the case before it; that the act of Congress purporting to expand the Court's jurisdiction over the matter at hand amounted to giving the Court more power than the people had authorized for it; and that, accordingly, the act of Congress was unconstitutional—the people had not given Congress that power. Thus, the Constitution is a document of positive law, to be sure; but its theory of legitimacy is grounded in the natural rights branch of natural law. It is the document through which the people, by right, granted, limited, and reserved their various natural powers.

Questions about the Court's authority or jurisdiction were at issue in the three cases mentioned above. In *Kennedy v. Louisiana*, Justice Anthony Kennedy, writing for himself and Justices John Paul Stevens, David Souter, Ruth Bader Ginsburg, and Stephen Breyer, held that the Eighth Amendment's ban on cruel and unusual punishments prohibited states from imposing the death penalty for the crime of child rape. The jurisdictional issue here is less clear than it was in *Marbury*, where mandamus was not among the categories of cases over which the Constitution had granted the Court original jurisdiction. Here the Court clearly had jurisdiction to decide whether Louisiana's statute authorizing capital punishment for child rape satisfied the Eighth Amendment. But the Court's exercise of its jurisdiction is what raises a further "jurisdictional" issue, as it were, bringing into question the Court's authority to rule as it did.

As with the Fourth Amendment's evaluative terms—"unreasonable" and "probable"—applying the Eighth Amendment's "cruel and unusual" involves policy questions and value judgments traditionally left to the discretion of the states and the political branches—except when such judgments go beyond the outer bounds those terms connote. There is no bright line here, to be sure, just as there is not in the jurisdictional questions that surround the political question doctrine, among other things. But that should not surprise: There are many vague matters of that kind that the people left to the political arena (state and federal), to be checked by the courts only in those exceptional cases that raise fairly clear constitutional concerns. Were it otherwise, were courts to make all or most of the competing policy judgments that surround the Eighth (and the Fourth) Amendment, they would be acting, in effect, like the political branches, yet would be immune from political accountability. That kind of judicial micromanagement is today upon us, of course, but not because the Constitution authorizes it. In fact, Justice Alito, writing for the dissent, chides the Court on just that point when he writes, sardonically, that, "in the end, what matters is the Court's 'own judgment' regarding 'the acceptability of the death penalty.'"

Those same issues arose in *District of Columbia v. Heller*, a decision Seventh Circuit Judge Richard Posner, writing in *The New Republic*, called "the most noteworthy of the Court's recent term." That it was, because in overturning the D.C. ban on handguns and functional firearms, the Court, for the first time in its history, set forth the contours of the Second Amendment. Yet Posner finds Justice Antonin Scalia's opinion for the Court, joined by Chief Justice Roberts and Justices Kennedy, Alito, and Clarence Thomas, to be "questionable in both method and result." Disparaging Scalia's use of history as well as his originalist method, Posner appears to make the not uncommon mistake of reading the amendment's militia clause as establishing not a sufficient but a necessary condition for there being a right to keep and bear arms. (In truth, his argument on the point is less than clear.) Thus, he concludes, notwithstanding Scalia's close parsing of the text, that the amendment "creates no right to the private possession of guns for hunting or other sport, or for the defense of person or property."

Posner's larger concern, however, is to urge what he calls "loose construction," a "flexible" method of interpretation "designed to adapt the Constitution (so far as the text permits) to current conditions," such as "the crime problem in the large crime-ridden metropolises of twenty-first-century America." Had the Court done what he wished it had and upheld the D.C. gun ban "it would merely have been leaving the issue of gun control to the political process." Yet Posner notes in conclusion that this "preference for judicial modesty—for less interference by the Supreme Court with the other branches of government—cannot be derived by some logical process from constitutional text or history." Rather, "it would have to be imposed" as "a discretionary choice by the justices."

Perhaps "judicial modesty" cannot be derived from constitutional text or history, but judicial authority surely can, at least in basic outline. The Court was authorized, instituted, and empowered for a reason, after all, which text and history speak to—not precisely, to be sure, but clearly enough for most justices to have understood, for a good part of our history, the scope and limits of their authority. And in *Heller*, I submit, the majority understood both. Leaving the issue of gun control to the political process, which the Court effectively did for over 200 years, worked well in most cases in most places, as Posner notes. But when and where it did not, where draconian restrictions like the District of Columbia's emerged from the political process, the individual rights the Second Amendment seemed to protect were ignored. Posner contends that *Heller* gives short shrift to federalism: "Why should the views of a national majority control?" he asks—and rightly so were this merely a political matter.

But it is not. As the *Heller* majority understood, the Second Amendment stands for something, and the Court had not only the authority but the duty to say what—and to make it clear too, as Scalia did, that the something for which the amendment stands cannot be diluted under the so-called rational basis test, which would reduce the amendment to a nullity. But the majority understood also that there are limits on the Court's authority. Inherent in the firearms issue are contextual value judgments concerning risk, about which reasonable people can reasonably disagree, much as in *Kennedy v. Louisiana* concerning punishment. Thus, having secured the principle of the matter and the general contours of the amendment, the Court did not attempt further to micromanage the details of our Second Amendment rights but left that, by implication, to the states and the political branches. There is already litigation over those details in lower courts, and over *Heller*'s application to state regulations. But if the Supreme Court respects the limits on its authority, a good many of those details will in fact be left to politics. As *Heller* co-counsel Clark Neily notes in his essay below, "relatively few firearms restrictions are likely to fall."

But if there is an area in which Posner's "loose construction" and its attendant deference to the political branches are in order, it is foreign affairs. Judge Posner's son, Professor Eric Posner, makes that clear in his essay below on *Boumediene v. Bush*, where once again questions about the authority of the Court and its limits come to the fore. As in previous volumes of this *Review*, when certain seriously contested decisions come down from the Court, we present opposing views—which is not to say that this Foreword remains neutral. Thus, the reader will find below that Professor Posner's essay, highly critical of the *Boumediene* decision, is followed by Professor David Cole's strongly supportive essay. Here I want simply to draw forth a few points about judicial authority and its limits as they emerge from the Court's opinion in the light shed by those essays.

In *Boumediene*, writing again for Justices Stevens, Souter, Ginsburg, and Breyer, Justice Kennedy held, as Posner states it, "that noncitizens held at Guantanamo Bay have the constitutional privilege of habeas corpus and that the review procedures established by the Detainee Treatment Act do not provide an adequate substitute." In crafting a detainee policy for the ongoing war on terror, the Bush administration had relied on the Court's 1950 decision in *Johnson v. Eisentrager* where, as Cole puts it, "the Supreme Court had expressly ruled that the writ of habeas corpus was unavailable to enemy fighters captured and detained abroad during wartime;" and, indeed, "both the district court and the court of appeals had found that decision to be controlling, and no subsequent case law had directly undermined its reasoning." The administration can be forgiven, then, for believing that, as Cole notes, "the government had precedent on its side."

But in a series of very recent sharply divided decisions, the Court has changed course. Briefly, by way of context, in 2004, in *Rasul v. Bush*, the Court held that *statutory* habeas reached Guantanamo Bay; and, in *Hamdi v. Rumsfeld*, it held that the detainees were entitled to contest their status as enemy combatants. Both the administration and Congress responded. The administration established Combatant Status Review Tribunals (CSRTs), which subsequently determined that the *Boumediene* petitioners were enemy combatants, prompting them to file the *constitutional* habeas writs at issue here. And Congress passed first the Detainee Treatment Act—limited by the Court in 2006 in *Hamdan v. Rumsfeld*—and then the Military Commissions Act, stripping federal district courts of jurisdiction over habeas writs filed by noncitizens held at Guantanamo Bay while giving the D.C. Circuit exclusive authority to conduct a limited review of CSRT determinations.

Thus, the *Boumediene* majority rejected not simply the administration's (and most others') understanding of the law, but also Congress's efforts to respond to the Court's changes in the law. Echoing the powerful dissents of Chief Justice Roberts and Justice Scalia, both Posner and Cole remark on how breathtaking a decision it was. Calling the decision "groundbreaking," Cole notes that (1) "for the first time in its history, the Supreme Court declared unconstitutional a law enacted by Congress and signed by the president on an issue of military policy in a time of armed conflict;" (2) "also for the first time, the Court extended constitutional protections to noncitizens outside U.S. territory during wartime:" indeed, to "'enemy aliens'—foreign nationals said to be associated with our enemy in wartime"—despite having said as recently as 2001 that "the Constitution was no solace for foreign nationals outside our borders;" and (3) "only on two prior occasions has the Court actually declared a jurisdiction-stripping law unconstitutional, and on both occasions there were rationales for doing so that were independent of the pure question of jurisdiction."

Yet for all the breathtaking lawmaking the five justices undertook, Cole offers us an all-but-breathless apology. "The real significance of the Court's decision" he writes, "lies not in whether it correctly applied or modified past precedent to a novel context, but in what it portends for modern-day conceptions of sovereignty, territoriality, and rights." It "reflects new understandings of these traditional conceptions, understandings that pierce the veil of sovereignty, reject formalist fictions of territoriality where the state exercises authority beyond its borders, and insist on the need for judicial review to safeguard the human rights of citizens and noncitizens alike." Indeed, *Boumediene* "fits comfortably within an important transnational trend of recent years," Cole points out, citing foreign courts that are playing "an increasingly aggressive role in reviewing and invalidating security measures that trench on individual rights"— rights drawn from the UN's Universal Declaration of Human Rights, the International Covenant on Civil and Political Rights, and the European Convention on Human Rights, among other sources.

But it is just that "significance" that most concerns Posner. To frame the issue he notes that while Justice Kennedy invokes separation-of-powers principles in reaching his conclusion, it is a focus on logistical concerns that looms largest in the opinion—there are just not that many *practical* problems with extending habeas rights to Guantanamo detainees. Yet in *Eisentrager* Justice Robert Jackson had rested his decision denying habeas on two main grounds: In Posner's words, "the interests of these overseas aliens do not 'count' like those of Americans, and the logistical demands on the military would be unreasonable." Kennedy "barely sees, and hardly acknowledges, the first point," Posner observes. "That leaves him with the logistical issue, which seems to melt away for Guantanamo Bay." But it leaves also a question: Why does Kennedy not see what seemed natural to Jackson, that nonresident aliens don't have the same rights as Americans? The answer, Posner says, is that "Justice Kennedy is a cosmopolitan."

"Judicial cosmopolitanism" stands for the idea that "judges have a constitutional obligation to protect the interests of noncitizens," as Posner puts it. To be sure, *resident* aliens have certain rights, both statutory and constitutional. But the idea that nonresident aliens have interests that deserve constitutional protection secured by American judges raises fundamental questions about the nature of the political community, questions that go well beyond the Court's increasing citations of foreign law as evidence of "evolving social values" in death penalty, gun control, and other such cases. Posner's essay is a theoretically sophisticated critique of the rationales one finds in the literature on the extraterritorial application of the Constitution. Drawing on democratic failure theory, and distinguishing arguments based on the systematic exclusion of certain groups from the political decisionmaking process, on one hand, and arguments based on net social welfare, on the other, he finds both wanting, if not impossible for judges to execute. And he concludes by asking whether Kennedy's cosmopolitan approach is wise, which raises policy questions more appropriately left to the political branches, not to judges with no special competence or role in such matters. Indeed, addressing commonly heard arguments based on "reciprocity" (if we respect their rights, they'll respect ours), Posner writes that "unilateral action by courts to grant unreciprocated benefits to noncitizens simply weakens the bargaining power of their own government."

Consequentialism aside, the argument against judicial cosmopolitanism is rooted at bottom in nothing less than the Constitution itself. As outlined above, the Constitution is a compact among "We the People of the United States." Foreigners are simply not party to it. The Constitution sets forth limited powers that have been delegated by the people and vested in certain offices. As *Marbury* made clear, power exercised beyond that delegated is *ultra vires* and hence unconstitutional—there, the power to hear a matter not authorized for the Court, and the power to grant that power through legislation. Judges are authorized to interpret and apply the law in cases or controversies properly before them, which may entail "discovering" rights "retained by the people" pursuant to the Ninth Amendment. But "the people" referenced in that amendment are the American people—"We the People of the United States," who ratified the Constitution and continue to consent to it, as best we can as a practical matter, by continuing to live under it. We delegated power over foreign affairs primarily to the executive branch, to be shared with Congress pursuant to its relevant enumerated powers.

It is those political branches that set foreign policy, checked by the courts when the policy is *ultra vires* or violates the rights of Americans or resident aliens. In that regard, Guantanamo Bay may have been a policy failure, Posner writes, "for which the Bush administration is responsible. Governments make policy mistakes all the time; it is not the role of the courts to correct them." But Cole would have judges securing human rights that "are predicated not on an individual's geographic location, nor on his or her relation to the state, but on human dignity." Set aside just where a judge is to "find" such rights ("periodic holidays with pay"?—article 24 of the UN Universal Declaration of Human Rights): Where does a judge find the *authority* to find those rights? According to our Declaration of Independence, to be "just" that power must be "derived from the Consent of the Governed." Where in the Constitution is such wide ranging judicial power enumerated? Cole tells us that "the international human rights regime insists that democracy is not the ultimate test of a legitimate government, but that respect for inalienable human rights is." That conflates moral and political legitimacy. And therein lies the Achilles' heel of this new "international human rights regime." It trades political legitimacy, which has been difficult enough to achieve over the long course of human history, for an undefined "moral legitimacy" tethered to the most evanescent and, indeed, disputed of institutions.

Our judges have a hard enough time discerning and applying American law. Do we need any better example than the *Boumediene* decision itself? Rather than defer to the political branches that had crafted a detainee policy in the give-and-take of politics, the Court majority rejected that political compromise; substituted its own "all-things-considered textual analysis [that] gives rise to few principles of law," as even Cole points out, leaving "government officials guessing" and "the Court a relatively free hand;" and then left the details for lower courts to work out. Well, barely a month after the decision came down we got a glimpse of how that process is working when the Fourth Circuit, sitting en banc in *Al-Marri v. Pucciarelli*, split 5–4 on the two questions before it, with only one of the judges in the majority on both questions, in a decision that generated seven separate opinions and ran on for some 216 pages. And of course the case is not finished but instead was remanded to the district court for further proceedings. There is a reason the Framers left foreign policy, and war in particular, mainly to the political branches. The increasing "judicialization of war," as it is known, raises anew the question whether the Court is any longer constrained by the Constitution.

# Introduction

*Ilya Shapiro**

This is the seventh volume of the *Cato Supreme Court Review*, the nation's first in-depth critique of the most recently completed Supreme Court term. We release this journal every year on September 17, Constitution Day, about two and a half months after the previous term concludes and two weeks before the next one begins. We are proud of the speed with which we publish this tome—authors of articles about the last-decided cases have little more than a month to provide us full drafts—and of its accessibility, at least insofar as the Court's opinions allow for that. This is not a typical law review, after all, whose 100-page articles use more space for footnotes than article text. (I say this somewhat shamelessly, as the author of both the longest article in this volume and the one with by far the most footnotes.) Instead, this is a book about law intended for everyone from lawyers and judges to educated laymen and interested citizens.

And we are happy to confess our biases: We approach our subject matter from a classical Madisonian perspective, with a focus on individual liberty, property rights, and federalism, and a vision of a government of delegated, enumerated, and thus limited powers. We also try to maintain a strict separation of politics (or policy) and law; just because something is legal does not mean it's good policy, and vice versa. Similarly, certain decisions must necessarily be left to the political process: We aim to be governed by laws, not lawyers. Just as a good lawyer will present all plausibly legal options to his client, a good public official will recognize that the ultimate buck stops with him.

Having said that, let's take a quick survey of the term that was. October Term 2007 was characterized, as many have been in recent years, by several high-profile 5–4 decisions—cases about the rights

*Senior Fellow in Constitutional Studies, Cato Institute, and Editor-in-Chief, *Cato Supreme Court Review*.

of detainees in Guantanamo, the Second Amendment, and capital child rape, for example. But, unlike last year, the term saw an even greater number of very high-profile, difficult, important cases that were decided by large majorities. This latter occurrence is in contradistinction to October Term 2006, when every major case—and a full third of the total 72 cases!—broke 5–4. That term, Justice Anthony Kennedy was in the majority for every single one of those narrow decisions, dissenting only twice altogether. The term just concluded saw fewer 5–4 splits—interestingly, there were also fewer unanimous and 8–1 decisions—and Chief Justice John Roberts was the leading majoritarian, voting 90 percent of the time on the winning side.

Given the relatively small number of decided cases—the Court filed a leisurely 67 opinions on the merits after argument, the lowest number since 1953—all these statistics need to be taken with a grain of salt. And for whatever the tealeaf-reading is worth, it's largely a function of the vagaries of the docket. The docket itself does seem to be changing as the Chief Justice and Justice Samuel Alito get settled on the Court; for reasons I won't go into here, we see relatively more business cases, as well as more technical issues of statutory interpretation (as opposed to hot-button constitutional disputes). And the cases tend to be decided along narrower grounds, perhaps reflecting the "minimalist" approach Chief Justice Roberts advocated at his confirmation hearings. So, even if Kennedy remains the "swing vote" on most of the cases making headlines, it is not wholly accurate to label this the "Justice Kennedy court."[1]

Turning to the *Review*, the volume begins, as always, with the text of the previous year's B. Kenneth Simon Lecture in Constitutional Thought, which in 2007 was given by Judge Janice Rogers Brown of the U.S. Court of Appeals for the D.C. Circuit. Judge Brown focuses on the First Amendment to build provocatively on an idea that often appears in these pages: that economic, personal, and political rights are indivisible. Invoking the likes of Tocqueville, Hayek, Lincoln, and Kurt Vonnegut's character Harrison Bergeron, she inveighs against the "new censors," the "new neutrals" and the "new moralists." These groups present challenges to the intellectual

---

[1] Linda Greenhouse, On Court That Defied Labeling, Kennedy Made the Boldest Mark, New York Times, June 29, 2008, at A1. (Full disclosure: Greenhouse quoted me in this article on a different point.)

freedom and marketplace of ideas that have spurred the American qua classical liberal rejection of speech regulation, but Judge Brown is hopeful that all is not lost.

We move then to the 2007 Term, beginning with a point-counter-point between Professors Eric Posner of the University of Chicago and David Cole of Georgetown on what was probably the most controversial issue of the past term: Whether enemy combatants captured abroad as part of the U.S.-led war on terror have a right to challenge their detention and, if so, what kind of review is appropriate. These sorts of national security cases form a growing part of the Court's docket (and even more so that of the D.C. Circuit) and highlight the fault lines among competing theories of executive, legislative, and judicial power. They also evince distinct ideas about the relationship between domestic and international law and consti-tutionalism more broadly.

Posner sees the Court's decision in *Boumediene v. Bush*, which held that noncitizen enemy combatants captured abroad and detained at Guantanamo have the constitutional privilege of habeas corpus, as a move toward "judicial cosmopolitanism." He posits that, more than resolving a relatively simple (though deep) disagreement over how the Constitution divides power among the branches of govern-ment, Justice Kennedy's opinion advanced "the emerging view that the interests of nonresident aliens deserve constitutional protection secured by judicial review." Kennedy's opinion might seem modest and relatively innocuous, but Posner shows how it threatens the entire American constitutional order—and indeed all of modern political theory.

In stark contrast, Cole agrees with *Boumediene* and suggests that it did not go far enough because it "merely decided . . . a question the Court seemed to have decided four years earlier." He notes that the case was nevertheless groundbreaking, for at least three reasons: 1) Never before has the Court struck down a law enacted by Con-gress and signed by the president on an issue of military policy in a time of armed conflict; 2) this is also the first time the Court extended constitutional protections to noncitizens outside U.S. terri-tory during wartime; and 3) the Court declared unconstitutional a federal law restricting federal court jurisdiction in the absence of rationales independent of the pure question of jurisdiction. Cole ultimately argues that, in moving away from traditional understandings of sovereignty, territoriality, and rights, the Court "ushers U.S. law into the 21st century."

Leaving issues of national security but staying in the realm of foreign affairs, I tackle the most complicated case of the year: *Medellín v. Texas*, which involved treaty interpretation, federalism, separation of powers, and criminal procedure. *Medellín's* convoluted factual and legal history take longer to explain than to analyze, but the significance of the case outstrips even its fascinating twists and turns. At bottom, the case centered on a ruling by the so-called World Court, and President George W. Bush's attempt to enforce it against Texas state courts. The Supreme Court held that neither an international judgment based on a non-self-executing treaty nor a presidential memorandum creates binding domestic law. This was a great victory for sovereignty, democracy, and federalism; but how long the Court can resist "global governance"—the complement to Posner's judicial cosmopolitanism—remains an open question.

Frequent *Review* contributor and Cato amicus brief author Erik Jaffe then looks at two cases dealing with the regulation of political parties and elections. The outcomes of the *López Torres* and *Washington State Grange* cases are not as important, he argues, as the weaknesses they reveal in how courts currently today protect speech and association rights in electoral contexts. The decisions "illustrate the First Amendment problems and confusion arising from the dual public and private roles, and excessive entanglement, of political parties in formal election mechanisms." Jaffe urges that parties be treated as the private expressive associations they are. Thus, courts and legislatures should separate the public function of regulating ballot access from the private associative advocacy and activities of political parties.

Next we have a thoroughly engaging walk through the instant classic "D.C. gun case," which has already generated follow-on litigation around the country over a part of the Constitution—the Second Amendment—that had lain dormant for so long. Clark Neily, senior attorney at the Institute for Justice and co-counsel in *District of Columbia v. Heller*, revisits the intellectual history interpreting the right "to keep and bear arms," the background to the suit he filed with Alan Gura and my Cato colleague Bob Levy, the case before the Court, and the aftermath of Justice Antonin Scalia's historic opinion striking down D.C.'s ban on functional firearms. In addition to lawsuits now pending in Chicago, San Francisco, and elsewhere, the case has also produced challenges to the substitute regulations the D.C. Council implemented in *Heller*'s wake.

Young scholar Edward Loya, about to join the Criminal Division of the U.S. Department of Justice, provides our lone contribution in the area of criminal law. Loya argues, through the spectrum of *Danforth v. Minnesota* and *Virginia v. Moore*, that the Roberts Court increasingly stands for judicial supremacy—that, for good or ill, the interpretative buck stops with the Supreme Court. Ultimately, whether dealing with a criminal defendant's right to confront his accuser or the right to be free from unreasonable search and seizure, "states can create and administer greater protections than those provided in [the] Constitution, [but] the application of the Constitution should remain the same in every state."

Next, appellate labor lawyers Bill Kilberg and Jennifer Schulp (Kilberg was the youngest-ever solicitor of the Department of Labor) take on *Chamber of Commerce v. Brown*. In *Chamber v. Brown*, the Court invalidated a California law that prohibited the recipients of state program funds—everything from MediCal reimbursements to payments on construction contracts—from using those funds to speak on unionization-related issues. The Court found the law preempted by the National Labor Relations Act because the state was regulating in an area Congress had "protected and reserved for market freedom." Aside from the technical labor law questions, the case also raised issues of a state's attaching unconstitutional conditions to employers' First Amendment rights to freedom of speech.

In the first of four articles on the Court's business docket, *Review* board member Adam Pritchard of the University of Michigan presents a fascinating analysis of the state of securities law in the wake of class action reform. *Stoneridge v. Scientific-Atlanta* was the biggest securities case to come before the Court in decades. While the Court correctly rejected an implied cause of action that would have exposed to liability third parties who made no fraudulent public statements, Pritchard argues that the way the Court thinks about securities cases generally is misguided as a matter of political economy. Congress and the SEC having also previously failed at reforming this area of law, Pritchard suggests that shareholders should take it upon themselves to amend articles of incorporation in a way that better deters fraud.

Experienced commercial litigators Dan Troy—previously chief counsel of the FDA, now general counsel at GlaxoSmithKline—and Rebecca Wood then survey the regulatory preemption cases before the Court. From a wide-ranging docket spanning important cases on medical device regulation, arbitration clauses, the aforementioned NLRA, and punitive damages relating to the Exxon Valdez oil spill, the authors find several trends: 1) a focus on statutory interpretation rather than constitutional conflict; 2) preemption where a case involves a special national interest or calibrated judgment by an expert federal agency; and 3) the Court's increasing comfort with an agency's having applied its considered judgment within the scope of its delegated power. All these trends point to greater uniformity in the justices' votes on preemption issues.

Administrative lawyers Richard Bress, Michael Gergen, and Stephanie Lim grapple with *Morgan Stanley Capital Group v. Public Utility District No. 1*, the most important energy regulation case in years. Arising out of the California electricity crisis of 2000–01, this case tested the integrity of contract law generally, with energy buyers wanting to modify previously negotiated contracts—whose prices were high relative to historic prices but lower than spot prices during the crisis—when prices dropped. While the Federal Energy Regulatory Commission rejected such ex post facto complaints, the Ninth Circuit ruled that, regardless even of a review for reasonableness, FERC must lower rates to protect consumer welfare. Bress, Gergen, and Lim explain how and why the Supreme Court disagreed, saying in essence that "a deal is still a deal."

Rounding out our business law quartet, Scott Kieff examines the latest in a continuing trend in patent cases of Supreme Court reversals of Federal Circuit decisions. The Court in *Quanta v. LG Electronics* decided that a patent license from LG to Intel that was limited to exclude Intel's customers (such as Quanta) would be treated as also giving patent permission to those Intel customers. Kieff argues, not uncontroversially, that the Court got it wrong—unanimously!—complicating future patent transactions and thereby preventing entrepreneurial efficiencies and innovation. One reading would limit the Court's holding to the failure of a poorly written contract in this particular case. If Kieff is right, lower courts would be well advised to take that narrow view.

Finally, SCOTUSblog founder and Supreme Court practitioner Tom Goldstein, along with SCOTUSblog contributor Ben Winograd, look ahead to October Term 2008. Possibly reversing a much-noted trend, the Court is now on pace to hear more cases than it has in over 20 years—and it has front-loaded its docket to buy time for opinion-writing at the end of the term. The Court will hear significant cases in the areas of voting rights, national security, the First Amendment (including private speech in a public forum and obscenity regulation), separation of powers (including a rare Appointments Clause case), and criminal law (Fourth and Sixth Amendments), as well as big-dollar business cases involving FDA preemption, punitive damages, and international trade. While there is no *Heller* or *Medellín* on the horizon, we're certainly in for another big year.

*      *      *

This is the first volume of the *Cato Supreme Court Review* that I have edited, and I could not have done it without more than a little help from many, many friends. I first need to thank our contributors—one of the most distinguished groups we've ever had—for sharing our pain of putting this *Review* together while colleagues are on vacation or otherwise enjoying the "easy living" of summertime. I should single out Tom Goldstein, not for hitting his deadlines or being easy to work with (though he was fine on both counts) but for creating and expanding SCOTUSblog, which is easily the most useful resource available for us Court-watchers. Following the Supreme Court is a bit like Kremlinology: Any lawyer worth his salt can analyze opinions after they come out, but you make your name by anticipating trends and noticing operational minutiae. SCOTUSblog is the best decoder ring around for understanding the machinations of One First Street and reading between the lines of its *Pravda*.

Thanks also to my colleagues at Cato's Center for Constitutional Studies, Bob Levy and Tim Lynch, who provided valuable counsel especially on the Second Amendment and criminal law, respectively. A big thanks to research assistant Jonathan Blanks for making the trains run on time, and to interns Seth Bailey, Adam Peshek, Roberto Valenzuela, and Curtis Waldo for doing some of the more thankless (except here) tasks. Neither the *Review* nor our Constitution Day conference would have gotten done without them. Finally, thanks to Roger Pilon, the founder and spiritual guru of this now well-established journal. Roger plucked me from the Big Law trenches and into a whole new career path; so far, so good.

As my predecessors Mark Moller and James Swanson did, I reiterate our hope that this collection of essays will deepen and promote the Madisonian first principles of our Constitution, giving renewed voice to the Framers' fervent wish that we have a government of laws and not of men. In so doing, we hope also to do justice to a rich legal tradition—now eclipsed by the modern regulatory state—in which judges, politicians, and ordinary citizens alike understood that the Constitution reflects and protects the natural rights of life, liberty, and property, and serves as a bulwark against the abuse of state power. In this uncertain time after the end of our post-Cold War "holiday from history," it is more important than ever to remember our humble roots in the Enlightenment tradition.

We hope you enjoy this seventh volume of the *Cato Supreme Court Review.*

# The Once and Future First Amendment

*Janice Rogers Brown**

I am delighted to present the Cato Institute's sixth annual B. Kenneth Simon Lecture in Constitutional Thought, appropriately named after such a generous supporter of individual liberty and constitutionalism. It is an honor to be asked to follow in the formidable wake of such luminaries as Judges Douglas Ginsburg and Danny Boggs, and Professors Walter Dellinger, Richard Epstein, and Nadine Strossen.

While I am certainly not in their league as a scholar, I want to take up a thread that I think has been part of the continuing dialogue promoted by this lecture series. Judge Ginsburg called on students of the Constitution to refocus attention upon its text;[1] Professors Dellinger[2] and Epstein[3] both argued, in essence, that economic, personal, and political rights are indivisible. In fact, one of Professor Dellinger's explicit premises was that disparaging the constitutional protection of economic liberties weakens the constitutional foundations of personal liberty.[4] I agree, of course. And today I will try to complete a bit more of this tapestry by considering from a different perspective the questions that undergird each of those discussions. Those questions pertain to the constant challenge of constitutionalism: Is the Constitution merely an emanation of "transformative overarching principles" uncontrolled by the text and disconnected from the political philosophy on which the text is based? Or must

---

*Judge, United States Court of Appeals for the District of Columbia Circuit. This article is a revised version of the sixth annual B. Kenneth Simon Lecture in Constitutional Thought, delivered at the Cato Institute on September 17, 2007.

[1] Douglas H. Ginsburg, On Constitutionalism, 2002–2003 Cato Sup. Ct. Rev. 7 (2003).

[2] Walter Dellinger, The Indivisibility of Economic Rights and Personal Liberty, 2003–2004 Cato Sup. Ct. Rev. 9 (2004).

[3] Richard Epstein, The Monopolistic Vices of Progressive Constitutionalism, 2004–2005 Cato Sup. Ct. Rev. 11 (2005).

[4] Dellinger, *supra* note 2.

9

a judge's attempt to interpret constitutional text be firmly anchored in the bedrock principles underlying a fixed constitution? Our difficulty is not only with the meaning of words; it is also with the more subtle problem of how we should approach interpretation. To paraphrase John Ciardi: How does our Constitution mean?[5] My particular focus will be on the relationship between the First and Fifth Amendments in the hope that history may show what future we need to re-invent.

## I. Parallels Between the First and Fifth Amendments

For a long time I have intuited a deep connection between the First and Fifth Amendments. Although we like to think of the First Amendment as a fixed point in our constitutional frame of reference, it is even now being transformed, in a way that shares troubling parallels to the demise of the Takings Clause of the late, great Fifth Amendment. The protection of private property was seriously diminished by people eager for government to redistribute wealth. Private space is slated for the same fate by people who want to redistribute ideas. Originally, I saw those efforts as similar—sharing an identifiable modus operandi—but largely separate and ad hoc instances of constitution bending. However, after deeper examination I understand that they are profoundly connected. Indeed, Ronald Coase and Aaron Director had by the early 1970s noted not only their near perfect symmetry but their philosophical congruence.

Proponents of economic liberty sought to limit the excesses of the redistributive state by arguing that the treatment of the First Amendment ought to serve as the model for state intervention. After all, if the benefit of the laissez faire approach in the marketplace of ideas is obvious, why should not the same rules apply to economic markets? Director and Coase argued for parity of the economic marketplace and the intellectual marketplace. "In this respect," Director contended, "the political economists have shown better insight into the basis of all freedom than the proponents of the priority of the marketplace for ideas."[6] He continued:

---

[5] John Ciardi, How Does a Poem Mean? (1959). Ciardi, an American poet, translator, and etymologist, celebrated for his ability to make poetry accessible to adults and children, once quipped: "The Constitution gives every American the inalienable right to make a damn fool of himself."

[6] Aaron Director, The Parity of the Economic Market Place, 7 J.L. & Econ. 1, 9 (1964).

The latter must of necessity rely on exhortation and on the fragile support of self-denying ordinances in constitutions. The former, on the other hand, have grasped the significance of institutional arrangements which foster centers of resistance against the encroaching power of coercive organization.[7]

Coase argued that there was "no fundamental difference between these two markets" and that the same considerations should influence both.[8] If, said Coase, "the government is as incompetent as is generally assumed in the market for ideas," we should seek to "decrease government intervention in the market for goods."[9] On the other hand, if it is as efficient as it is often implicitly assumed to be in the market for goods, we ought to "increase government regulation in the market for ideas."[10]

Of course, it is not only conservatives and libertarians who have noticed the evident parallelism between the economic marketplace and the marketplace of ideas. Acknowledging that Coase and Director "have confronted New Deal liberals with the free speech tradition in order to remind them of the virtues of laissez faire and to build a case against state intervention in economic matters," Owen Fiss confesses that his inclination is "just the reverse."[11] Fiss explains:

It occurred to me that if Coase and Director can celebrate the libertarian element in the free speech tradition as a way of arguing against state intervention in the economic sphere, we should be able to start at the other end—to begin with the fact of state intervention in economic matters, and then use that historical experience to understand why the state might have a role to play in furthering free speech values.[12]

The proponents of this view ignore Coase's challenge to demonstrate the state's competence first. There was no pure liberal/conservative divide on the issue. Judge Robert Bork, a staunch defender

---

[7] *Id.*

[8] R. H. Coase, The Economics of the First Amendment: The Market for Goods and the Market for Ideas, 64 Am. Econ. Rev. 384, 389 (1974).

[9] *Id.* at 390.

[10] *Id.*

[11] Owen Fiss, Why the State?, 100 Harv. L. Rev. 781, 783 (1987).

[12] *Id.*

of government restraint in the marketplace, has argued that the First Amendment should protect only speech involving the "discovery and spread of political truth,"[13] and all other forms of speech should be subject to government regulation. More recently, Professor Cass Sunstein has called for a "New Deal for Speech" that would authorize dramatic government regulation of undeserving speech.[14] In the same way that economic regulation enlists government on the side of the poor, the vulnerable, or the numerous, Sunstein would have government take sides in the marketplace of ideas, amplifying powerless voices, squelching the impulses of crass commercialism, and regulating the content of broadcasts.

Sunstein goes beyond the strict parallel between regulation of the market for goods and regulation of the market for ideas. He traces the provenance of his ideas back to *Lochner*.[15] According to Sunstein, "for purposes of speech, contemporary understandings of neutrality and partisanship, or government action and inaction, are identical to those that predate the New Deal."[16] Thus, the rejection of *Lochner* effectively erased the separation between the public and private spheres. By overruling *Lochner*, the Supreme Court conceded that the Constitution does not require the government to remain neutral toward activities in the private sector or to protect the private status quo.[17] Sunstein's New Deal for speech would "replace neutrality— which entails the protection of individual privacy and intellectual autonomy—with paternalism—which entails a substantial measure of governmental intrusion into individual thought and action."[18]

Sunstein's argument is interesting because, in many ways, it is the most candid and most complete. He embraces the true heart of the progressive agenda, finding no principled basis for exempting speech from regulation.

[13] Robert H. Bork, Neutral Principles and Some First Amendment Problems, 47 Ind. L.J. 1, 26 (1971).

[14] Cass R. Sunstein, A New Deal for Speech, 17 Hastings Comm. & Ent. L.J. 137 (1994).

[15] Lochner v. New York, 198 U.S. 45 (1905); Cass R. Sunstein, Lochner's Legacy, 87 Colum. L. Rev. 873 (1987).

[16] Sunstein, *supra* note 14, at 138–139.

[17] *Id.* at 140.

[18] Steven G. Gey, The Case Against Postmodern Censorship Theory, 145 U. Pa. L. Rev. 193, 261 (1996).

Those who now challenge America's historically robust hands-off approach to speech get high marks for consistency. They acknowledge the powerful parallelism between the economic market and the market for ideas. Generally, they simply choose the interventionist state across the board, favoring a more limited notion of protected speech. The ranks of those who think the government should regulate what people see, hear, and say is growing, encompassing a broad spectrum of political views—from conservatives who would treat pornography like smoke pollution to critical feminists, such as Catherine McKinnon, who would have the government pursue us even into our dreams (to ferret out erotic fantasies). The new censors would scrub the minds of citizens of all antisocial thoughts—sexism, racism, homophobia, and pornography. The old censors would treat pornography as a nuisance that degrades the quality of life—a nuisance from which the majority may rationally decide to protect society. The difference between the new and the old censors is that the new would impose an elite vision, the tyranny of the minority, whereas the old would enshrine the tyranny of the majority.

## II. Current Challenges

The various challenges to the First Amendment have been nothing if not heterodox. For convenience and brevity, I divide the various arguments into three categories: the new censors, the new neutrals, and the new moralists. None of these categories is impermeable and thus considerable cross-pollination occurs.

### A. The New Censors

Not surprisingly, the new censors are the most adept practitioners of postmodern cant—"doublethink" and "newspeak." Echoing Orwell: Freedom is slavery and slavery is freedom, and so on. This school of thought can be summarized very succinctly: There is no such thing as free speech—freedom of expression becomes just another "political device to promote particular agendas."[19] Thus, "free speech" is just "the label" we "want [our] favorites to wear."[20] To put it another way: "[S]peech and conduct are continuous; ideas construct reality and reflect it back. Therefore, both are equally

[19] David E. Bernstein, You Can't Say That! 21 (2003).

[20] *Id.* (quoting Stanley Fish, There's No Such Thing as Free Speech 102 (1994) (internal quotation marks omitted)).

13

regulable if regulation serves desirable ends."[21] Speech that makes our society more sexist, more racist, or more violent may not merely cause harm; it *is* harm. Such a view justifies eliminating the speech and reeducating or transforming the speaker. After all, "[i]f you want to change reality, you have to change the speech that constructs it."[22]

## B. The New Neutrals

In contrast, the new neutrals don't seem so radical. Indeed, they purport to accept one of the principal tenets of traditional First Amendment doctrine—neutrality. Under traditional doctrine, except in limited circumstances, government may not suppress or regulate speech merely because its content is objectionable. Permissible government regulation does not take sides and any collateral restriction of speech must be neutral.

But often, when contested questions are involved, neutrality is in the eye of the beholder. As Professor Laurence Tribe notes, sometimes "one man's discrimination is another's expression of a moral view."[23] Thus, the application of anti-discrimination laws to a private association such as the Boy Scouts[24] may not be a neutral instance of error-correction, but instead "a direct clash of competing images of 'the good life.'"[25]

Is government really being neutral in the clash of ideas when it denies subsidies or benefits on the basis of pejorative labels? Or requires religious organizations to adopt practices fundamentally at odds with their core beliefs?[26] Or even when it seeks to exponentially increase a criminal sentence because of perceived "hatred" toward

---

[21] Kathleen M. Sullivan, Free Speech Wars, 48 SMU L. Rev. 203, 210 (1994).

[22] *Id.*

[23] Laurence H. Tribe, Disentangling Symmetries: Speech, Association, Parenthood, 28 Pepp. L. Rev. 641, 651 (2001).

[24] See, e.g., Boy Scouts of America v. Wyman, 335 F.3d 80 (2d Cir. 2003); Evans v. City of Berkeley, 129 P.3d 394 (Cal. 2006).

[25] Tribe, *supra* note 23, at 651.

[26] See, e.g., Catholic Charities of Sacramento, Inc. v. Superior Court, 85 P.3d 67 (Cal. 2004) (upholding a California law requiring Catholic Charities to provide its employees prescription coverage for contraceptives); John Garvey, State Putting Church Out of Adoption Business, Boston Globe, Mar. 14, 2006, at A15.

some protected group?[27] If the power to tax is the power to destroy, in the modern state the power to officially label may be equally pernicious.[28]

## C. The New Moralists

Finally, we come to the new moralists. In this camp, I include the civic republicans, the advocates of campaign finance regulations (including those who would regulate speech in the name of fairer and more enlightening public debate), and those who clamor for government subsidies of underfinanced views or compelled speech by broadcasters. A chorus of voices calling for a return to the Fairness Doctrine is growing,[29] and regulation of campaign speech continues to proliferate despite the Supreme Court's fiery declamation in *Buckley v. Valeo* that "the concept that government may restrict the speech of some elements of our society in order to enhance the relative voice of others is wholly foreign to the First Amendment."[30]

The argument for economic equality transforms easily into an argument for political equality. If government has an obligation to burden the property of the rich in order to help the poor, why is it not equally obliged to dampen the political influence money can buy? Thus, speech—even (or should I say, *especially*) political speech—must be treated the same way property is treated: "as something that is really owned by government, and which citizens are only permitted to use or engage in when they meet conditions established by government to promote fairness and justice."[31]

---

[27] See, e.g., Posting of Eugene Volokh to The Volokh Conspiracy, The Shmulevich Case—Facts and New York Law, As I Can Best Figure Them Out, http://volokh.com/posts/1185829677.shtml (July 30, 2007, 5:07 p.m.) (relating the story of a man charged with hate crimes under New York law for placing two stolen Korans in a toilet).

[28] See Tribe, *supra* note 23, at 653.

[29] See, e.g., Center For American Progress & Free Press, The Structural Imbalance of Political Talk Radio, http://www.americanprogress.org/issues/2007/06/talk_radio.html (June 21, 2007); Posting of Tom Regan to NPR News Blog, http://www.npr.org/blogs/news/2007/06/some_conservatives_fear_return.html (June 22, 2007, 2:02 p.m.).

[30] 424 U.S. 1, 48–49 (1976).

[31] Thomas G. West, The Liberal Assault on Freedom of Speech, The Claremont Institute, http://www.claremont.org/publications/pubid.323/pub_detail.asp (Feb. 4, 2004).

15

In summary, how zealous the public or the courts will be about defending First Amendment protections seems to depend on the way the challenge is marketed. Direct restrictions, such as campus speech codes or statutes explicitly limiting a particular kind of speech, are likely to be rejected. However, ostensibly neutral and generally applicable restrictions on speech or associational rights easily trump the First Amendment.

## III. Half a Loaf?

Of course, as always, there are those who posit a third way. Not all progressives are eager to dismantle the First Amendment; some see no contradiction between a libertarian First Amendment and an economically interventionist state. Economic regulation, they say, is qualitatively different. The government's interference with contract and property rights should be deemed constitutionally inoffensive on pragmatic and pluralist grounds. The key is not paternalism; it is the democratic imperative. As Steven Gey explains, after *Lochner*, "the political majority" was free to do whatever it deemed necessary "to further its own self-interest through government action."[32] Gey clings to a critical distinction between the government asserting "the ability to discern the 'true' wishes of workers who have not yet realized their self-interest" and the government acting on "behalf of workers who exercise their political clout in the pursuit of very specific goals."[33] This distinction fails to explain why the majority should be able to overrule constitutional protections in the economic realm but not in the realm of ideas.

As Professor Dellinger noted in his Simon Lecture, "[e]conomic rights, property rights, and personal rights have been joined, appropriately, since the time of the founding."[34] Scholars as disparate as Stephen Macedo and Bernard Siegan have argued that economic rights are as clearly entitled to constitutional protection as political rights. "The modern Court's double standard, which neglects economic liberties and protects other 'personal' liberties, like privacy, is

[32] Gey, *supra* note 18, at 263 n.212.

[33] *Id.*

[34] Dellinger, *supra* note 2, at 19.

incoherent and untenable."[35] Occasionally, even the Supreme Court itself acknowledges the muddle, admitting "the right to enjoy property without unlawful deprivation" is as much a personal right as any other.[36]

The withdrawal of constitutional protection from economic activity happened because it was necessary to implement the social democratic ideal of the New Deal. This meant the spontaneous order created by the exercise of property rights should be subject to "perpetual revision" and control through central government.[37] And although the architects of the new consensus could self-consciously carve out a private sphere ostensibly protected by the First Amendment, nothing in the new vision compelled allegiance to the idea of a permanent separation between the public and private spheres. The collective governance rationale had cachet only so long as it seemed to serve the purposes of the architects.

Alexis de Tocqueville recognized this reality when he spoke out against the revolutionary fervor of 1848—the first broadly socialist revolution in Europe—warning that socialism challenged civilization's very foundation and "was nothing less than a new 'road to servitude' because it makes the state 'the sole owner of property,' unleashes man's crudest material passions, and shows 'a deep distrust of liberty, of human reason, a profound scorn for the individual in his own right.' "[38] He saw democracy as the source of individuality and freedom. He said: "Democracy attaches all possible value to each man; socialism makes each man a mere agent, a mere number. Democracy and socialism have nothing in common but one word: equality. But notice the difference: while democracy seeks equality in liberty, socialism seeks equality in restraint and servitude."[39]

---

[35] Scott Gerber, To Secure These Rights 191 (1995) (quoting Stephen Macedo, The New Right v. The Constitution 47 (2d ed. 1987)); see also Bernard H. Siegan, Economic Liberties and the Constitution (1980).

[36] Lynch v. Household Fin. Corp., 45 U.S. 538, 552 (1972).

[37] John O. McGinnis, The Once and Future Property-Based Vision of the First Amendment, 63 U. Chi. L. Rev. 49, 51 (1996).

[38] Daniel J. Mahoney, A Noble and Generous Soul, Claremont Rev. of Books (Summer 2007) (available at http://www.claremont.org/publications/crb/id.1398/article_detail.asp) (quoting, as translated, Alexis de Tocqueville, Discours Prononcé à l'Assemblée Constituante le 12 September 1848 Sur la Question du Droit au Travail, in Etudes Economiques Politiques et Littéraires (1866)).

[39] Friedrich A. Hayek, The Road to Serfdom 29 (1994 ed.) (quoting, as translated, Tocqueville, *supra* note 38).

17

Tocqueville was not quite prescient. He did not perceive how the collectivist impulse might deform democracy. One hundred years later, Friedrich Hayek laments the inevitable consequence of unlimited democracy: "So long as it is legitimate for government to use force to effect a redistribution of material benefits . . . there can be no curb on the rapacious instincts of all groups." He goes on to say: "Once politics becomes a tug of war for shares in the income pie, decent government is impossible."[40]

Do the same insights apply to the intellectual marketplace? I think they might. We can now broadly identify three different philosophical camps: those who see free speech as an instrument (a means) to a collective good, one that can be jettisoned whenever they perceive circumstances have changed; those who see free speech as instrumental, but argue that it has enduring but limited utility; and those who argue that expressive man and economic man are indivisible and that strong protection of speech, property, and other rights is the end for which government exists. The folks in the middle think we can have it both ways. They insist that the regulation of products and the regulation of speech "pose quite different problems for democratic self-governance."[41] But the difference is more illusory than real. While it is accurate to say that speech regulations are intended to permanently alter "the thought patterns of citizens living under the control of the government,"[42] it is equally true that economic regulations of the welfare state are intended to permanently transform citizens from being the government's master to subsisting as its ward.

So the more familiar argument made for intellectual freedom applies with equal potency to economic freedom. The attempted distinction cannot be sustained because there is no single road to serfdom. Like the path to hell, the way is broad and paved with good intentions. You can begin by undermining property, or objective moral value, or the family, or by attempting to control ideas directly.

---

[40] Friedrich A. Hayek, Law, Legislation and Liberty, Vol. III, at 150 (U. of Chi. Press 1979).

[41] Gey, *supra* note 18, at 267.

[42] *Id.* at 269.

To be sure, the economic revolution is easier to justify on democratic principles. After all, the great leveling impulse is widespread. Being free requires human beings to live in a fierce and irresolvable tension—to accept imperfection and to risk failure. In contrast, slavery in the welfare state—the permissive cornucopia of modern tyranny—exudes the seductive thrall of a crack pipe. Comforting, mind-numbing, solidly addictive—it whispers constantly that you deserve more and you need not tally the cost, for the accounting will be someone else's problem. It is freedom that is the hard sell. It has a short shelf life. Only entitlements last forever.

## IV. The Soul of the Old and the Future Regime

A constitutional republic cannot be sustained without the commitment of virtuous citizens. The founding generation made this point repeatedly. Despite great theological diversity, the Founders unanimously "endorsed ancient ideas concerning the central roles of morality, virtue, the family, and property," and took an "intrinsically religious approach to government."[43]

George Washington, in his farewell address, identified "religion and morality" as "indispensable supports" of "political prosperity."[44] John Adams, the nation's second president, put it just as bluntly: "Our Constitution was made only for a moral and religious people. It is wholly inadequate to the government of any other."[45]

The mistake for the would-be regulators on both the right and the left is the misplaced confidence that the state itself should be the source of virtue. No branch of government is competent to coerce virtue—whether virtue is defined as a redistributive notion of compassion; a substantive political dialogue that leads to public consensus; or a society free of bias, bigotry, and prejudice. The inculcation of virtue is beyond the sustained ability of the state. "[V]irtue cannot be enforced or brought about by political means."[46] Virtue, like faith, must be a free choice or it is not virtue. As John Locke writes in *A Letter Concerning Toleration*: "[S]uch is the nature

---

[43] Sidney E. Mead, The Nation with the Soul of a Church 45 (1975).

[44] Michael W. McConnell, The Origins and Historical Understanding of Free Exercise of Religion, 103 Harv. L. Rev. 1409, 1441 (1990).

[45] Edward J. Eberle, Religion in the Classroom in Germany and the United States, 81 Tul. L. Rev. 67, 89 n.145 (2006).

[46] Frank S. Meyer, Leviathan, in In Defense of Freedom 127 (1996).

of the understanding that it cannot be compelled to the belief of anything by outward force."[47]

The shifting consensus on the value of the First Amendment brings us face to face with our real difficulty. It is the reason the arguments offered for diminishing the protections of the First Amendment seem like déjà vu all over again. Tocqueville, as usual, seems to have a unique insight. His 1848 speech may be the first time socialism is explicitly linked to a "distrust of reason, a profound scorn for the individual in his own right."[48] The link is not immediately obvious. Superficially, at least, socialism seems the implementation of pure reason—perhaps the most prominent example of what Harvey Mansfield calls "rational control."[49] But it is precisely this notion of rational control that Hayek rejects as a dangerous illusion, the belief that we can deliberately create the future of mankind. He recognizes the demand for just distribution, whether of wealth, ideas, or information, as "strictly an atavism, based on primordial emotions."[50] Ironically, it is the progressive movement that harkens back to the days of lethal superstition, the evil eye and the bloody sacrifice, to the old gods of envy, jealousy, and guilt.[51] Neither innovation nor virtue can thrive in such an environment.

## V. Conclusion

The politics of envy have no principled stopping point. The demand for redistribution of material goods is the place such discussions begin, but the demand must inevitably expand to encompass intellectual and physical inequalities as well. There can never be a society in which there is nothing left to envy. Even when we have the same clothes and cars and faces, there will still be envy for "those

[47] John Locke, A Letter Concerning Toleration 7 (William Pope trans. 1689) (available at http://www.constitution.org/jl/tolerati.htm) (last visited July 14, 2008).

[48] As quoted in Mahoney, *supra* note 38.

[49] Harvey C. Mansfield, Rational Control: Or, Life Without Virtue, 25 The New Criterion 39 (Sept. 2006). According to Mansfield, this is the big idea of modernity, an idea that requires us to subject our entire lives, "holding nothing back—which means holding nothing sacred as exempt—to an examination by reason as to whether we can live more effectively."

[50] Hayek, *supra* note 40, at 165.

[51] Helmut Schoeck, Envy: A Theory of Social Behavior 328–329, 361, 363–364 (Liberty Fund 1987) (1966).

imagined, innermost feelings."[52] There may be no way out of the dilemma in liberal democracies. The great leveling impulse turns out not to represent progress at all. Instead it signals a return to one of the most primitive aspects of the human psyche.[53] In sum, state enforcement of public virtue threatens to undo individual liberty.[54]

If we are not vigilant, if we do not think—as Abraham Lincoln warned us in another time of great peril—as we have never thought before, we might find ourselves in the real world of Harrison Bergeron, in the year 2081, when everybody is "finally equal" because all advantages of energy, imagination, effort, or genetics have been erased by the intervention of a ruthlessly efficient Handicapper General.[55]

The same impulse that felled the Takings Clause of the Fifth Amendment now seems poised to undermine freedom in the intellectual marketplace. The First Amendment's fall from favor is just another manifestation of the collectivist impulse that has already undermined much of our constitutional order as originally conceived. And it may accurately predict the future of any other constitutional imperative that stands in the way of what is variously called progressivism, radical egalitarianism, the general will, elite opinion, or (my personal favorite) the tyranny of the anointed. "The partisans of equal subordination to the claims of politics have always been driven to crush what stood in their way: religion, talent, property, science and most of all, liberty."[56]

I am not without sympathy for the concerns expressed by those who see high risk in a robust First Amendment. As does all of existence, freedom has its risks. "Unless men are free to be vicious" as well as vulgar, "they cannot be virtuous."[57] As Hayek reminds us, "freedom can be preserved only if it is treated as a supreme principle which must not be sacrificed" because when "the choice

---

[52] *Id.* at 15.

[53] *Id.* at 363–364.

[54] Frank S. Meyer, Western Civilization: The Problem of Political Freedom, in In Defense of Freedom 220–222 (1996).

[55] Kurt Vonnegut, Harrison Bergeron (1950), reprinted in Welcome to the Monkey House 7 (Dial Press 1998).

[56] Charles Fried, The New First Amendment Jurisprudence: A Threat to Liberty, 59 U. Chi. L. Rev. 225, 230 (1992).

[57] Frank S. Meyer, The Locus of Virtue, in In Defense of Freedom 148 (1996).

between freedom and coercion is treated as a matter of expediency," freedom loses.[58]

The American ideal of freedom faces challenges, externally and internally. Democracy is a fragile form of government; liberal democracy is more delicate still. We have a constitution. It may not be possible to retrieve what has been lost, but I haven't given up on that yet. What is at stake now is clear. And we do know how our Constitution means. It was intended as a blueprint for liberty. We are now on the cusp of another constitutional moment. We have a chance to think anew, again. Perhaps this time we will "fail better."

[58] Friedrich A. Hayek, Law, Legislation and Liberty, Vol. I, at 57 (U. of Chi. Press 1983).

# *Boumediene* and the Uncertain March of Judicial Cosmopolitanism

*Eric A. Posner*[1]

In *Boumediene v. Bush*, the Supreme Court held that noncitizens detained at Guantanamo Bay have the constitutional privilege of habeas corpus and that the review procedures established by the Detainee Treatment Act do not provide an adequate substitute. Justice Anthony Kennedy rests his majority opinion on what he calls a theory of separation of powers, but on inspection it becomes clear that the real basis of the opinion lies elsewhere. The holding turns on an implicit theory about the rights of noncitizens, a theory that is *prior* to the conception of separation of powers and is essentially about who belongs to the political community or *demos*. Justice Kennedy's theory is a cosmopolitan theory.

Shortly after 9/11, Congress passed the Authorization for Use of Military Force, which authorized the president "to use all necessary and appropriate force against those nations, organizations, or persons he determines planned, authorized, committed, or aided the terrorist attacks that occurred on September 11, 2001, or harbored such organizations or persons, in order to prevent any future acts of international terrorism against the United States by such nations, organizations or persons."[2] The Bush administration claimed that the AUMF authorized the military to detain and hold "enemy combatants," a position that was accepted by the Supreme Court in *Hamdi v. Rumsfeld*.[3] But the Court also held that the detainees were entitled to a procedure that allows them to contest their status as

[1] Kirkland & Ellis Professor, University of Chicago Law School. Many thanks to Scott Anderson, Curt Bradley, Mary Anne Case, Adam Cox, Mark Heyrman, Jens Ludwig, Madhavi Sunder, Adrian Vermeule, and participants at a workshop at the University of Chicago, for helpful comments, and Ben Burry for research assistance.

[2] Authorization for Use of Military Force, Pub. L. No. 107-40, 115 Stat. 224 (2001).

[3] 542 U.S. 507, 509 (2004).

23

enemy combatants. The Bush administration attempted to comply by establishing Combatant Status Review Tribunals. CSRTs determined that the petitioners in *Boumediene* were enemy combatants, whereupon they filed writs of habeas corpus.

Meanwhile, Congress passed the Detainee Treatment Act, which stripped federal district courts of jurisdiction over writs of habeas corpus filed by noncitizens held at Guantanamo Bay and gave the D.C. Circuit the exclusive authority to conduct a limited review of the determinations of CSRTs.[4] After the Supreme Court held, in *Hamdan v. Rumsfeld*,[5] that these provisions did not apply to petitions filed before the DTA was enacted, Congress passed the Military Commissions Act, which provided that the habeas-stripping provision of the DTA would apply to pending petitions as well.[6]

The government's argument in *Boumediene* was that under the 18th-century common law understanding of habeas corpus, the writ was not available to detainees held outside sovereign territory, that this understanding of habeas corpus was incorporated into the U.S. Constitution's suspension clause, and that Guantanamo Bay is not American sovereign territory.[7] Finding no historical evidence that the writ of habeas corpus was available to enemy aliens held abroad, and also no evidence that the writ was *not* available to enemy aliens held abroad, Justice Kennedy declined to rest his holding on historical understandings.[8] Instead, he applied what he called principles of separation of powers.

I argue first that the significance of Justice Kennedy's opinion has less to do with separation-of-powers theory than with a commitment to protecting the interests of noncitizens overseas. Second, I argue that this commitment reflects an emerging type of jurisprudence—which I call "judicial cosmopolitanism." Judicial cosmopolitanism is the view that judges have a constitutional obligation to protect the

---

[4] Pub.L. 109-148, div. A, tit. X, §§ 1001–1006, 119 Stat. 2680, 2739–44 (2005) (codified in part at.42 U.S.C. § 2000dd (2007) and 28 U.S.C. § 2241(e) (2008)).

[5] 548 U.S. 557 (2006).

[6] Pub. L. No. 109-366, 120 Stat. 2600 (2006) (to be codified in scattered sections of 10, 18, 28, and 42 U.S.C.).

[7] Boumediene v. Bush, 553 U.S. ____, 128 S. Ct. 2229, 2251 (2008).

[8] *Id.*

interests of noncitizens.[9] After explaining its role in the *Boumediene* opinion and its novelty in Supreme Court jurisprudence, I briefly criticize it.

### I. *Johnson v. Eisentrager*

In *Johnson v. Eisentrager*, the Supreme Court held that nonresident alien combatants captured in a theater of war and convicted of war crimes by a military commission did not have the right to petition for habeas corpus in American courts.[10] American forces had captured German soldiers who were giving assistance to the Japanese after the surrender of Germany but before the surrender of Japan.

Justice Jackson's opinion contains a number of reasons for its holding, but in summary form, inviting speculation about what he meant. At least the following factors, in some combination, played a role, though it is not clear whether all or some of them were necessary to the result, or whether the result occurred as a consequence of their cumulative effect in some sort of balancing test.

First, Justice Jackson emphasized the petitioners' alien status: They did not have habeas rights because they were aliens outside American territory, or perhaps *enemy* aliens (whether or not outside American territory). By contrast, (non-enemy?) resident aliens obtain rights as a result of their "preliminary declaration of intention to become a citizen,"[11] implying that rights go to those who appear (increasingly) loyal to the United States or who are located on American territory (where the power of American courts is at its height).

Underlying this inquiry is an idea about political community. People in the American political community are entitled to certain rights that are denied to those outside it. Aliens overseas, and certainly enemy aliens overseas, do not belong to the American political community and therefore are entitled to no, or few, rights. American

---

[9] The term has been used by others in a broader sense—to refer to the use of foreign sources for the purpose of constitutional interpretation. See, e.g., Ken I. Kersch, The New Legal Transnationalism, The Globalized Judiciary, and the Rule of Law, 4 Wash. U. Global Stud. L. Rev. 345 (2005), who appears to be the first to use the term in this way. I will discuss the relationship between these two types of judicial cosmopolitanism below. Kennedy, of course, is known for his cosmopolitan tendencies. See, e.g., Roper v. Simmons, 543 U.S. 551 (2005); Lawrence v. Texas, 539 U.S. 558, 568–74 (2003); United States v. Verdugo-Urquidez, 494 U.S. 259, 275 (1990) (Kennedy, J., concurring).

[10] 339 U.S. 763 (1950).

[11] Eisentrager, 339 U.S. at 770.

citizens do belong to that community, even those who have joined the enemy. Aliens on American territory occupy an ambiguous middle ground because many of them do plan to become Americans, or have otherwise sunk roots into—and to some extent participate in—the American political community as quasi-citizens.

Second, in a famous passage, Justice Jackson speculated about the practical and logistical difficulties that would follow if enemy aliens were given habeas rights:

> A basic consideration in *habeas corpus* practice is that the prisoner will be produced before the court. . . . To grant the writ to these prisoners might mean that our army must transport them across the seas for hearing. This would require allocation of shipping space, guarding personnel, billeting and rations. It might also require transportation for whatever witnesses the prisoners desired to call as well as transportation for those necessary to defend the legality of the sentence. The writ, since it is held to be a matter of right, would be equally available to enemies during active hostilities as in the present twilight between war and peace. Such trials would hamper the war effort and bring aid and comfort to the enemy. They would diminish the prestige of our commanders, not only with enemies but with wavering neutrals. It would be difficult to devise more effective fettering of a field commander than to allow the very enemies he is ordered to reduce to submission to call him to account in his own civil courts and divert his efforts and attention from the military offensive abroad to the legal defensive at home. Nor is it unlikely that the result of such enemy litigiousness would be a conflict between judicial and military opinion highly comforting to enemies of the United States.
>
> Moreover, we could expect no reciprocity for placing the litigation weapon in unrestrained enemy hands. The right of judicial refuge from military action, which it is proposed to bestow on the enemy, can purchase no equivalent for benefit of our citizen soldiers. Except in England, whose law appears to be in harmony with the views we have expressed, and other English-speaking peoples in whose practice nothing has been cited to the contrary, the writ of *habeas corpus* is generally unknown.[12]

[12] *Id.* at 778–79.

Here we see concerns about the sheer financial cost of habeas hearings when prisoners, custodians, and witnesses are overseas; the military risk of transporting such people; the positive morale effect for the enemy and the negative morale effect for Americans; interference with command; and the absence of any reciprocal benefit that would be conferred upon the United States by the enemy if habeas rights were recognized. Justice Jackson does not express doubts about the capacity of judges to evaluate the military's reasons for detention, but he hints that disagreement between the judiciary and the military is likely to occur—which would be "comforting" to the enemy.

This concern about logistics involves a more familiar and uncomplicated national interest analysis than the political community question does. Supposing that a habeas petitioner does belong to the political community, or does so to a sufficient extent—because he is an American, or an alien on American territory—what rights protections are reasonable given the conflicting interest of national security? Depending on the setting, it will be more or less costly, difficult, and dangerous for the military to comply with the requirements of a habeas hearing. Normal procedural protections can be compromised in light of these problems. Indeed, the entire military justice system reflects such compromises.

Third, Justice Jackson might have believed that the petitioners did not have habeas rights because the military commissions gave them adequate process.[13] This interpretation was advanced by Justice Kennedy in *Boumediene*, who says that one of the reasons that Justice Jackson refused to extend habeas rights to the petitioners in *Eisentrager* is that the petitioners there benefited from the military commissions, which provided "a rigorous adversarial process to test the legality of their detention," whereas the CSRTs that heard the petitioners' case provided more limited process.[14] This seems to be a misreading of *Eisentrager*. In the section of the opinion that explains the holding, Justice Jackson does not say that the military commissions provide adequate process. Justice Kennedy cites a passage

---

[13] It is sometimes said that the result turned on the fact that the petitioners did not contest their status as enemy combatants. If that is the case, then *Eisentrager* was a trivial decision because no one would make that mistake again.

[14] Boumediene, 128 S. Ct. at 2259–60.

where Justice Jackson merely summarizes the factual setting, and the reference to the military commission seems to be intended merely to show how exotic the petitioners' claim is.[15]

## II. *Boumediene*

### A. *A Narrow Reading*

One reading of *Boumediene* is that it does not advance the law at all, and simply applies the *Eisentrager* precedent to a novel set of facts. *Eisentrager* said that aliens held outside American sovereign territory have no habeas rights, and the question in *Boumediene* was whether Guantanamo Bay should be considered part of America's sovereign territory. The government misinterpreted the *Eisentrager* test as turning on de jure sovereignty; in fact, the right interpretation of *Eisentrager* is "effective control." *Rasul* had already addressed this issue within the statutory habeas framework and held that Guantanamo Bay is, for habeas purposes, part of America's territory.[16] *Boumediene* comes to the same conclusion as a matter of constitutional law.

On this view, the jurisprudential significance of *Boumediene* is nil or close to it, though it might be practically important. All that it did was change the *form* of the law: it changed the *Eisentrager* rule into a standard by converting the reasons behind the *Eisentrager* rule into governing law. The government had manipulated the *Eisentrager* rule, according to Justice Kennedy, by holding the detainees in territory over which the United States had de facto but not de jure control: we shouldn't care about the rule but the reasoning behind it, and so such manipulation can't be tolerated. This is, of course, a common response among judges when they see rules being manipulated, and although the response is understandable, it inevitably undervalues the reasons for rules—their predictability. So the government loses the power to manipulate but also to engage in reasonable planning. Whether Justice Kennedy was right to think that the balance between decision and error costs favored a standard in this case rather than a rule will become clear only with time.

But what was the standard that was embodied in the reasoning of *Eisentrager*? Justice Jackson gave reasons for his rule; he did not

---

[15] *Id.*, 128 S. Ct. at 2259 (quoting Eisentrager, 399 U.S. at 777).

[16] Rasul v. Bush, 542 U.S. 466, 481–84 (2004).

state a standard. He might have offered these reasons in the alternative or he might have thought they were mutually reinforcing. In drawing a standard from Justice Jackson's reasoning, Justice Kennedy had the opportunity to change the emphasis among these reasons, and thus change the substance of the law. He took this opportunity.

## B. A Broader Reading

Justice Kennedy argues that the writ of habeas corpus serves the principles of separation of powers by creating a judicial check on the political branches. The theory is stated about halfway through the discussion:

> The necessary implication of the [government's] argument is that by surrendering formal sovereignty over any unincorporated territory to a third party, while at the same time entering into a lease that grants total control over the territory back to the United States, it would be possible for the political branches to govern without legal constraint.
>
> Our basic charter cannot be contracted away like this. The Constitution grants Congress and the President the power to acquire, dispose of, and govern territory, not the power to decide when and where its terms apply. Even when the United States acts outside its borders, its powers are not "absolute and unlimited" but are subject "to such restrictions as are expressed in the Constitution." Murphy v. Ramsey, 114 U.S. 15, 44 (1885). Abstaining from questions involving formal sovereignty and territorial governance is one thing. To hold the political branches have the power to switch the Constitution on or off at will is quite another. The former position reflects this Court's recognition that certain matters requiring political judgments are best left to the political branches. The latter would permit a striking anomaly in our tripartite system of government, leading to a regime in which Congress and the President, not this Court, say "what the law is." Marbury v. Madison, 1 Cranch 137, 177 (1803).[17]

As an aside, note that it is questionable that the writ of habeas corpus can be understood as a check on *both* the political branches

---

[17] Boumediene, 128 S. Ct. at 2258–59.

given that Congress has the power to suspend the writ. True, Congress did not (formally) suspend the writ after 9/11, but it probably could have,[18] in which case the petitioners would have no claim and the reference to *Marbury v. Madison* is hollow. The writ is a check on the executive *acting alone*, without the concurrence of Congress. Yet the court ends up striking down a statute that Congress had enacted. Perhaps the best that can be said for this argument is that the requirement that Congress "formally" suspend the writ serves as a check on Congress. A formal suspension might be more politically costly than a de facto suspension, even though a de facto suspension will often be clear enough, as was the case here. But normally the Supreme Court does not require Congress to utter magic words in order to discharge its constitutional responsibilities.[19]

Regardless, my focus is Justice Kennedy's use of *Eisentrager*. Justice Kennedy places all weight on the logistical concern in *Eisentrager*, and very little—perhaps none—on the political community concern. Justice Kennedy summarizes what he calls the "functional" test of *Eisentrager* as follows:

> (1) the citizenship and status of the detainee and the adequacy of the process through which that status determination was made; (2) the nature of the sites where apprehension and then detention took place; and (3) the practical obstacles inherent in resolving the prisoner's entitlement to the writ.[20]

Notably, Justice Kennedy's discussion of the first factor omits any reference to the petitioners' status as aliens, or enemy aliens, and instead focuses entirely on the adequacy of process question, which, as I argued earlier, he mistakenly reads into *Eisentrager*. Otherwise, Justice Kennedy addresses the logistical question. Because Guantanamo Bay is fully under the control of the United States military, diplomatic frictions will not arise if courts exercise habeas jurisdiction; nor will there be any serious military risks.[21] By contrast, in

---

[18] Some commentators may think that Congress cannot suspend the writ unless there is an emergency of a sufficient magnitude, and that courts would review suspension of the writ rather than defer. If so, then Justice Kennedy's view is correct.

[19] For example, there is no rule that Congress must echo the text and announce a declaration of war in order to authorize hostilities.

[20] Boumediene, 128 S. Ct. at 2259.

[21] *Id.*, 128 S. Ct. at 2260–61.

*Eisentrager*, the occupation zone was larger and covered more people; more U.S. military resources were involved; the U.S. shared control of the prison with other countries; and there were potential threats from the defeated.

The focus on logistics may not have been adventitious. It is hard to imagine a weaker case for the logistics argument than Guantanamo Bay, at least compared to other foreign territories. Located only about 500 miles from Florida, it would not seem particularly difficult to transport prisoners and soldiers to a federal district court. Nor does the type of risk involved seem measurably greater than the risk of transferring a dangerous criminal from a prison to a court. True, many of the witnesses are in Afghanistan, Iraq, and elsewhere throughout the world. But witness availability issues also arise in ordinary criminal cases, and are not a reason to foreclose habeas. Justice Kennedy notes that the habeas court will give deference to the government when deference is justified, and this forecloses—at least until experience proves otherwise—the argument that habeas hearings are logistically impossible or unreasonable.[22]

Unmentioned is the status of the noncitizen. An oblique reference can be found in this passage only:

> It is true that before today the Court has never held that noncitizens detained by our Government in territory over which another country maintains *de jure* sovereignty have any rights under our Constitution. But the cases before us lack any precise historical parallel. They involve individuals detained by executive order for the duration of a conflict that, if measured from September 11, 2001, to the present, is already among the longest wars in American history.[23]

Why should it matter that this conflict is among the longest wars in American history? The only possible answer is that the interests of the detainee must be taken into account, and it is worse to be detained for a very long conflict than it is to be detained for a short conflict.

---

[22] *Id.*, 128 S. Ct. at 2261–62. A similar focus on logistics appeared in Justice Kennedy's concurring opinion in *Verdugo-Urquidez*, which involved the extraterritorial application of the Fourth Amendment. See Verdugo-Urquidez, 494 U.S. at 278.

[23] Boumediene, 128 S. Ct. at 2262.

So here is a theory: Justice Jackson refused to extend habeas rights to overseas enemy aliens for two reasons—the interests of these overseas aliens do not "count" like those of Americans, and the logistical demands on the military would be unreasonable. Justice Kennedy barely sees, and hardly acknowledges, the first point, and is not willing to countenance it. That leaves him with the logistical issue, which seems to melt away for Guantanamo Bay, with its convenient location and status as a de facto American territory, and the consideration that courts can always make concessions to logistics on a case-by-case basis, deferring to the military when they must but not otherwise.

Logistics just won't get one very far; the crucial assumption in *Eisentrager* is that overseas noncitizens are not entitled to judicial process, logistics or no logistics. Why doesn't Justice Kennedy confront what seemed like a natural assumption to Justice Jackson— that nonresident aliens just don't have the rights that Americans have, and thus don't deserve judicial protection of any sort? The answer is that Justice Kennedy is a cosmopolitan.

## III. The Application of the Constitution Overseas

The main question posed by *Boumediene* is this: Should nonresident aliens be treated as Americans, or at least be given some of the rights of Americans?

The relevant literature is not the separation-of-powers literature, but the literature on the extraterritorial application of the Constitution. The literature arises from a series of cases, some but not all of them discussed in *Boumediene*,[24] that have questioned whether the Constitution—or certain provisions of it—constrains the U.S. government when it operates abroad. The answer, for the most part, is "no," except when government action affects Americans, or resident aliens who have partially joined the political community, or quasi-Americans who live in territories that the United States has acquired.[25] But tantalizing hints in some of the cases suggest that

---

[24] Justice Kennedy furiously distinguishes away the contrary cases but never explicitly recognizes the cosmopolitan implications of his holding.

[25] See In re Ross, 140 U.S. 453 (1891); Eisentrager, 339 U.S. 763 (1950); Reid v. Covert, 354 U.S. 1 (1957); Verdugo-Urquidez, 494 U.S. 259 (1990).

the "no" is not a hard "no,"[26] and *Boumediene* has, for the first time, suggested that in fact the "no" is a "yes."

Therein lies the significance of *Boumediene*. It is the first Supreme Court case that appears to recognize that noncitizens on foreign soil have constitutional rights secured by judicial oversight.[27] It is possible that *Boumediene* will have little effect in the future. Courts that hear habeas petitions coming from abroad might give deference to the military,[28] or not recognize any substantive constitutional rights beyond the habeas right itself. It is also possible that in a future case, the Court will confine *Boumediene* to the facts, treating Guantanamo Bay as unique because U.S. control is complete and Cuban sovereignty so clearly fictional. But in a more general jurisprudential sense, the opinion signifies the increasing influence of cosmopolitanism on the Court.

## A. What Is Judicial Cosmopolitanism?

There has been much talk of judicial cosmopolitanism in recent years, stimulated by a handful of Supreme Court cases that cite foreign and international law in the context of constitutional interpretation, including a pair of Eighth Amendment cases where the Supreme Court relied on international or foreign sources in order to ascertain whether evolving norms prohibited certain types of punishment.[29] The concept can be given various interpretations.

*1. A Global Constitution.* Governments must obey a global constitution, one that sets the limits of power for all governments around the world. These limits are universal; perhaps they are embodied in human rights treaties. By applying to all governments, the global constitution protects all people, regardless of nationality. This does not necessarily mean that a government must treat noncitizens and

---

[26] See especially Reid v. Covert, 354 U.S. at 6 (noting government "can only act in accordance with all the limitations imposed by the Constitution"). See also Rasul, 542 U.S. at 484 n. 15; and J. Andrew Kent, A Textual and Historical Case Against a Global Constitution, 95 Geo. L.J. 463, 478 (2007); Paul B. Stephan, Constitutional Limits on the Struggle Against International Terrorism: Revising the Rights of Overseas Aliens, 19 Conn. L. Rev. 831 (1987).

[27] With the ambiguous exception of the Insular cases, on which see below.

[28] But this is unlikely if *Parhat* is any indication. See Parhat v. Gates, No. 06-1397 (D.C. Cir. 2008).

[29] Roper v. Simmons, 543 U.S. 551 (2005); Atkins v. Virginia, 536 U.S. 304 (2002).

citizens the same in all respects, just that noncitizens and citizens have certain identical basic rights.[30]

2. *A Cosmopolitan-American Constitution.* The U.S. Constitution itself embodies certain global constitutional commitments, including the commitment to respect the rights of all people, regardless of nationality. Thus, any rights in the U.S. Constitution that protect Americans also protect noncitizens. Observed limits on rights granted to nonresident aliens are the result of logistical constraints, not lower constitutional status of noncitizens.[31]

3. *Residual Constitutionalism.* The U.S. Constitution does not apply in foreign countries that have governments, but it does apply in places, like Guantanamo Bay, where there is no government. Nation-states and sovereigns get priority otherwise.[32]

These definitions differ as to the strength of the rights granted to nonresident aliens under the U.S. Constitution, but they agree that they do have at least some rights, and that is the minimalist sense in which I will use the term judicial cosmopolitanism.[33]

## B. What Is the Justification for Judicial Cosmopolitanism?

What should we think of judicial cosmopolitanism? The literature is overwhelmingly favorable. The relevant historical and textual sources are sporadic and ambiguous, however, and authors end up

---

[30] I have not found an American scholar who has made this claim in quite so bald a form, because it would be inconsistent with Supreme Court jurisprudence as it currently exists. But this idea has currency among foreign scholars. See, e.g., Ernst-Ulrich Petersmann, Constitutional Functions and Constitutional Problems of International Economic Law (1991). American scholars usually refer to the idea of "dialogue" between the Supreme Court and foreign courts, but it is not clear what this term means. See, e.g., Gerald L. Neuman, The Uses of International Law in Constitutional Interpretation, 98 Am. J. Int'l L. 82, 87 (2004). There is a less ambitious epistemic interpretation of *Roper*, which does not rely on any version of judicial cosmopolitanism: aliens are a source of information only. See Eric A. Posner & Cass R. Sunstein, The Law of Other States, 59 Stan. L. Rev. 1309 (2007).

[31] Cf. Verdugo-Urquidez, 494 U.S. at 275 (Kennedy, J., concurring). This is what Neuman calls "mutualism." See Gerald L. Neuman, Strangers to the Constitution: Immigrants, Borders, and Fundamental Law (Princeton University Press, 1996).

[32] Cf. Munaf v. Geren, 553 U.S. ____, 128 S. Ct. 2207 (2008), where the Supreme Court refused to prevent the U.S. military from turning over American criminal suspects in Iraq to the Iraqi government, because the Iraqi government was sovereign.

[33] "Judicial cosmopolitanism" is essentially the same as "global constitutionalism." See Kent, *supra* note 26.

relying on a claim that human rights are universal and judges should ensure that the U.S. government does not violate any human rights.[34] I will address this theory shortly. But first some theoretical throat-clearing.

One cannot address judicial cosmopolitanism without a theory of the judicial role in the constitutional system. There are as many such theories as there are constitutional theorists, and to keep the argument simple, I will focus on the simplest and most plausible of these theories—the democratic failure theory associated with John Hart Ely and footnote 4 of *Carolene Products*.[35] According to this theory, our majoritarian political system can survive and prosper only if courts guard against "democratic failures." This idea can be cashed out in two ways. First, a democratic failure exists when a particular group is systematically excluded from the political decisionmaking process, as African-Americans were during the Jim Crow era. Second, a democratic failure exists when the political process does not generate policies that satisfy a relatively uncontroversial welfarist principle—for example, a principle that bars transferring resources from out-of-power groups to in-power groups while reducing, or not increasing, total social welfare. The overall concern is that groups within any given democracy obtain control of the government through democratic means but then use the power at their disposal to weaken democratic institutions so as to undermine political competition.

The immediate problem that the usual analysis skirts is the scope of the *demos*.[36] In the first case, which emphasizes exclusion of groups from political decisionmaking, we need to know which groups count as a part of the *demos*. If Congress passes a tariff that advances the political interests of constituents, while injuring people who live in

---

[34] See, e.g., Neuman, *supra* note 30; David Cole, Are Foreign Nationals Entitled to the Same Constitutional Rights as Citizens?, 25 T. Jefferson L. Rev. 367 (2003); Kal Raustiala, The Geography of Justice, 73 Fordham L. Rev. 2501 (2005)). For dissent, see Stephan, *supra* note 26; Kent, *supra* note 26.

[35] John Hart Ely, Democracy and Distrust: A Theory of Judicial Review (1980); United States v. Carolene Products Co., 304 U.S. 144, 153 n.4 (1938).

[36] For a discussion of this problem in the context of the treatment of resident aliens, see Eric A. Posner & Adrian Vermeule, Terror in the Balance: Security, Liberty, and the Courts 275 (2007).

Haiti, one would not normally call this tariff the result of a democratic failure. Quite the contrary, Congress advances the interests of the American public. However harmful the law for Haitians, they can't complain that they have been unfairly excluded from the *demos* because they are not American citizens.

Some scholars have rejected this argument. Some have argued, at least with respect to resident aliens, that they should have a vote because they are regulated by the government.[37] The principle seems to be that anyone who is directly affected by government policy should have a say in it. The logic of this argument would seem to imply that Haitians should have a vote in American elections, or at least a vote in decisions that affect Haiti. Few people take this view, and so I will put it aside for reasons of space.[38]

Another view is that courts should grant constitutional protections to noncitizens just because they cannot vote, and therefore they belong to a minority that can be exploited by the vote-holding majority. This view has been prominent among advocates for resident aliens, and the Supreme Court has indeed given them many rights.[39] But this view, like the earlier one, is question-begging. If resident aliens should be considered part of the political community, then they should have the right to vote as well as other constitutional rights. If not, and therefore they are not entitled to the right to vote, it's not clear why they should enjoy the other rights protections. Put differently, if we are concerned that citizens will abuse resident aliens, then the democratic failure argument is just that resident aliens should be given citizenship.

Another theory tries to evade these problems by asserting that everyone in the world has human rights, and that it is the obligation of courts to protect the human rights of aliens against policies of the U.S. government that harm them. Even if so, the question, which I will address in Part IV, is whether there is reason in constitutional theory for courts to force the political branches to respect human

---

[37] Joseph H. Carens, Culture, Citizenship and Community: A Contextual Exploration of Justice as Evenhandedness, Oxford University Press Inc, New York (2000).

[38] See, e.g., Robert E. Goodin, Enfranchising All Affected Interests, and Its Alternatives, 35 Philosophy & Pub. Aff. 40 (2007). Various philosophers have argued for world government or a version of it, which could in theory solve this problem. For now, and the foreseeable future, however, world government is not in the cards.

[39] See Ely, *supra* note 35.

rights. The human rights treaties have been negotiated and ratified by the political branches, which have declared that the courts may not enforce them except insofar as they are incorporated in domestic law. Under the human rights treaties, states have an obligation to refrain from arbitrary detentions, but they don't have an obligation to give habeas rights to victims of arbitrary detentions. If states seek to comply with their treaty obligations by authorizing courts to review detentions of noncitizens captured overseas, they are free to do so. A constitutional theory would need to show that American judges should compel the U.S. government to go beyond its treaty commitments, perhaps because human rights exist in natural law and courts have a constitutional obligation to compel the government to obey this source of law.

Now turn to the welfarist approach. Initially, we must distinguish between two types of welfarism: national and global. For national welfarism, the social welfare function includes only citizens of the nation-state. For global welfarism, the social welfare function includes everyone in the world.

National welfarism provides the cleanest explanation for the traditional view that constitutional rights stop at the shoreline. Americans "count" in the social welfare function; non-Americans do not. Courts thus have no reason to extend protections to non-Americans. *Eisentrager* reflects this approach. Recall Justice Jackson's brief comment that "the right of judicial refuge from military action, which it is proposed to bestow on the enemy, can purchase no equivalent for benefit of our citizen soldiers."[40] He is saying that there could be a policy reason to extend habeas corpus to enemy soldiers, namely, that if we do so, enemy courts might be opened to American soldiers. This type of reciprocal logic is the traditional basis for the laws of war, where we treat enemy POWs humanely so that the enemy treats American POWs humanely. The humane treatment of enemy soldiers is derived entirely from gains to Americans; the enemy soldiers themselves don't count in the social welfare function.

National welfarism is philosophically disreputable but has the offsetting advantage of empirical accuracy. There is little doubt that the American political system as a whole favors Americans, greatly

---

[40] Eisentrager, 339 U.S. at 779.

at the expense of people who live in other countries.[41] But if national welfarism is the premise upon which the democratic failure theory rests, then it follows that courts have no business granting rights to noncitizens. The political branches, acting for the benefit of the citizenry, can certainly make deals with foreign governments—including that of making habeas available to foreign citizens in return for similar treatment of Americans by foreign governments—but courts have no reason to compel such an outcome on their own. The one exception would be for the extremely unlikely case that the failure to do so could be traced to domestic laws that reduce the welfare of Americans.

That leaves global welfarism. A global welfarist argument for extraterritorial constitutionalism is that the political branches have no, or very weak, incentives to take account of the well-being of noncitizens because noncitizens don't vote. Democratic failure arises because the *demos* consists of the global population but only a small fraction of it—American citizens—can vote for American government officials who affect the greater *demos*. Americans have strong incentives to compel their leaders to adopt policies that effect transfers from the rest of the world to the United States. Courts can block these transfers, or at least the worst of them—including detentions of people on the basis of weak evidence of dangerousness.

One might object that, if this is really a problem, judges should compel the political branches to grant the vote to foreigners living in foreign countries. The obvious (and sufficient) response is that this would be impractical, whereas judges do seem to have the power to compel the political branches to respect at least some minimal rights—such as the right not to be arbitrarily detained. So why shouldn't they do this?

One conjectures that Justice Kennedy and the four justices who signed his opinion would, if forced to answer this question, agree that the U.S. government should respect the rights of nonresident aliens, subject to logistical and other practical constraints.[42] Whether or not they think that aliens "count" in the social welfare function

---

[41] See Wojciech Kopczuk, Joel Slemrod, and Shlomo Yitzhaki, The Limitations of Decentralized World Redistribution: An Optimal Taxation Approach, 49 Eur. Econ. Rev. 1051 (2005).

[42] See also Verdugo-Urquidez, 494 U.S. at 275 (Kennedy, J., concurring).

to the same extent that Americans do, they surely think that they "count" at least a little, and therefore the *demos* for purposes of the democratic failure theory extends across the world. Or perhaps they do not think in welfarist terms, but just think that nonresident aliens have certain basic rights. Nonresident aliens are not treated as the classic discrete and insular minority, regulation of whom requires strict scrutiny. They are not citizens, after all; perhaps one should call them second-class citizens. Their interests must be given some weight; the government, influenced entirely by voters, has no incentive to give those interests any weight; and therefore, judicial intervention is justified.

## C. *The Connection Between* Boumediene *and the Foreign Law Debate*

From this perspective, we can reconsider the style of cosmopolitanism seen in cases like *Roper v. Simmons*, where, in another Kennedy opinion, the Supreme Court cited foreign and international law sources in the course of holding that the Eighth Amendment bars the death penalty for crimes committed by juveniles.[43] This practice can be defended on purely epistemic grounds—the laws of other states might provide relevant information for judicial decisionmaking where local law authorizes judges to use such information. This justification for using foreign law sources is not cosmopolitan: One uses information from abroad, but not in order to protect the interests of noncitizens or show respect for them. Nor does this justification have much to do with *Boumediene*.[44]

The more ambitious and cosmopolitan justification for use of foreign law goes farther. Consider, for example, this statement by Justice Sandra Day O'Connor:

> Doing so [citing foreign sources] may not only enrich our own country's decisions; it will create that all important good impression. When U.S. courts are seen to be cognizant of other judicial systems, our ability to act as a rule-of-law model for other nations will be enhanced.[45]

---

[43] Roper, 543 U.S. 551 (2005). See also Lawrence, 539 U.S. 558 (2003); Atkins, 536 U.S. 304 (2002).

[44] See Posner & Sunstein, *supra* note 30.

[45] Sandra Day O'Connor, Assoc. Justice, U.S. Supreme Court, Remarks at the Southern Center for International Studies (Oct. 28, 2003) (transcript available at http://www.southerncenter.org/OConnor_transcript.pdf).

The statement, taken literally, suggests a vision of U.S. courts interpreting the American Constitution in a manner that, at least at the margin, defers to foreign sensibilities, in return for which foreign courts follow American jurisprudence—again, at least at the margin. On the American side, the Court would cut back on constitutional norms that many Americans approve of—say, freedom of speech or the permissibility of the death penalty. On the foreign side, American constitutional norms would increasingly influence foreign law—stronger abortion rights, say, or a right to bear arms.

What is the justification for this approach? American judges confer benefits on Americans—perhaps, strengthening their rights in foreign countries, or perhaps advancing their presumed political/constitutional interests in those lands—in return for which American judges accept constraints on American constitutional norms at home. In a stronger form, perhaps it is not even necessary for American norms to travel abroad. In the weaker form, reciprocity occurs, albeit of an odd sort. From our perspective (not theirs), foreigners benefit from the extension of American constitutional norms to their states, while from their perspective (not ours) we benefit from the extension of their norms to our state. We want them to accept our norms; they want us to accept theirs. All these notions are outside traditional American jurisprudence.[46] We are used to encouraging other countries to adopt American constitutional norms, but we have never accepted the idea that we should adopt theirs—and even less, the idea that this adoption of foreign constitutional norms should take place at the hands of our judges.

Now one could think of the reciprocal version of this idea—we give up some of our constitutional norms and you give up some of yours—as not really cosmopolitan because, in theory, Americans gain from a kind of constitutional-level bargain. But in practice the willingness to even consider such a bargain in the first place, against the background of American exceptionalism, suggests an openness

---

[46] Mark Tushnet refers to a tradition of American "engagement" but cites political documents, not judicial opinions, and seems to acknowledge the novelty of the reciprocity idea. Mark Tushnet, When Is Knowing Less Better Than Knowing More? Unpacking the Controversy over Supreme Court Reference to Non-U.S. Law, 90 Minn. L. Rev. 1275, 1292 (2006) ("Perhaps merely explaining ourselves might have been enough in 1776 or 1862. But today, others will not listen unless we display some reciprocity.").

to alien norms, and a concern about showing respect to noncitizens, that is the essence of cosmopolitanism. The nonreciprocal version of this idea—we give up some of our constitutional norms just because they diverge from yours—is just a more extreme version of this openness.

So *Roper* and cases like it take the interests of nonresident aliens seriously—seriously enough to permit their moral interests to influence American constitutional law—not just the common law, which of course can be easily changed. *Boumediene* does the same. Although *Roper* cited foreign law to protect Americans, and *Boumediene* cited American law to protect foreigners, the thrust of both cases was that of advancing the interests of noncitizens—their moral interest in limiting the death penalty and arbitrary detention, their individual interests in freedom—at the expense of traditional American constitutional understandings.

There are two earlier sets of cases that are relevant but that did not go so far as the modern cases. First, there are the Insular Cases, but in those cases, the affected people, while not Americans, were not aliens either.[47] They were subject to no foreign government, and in those days few people would have claimed that the international community had any interest in their well-being. They were colonial subjects, and although the Court—by granting them some constitutional rights—was more cosmopolitan than the political branches responsible for their conquest and subjugation, this was a minimal type of cosmopolitanism indeed.

Second, there are cases that grant constitutional rights, albeit of a limited sort, to noncitizens on American soil. I mentioned earlier that noncitizens on American soil enjoy habeas rights as well as other constitutional rights—a point that Justice Jackson noted in *Eisentrager*. This has led to the following chain of reasoning: If noncitizens on sovereign American territory have constitutional rights, then it can't be the case that the Constitution draws a line between noncitizens and American citizens, and gives rights only to the

---

[47] There is no authoritative list of Insular Cases; the term at a minimum applies to a group of 1901 cases such as DeLima v. Bidwell, 182 U.S. 1 (1901); Goetze v. United States, 182 U.S. 221 (1901); Armstrong v. United States, 182 U.S. 243 (1901); Downes v. Bidwell, 182 U.S. 244 (1901); Huus v. New York & Porto Rico S.S. Co., 182 U.S. 392 (1901); Dooley v. United States, 183 U.S. 151 (1901); and Fourteen Diamond Rings v. United States, 183 U.S. 176 (1901). Certain later decisions are sometimes also included.

latter. If that is the case, then the Constitution is not "nationalistic"; it is already cosmopolitan, and has been recognized as such for many years. It follows that the only possible explanation for traditional judicial reluctance to extend habeas to noncitizens abroad is that of logistics, and therefore it would be wrong to assume that *Eisentrager* drew a sharp line between noncitizens and American citizens. And so where logistics do not pose an insurmountable problem, habeas and other constitutional rights should be granted to noncitizens. On this view, *Boumediene* did no more than follow *Eisentrager*, a version of the narrow interpretation discussed in Part II.A.

Americans abroad enjoy greater rights than noncitizens abroad do, however, and Americans at home enjoy greater rights than noncitizens at home do (including, in particular, the right to vote, but also many constitutional protections). So as a matter of tradition noncitizens "count" less than Americans do; it's just that the noncitizen's disadvantage is greater when he or she is abroad than when he or she is on American territory. *Boumediene* certainly does not erase this disadvantage, but it does erode it (or portend such an erosion), assuming that in subsequent years the Court does not reverse course and refuse to grant substantive constitutional rights to nonresident aliens.

Still, the question can be asked: What is the constitutional reason for granting resident noncitizens any rights at all? The best answer probably would start from the premise that there is no reason to think that all people can be divided into two categories, citizen and noncitizen. There is a hazy third category, the quasi-citizen, that consists of people who have partly but not fully committed themselves to a polity. In the United States, these people are lawfully admitted noncitizens and, in particular, lawful permanent residents. Courts have granted these people (some) rights because they have made their way (partly) into the *demos*, and thus are (partly) vulnerable to democratic failure. This is not cosmopolitan or only ambiguously cosmopolitan—much like an open immigration law itself—because the status of the long-term resident is not clearly alien.[48]

---

[48] On the correlation between level of constitutional protection and extent to which a person has entered the *demos*, see, e.g., David A. Martin, Graduated Constitutional Protections for Aliens: The Real Meaning of *Zadvydas v. Davis*, 2001 Sup. Ct. Rev. 47.

## IV. A Brief Critique

The broad reading of *Boumediene,* which suggests a sneaking cosmopolitanism in Supreme Court jurisprudence, raises the question of whether Justice Kennedy's cosmopolitan approach to habeas is wise. One cannot answer this question without taking a position on whether the *demos* is national or global; I will start with the first assumption.

The national *demos* consists of American citizens at home and abroad, plus various quasi-citizens, such as lawful permanent residents. These people have values and interests that no doubt concern people living abroad. Some of these interests are intrinsic, while others are instrumental. Some Americans care about the well-being of the poor in other countries. This concern appears as government foreign aid and related projects, which though no doubt reflecting other motivations as well, at least partly reflect altruistic or cosmopolitan commitments. In addition, Americans benefit when their government makes deals with foreign governments, including trade deals, for example; here, noncitizens benefit but only as a means toward benefiting Americans.

None of these values and interests implies a constitutional role for the courts. As noted in Part III.B, the U.S. government has normal electoral incentives to respect altruistic interests of citizens, and to make deals with foreign governments in order to advance Americans' interests. Sometimes such deals are possible, sometimes they are not. As Justice Jackson recognized, the United States gains by extending habeas protections to enemy soldiers only if foreign states grant similar protections to Americans. There was no reason in Justice Jackson's time to think that they would, and there is no reason to think so today. Reciprocal rights are extended through negotiations between governments. Unilateral action by courts to grant unreciprocated benefits to noncitizens simply weakens the bargaining power of their own government.

Justice O'Connor hinted that the exchange of rights occurs at the constitutional level and is handled by judges rather than politicians. But she does not explain why judges should have this role, or even if the purported exchanges go through as intended. What will Americans obtain as a result of the Court's grant of habeas protections to noncitizens in Guantanamo Bay? What exactly did they receive in return for giving up the juvenile death penalty? Europeans seem no more inclined to adopt American religious freedoms than in the past—and would we really gain if they did?

These questions are not meant to deny the benefits that result when governments reciprocally advance the interests of noncitizens. The question is one of judicial competence and constitutional theory. In the framework of the democratic failure theory with a national *demos*, we would need to suppose that American judges restrain the American government because otherwise the American government would shun opportunities to advance the rights and interests of a discrete and insular minority of Americans by making deals with foreign governments. Because of democratic failure, the U.S. government neglects to protect Americans abroad by offering fair process to detainees, and the U.S. government (or state governments) neglects to influence European constitutional norms by rejecting the juvenile death penalty. Neither of these propositions has any plausibility. Because these benefits—protection of Americans abroad, influence on Europe—would go to Americans generally, rather than to a particular minority, these failures are not democratic failures.[49] If Guantanamo Bay has been a failure—if it has caused more harm to the United States than good—this is just a policy failure for which the Bush administration is responsible. Governments make policy mistakes all the time; it is not the role of courts to correct them.

Even if we were to accept the idea that courts should make constitutional deals directly with foreign constitutional courts, with our courts restraining our government for the sake of foreign interests so that foreign courts restrain their government for the sake of American interests, there is no evidence that Americans are getting anything out of these bargains. Indeed, most foreign courts do not have the power to deliver their governments. This leaves the suspicion that there are no exchanges—that the influence is really going only one way—so that noncitizens are being invited into our *demos* without our being invited into theirs. The interests of noncitizens are treated as constitutional ends; protection of those interests is not merely an instrument for securing the constitutional interests of

---

[49] Cf. Roger P. Alford, In Search of a Theory for Comparative Constitutionalism, 52 UCLA L. Rev. 639 (2005). Alford similarly doubts that democratic failure theory justifies reliance on foreign law for constitutional interpretation.

Americans overseas. If the *demos* is national, there is no justification for such an outcome.

Let us turn to a more promising basis for judicial cosmopolitanism: that the *demos* is actually global, not national. Hence democratic failure occurs because the U.S. government has no electoral incentive to take account of the interests of people living abroad. Courts should therefore strike down laws and block other government actions that (for example) unreasonably burden noncitizens abroad. This is a perfectly coherent view, albeit subject to a series of standard pragmatic objections. Courts that take this position run the risk that they hamstring their own government's ability to advance the interests of Americans by weakening its bargaining power. But they also would be concerned that when the government advances the interests of Americans, it harms the interests of others. Courts might also worry that they do not have the institutional competence to understand the interests of people living in other countries, their values and priorities, the reliability of their governments' claims about them, and so forth. But these are pragmatic issues, and conceivably a cosmopolitan judge would be justified in ignoring them—especially if he or she thinks that the American government's regard for nonresident aliens falls well short of what is morally required.

This view would take the Court far beyond anything it has done before. Consider a new tariff bill that harms some exporters in Haiti but benefits some export-competitors in Haiti, while benefiting some workers in the Dominican Republic because of trade diversion—with both governments offering to raise or lower cooperation with respect to various diplomatic initiatives in the Caribbean if the U.S. Congress does (or does not) pass the bill. Should the Court review this law in order to ensure that the interests of noncitizens are appropriately taken into account? No one seems to think so. Yet the hardship imposed on the Haitians thrown out of work could be just as significant as a detention, and would be constitutionally suspect under the democratic failure theory assuming a global *demos*. If a law strips habeas protections of noncitizens, so that Americans and some noncitizens benefit from the increased security while other noncitizens—including the detainees—are harmed, the question is no easier. And these questions are not very different from the question of whether Europeans would, in general, benefit or be harmed if the United States eliminated the death penalty, and to what extent.

Some noncitizens would be, others not; again all questions that are beyond judicial competence under any reasonable conception of it.

Whatever its merits, one doubts that such an approach is sustainable. Aside from the sheer complexity of evaluating American laws that affect foreigners abroad, it gives courts the difficult task of resisting the political interests of government, whichever party controls it. Many scholars believe that the Supreme Court maintains its power by staying close to the political center. Protecting noncitizens, by contrast, will put the Supreme Court outside the mainstream— regardless of which party is in power—unless the cases have little practical importance. *Boumediene* itself has received praise from Democrats, but it seems doubtful that more aggressive efforts by courts to protect the interests of nonresident aliens would be welcome, even if Democrats take control of the presidency.[50] If the Court must stay close to the political center, then even approaches to the Constitution that incorporate moral principles must rely on a morality rooted in the sensibilities of citizens, who are not themselves notably cosmopolitan.

## V. Conclusion

If the *Boumediene* case is remembered, it will be remembered not as a separation-of-powers case, but as one more step in the march of judicial cosmopolitanism—the emerging view that the interests of nonresident aliens deserve constitutional protection secured by judicial review. The constitutional basis for this view remains to be worked out. Although it may be good policy for the American government to respect—or at least take account of—the interests and values of foreigners, it is not clear why American judges should compel the government to do so by giving overseas aliens the right to bring actions against it in American courts, or by incorporating foreign norms into American constitutional law.

---

[50] See, e.g., the Clinton administration's treatment of Haitian refugees, who were also detained in Guantanamo Bay.

# Rights over Borders: Transnational Constitutionalism and Guantanamo Bay

*David D. Cole\**

In June 2008, more than six years after the first prisoners were brought to a makeshift military prison camp at Guantanamo Bay, Cuba—bound, gagged, blindfolded, and labeled "the worst of the worst"—the Supreme Court in *Boumediene v. Bush*[1] declared that they have a constitutional right to challenge the legality of their detention in federal court. The detainees may be excused if they did not leap for joy at the result. After all, the Court ordered no one released, did not address the question of whether the detainees were lawfully detained or treated, and merely decided as a threshold matter that they had a right to take their cases to a federal district court—a question the Court seemed to have decided four years earlier in the first Guantanamo case it considered, *Rasul v. Bush*.[2] Yet the decision was in fact a profound—and in many respects surprising—defeat for the Bush administration in the legal "war on terror." It means that Guantanamo is no longer a "law-free zone"— and that the courts will play a vital role in ensuring that the rule of law applies to the ongoing struggle with Al Qaeda. As critically important as the *Boumediene* decision is for the place of law in the war on terror, however, its most profound implications may lie in what it reflects about altered conceptions of sovereignty, territoriality, and rights in the globalized world.

## I.

*Boumediene* is groundbreaking in at least three respects. First, for the first time in its history, the Supreme Court declared unconstitutional a law enacted by Congress and signed by the president on

---

*Professor, Georgetown University Law Center.
[1] 553 U.S. ____ , 128 S. Ct. 2229 (2008).
[2] 542 U.S. 466 (2004).

an issue of military policy in a time of armed conflict. While the Court has on rare occasions found that presidents exceeded their powers where they acted *contrary* to congressional will during wartime, as in *Youngstown Sheet & Tube Co. v. Sawyer*[3] and *Little v. Barreme*,[4] this decision went much further, upending the joint decision of the political branches acting together on a military matter during a time of military conflict.

Second, and also for the first time, the Court extended constitutional protections to noncitizens outside U.S. territory during wartime. As recently as 2001, the Court had stated—without reasoning—that the Constitution was no solace for foreign nationals outside our borders, articulating a traditional understanding of the Constitution as guided by territory and citizenship.[5] Yet in *Boumediene* the Court extended the constitutional right of habeas corpus not only to foreign nationals outside our borders, but to what some might call the modern-day equivalent of "enemy aliens"—foreign nationals said to be associated with the enemy in wartime.

Third, the Court declared unconstitutional a law restricting federal court jurisdiction. The Court has traditionally sought to avoid such confrontations through the application of statutory interpretation, bending over backward to interpret statutes to preserve judicial review where it might be unconstitutional to deny such review.[6] Only on two prior occasions has the Court actually declared a jurisdiction-stripping law unconstitutional, and on both occasions it

---

[3] 343 U.S. 579, 609 (1952). In *Youngstown*, the Supreme Court invalidated President Truman's seizure of the steel mills during the Korean War, where Congress had "rejected an amendment which would have authorized such governmental seizures in cases of emergency." *Id.* at 586; see also *id.* at 597–609 (Frankfurter, J., concurring); *id.* at 656–660 (Burton, J., concurring); *id.* at 662–666 (Clark, J., concurring in the judgment).

[4] 6 U.S. (2 Cranch) 170 (1804). In *Little*, the Court held unlawful a seizure pursuant to presidential order of a ship during the "Quasi War" with France. The Court found that Congress had authorized the seizure only of ships going *to* France, and therefore the president could not unilaterally order the seizure of a ship coming *from* France.

[5] Zadvydas v. Davis, 533 U.S. 678, 693 (2001) ("It is well established that certain constitutional protections available to persons inside the United States are unavailable to aliens outside of our geographic borders.").

[6] See, e.g., INS v. St. Cyr, 533 U.S. 289, 304 (2001).

found reasons for doing so that were independent of the pure question of jurisdiction.[7] The courts have traditionally avoided enforcing constitutional limits on Congress's control over jurisdiction because congressional control is seen as important in conferring democratic legitimacy on an unelected institution. Yet in *Boumediene*, despite the availability of statutory constructions that could have saved the statute, the Court declared Congress's repeal of habeas corpus unconstitutional.

The result in *Boumediene* was also surprising because the government had precedent on its side. In 1950, the Supreme Court had expressly ruled that the writ of habeas corpus was unavailable to enemy fighters captured and detained abroad during wartime.[8] Both the district court and the court of appeals had found that decision, *Johnson v. Eisentrager*, to be controlling, and no subsequent case law had directly undermined its reasoning.

Critics will point to these features as evidence that the Court's decision was illegitimately "activist." To many observers, there are good reasons for judicial reticence in military matters, especially where the political branches act in concert;[9] good reasons not to extend constitutional protections to foreign nationals;[10] and good reasons for the Court to avoid a direct confrontation with Congress over the scope of its jurisdiction. Justice Antonin Scalia charged in dissent that "[w]hat drives today's decision is neither the meaning

[7] In US v. Klein, 80 U.S. 128 (1871), the Court struck down a statute stripping federal court jurisdiction over claims by former rebel soldiers during the Civil War who had obtained presidential pardons, but the decision can be seen as resting on the impermissibility of interfering with the president's pardon power. And in Plaut v. Spendthrift Farm, 514 U.S. 211 (1995), the Court invalidated a statute that sought to reopen prior final judgments under the Securities and Exchange Act, on the narrow ground that it violates the separation of powers for Congress to reopen a final judgment of the courts.

[8] Johnson v. Eisentrager, 339 U.S. 763 (1950).

[9] Samuel Issacharoff & Richard H. Pildes, Between Civil Libertarianism and Executive Unilateralism: An Institutional Process Approach to Rights During Wartime, 5 Theoretical Inquiries in Law 1 (2004) (available at http://www.bepress.com/til/default/vol5/iss1/art1/); Eric Posner and Adrian Vermeule, Terror in the Balance: Security, Liberty and the Courts (2007); John Yoo, War By Other Means: An Insider's Account of the War on Terror (2007).

[10] J. Andrew Kent, A Textual and Historical Case Against a Global Constitution, 95 Geo. L. J. 463 (2007).

of the Suspension Clause, nor the principles of our precedents, but rather an inflated notion of judicial supremacy."[11]

At the same time, the decision was not entirely unprecedented. It vindicated the right to a "writ of habeas corpus," an ancient form of judicial remedy that finds its origins in the Magna Carta, and that the Framers deemed so fundamental that they included it in the main body of the Constitution at a time when they considered a "Bill of Rights" unnecessary.[12] Habeas corpus gives prisoners the right to challenge the legality of their detentions in court, and is both an essential part of the separation of powers and the "stable bulwark of our liberties."[13] It is fundamental to the protection of all other rights, because no right can be safely exercised if the government is free to imprison people without judicial recourse.

In addition to enforcing a fundamental and long-standing right, the Court applied established doctrine—albeit in a new setting. In assessing whether the constitutional right of habeas corpus extended to Guantanamo, the Court applied a contextual and pragmatic inquiry that it had developed and applied in assessing whether constitutional rights extend to "unincorporated territories," jurisdictions over which the United States exercises control but does not intend to incorporate as states. That test asks whether the application of a given constitutional right would be "anomalous or impracticable" in light of the particular circumstances of the jurisdiction, and applies those rights that would not create serious anomalies or impracticalities.

The real significance of the Court's decision in *Boumediene*, however, lies not in whether it correctly applied or modified past precedent to a novel context, but in what it portends for modern-day conceptions of sovereignty, territoriality, and rights. For all its assertions that "everything changed" after the terrorist attacks of September 11, the Bush administration relied on old-fashioned conceptions

---

[11] Boumediene, 128 S. Ct. at 2302 (Scalia, J., dissenting). Chief Justice Roberts similarly declared that "[a]ll that today's opinion has done is shift responsibility for those sensitive foreign policy and national security decisions from the elected branches to the Federal Judiciary." *Id.* at 2280 (Roberts, C.J., dissenting).

[12] The Bill of Rights was drafted subsequently as the first 10 amendments to the Constitution, at the insistence of the ratifying conventions.

[13] Boumediene, 128 S. Ct. at 2245 (quoting 1 William Blackstone, Commentaries *137).

of sovereignty and rights in arguing that habeas corpus jurisdiction did not extend to Guantanamo, and that federal courts should have no constitutionally recognized role there. The Court's decision, by contrast, reflects new understandings of these traditional conceptions, understandings that pierce the veil of sovereignty, reject formalist fictions of territoriality where the state exercises authority beyond its borders, and insist on the need for judicial review to safeguard the human rights of citizens and noncitizens alike.

While *Boumediene* may appear unprecedented from a domestic standpoint, it fits quite comfortably within an important transnational trend of recent years, in which courts of last resort have played an increasingly aggressive role in reviewing (and invalidating) security measures that trench on individual rights. The Law Lords in Britain, the Supreme Courts of Canada and Israel, the European Court of Human Rights, and the Constitutional Court of Germany have all issued major decisions restricting political prerogative on issues of terrorism and national security in the name of individual rights.[14]

---

[14] In Great Britain, the Law Lords, the equivalent of our Supreme Court, have since 9/11 issued three decisions rejecting counterterrorism measures in whole or in part. They declared invalid a law authorizing indefinite preventive detention of foreign terror suspects, A and others v Secretary of State for the Home Department, 2 A.C. 68 (U.K.H.L. 2005); barred any consideration of evidence obtained by torture, even when British authorities played no part in the torture, A and others v Secretary of State for the Home Department (No 2), 2 A.C. 221 (U.K.H.L. 2005); and barred the use of secret evidence in procedures employed to justify imposing curfews on terror suspects, Secretary of State for the Home Department v MB, [2008] A.C. 48 (U.K.H.L. 2008).

In 2007, Canada's Supreme Court ruled that the use of secret evidence to detain foreign nationals suspected of terrorist activities was unconstitutional. Charkaoui v. Minister of Citizenship and Immigration, 2000 S.C.R. LEXIS 9 (Can. 2000). And in 2008, the Court unanimously ordered the Canadian government to disclose to Omar Khadr, a Canadian held at Guantanamo, evidence that Canadian authorities had obtained from him when they interviewed him there. Minister of Justice v. Khadr, 2008 Can. Sup. Ct. LEXIS 32 (Can. 2008).

Israel's Supreme Court has barred the use of coercive interrogation tactics against Palestinian terror suspects, HCJ 5100/94 Public Committee Against Torture in Israel v. State of Israel [1999] IsrSC _____ , forbade detention of Palestinians as "bargaining chips" to seek the release of Israeli hostages, CrimFH 7048/97 A v. Minister of Defence [2000] IsrSC 44(1) 721, and restricted when the military may seek to kill suspected terrorist leaders. HCJ 769/02 The Public Committee against Torture in Israel v. The Government of Israel [2005] IsrSC _____ .

The European Court of Human Rights has barred countries from deporting terror suspects to countries where they face a risk of cruel, inhuman or degrading treatment. Saadi v Italy, [2008] Eur. Ct. H.R. 37201/06.

These increasingly confident judicial assertions of authority in turn reflect global transformations in international law since the end of World War II, including most significantly international human rights law. The latter half of the 20th century and the beginning of the 21st have witnessed an extraordinary explosion of human rights, beginning with the UN's Universal Declaration of Human Rights, and finding reflection in international treaties such as the International Covenant on Civil and Political Rights, the Geneva Conventions, and the Convention Against Torture. This trend is reinforced by regional agreements for the establishment and enforcement of human rights, especially the European Convention on Human Rights; the growth in influence and power of nongovernmental human rights groups; the increasing resort by domestic courts to international and comparative standards in the interpretation of their own laws;[15] and the recognition of "universal jurisdiction" as a way of holding abusers of certain fundamental human rights accountable wherever they are found.[16]

These developments have transformed international law from a subject that concerned only state-to-state relations to one that focuses just as significantly on the relations of states to their own citizens, and to others subject to their authority. In particular, international human rights law has made substantial inroads on traditional notions of sovereignty and territoriality that once left states both unaccountable to outsiders for what they did to their own citizens inside their borders, and unaccountable to domestic law for what they did to others outside their borders. The lasting significance of *Boumediene* will rest on its recognition of, and critical role in, the transformation of our understandings of this interplay between sovereignty, territoriality, and human rights.

---

And Germany's highest court has twice in recent years ruled that computer "data mining" measures designed to identify terrorists violate privacy rights. Bundesverfassungsgericht [BVerfG] [Federal Constitutional Court] Apr. 4, 2006, 1 BvR 518/02 (F.R.G.); Bundesgerichtshof [BFG] [Federal Court of Justice] Oct. 26, 2006, III ZR 40/06 (F.R.G.).

[15] See, e.g., Roper v. Simmons, 543 U.S. 551 (2005); Lawrence v. Texas, 539 U.S. 558, 573 (2003).

[16] See, e.g. Filártiga v. Peña-Irala, 630 F.2d 876 (2d Cir. 1980) (holding that U.S. courts could hold a Paraguayan official liable for torturing a Paraguayan in Paraguay); Kenneth Roth, The Case for Universal Jurisdiction, 80 Foreign Affairs 5 (Sept./Oct. 2001).

## II.

The central issue in *Boumediene* was whether the privilege of habeas corpus protects foreign nationals captured abroad and held as enemy combatants at Guantanamo. The Bush administration consciously chose to house its detainees at Guantanamo, a military base in Cuba that we have the right to lease as long as we choose, because it thought its location beyond our borders would afford it a "law-free zone."

In 2004, the Court ruled in its first Guantanamo case, *Rasul v. Bush*, that the existing federal habeas statute provided review to persons held at Guantanamo.[17] But that decision was superseded when, in the Military Commissions Act, Congress stripped the courts of habeas jurisdiction over detainees' claims.[18] As a result, the Court in *Boumediene* was confronted with the question of whether Guantanamo detainees have a *constitutional* right to habeas corpus—that is, one that cannot be taken away unless Congress suspends the writ in times of "rebellion or invasion." The Court in *Rasul* had simply employed statutory interpretation, and as such left Congress free to respond, as it did, by changing the law. In *Boumediene*, however, the Court thwarted the will of the president and Congress acting together, and did so on constitutional grounds—which are far less susceptible to a political override.

In arguing that habeas did not extend to Guantanamo, the administration invoked traditional territorial conceptions of national sovereignty and rights. While the Constitution is unquestionably supreme within U.S. sovereign territory, courts have generally been reluctant to extend its protections beyond our borders, even to restrict our own government's actions. For example, the Court has held that the Fourth Amendment does not apply to a search by U.S. agents of a Mexican national's home in Mexico,[19] and that the Fifth Amendment's Due Process Clause does not protect foreign nationals with respect to admission to the United States, even if they have been

---

[17] 542 U.S. 466.

[18] The Military Commission Act provided that "[n]o court, justice, or judge shall have jurisdiction to hear or consider an application for a writ of habeas corpus filed by or on behalf of an alien detained by the United States who has been determined by the United States to have been properly detained as an enemy combatant or is awaiting such determination." 28 U.S.C.A. § 2241(e)(1) (Supp. 2007).

[19] United States v. Verdugo-Urquidez, 494 U.S. 259 (1990).

detained on Ellis Island for years.[20] And in *Johnson v. Eisentrager*, the Court noted that the foreign prisoners had committed their offenses abroad, been captured abroad, tried abroad, and had never been inside U.S. territory, in declining to extend habeas corpus to them.[21]

The government also stressed the status of the detainees as foreign enemies of the state. Even if the constitutional right of habeas corpus might extend to a U.S. citizen held by the United States abroad, the government maintained, it should not reach foreigners deemed to be enemies in a military conflict. The Supreme Court had previously extended constitutional protections to U.S. citizens abroad,[22] but the government argued that those cases rested on the ties of citizenship and could not be extended to foreign nationals—much less those associated with the enemy.

The *Boumediene* Court ruled that at least some constitutional rights can reach beyond U.S. borders to foreign nationals. As a formal matter, it did so by looking back, not forward. It initially examined the historical evidence regarding the scope of habeas corpus under English common law at the time of the Founding, and concluded that the evidence was ambiguous. British courts had exercised habeas jurisdiction over claims of alleged "enemy aliens" during wartime, but they had generally been in custody in England at the time. British courts had also exercised habeas jurisdiction over India and Ireland, but had declined to do so over Scotland. The Court ultimately concluded that this historical evidence left the issue open: There were no clear precedents establishing or denying habeas corpus jurisdiction in analogous circumstances (in large part because there were no precisely analogous circumstances).

The Court then turned to its own jurisprudence concerning the application of the Constitution to so-called unincorporated territories—areas such as Guam or the Philippines that were (for a time) under U.S. control, but were not intended to be "incorporated" as states into the Union. The Court held that the Constitution applies of its own force in full to "incorporated" territories destined to

---

[20] United States ex rel. Knauff v. Shaughnessy, 338 U.S. 537 (1950); Shaughnessy v. United States ex rel. Mezei, 345 U.S. 206 (1953).

[21] Johnson v. Eisentrager, 339 U.S. 763, 778 (1950).

[22] See, e.g., Reid v. Covert, 354 U.S. 1 (1957).

become states, but applies only in part to "unincorporated" territories. The selective application of the Constitution to unincorporated territories was motivated by the need to be respectful of the territory's own legal tradition and culture. Accordingly, the Court—in what have come to be known as the *Insular Cases*—undertook a context-specific inquiry that asks "whether judicial enforcement of the provision would be 'impracticable and anomalous.'"[23]

The *Boumediene* Court read *Johnson v. Eisentrager* within this doctrinal tradition, noting that the *Eisentrager* decision had cited a variety of pragmatic factors in concluding that habeas corpus should not extend to prisoners of war held at Landsberg Prison in Germany, including "the difficulties of ordering the Government to produce the prisoners in a habeas corpus proceeding."[24] The United States argued in *Boumediene* that the key to *Eisentrager* was that the prisoners were not and had never been within U.S. sovereign territory, and that because Guantanamo was subject to Cuban, not U.S., sovereignty, a similar result should obtain. The Court rejected this argument on two grounds. First, the *Eisentrager* Court had cited the petitioners' relationship to U.S. sovereign territory only briefly, while employing other arguments that seemed in keeping with the broader functional inquiry used in the *Insular Cases*. Second, and more significantly, the Court noted that because "sovereignty" was determined by the political branches, making sovereignty the linchpin for rights protections would make it "possible for the political branches to govern without legal constraint"[25]—or in other words, to establish "law-free zones." Accordingly, the Court concluded, questions of extraterritorial application of the Constitution "turn on objective factors and practical concerns, not formalism."[26]

The majority then determined that several factors distinguished *Eisentrager* and made application of habeas corpus to the Guantanamo detainees neither anomalous nor impracticable. *Eisentrager* concerned individuals who did not dispute their status as "enemy aliens" captured during a declared war; the Guantanamo detainees,

---

[23] Boumediene, 128 S. Ct. at 2255 (quoting Reid, 354 U.S. at 74–75) (Harlan, J., concurring in result)).

[24] *Id.* at 2257.

[25] *Id.* at 2258–59.

[26] *Id.* at 2258.

by contrast, were not citizens of any state with which the United States is at war, and denied that they had been correctly identified as "enemy combatants." The *Eisentrager* petitioners had been convicted of war crimes after a full-fledged criminal trial; the Guantanamo detainees had received only the summary procedure of a Combatant Status Review Tribunal, the procedural shortcomings of which made habeas corpus review more essential. The *Eisentrager* petitioners were held in Landsberg Prison in Germany, which was subject to the control of the Allied Powers, while the United States exercises exclusive jurisdiction and control over Guantanamo. And while the United States faced significant security threats in Germany at the end of World War II, the government cited no security obstacles to extending habeas jurisdiction to Guantanamo, an isolated location thousands of miles from any battlefield.

As the dissenting justices pointed out, however, this sort of all-things-considered contextual analysis gives rise to few general principles of law. As a result, it leaves government officials guessing as to which, if any, constitutional constraints will apply to official action abroad, and gives the Court a relatively free hand in future cases. Moreover, as Justice Scalia illustrates in his dissent, one could read both the British and the U.S. precedent to preclude extension of habeas corpus to foreign nationals held as enemy combatants outside U.S. borders.

## III.

The real significance of the *Boumediene* decision, however, lies not in how it reads the past, but in what it says about the present and the future. Although the decision rested entirely on domestic constitutional grounds, the Court's ruling reflects important modern-day developments in conceptions of sovereignty, rights, and judicial review—each of which has been profoundly transformed by the human rights revolution of the past half century.

As noted above, the worldview underlying the government's position in *Boumediene* was decidedly old-fashioned. It treated sovereignty as absolute, and strictly tied to territory; and viewed rights as derivative of sovereignty, and therefore also territorially limited. Within our borders, the United States is sovereign, and the governing sovereign law, the Constitution, establishes rights that are subject to judicial protection and enforcement. Guantanamo, however, lies outside our borders and is subject to the absolute sovereignty of another nation, Cuba. The government argued, therefore, that constitutional rights cannot govern there, even if the United States, as a practical matter, exercises exclusive jurisdiction and control.

This worldview is consistent with traditional conceptions of sovereignty and international law. At the time of the Constitution's framing, for example, nations were seen as independent sovereigns and sovereignty was seen as virtually impregnable. It followed, almost as a corollary, that national sovereignty was territorially limited. If sovereignty is absolute, it cannot coexist with the sovereignty of another nation, and so territorial lines are necessary to demarcate the beginning of one nation's absolute sovereignty and the end of another's.

Traditionally, the realms of domestic and international law were similarly defined by borders. A state's domestic laws were presumptively limited to its territory, and only in limited contexts could domestic law extend extraterritorially—as such an extension would risk interfering with the absolute sovereignty of another state. And as a traditional matter international law addressed relations among, not within, states. The objects of international and domestic law were thus strictly divided. International law concerned external relations between nation-states as such, while domestic law concerned the relation between "the people" and their government. Individual rights were accordingly a domestic matter, subject to the will of the sovereign, and not a concern of international law.

The Bush administration's arguments rested on these notions: Sovereignty is territorially defined, and individual rights are a matter of the sovereign's domestic law. That domestic law generally does not extend beyond our borders, except (and even this exception is a post-constitutional development) when the state's actions affect its own citizens abroad. As domestic law, the Constitution should not extend beyond our borders to another sovereign's territory unless the extension is based on the (domestic) tie between the state and its own citizens.

This understanding still largely governed international and domestic law at the time *Eisentrager* was decided. Long before September 11, however, these conceptions had begun to change. International human rights, globalization, and modern communications and transportation have rendered borders and sovereignty considerably less sacrosanct, while simultaneously providing new bases for the protection of rights. Sovereigns no longer enjoy absolute supremacy within their own borders, but are subject to the limits of inalienable human rights.[27] Those rights in turn are predicated not on an individual's geographic location, nor on his or her relation to the state, but on human dignity, a quality that exists independently of both territory and citizenship.

International human rights norms have increasingly been interpreted as applicable beyond a nation's own borders, wherever the nation exercises effective control over a place or a person.[28] The Inter-American Human Rights Commission, for example, has stated that the obligations of the Inter-American Convention on Human Rights apply wherever a state exercises effective control over an individual, regardless of territorial considerations. It reasons that the rights articulated in the Convention inhere in human dignity, and therefore it should not matter where the individual is found.[29] If a Convention state exercises control over the individual, it must respect his rights under the treaty. The European Court of Human Rights has similarly ruled that the obligations of the European Convention apply wherever a state exercises effective control over a particular jurisdiction, and in some instances, over a particular individual.[30] Applying this

---

[27] See, e.g., Philip Bobbitt, Terror and Consent: The Wars for the Twenty-First Century 452–83 (2008).

[28] Sarah Cleveland, Geography or Control? International Jurisdiction and Constitutional Protection for Aliens Abroad, presented at Georgetown University Law Center Symposium on Human Rights and Immigrants' Rights (2007) (manuscript on file with author).

[29] Coard and Others v. the United States ('US military intervention in Grenada'), IACHR Report No. 109/9, Case No. 10.951, Sec. V, ¶ 37 (Sept. 29, 1999) (available at http://www.cidh.oas.org/annualrep/99eng/Merits/UnitedStates10.951.htm).

[30] The Court has stated that the obligations of the European Convention on Human Rights are primarily territorial, but extend where a state, "through the effective control of the relevant territory and its inhabitants abroad as a consequence of military occupation or through the consent, invitation or acquiescence of the government of that territory, exercises all or some of the public powers normally to be exercised by that government." Bankovíc and Others v. Belgium and 16 Other Contracting States, Eur. Ct. H.R. appl. No. 52207/99; Adm. Dec., ¶ 71 (Dec. 12 2001). And in a case involving Turkey's abduction of a terror suspect from Kenya, the Court held that Turkey's obligations were triggered by the suspect's abduction, even though it took place in Kenya. Öcalan v. Turkey, ¶ 93, Eur. Ct. H.R. appl. No. 46221/99, Judgment ¶ 93 (Mar. 12, 2003).

principle, the United Kingdom's Law Lords held that the European Convention on Human Rights applied to a British prison maintained in Basra, Iraq, because the British Army exercised effective control over the prison.[31]

Even though the United States has been a leader in pressing for many of these international developments, it has found the implications for its own conduct difficult to accept. When the Senate has ratified human rights treaties, for example, it has generally insisted on reservations that ensure that the treaty's obligations do no more than duplicate those already imposed by our own Constitution.[32] Moreover, the Bush administration has relied on territorial and citizenship arguments to shield other "war on terror" initiatives from legal constraint. Thus it maintained that the international treaty prohibition on cruel, inhuman, and degrading treatment did not protect foreign nationals waterboarded and otherwise abused by the CIA in secret "black sites" abroad.[33] And it has argued that federal officials' "renditions" of foreign nationals to other countries to be interrogated under torture there implicate no constitutional rights so long as the individual was not admitted to the United States when the rendition occurred.[34]

[31] R. (on the application of Al-Skeini and others) v. Sec'y of State for Defence, 1 A.C. 153 (U.K.H.L. 2007).

[32] Ryan Goodman, Human Rights Treaties, Invalid Reservations, and State Consent, 96 Am. J. Int'l L. 531 (2002); William A. Schabas, Invalid Reservations to the International Covenant on Civil and Political Rights: Is the United States Still a Party? 21 Brook. J. Int'l L. 277, 295–96 (1995).

[33] This interpretation, adopted in secret, was disclosed in response to questions put to Alberto Gonzales when the Senate was considering whether to confirm him as attorney general. See, e.g., Transcript of Confirmation Hearing on the Nomination of Alberto Gonzales to be U.S. Attorney General: Hearing Before the S. Comm. on Judiciary, 109th Cong. (Jan. 6, 2005) (available at http://www.washingtonpost.com/wp-dyn/articles/A53883-2005Jan6.html). When Congress learned that the administration had adopted this interpretation, it overruled it in what came to be known as the McCain Amendment, which insisted that the obligation to desist from cruel, inhuman, and degrading treatment applied to everyone held in U.S. custody, no matter what their citizenship and no matter where they are held. The McCain Amendment was included as Title X in Division A of the Department of Defense, Emergency Supplemental Appropriations to Address Hurricanes in the Gulf of Mexico, and Pandemic Influenza Act, H.R. 2863, 109th Cong. (2006) (available at http://www.govtrack.us/congress/billtext.xpd?bill=h109-2863).

[34] U.S. Brief in Arar v. Ashcroft, 532 F.3d 157, No. 06-4216-cv, 27–35 (available at http://ccrjustice.org/files/US%20Appellee%20Brief%202.22.07.pdf) (2d Cir. en banc review pending).

The *Boumediene* decision suggests that the Court is more open to these transformations in international legal culture than is the administration. That in turn may be because under the modern conception of international law, the legitimacy of judicial review has itself been reinforced in important ways. The international human rights regime insists that democracy is not the ultimate test of a legitimate government, but that respect for inalienable human rights is. And democracies are not particularly likely to protect human rights when the majority feels threatened by outsiders or by a minority group. In those settings, as in the "war on terror," the political branches, responsive as they are to majoritarian desires, are likely to sacrifice the rights of those without a powerful voice in the political process in the name of preserving the security of the majority.[35] This is not a flaw unique to the United States, but is an inevitable feature of a majoritarian process. Precisely for that reason, courts have an essential role to play in protecting individual rights on behalf of those without a voice in the political process.[36]

The transnational trend referred to above, in which courts have restrained the national security measures of political branches, reflects an increasingly broad acceptance of the importance of individual rights, and of the appropriate role of courts in enforcing them. When the Israeli Supreme Court barred coercive interrogations of Palestinian terror suspects, the Law Lords deemed incompatible with human rights obligations a U.K. law authorizing indefinite detention of foreign terror suspects, or the European Court of Human Rights ruled that nations may not deport a foreign national suspected of terrorist ties to a country where he faces a risk of cruel, inhuman, or degrading treatment, they were insisting on the propriety—and indeed the *necessity*—of meaningful judicial review where states take action against outsiders in the name of national security. The Supreme Court's decision in *Boumediene* does the same. Chief Justice John Roberts's complaint that the majority gave "unelected, politically unaccountable judges" an inappropriate role in overseeing "the Nation's foreign policy"[37] misses the point of the last half century.

[35] See David Cole, Enemy Aliens: Double Standards and Constitutional Freedoms in the War on Terrorism (2005).

[36] John Hart Ely, Democracy and Distrust: A Theory of Judicial Review (1980).

[37] Boumediene, 128 S. Ct. at 2293 (Roberts, C.J., dissenting).

The protection of fundamental human rights requires not only the piercing of once-impermeable sovereign borders, but also the robust intervention of unelected courts.

## Conclusion

The United States' legal defense of Guantanamo in the *Boumediene* case turned ultimately on outmoded claims about sovereignty, territoriality, and rights. The Court's rejection of those arguments in turn is in keeping with a global shift in modern understandings of these concepts. Sovereignty is no longer absolute, territorial, and sacred, but conditional and limited by legal obligations to the individual that simultaneously pierce the border—insisting that a state respect the rights of those within its own jurisdiction—and extend beyond the border, limiting the state's range of choice wherever it exercises effective control over an individual or place. At the same time, the Court's confident assertion of its own role in enforcing rights is also in keeping with a transnational understanding that, while democracy is good for many things, it is not the sine qua non of legitimate government; respect for individual autonomy and human rights is. Because democracies are not particularly good at protecting the rights of unpopular minorities, especially those minorities outside the polity, the courts have an essential role to play. Extending habeas corpus to Guantanamo detainees as a constitutional matter insists on the rights of individuals over formal conceptions of sovereignty and territoriality, and on the role of courts in ensuring that democracies respect human rights. It ushers U.S. law into the 21st century.

# Medellín v. Texas and the Ultimate Law School Exam

*Ilya Shapiro**

## Introduction

Commentators often fall in love with the object of their analysis and thereby lose perspective. After being immersed for so long in the minutia of a given topic, and investing so much in a particular narrative or thesis, it becomes difficult not to overstate the importance of the subject matter. In recognizing this bias with respect to *Medellín v. Texas*,[1] I hope to avoid it. Having said that, I don't believe it's an exaggeration to call this the most intellectually interesting case of the term. It is also probably the one with the broadest implications for American jurisprudence, coming at the increasingly topical intersection of international and constitutional law.

*Medellín* presented the Court with a law school exam of a case, combining questions of treaty interpretation and application, federalism, separation of powers, and criminal procedure. It forced the justices to grapple with tensions between international and domestic law (and what that means for the Constitution's Supremacy Clause), federal and state government, and the president and three separate institutions: Congress, the Supreme Court, and—in what then-Texas Solicitor General Ted Cruz (who argued the case) has called a "Mobius twist"—state courts. In short, this remarkable case raised issues touching on every axis of governmental structure, checks and balances, and the design of political institutions.

---

*Senior Fellow in Constitutional Studies, Cato Institute, and Editor-in-Chief, *Cato Supreme Court Review*.

[1] 552 U.S. ____, 128 S. Ct. 1346 (2008). All citations styled as "Medellín" that do not include the other party to the case (i.e., lower court, state, and previous Supreme Court rulings) refer to this opinion.

The case arose out of a lawsuit that Mexico filed against the United States in the International Court of Justice (often called the "World Court") regarding the interpretation of the Vienna Convention on Consular Affairs[2] and its Optional Protocol[3]. The ICJ issued an extraordinary order, directing the United States to reopen and review the convictions and death sentences of 51 Mexican nationals who had not been apprised of their consular rights.[4] It was a rare instance of a foreign tribunal attempting to assert the authority to bind American judges, and so the first issue for the Supreme Court to resolve was whether it could do so.

The case took a further strange twist in 2005, when President George W. Bush wrote a two-paragraph memorandum to then-Attorney General Alberto Gonzalez (formerly of the Texas Supreme Court) directing the Texas courts to put the ICJ order into effect. There was no precedent for a U.S. president to do something like that, either in the name of international comity or in fulfillment of a treaty obligation. The second issue was thus whether the president can direct state courts to follow an ICJ judgment regarding the consular rights of a convicted felon.

The Court found for the state of Texas, holding that the ICJ cannot make Vienna Convention rights—the alleged violation of which was not raised until post-conviction state habeas review four years after the original trial—legally cognizable without congressional legislation (cannot make them "self-executing"); but regardless, the Court further held, President Bush stepped beyond his lawful authority in trying to enforce the ICJ judgment against state courts.

Not surprisingly, the multi-layered legal controversy produced the oddest of bedfellows: On one side, Texas was supported by states not typically known to hold the Lone Star State's view of law or policy—and one amicus brief brought together Erwin Chemerinsky and John Yoo, scholars not often on the same side of a legal dispute. On the other, President Bush found himself supported by

[2] Apr. 24, 1963, [1970] 21 U.S.T. 77, T.I.A.S. No. 6820.

[3] Optional Protocol Concerning the Compulsory Settlement of Disputes to the Vienna Convention, Apr. 24, 1963, [1970] 21 U.S.T. 325, 326, T.I.A.S. No. 6820 (granting the ICJ exclusive jurisdiction over disputes regarding the Vienna Convention).

[4] Case Concerning Avena and Other Mexican Nationals (Mexico v. United States of America), 2004 I.C.J. 12 (Judgment of Mar. 31).

death penalty abolitionists and progressive transnationalists (and 81 countries joined briefs supporting the U.S. position).

This article presents the lead-up to the case, analyzes the opinion and its aftermath, and evaluates *Medellín*'s implications for international law and executive authority. I begin in Part I with the factual and procedural background to the case, the legal developments that led to this intersection of international and constitutional law, and the course of litigation before the Supreme Court. In Part II, I parse the *Medellín* opinion, concentrating of course on Chief Justice John Roberts's opinion for the Court, but also noting salient points from Justice John Paul Stevens's concurrence and Justice Stephen Breyer's dissent. Part III details subsequent legal action and Medellín's execution. In Part IV, I look at the future of international law and executive power in U.S. courts and propose how a president could act in similar circumstances if an issue like this ever arises again.

## I. Background

### A. Legal Developments

The United States ratified the Vienna Convention and its Optional Protocol in 1969. Article 36 of the Convention "facilitate[s] the exercise of consular functions" and provides that if a foreign person detained by a party country "so requests, the competent authorities of the receiving State shall, without delay, inform the consular post of the sending State" of such detention, and "inform the [arrested person] of his right[]" to consular assistance.[5] This right is meant to "contribute to the development of friendly relations among nations."[6] Under the Optional Protocol, disputes over the application of the Vienna Convention "shall lie within the compulsory jurisdiction of the [ICJ]" and can be brought "by any party to the dispute" who is a party to the Protocol.[7]

The ICJ is "the principal judicial organ of the United Nations"[8] and is governed by a part of the UN Charter known as the ICJ Statute.[9] Each UN member "undertakes to comply with the decision

[5] Art. 36(1), 21 U.S.T. at 100–01.

[6] Preamble, 21 U.S.T. at 79.

[7] Art. I, 21 U.S.T. at 326.

[8] UN Charter, art. 92, 59 Stat. 1051, T.S. No. 993 (1945).

[9] *Id.*, art. 59, 59 Stat. 1062.

of the [ICJ] in any case to which it is a party."[10] ICJ jurisdiction, however, depends on the parties' consent, either generally to any question of international law or treaty or specifically over a particular category of cases under a particular treaty.[11] The United States consented to the ICJ's general jurisdiction until 1985, at which point its continuing adherence to the Optional Protocol constituted consent to the specific jurisdiction over Vienna Convention claims. About a year after the *Avena* decision (referenced above and discussed below), the United States withdrew from the Optional Protocol altogether.[12]

As it happens, the instant case is not the first time that the Supreme Court has grappled with the meaning of the Vienna Convention and its relationship to state criminal law. In 1998, the Court in *Breard v. Greene* considered a petition to stay the execution of a rapist-murderer to allow time for the consideration of his claim that he had not been informed of his right to contact his consulate.[13] The Court ruled that the defendant could not raise his Vienna Convention claim for the first time at this late stage (not having argued it at trial, appeal, or state habeas proceedings) and added that even if he were not procedurally defaulted, it was "extremely doubtful" that the alleged violation had any effect on his trial that would result in the overturning of his conviction.[14] In an interesting wrinkle—and in response to the intervention of the government of Paraguay, its ambassador, and its consul general—the Court also found that the Vienna Convention did not give a foreign nation a private right of action in U.S. courts.[15]

Then, between *Avena* and this latest iteration of the Medellín saga, the Court had a further opportunity to interpret the Vienna Convention's Article 36, in a case unrelated to the individuals named in the

[10] *Id.*, art. 94(1), 59 Stat. 1051.

[11] *Id.*, art. 36, 59 Stat. 1060.

[12] Letter from Condoleezza Rice, U.S. Secretary of State, to Kofi Annan, UN Secretary-General, March 7, 2005; Charles Lane, U.S. Quits Pact Used in Capital Cases, Washington Post, March 10, 2005, at A01.

[13] 523 U.S. 371 (1998) (per curiam). While per curiam ("by the court") opinions are typically unanimous and uncontroversial, this one generated separate dissents from Justices Stevens, Ginsburg, and Breyer, as well as a bizarre "statement" (not concurrence nor dissent) from Justice Souter.

[14] *Id.* at 377.

[15] *Id.*

ICJ suit. The consolidated 2006 case of *Sanchez-Llamas v. Oregon* involved two murderers who argued that their respective convictions should be overturned because their consular rights had been violated.[16] The Oregon Supreme Court had affirmed, on direct appeal, the denial of the Mexican defendant's motion to suppress his own incriminating statements, holding that Article 36 did not create judicially cognizable rights.[17] The Virginia Supreme Court, meanwhile, had affirmed the denial of the Honduran defendant's state habeas petition in part because he had not previously made the consular rights argument (and so had waived it).[18] The U.S. Supreme Court, in an opinion by Chief Justice Roberts (then completing his first term), agreed with both states' judiciaries, holding that: 1) the Vienna Convention did not override state default rules—the standard principle of criminal (and civil) procedure that issues not raised before the trial court could not later be raised on appeal—and 2) even if the Convention created privately enforceable rights that were violated here, the exclusionary rule (which was designed to remedy federal constitutional violations) was not an appropriate remedy.[19] The Court left to another day the question of whether the Vienna Convention did indeed create rights that could—after the ICJ adjudicated them—be individually enforced in state or federal court. That day came with the *Medellín* case.

## B. Facts of the Case

This case, which would gain worldwide infamy, move both the Supreme and World Courts to action, and rebuke the "leader of the free world," began with a grisly gang rape and double murder. They were brutal crimes, but ones not normally meriting national—let alone international—attention. It was only the later (and latest) legal machinations that make this much more than a personal tragedy for the families of the victims.

In June 1993, then-18-year-old José Ernesto Medellín, who was born in Mexico but came to the United States when he was three, growing up in Houston, participated in a particularly depraved gang initiation. As 14-year-old Jennifer Ertman and 16-year-old Elizabeth

---

[16] Sanchez-Llamas v. Oregon, 548 U.S. 331 (2006).

[17] State v. Sanchez-Llamas, 108 P.3d 273 (Or. 2005).

[18] Shackleford v. Commonwealth, 547 S.E.2d 899 (Va. 2001).

[19] Sanchez-Llamas, 548 U.S. at 360.

Peña walked home, they encountered Medellín and his fellow gang members, who began teasing them. The girls tried to run away but were soon caught. Ertman tried to help her friend, whom Medellín had thrown to the ground. The gang proceeded to rape both girls for over an hour. Then, to prevent their victims from being able to get them in trouble, the gang killed the girls and left their bodies in a wooded area. Medellín himself strangled one of the girls with her own shoelace. The gang then divided up the girls' money and jewelry; Medellín kept Ertman's ring while his brother took a Disney watch. Later that evening, at the home of the brother of one of the gang members, Medellín boasted of the "fun" they had had.

Authorities found the girls' decomposing remains four days later. The police arrested Medellín the day after that. He confessed almost immediately—the timing would become an important detail—signing a detailed statement after being given his *Miranda* warnings. Medellín was convicted of capital murder and sentenced to death by lethal injection, which conviction and sentence were duly affirmed on appeal in May 1997.[20]

Medellín next filed for habeas corpus in state court (seeking post-conviction relief for procedural irregularities at trial and on direct appeal), arguing inter alia that his arresting officers never informed him of his right under the Vienna Convention to notify the Mexican consulate. The state district court ruled the claim procedurally waived because he had not previously raised it, but also reached the merits to find that Medellín had not presented any evidence that the violation of his consular rights somehow affected the outcomes of his trial and appeals.[21] (The ICJ later found that the Vienna Convention is satisfied when the detaining state provides the detainee's consulate with notice of detention within three working days of arrest.[22] Here, Medellín confessed within three hours of arrest, well before the deadline by which Texas had to vindicate his consular rights.[23]) Nearly four years after Medellín did his deeds, the Texas Court of Criminal Appeals affirmed the habeas denial.[24]

[20] Medellín v. State, No. 71,997 (Tex. Crim. App., May 16, 1997).

[21] Ex parte Medellín, No. 675430-A (339th Dist. Ct., Jan. 22, 2001).

[22] Avena, 2004 I.C.J. 12, 52 ¶ 97 (Judgment of Mar. 31). See also Sanchez-Llamas, 548 U.S. at 362 (Ginsburg, J., concurring in the judgment).

[23] Medellín v. Texas, 128 S. Ct. at 1355 n.1.

[24] Ex parte Medellín, No. WR-50, 191–02 (Tex. Crim. App. Oct. 3, 2001).

Medellín then filed for habeas in federal district court. That petition was also denied, again because 1) the Vienna Convention claim was procedurally defaulted and 2) Medellín had failed to show that he had been prejudiced by any such violation.[25]

While Medellín sought to appeal this ruling in the Fifth Circuit—rejections of collateral attacks on state convictions are not entitled to appeal as of right—the ICJ issued *Avena*. The court held that the United States had indeed violated the Vienna Convention rights of 51 Mexicans, including Medellín. The United States was thus obligated "to provide, by means of its own choosing, review and reconsideration of the convictions and sentences"[26] without regard to state procedural default rules.[27]

Nevertheless, the Fifth Circuit denied a certificate of appealability, following its own precedent and concluding that the Convention did not confer individually enforceable rights.[28] It further held that it was bound not by the ICJ but by the Supreme Court's ruling in the *Breard* decision that Vienna Convention claims are indeed subject to procedural default rules.[29]

The Supreme Court granted certiorari to resolve the seeming conflict between the ICJ and America's treaty obligations on the one hand and Court precedent and Texas criminal procedure on the other. After briefing but before oral argument, President Bush reversed his administration's previous position—which, far from endorsing *Avena*, involved filing a brief supporting Texas—and issued a remarkable memorandum to Attorney General Gonzales. The memorandum, dated February 28, 2005, and titled "Compliance with the Decision of the International Court of Justice in *Avena*," read, in its entirety:

[25] Medellín v. Cockrell, Civ. Action No. H-01-4078 (S.D. Tex., June 26, 2003).

[26] Avena, 2004 I.C.J. at 72.

[27] *Id.* at 56–57.

[28] Medellín v. Dretke, 371 F.3d 270, 280 (5th Cir. 2004). For purposes of full disclosure, I should note that I was clerking for a Fifth Circuit judge while this case was pending. My judge was not on the panel that decided the case, but I had the opportunity to read the slip opinion and confer with my judge before the mandate issued. (While the procedure varies by circuit, at the federal appellate level judges can "hold" the mandate of opinions in cases decided by their colleagues to study the issues further and potentially call for a vote as to whether to have the case re-argued en banc.)

[29] *Id.* (citing Breard, 523 U.S. at 375).

> The United States is a party to the Vienna Convention on Consular Relations (the "Convention") and the Convention's Optional Protocol Concerning the Compulsory Settlement of Disputes (Optional Protocol), which gives the International Court of Justice (ICJ) jurisdiction to decide disputes concerning the "interpretation and application" of the Convention.

> I have determined, pursuant to the authority vested in me as President by the Constitution and the laws of the United States of America, that the United States will discharge its international obligations under the decision of the International Court of Justice in *Avena*, by having State courts give effect to the decision in accordance with general principles of comity in cases filed by the 51 Mexican nationals addressed in that decision.[30]

That is, the president purported to use his executive power over foreign affairs to enforce U.S. obligations under international law, all in the interest of "comity."

Relying on both this presidential memorandum and *Avena*, Medellín filed a *second* petition for state habeas, arguing that Texas's violation of the Vienna Convention deprived him of assistance during sentencing, in developing mitigating evidence. Not wanting to tread on state court jurisdiction (and because Medellín's federal claims might turn out to be barred), the Supreme Court dismissed the cert petition as improvidently granted (a move known as a "DIG," an acronym combining the action's operative words).[31]

Texas courts again denied Medellín's petition, in part because he had received consular assistance in preparing his first habeas filing and failed to raise the mitigation argument, but more importantly because neither *Avena* nor the presidential memorandum was "binding federal law" that could overcome state limitations on successive habeas petitions.[32]

Medellín again filed for certiorari, and the Supreme Court again granted it.

---

[30] Memorandum from President George W. Bush to the Attorney General of the United States (Feb. 28, 2005) (available at http://www.whitehouse.gov/news/releases/2005/02/20050228-18.html).

[31] Medellín v. Dretke, 544 U.S. 660, 664 (2005) (per curiam). For an analysis of *Medellín*'s previous trip to the Court, see A. Mark Weisburd, International Judicial Decisions, Domestic Courts, and the Foreign Affairs Power, 2004–2005 Cato Sup. Ct. Rev. 287 (2005).

[32] Ex parte Medellín, 223 S.W.3d 315, 352 (Tex. Crim. App., Nov. 15, 2006).

## C. *The Case before the Supreme Court*

Medellín presented four basic arguments to the Court: 1) that the United States is bound to comply with the *Avena* judgment by virtue of being a party to the UN Charter, the Vienna Convention, and the Optional Protocol—and states cannot enact policies contrary to U.S. treaties;[33] 2) the Constitution's Supremacy Clause makes duly ratified treaties a part of federal law, which states are bound to enforce (and which President Bush was enforcing);[34] 3) President Bush's memorandum was a valid and binding exercise of the federal executive's authority over foreign affairs;[35] and 4) Texas's procedural bar (the issue of Medellín's having waived his consular rights claim by not having raised it earlier) is preempted by U.S. treaty obligations, as incorporated into federal law by the Supremacy Clause.[36] Simply put, Texas was bound by the judgment of a court whose jurisdiction it fell under as a result of U.S. treaty commitments.

Texas had several options for opposing that argument, with potential emphases on sovereignty (American and Texan), federalism (the federal government's stepping on state prerogatives), and separation of powers (the president's encroaching on Congress, the federal judiciary, and state courts). While each of these issues would be aired in the briefs and at oral argument, it is no coincidence that Texas focused on the last, presenting this complex matter as essentially a grade-school civics lesson on checks and balances. That is, Texas's main arguments were that President Bush, through his memorandum: 1) purported to create law and thus intruded on congressional authority;[37] 2) usurped the courts' (federal and state) role in saying what the law is, particularly in light of *Sanchez-Llamas*;[38] and 3) interfered with state control over criminal law while conscripting states to implement federal obligations.[39] Texas raised five other points that underscore its theme that President Bush vastly exceeded his powers, including that the federal government's position admits

---

[33] Petitioner's Brief, 2007 WL 1886212, at *19–26.

[34] *Id.* at *26–33.

[35] *Id.* at *34–42.

[36] *Id.* at *43–44.

[37] Respondent's Brief, 2007 WL 2428387, at *13–34.

[38] *Id.* at *34–38.

[39] *Id.* at *38–42.

of no limiting principles to presidential authority; the executive branch can comply with *Avena* in other ways;[40] *Avena*, even if binding, is not enforceable by a private party in a domestic court; and Medellín already received the judicial review the ICJ ordered.[41]

Had the state defended the case otherwise, the narrative on the other side would have been about "those cowboys," defying the world and even its own former governor—not to mention how "crazy" Texans are about the death penalty. That is how the case still appears to many in the foreign media.[42] It would have been much more difficult to win. Instead, Texas's lawyers articulated Congress's authority to ratify treaties and make them have domestic effect, and the power of the Supreme Court to make decisions about the Constitution. To paraphrase what Ted Cruz says when he discusses the case in public: How many times in your legal career do you get to cite *Marbury v. Madison* as a principal authority?

The argument before the Court proceeded along expected lines. Justice Antonin Scalia and Chief Justice Roberts questioned Medellín's counsel about the enforceability of the treaties at issue. "The thing that concerns me . . . is that it seems to leave no role for this Court in interpreting treaties as a matter of federal law," the Chief explained, posing a hypothetical where the ICJ ordered a five-year prison term for the officers who violated Medellín's consular right.[43] Justice Anthony Kennedy expressed "interest[]" in the answer to this hypothetical but inferred that, in any event, the president's determination "is not conclusive."[44] Moreover, Kennedy expressed his belief that "Medellín did receive all the hearing he's entitled to under [*Avena*] anyway."[45]

On the other hand, Justice Breyer offered that the Court could decline to enforce an ICJ ruling that "violate[d] something basic in

---

[40] See Part IV.B, *infra*.

[41] *Id.* at *43–50.

[42] See Part III, *infra*.

[43] Argument Transcript, 2007 WL 2945736, at *4.

[44] *Id.* at *6, *10.

[45] *Id.* at *20.

our Constitution" but otherwise appeared willing to enforce the World Court's ruling.[46] And Justice Ruth Bader Ginsburg suggested that the agreement to submit the *Avena* dispute to the ICJ's exclusive jurisdiction required state courts to give the ruling the equivalent of "full faith and credit."[47]

Justice Stevens agreed with Justice Breyer's answer to Chief Justice Roberts's hypothetical but then posited a situation whereby the ICJ ordered that Medellín's sentence be commuted and reduced.[48] Medellín's counsel seemed flustered by that change-up and the ensuing pile-on by Justices Samuel Alito and Scalia and the Chief Justice. Justice David Souter clarified that, in any event, Medellín's position was not that federal law (or the ICJ ruling) trumped state jurisdiction, but that it preempted it.[49]

The questioning of Solicitor General Paul Clement focused on presidential authority, because the government's position was that the Court would have no obligation to enforce *Avena* but for President Bush's memorandum.[50] Justice Scalia pointed out the seeming weakness in the government's split-the-baby position: The ICJ judgment was not self-enforcing, but the president, acting without Congress (which typically passes the legislation enforcing such non-self-enforcing treaties), can enforce it himself.[51] Chief Justice Roberts and Justice Alito then questioned the solicitor general on the limits to the president's power to enforce treaties that didn't enforce themselves. Clement explained that here the president was enforcing the Optional Protocol and not the Vienna Convention itself, which he conceded the Court had already determined in *Sanchez-Llamas* not to mean what the ICJ said it did.[52]

Roberts and Scalia then raised the issue of how Medellín gained any personal rights from *Avena* when he was not a party to a case, but only named in the suit.[53] Before Clement could respond, Justice

---

[46] *Id.* at *9.

[47] *Id.* at *12.

[48] *Id.* at *13.

[49] *Id.* at *17.

[50] U.S. Brief at 27–29; Argument Tr., 2007 WL 2945736, at *23.

[51] Argument Tr. at *25.

[52] *Id.* at *26–29.

[53] *Id.* at *29–30.

Ginsburg interrupted with a long colloquy centering on the United States' having submitted to ICJ jurisdiction.[54] Justice Kennedy steered a middle ground, saying that "we should give [the president's] determination great weight, but that's something different from saying that he can displace the authority of this Court on that issue of law."[55] Clement concluded by first referring to a John Marshall speech on an extradition case that seemed to suggest that the president can act to enforce a treaty when Congress doesn't, then by invoking international comity.[56]

Ted Cruz began with the uncomfortable truism that "the United States's argument is predicated on the idea that the President's two-paragraph memorandum is in and of itself binding federal law."[57] Justice Souter pointed out that if *Avena* is directly binding, then the executive power question is obviated—which Cruz readily conceded, but added that the United States explicitly disclaimed the treaties in question as the source of presidential authority and expressly agreed with the holding of *Sanchez-Llamas*.[58] Justice Breyer, later joined by Justice Ginsburg, led a long discussion challenging Cruz on why Texas was not bound by *Avena* by operation of the Supremacy Clause in light of the United States' having submitted itself to the ICJ's jurisdiction.[59] Cruz, supported by Justice Scalia, explained that this was "jurisdiction" for political (or international obligation) purposes, not for enforcement of a judgment in domestic court.[60]

Justice Stevens jumped in to ask Cruz why *Avena* is not an ordinary enforceable judgment, and Cruz—in his longest uninterrupted period at the podium—listed six reasons, concluding again with the idea that "the entire purpose of this [ICJ] adjudication is not to resolve something finally in a court of law, but it is rather a diplomatic measure."[61] Justice Kennedy suggested that the heart of the

---

[54] *Id.* at *30–32.

[55] *Id.* at *33.

[56] *Id.* at *38 (referring to 10 Annals of Cong. at 611, reprinted in 18 U.S. (5 Wheat.) 1 App. at 24 (1800) (statement of Rep. John Marshall on the extradition of Thomas Nash)).

[57] *Id.* at *39.

[58] *Id.* at *40.

[59] *Id.* at *40–44.

[60] *Id.* at *44–45.

[61] *Id.* at *49–50.

case is that "for 200 years we have had some treaties that are very important, but they're not self-executing . . . there is no obligation on the part of the State to comply with" a law that is "not self-executing."[62] Cruz agreed with that characterization and went on to clarify that "the Vienna Convention was self-executing in the sense that it didn't require legislation to go into effect, but it was not self-executing in the sense that it provided judicially cognizable rights."[63]

The remainder of the argument reinforced the back-and-forth between the Breyer/Ginsburg/Souter line regarding submission to binding ICJ jurisdiction and the Scalia/Kennedy line regarding non-self-execution. At one point, Justice Kennedy asked whether Texas would have to lose if the Court determined—as it had assumed, without deciding, in *Breard* and *Sanchez-Llamas*—that the Vienna Convention created individually enforceable rights. Cruz replied in the negative because Medellín had defaulted his claim to those rights, which result *Sanchez-Llamas* held was fully constitutional.[64] And when Justice Ginsburg prodded Cruz to explain what the president could have done to enforce the Vienna Convention, Cruz suggested a new statute providing for a federal right of review in consular rights cases; even Texas's procedural bar allows an exception for a new law.[65] This would get Congress involved and avoid problems like those raised by unilateral executive authority in *Hamdan* (which the Court struck down even though there the president was "at the height of his war powers authority").[66]

It appeared by the end of the argument that the decision in the case would be exceedingly close, but Justice Kennedy's skepticism toward the position that the ICJ ruling was directly binding suggested that Medellín had lost on that point. And if Texas won there, it was hard to conceive of a scenario whereby five justices (or even one) would be willing to establish the precedent that a two-paragraph presidential memorandum could overrule state criminal court decisions that had already found both that the claim was procedurally defaulted and that any error was harmless.

---

[62] *Id.* at *50.

[63] *Id.* at *51.

[64] *Id.* at *58–59.

[65] *Id.* at *63–65.

[66] *Id.* at *65–66 (referring to Hamdan v. Rumsfeld, 548 U.S. 557 (2006)).

## II. The *Medellín* Decision

Remarkably, it was a 6–3 decision. The Court, in a magisterial opinion by Chief Justice Roberts, made two main points: 1) The so-called World Court has no authority to bind the United States' (let alone an individual state's) justice system, and 2) the president does not have the power to tell state courts what to do. In short, it is the Constitution and the Supreme Court that define American law, not international tribunals or chief executives. Chief Justice Roberts's majority opinion is a tour de force of separation of powers, federalism, and international law. Justice Stevens's concurrence—preventing this from being another highly charged 5–4 split—agreed with the majority's judgment but recommended that Texas nevertheless comply with the (otherwise non-binding) ICJ decision. Justice Breyer's dissent, meanwhile, found both the Vienna Convention's consular rights and the ICJ ruling judicially enforceable without further legislative (or other) action but, interestingly, declined to speak definitively on the executive power issue.

The Chief Justice's legal analysis begins with the question of whether *Avena* is directly binding on U.S. courts.[67] The ICJ ruling would have to be binding on both federal and state courts for this to be the end of the habeas inquiry because: a) It would be bizarre for an international treaty to bind national courts but not those of a sub-national jurisdiction such as a state, and, conversely; b) under the U.S. Constitution, federal courts cannot simply order state courts to do something without some preempting force of law. Here such a preemptory authority would be the Supremacy Clause, which in relevant part says that "all Treaties made . . . under the Authority of the United States, shall be the supreme Law of the Land; and the Judges in every State shall be bound thereby" notwithstanding any state law or constitution.[68] That is, if the duly authorized treaties require that an ICJ ruling be treated as co-equal with the Constitution and federal law—setting aside for now the question of what would happen if the ICJ ordered an unconstitutional action—there is nothing the Supreme Court (let alone a state court) could do but honor *Avena*.

---

[67] Medellín, 128 S. Ct. at 1356.

[68] U.S. Const. art. VI.

Clearly the Supreme Court was not going to stand for such a limitation on its powers. (Recall that, whether led by "liberals"— as in, say, *Boumediene v. Bush* or *Kennedy v. Louisiana*—or "conservatives"—here—the Court this term, and indeed throughout modern history, rarely acts to constrain its own jurisdiction when given the opportunity to do so.)[69] And so Roberts explains that even as *Avena* indisputably creates an *international* law obligation on the United States, that obligation does not automatically become binding and privately enforceable *domestic* law. From its earliest days, the Court has recognized "the distinction between treaties that automatically have effect as domestic law, and those that—while they constitute international law commitments—do not by themselves function as binding federal law."[70] In other words, some treaties bind the U.S. government generally—the nation violates the commitments it has made to its treaty partners if it does not fulfill the treaty terms— but do not have any legal effect in the courts, let alone creating a right of action for an individual litigant.

Chief Justice Marshall himself found a treaty to be directly binding only when it "operates of itself without the aid of any legislative provision."[71] Half a century later, the Court explained the converse, that when treaties "can only be enforced pursuant to legislation to carry them into effect" they are not "self-executing"—applying that term for the first time in the context of treaty interpretation.[72] *Medellín* synthesizes this line of precedent by adopting the First Circuit's formulation that treaties do not constitute domestic law "unless Congress has either enacted implementing legislation or the treaty itself conveys an intention that it be 'self-executing' and is ratified on those terms."[73] In what will likely stand as the most consequential

---

[69] For a discussion of judicial supremacy in criminal law, see Edward J. Loya Jr., Judicial Supremacy and Federalism: A Closer Look at *Danforth* and *Moore*, 2007–2008 Cato Sup. Ct. Rev. 161 (2008).

[70] Medellín, 128 S. Ct. at 1356.

[71] Foster v. Neilson, 27 U.S. (2 Pet.) 253, 314 (1829) (title dispute hanging on whether Spain ceded titles to land upon signing a certain treaty), overruled on other grounds, United States v. Percheman, 7 Pet. 51 (1833).

[72] Whitney v. Robertson, 124 U.S. 190, 194 (1888) (import duty applications and obligations of a treaty between the United States and the Dominican Republic).

[73] Medellín, 128 S. Ct. at 1356 (quoting Igartúa-De La Rosa v. United States, 417 F.3d 145, 150 (1st Cir. 2005) (en banc)).

footnote in treaty interpretation—as with *Carolene Products* footnote 4, some of the most revealing Supreme Court nuggets are dropped in footnotes—Chief Justice Roberts makes it clear that the term "self-executing" refers to a treaty provision that has "automatic domestic effect as federal law upon ratification," without regard to implementing legislation.[74]

Roberts next cites the *Head Money Cases*, a set of 19th-century cases argued together that established the principle that a treaty, while the "law of the land," is "primarily a compact between independent nations"; it does not hold a privileged position over—and indeed is "subject to"—other acts of Congress that may affect its "enforcement, modification, or repeal."[75] He observes that only "[i]f the treaty contains stipulations which are self-executing, that is, require no legislation to make them operative, [will] they have the force and effect of a legislative enactment."[76] And even when treaties are self-executing, "the background presumption is that '[i]nternational agreements, even those directly benefiting private persons, generally do not create private rights or provide for a private cause of action in domestic courts.'"[77] Finding that neither the Optional Protocol nor the UN Charter (or any other ICJ-relevant treaty) "creates binding federal law in the absence of implementing legislation," the Court concludes that *Avena* was not "automatically binding domestic law."[78] In another passing footnote, the Court notes that the ICJ itself

[74] *Id.*, 128 S. Ct. at 1356 n.2. Roberts goes on to say that "[a] non-self-executing treaty, by definition, is one that was ratified with the understanding that it is not to have domestic effect of its own force." *Id.* at 1369.

[75] 112 U.S. 580, 598–99 (1884). See also The Federalist No. 33, p. 207 (J. Cooke ed. 1961) (A. Hamilton) (comparing laws that individuals are "bound to observe" as "the supreme law of the land" with "a mere treaty, dependent on the good faith of the parties") (as quoted in Medellín, 128 S. Ct. at 1357).

[76] Medellín, 128 S. Ct. at 1357 (quoting Whitney, 124 U.S. at 194).

[77] *Id.* at 1357 n.3 (quoting 2 Restatement (Third) of Foreign Relations Law of the United States § 907, Comment a, p. 395 (1986)) (going on to cite opinions from six Courts of Appeals holding that "treaties do not create privately enforceable rights in the absence of express language to the contrary"). That the Court was able to cite the Restatement for this proposition is telling, because the Restatement is generally favorable to the application of international law in U.S. courts.

[78] *Id.* at 1357. Interestingly, because the issue presented was whether *Avena* has binding effect in domestic courts under the Optional Protocol, ICJ Statute, and UN Charter, the Court declined to decide whether the Vienna Convention itself is self-executing, simply assuming as it did in *Breard* and *Sanchez-Llamas* that for purposes

does not seem to see *Avena* as directly enforceable because it ordered the United States to review and reconsider the convictions and sentences "by means of its own choosing"—a strange formulation for a binding legal instrument.[79]

Chief Justice Roberts then turns to the executive power issue. Recall that while the U.S. position to this point accords with the Court, here the government joined Medellín's argument that, regardless of the *Avena* decision's direct applicability, the presidential memorandum made it binding domestic law. The majority opinion initially sets out as a first principle that presidential authority "as with the exercise of any governmental power 'must stem either from an act of Congress or from the Constitution itself.'"[80] It invokes Justice Robert Jackson's classic formulation that: 1) presidential authority reaches its zenith when Congress authorizes the particular action (because it includes his own vested powers "plus all that Congress can delegate"); 2) when Congress has not spoken on a given matter, the president must rely on his own independent powers (some of which may overlap with Congress's in a "zone of twilight"); and 3) the president's power is "at its lowest ebb" when he acts in contravention to the "expressed or implied will of Congress."[81]

Next, the Court dispatches the multifarious arguments about presidential authority with the stark statement that while the president "has an array of political and diplomatic means available to enforce international obligations[,] unilaterally converting a non-self-executing treaty into a self-executing one is not among them."[82] Instead, that responsibility is reserved to Congress.[83] The president "makes" treaties and the Senate ratifies them; if a treaty is not self-executing—lacks domestic legal effect without further domestic lawmaking—its ratification signals that Congress has reserved the decision to craft enabling legislation (rather than somehow granting the president the

---

of the instant litigation the Convention grants an individually enforceable right to consular notification.

[79] *Id.* at 1361 n.9 (citing Avena, 2004 I.C.J. at 72).

[80] *Id.* at 1368 (quoting Youngstown Sheet & Tube Co. v. Sawyer, 343 U.S. 579, 585 (1952) and citing Dames & Moore v. Regan, 453 U.S. 654, 668 (1981)).

[81] *Id.* (quoting and citing Youngstown, 343 U.S. at 635–38 (Jackson, J., concurring)).

[82] *Id.*

[83] *Id.* (citing Foster, 27 U.S. at 315; Whitney, 124 U.S. at 194; Igartúa-De La Rosa, 417 F.3d at 150).

unilateral power to do so independently). That is, "the non-self-executing character of the relevant treaties not only refutes the notion that the ratifying parties vested the President with the authority to unilaterally make treaty obligations, but also implicitly prohibits him from doing so."[84] Here President Bush was in Justice Jackson's third category, the Chief Justice concludes, and could not execute *Avena* without involving Congress.[85]

All the above does not mean that the Court has precluded the president, in the absence of implementing legislation, from acting to comply with international legal obligations arising from non-self-executing treaties. It simply means that "the Executive cannot unilaterally execute a non-self-executing treaty by giving it domestic effect," because a treaty's "non-self-executing character" is a check on presidential power.[86] And the president has other means at his disposal to ensure U.S. compliance with its international obligations.[87]

Finally, the Court quickly disposes of the claim that the memorandum was a valid exercise of the president's authority to resolve disputes with foreign countries. In making this argument, the United States relied on a line of precedent whereby the Court had upheld the exercise of the president's foreign affairs power "to settle foreign claims pursuant to an executive agreement."[88] The Court distinguishes this power as involving instances of making "executive agreements to settle civil claims between American citizens and foreign governments or foreign nationals."[89] Unlike such actions, there is no precedent for a president's issuing a directive to state courts that purports to "reopen final criminal judgments and set

---

[84] *Id.* at 1369.

[85] *Id.* at 1368, 1370 n.14 (referencing the president's previous resolution of numerous ICJ controversies, including two Vienna Convention cases, that did not involve "transforming an international obligation into domestic law and thereby displacing state law").

[86] *Id.* at 1371.

[87] *Id.* For some suggestions on what the president could have done in this case—and options available for similar situations in future—see Part IV.B, *infra*.

[88] *Id.* at 1372 (citing American Ins. Ass'n v. Garamendi, 539 U.S. 396, 415 (2003); Dames & Moore v. Regan, 453 U.S. 654, 679–80 (1981); United States v. Pink, 315 U.S. 203, 229 (1942); United States v. Belmont, 301 U.S. 324, 330 (1937)).

[89] *Id.* at 1371 (citations omitted).

aside neutrally applicable state laws."[90] Nor is the memorandum somehow empowered by the "Take Care" clause, which "allows the President to execute the laws, not make them."[91]

Justice Stevens concurs in the judgment but does not join the majority opinion, saying that "[t]here is a great deal of wisdom in Justice Breyer's dissent" and that "this case presents a closer question than the Court's opinion allows."[92] He agrees with Breyer that the Supremacy Clause and the Court's treaty interpretation precedent "do not support a presumption against self-execution" and that the Vienna Convention is self-executing and judicially enforceable.[93] In the end, however, he determines that "the relevant treaties do not authorize this Court to enforce [*Avena*]" because the operative phrase "undertakes to comply" is "a promise to take additional steps to enforce ICJ judgments" rather than the automatically binding language of a self-executing treaty.[94]

Importantly, Justice Stevens notes that under the governing treaties, an ICJ decision "has no binding force except between the parties and in respect of that particular case."[95] By the terms of the Optional Protocol (and the ICJ Statute generally), only countries can be party to ICJ cases, whose judgments are only binding on those country-parties and cannot be used by individuals to sue in domestic courts. That amounts, ultimately, to saying the same thing the majority did: An ICJ judgment is binding as a matter of international law, but has no domestic legal effect. Still, Stevens adds that even though the presidential memorandum is not binding law for the reasons the majority cites, the United States is not released from "its promise to take action necessary to comply with [*Avena*]."[96] Thus, while the Court has no legal basis for ordering Texas courts to enforce the ICJ judgment, Stevens strongly urges Texas to save the United States from (further) treaty violations: "Texas would do well to recognize

[90] *Id.* at 1372.

[91] *Id.* (referencing U.S. Const art. II, § 3). The Court uses but one paragraph—four sentences—to dispose of this last argument, lauding the United States for not joining Medellín in making it.

[92] *Id.* (Stevens, J. concurring).

[93] *Id.*

[94] *Id.* at 1372–73.

[95] *Id.* at 1374 (citing the ICJ Statute, *supra* at note 10).

[96] *Id.*

that more is at stake than whether judgments of the ICJ, and the principled admonitions of the President of the United States, trump state procedural rules in the absence of implementing legislation."[97]

Justice Breyer dissents (joined by Justices Souter and Ginsburg[98]), applying the simple logic that the judgment of a court whose jurisdiction the United States has accepted via duly ratified treaty necessarily binds U.S. courts "no less than 'an act of the [federal] legislature.'"[99] Looking at the Court's history of treaty-related cases' interpreting the Supremacy Clause, Breyer concludes that no implementing legislation is required. Breyer uses a 1796 case as a vehicle for illustrating the point that the Founders intended the Supremacy Clause to mean that ratified treaties were self-executing.[100] He traces the development of the law from Chief Justice Marshall's opinion in *Foster v. Neilson* through at least some recognition by 1840 that "it would be a bold proposition" to assert "that an act of Congress must be first passed" to make a treaty the supreme law of the land.[101] Breyer then refers to an appendix listing, as examples, 29 cases where the Court held or assumed that particular treaty provisions were self-executing. Of course, this whole discussion shows only that it is not unusual for treaties to be self-executing and that the Supremacy Clause ensures that treaties sometimes have different domestic legal effect

---

[97] *Id.* at 1375.

[98] It was not a shock that Justice Ginsburg dissented here, but it would also not have been too surprising to see her come out the other way in light of her concurrence in *Sanchez-Llamas*. While agreeing with Justice Breyer's dissenting opinion that the Vienna Convention grants privately enforceable rights, Justice Ginsburg found that the exclusionary rule was not appropriate on the facts of that case because the defendant, "who indicated that he understood" the *Miranda* warnings he was given in both English and Spanish, and "with his life experience in the United States," "would have little need to invoke the Vienna Convention." Sanchez-Llamas, 548 U.S. at 361 (Ginsburg, J., concurring in the judgment). Apparently this reasoning does not apply to death penalty cases.

[99] Medellín, 128 S. Ct. at 1376 (Breyer, J., dissenting) (quoting Foster, 27 U.S. at 314) (edited text in original).

[100] *Id.* at 1377–78 (discussing *Ware v. Hylton*, 3 Dall. 199, 272–77 (1796), with a focus on Justice Iredell's opinion that, unlike in the pre-Constitutional era—or the state of the law in Britain—the Supremacy Clause obviated the need for legislative action on ratified treaties).

[101] *Id.* at 1379 (citing Foster, 27 U.S. at 310 and quoting Lessee of Pollard's Heirs v. Kibbe, 14 Pet. 353, 388 (1840) (Baldwin, J., concurring)).

in the United States than in other countries—which Breyer admits as he turns to the interpretive tools available to the Court.[102]

Justice Breyer argues that the determination of whether a particular treaty provision is self-executing should go beyond the typical "clear statement" presumptions undergirding textual analysis. Referring to cases where the Court found implicit self-execution, Breyer states that "the absence or presence of language in a treaty about a provision's self-execution proves nothing at all."[103] "At worst it erects legalistic hurdles that can threaten the application of provisions in many existing [treaties] and make it more difficult to negotiate new ones."[104]

Next, Justice Breyer suggests certain context-specific criteria for the Court to use, such as the treaty's subject matter. If the treaty declares peace or promises not to engage in war, then clearly it is addressed to the political branches (and is not justiciable).[105] If, on the other hand, it "concern[s] the adjudication of traditional private legal rights such as rights to own property, to conduct a business, or to obtain civil tort recovery," it is more likely to have direct legal effect in U.S. courts.[106] Similarly, if a treaty confers "specific, detailed individual legal rights" or presents "definite standards that judges can readily enforce," its provisions are more likely to be available for private domestic litigation.[107] Glossing over other potential factors, Breyer clearly favors a balancing test here rather than a bright line rule (or "magic formula," as he calls it).

Applying the above principles to the instant case, Justice Breyer concludes his analysis of the international law issue with seven reasons that militate for holding *Avena* to be a self-executing judgment: 1) The language of the relevant treaties supports direct enforceability because they contemplate mandatory ICJ adjudication;[108] 2) the Vienna Convention itself, without the Optional Protocol, is self-executing;[109] 3) "logic suggests that a treaty provision

[102] *Id.* at 1381.

[103] *Id.*

[104] *Id.* at 1381–82.

[105] *Id.* at 1382 (citing Ware, 3 Dall. At 259–62 (opinion of Iredell, J.)).

[106] *Id.*

[107] *Id.* (citations omitted).

[108] *Id.* at 1383.

[109] *Id.* at 1385–86 (referencing, inter alia, the State Department's report after ratification that the Convention is "considered entirely self-executive and does not require any implementing or complementing legislation" S. Exec. Rep. No. 91-9, p. 5 (1969)).

providing for 'final' and 'binding' judgments that 'settl[e]' treaty-based disputes is self-executing insofar as the judgment in question concerns the meaning of an underlying treaty provision that is itself self-executing";[110] 4) the majority's approach has "seriously negative practical difficulties" in terms of the (at least 70) treaties providing for ICJ dispute resolution;[111] 5) the particular requirements of the judgment at issue here—evaluation of the prejudice Medellín faced from a violation of his rights—is particularly suited to judicial (rather than legislative) action;[112] 6) finding U.S. treaty obligations self-executing neither upsets constitutional structures nor creates a new private right of action;[113] and 7) neither the executive nor legislative branch has "expressed concern about direct judicial enforcement of the ICJ decision."[114] Having thus decided that *Avena* is self-executing and judicially enforceable, Breyer briefly explains that the proper means of enforcing it is to remand the case back to the Texas courts to provide further hearings on whether Medellín was prejudiced by having been denied his consular rights.[115]

Justice Breyer curiously avoids taking a position on the presidential authority question, instead engaging in some brief ruminations on the foreign affairs power. He mentions in passing that President Bush's authority here lies in Justice Jackson's "middle range" because Congress has "neither specifically authorized nor specifically forbidden" the action at issue.[116] Then he raises various hypothetical situations whereby, potentially, the president could legitimately set aside state law. "On the other hand, the Constitution must impose significant restrictions upon the President's ability, by invoking Article II treaty-implementation authority, to circumvent ordinary legislative processes and to pre-empt state law."[117] Ultimately, because the Court has "reserved judgment" as to "the 'scope

[110] *Id.* at 1386. That is, because *Avena* interpreted the self-executing Vienna Convention, and the United States agreed that ICJ adjudication of the Convention would be binding, the judgment is itself self-executing.

[111] *Id.* at 1387.

[112] *Id.* at 1388.

[113] *Id.*

[114] *Id.* at 1389.

[115] *Id.* at 1390.

[116] *Id.* (citing Youngstown, 343 U.S. at 637 (Jackson, J., concurring)).

[117] *Id.*

of the President's power to preempt state law pursuant to authority delegated by . . . a ratified treaty,'" Breyer would "leave the matter in the constitutional shade from which it has emerged."[118]

Justice Breyer concludes that the Court unnecessarily complicates both the president's foreign affairs power and U.S. foreign relations generally, as well as putting American citizens at risk abroad and upsetting constitutional structures.[119] Citing among other things "the views of the Founders," he laments that the Court is now complicit in breaking U.S. treaty obligations that the president tried to enforce and in regards to which Congress has been silent.[120]

## III. Aftermath and Execution

While *Medellín v. Texas* provided rich material for debating legal theory and speculating about the course of future litigation involving international treaties, this case did not end when Chief Justice Roberts read the Court's opinion in open court. Instead, the fate of José Medellín, and of the issues he raised, took one more journey through the Texas, World, and Supreme courts. These developments showcased the interaction between abstruse jurisprudence and contemporary political debates. In particular, and unfortunately for the rule of law, they revealed that much of the support for Medellín—who never retracted his confession, and whom nobody believes to be innocent—was a) support for "global governance" by unelected and unaccountable international institutions, and b) back-door death penalty abolitionism.

Medellín was ultimately executed, as would have happened had nothing more been filed after the opinion came down. But to say that nothing happened in the interim would be to leave this ultimate law school exam fact pattern unfinished. Here is a brief summary of events from March 25, 2008, the date of the opinion's release, to Medellín's execution in early August.

On May 5, soon after the Supreme Court lifted its de facto death penalty moratorium by deciding that the most common method of

---

[118] *Id.* at 1391 (quoting Barclays Bank PLC v. Franchise Tax Bd. of California, 512 U.S. 298, 329 (1994)).

[119] *Id.*

[120] *Id.* at 1392.

lethal injection was not unconstitutional,[121] a Texas state judge ordered a new execution date set for Medellín: August 5. A month later, on June 5, Mexico returned to the ICJ, claiming that all parts of U.S. government—national and state—had been involved in violating the Vienna Convention, so all must take steps to prevent the imminent executions of Medellín and four others (the only five on Texas's death row whose appeals had concluded). Mexico relied on a provision in the ICJ Statute that allows the court to elaborate on a ruling if any part of the ruling is in dispute. The United States responded that there is no dispute—that Texas had indeed violated the Mexicans' consular rights—so the World Court had no authority to issue new orders. Mexico contended that there was a continuing dispute because not all governmental actors (such as Congress and the states) had implemented *Avena*.

On June 17, before the World Court could rule, Attorney General Michael Mukasey and Secretary of State Condoleezza Rice wrote to the governor of Texas, Rick Perry, to ask for help in carrying out the World Court's previous ruling (*Avena*). Governor Perry, echoing the Supreme Court, replied that Texas was not bound by *Avena* and it was up to the federal government to comply with international obligations. Other efforts by the administration had led other states with Mexicans on their death rows (such as Oklahoma) to newly review their cases.

On July 14, leading Democrats in the U.S. House of Representatives introduced a bill to create rights for Medellín and others covered by the World Court's rulings, to wit "a civil action to provide judicial remedies to carry out certain treaty obligations of the United States under the Vienna Convention [and Optional Protocol]."[122] Later that week, the current and past presidents of the American Society of International Law wrote to Congress, urging action to "ensure that the United States lives up to its binding international legal obligations."[123]

On July 16, the ICJ voted 7–5 that the U.S. government had not done enough to ensure the consular rights of Mexican nationals

---

[121] Baze v. Rees, 553 U.S. _____ , 128 S. Ct. 1520 (2008).

[122] Avena Case Implementation Act of 2008, H.R. 6481, 110th Cong. (2d Sess. 2008).

[123] Letter from Lucy Reed, President, ASIL, et al., to Senator Harry Reid, et al. (July 17, 2008) (available at http://www.asil.org/pdfs/presidentsletter.pdf).

convicted of capital murder, and ordered it to stop five imminent executions in Texas, including Medellín's.[124] The court agreed with Mexico that there remained a dispute over *Avena*'s scope—and did so by relying on the French version of the ICJ Statute, rather than the English one.[125] Leaving it up to the United States to choose the way to carry out the order, the ICJ ordered the United States to "take all measures necessary" to ensure that Texas did not execute Medellín and four others.[126] This ruling was essentially a directive to keep the five individuals alive pending the full resolution of Mexico's arguments regarding the U.S. government's treaty obligations. The ICJ ruling also included 11–1 votes ordering the United States to inform the World Court of its complying measures and maintaining jurisdiction over the case. The American judge, Thomas Buergenthal, dissented on all points, but was joined by judges from Japan, New Zealand, Russia, and Slovakia on the issue of whether to stay the executions.

On July 22, a federal court rejected a new (second federal) habeas petition by Medellín because, under the relevant statute, he had no legal right to pursue that new claim without first getting permission from the Fifth Circuit. The Fifth Circuit would later deny Medellín's motion for leave to file a successive habeas petition because, contrary to Medellín's contention, the Supreme Court's March 25 decision did not create a "new rule of constitutional law" such that he could make out a previously unavailable claim.[127] On July 24, the Inter-American Commission on Human Rights, a part of the Organization of American States, issued a preliminary report finding that Medellín's rights were violated by denial of access to Mexican diplomats while his case went forward to Texas courts.

---

[124] Avena and Other Mexican Nationals (Mexico v. United States of America), 2008 I.C.J. 3, Request for Interpretation of the Judgment of 31 March 2004 (Order of July 16, 2008).

[125] *Id.* at 3. The French version gives the ICJ the power to issue interpretations where there is a *"contestation,"* while the English version does so when there is a "dispute." The court concluded that a *"contestation"*—which it found currently exists—is broader than a "dispute." Whether an international (or any) court can arbitrarily decide that different translations of what is obviously meant to be the same text can have different legal weights is a topic beyond the scope of even this polymathic article.

[126] *Id.* at 6.

[127] Medellín v. Quarterman, No. 08-20495, slip op. at 4 (5th Cir. Aug. 4, 2008) (unpublished) (citing 28 U.S.C. § 2244(b)(2)(A)).

On July 28, after the federal habeas plea was dismissed, Medellín's lawyers filed another (third state) habeas petition in the Texas Court of Criminal Appeals. Not having gotten a response by (Friday) August 1, the same lawyers lodged a mass of filings with the U.S. Supreme Court. The papers included: a motion to recall and stay the mandate in *Medellín v. Texas* (to give the political branches time to afford *Avena* domestic legal effect); a new petition for habeas; and a new cert petition (in the event the Texas court denies relief); along with an application to stay Medellín's execution pending the resolution of these other claims. As is appropriate with this type of filing, the stay request was addressed to Justice Scalia as circuit justice for the Fifth Circuit. Scalia had authority to act alone but, not surprisingly, referred it to the whole Court.

In asking the Court to pull back its March decision, Medellín's counsel said they were not seeking to reopen previously resolved issues, but merely wanted the mandate held "until Congress has had a reasonable opportunity to enact legislation consistent with this Court's decision."[128] "Federal and state actors at the highest levels of government have been engaging in unprecedented efforts to bring the Nation into compliance by providing a judicial forum to grant [Medellín] the review and reconsideration to which he is entitled," they noted.[129] Medellín's attorneys also alerted the Court to the pending House bill and that Secretary Rice and Attorney General Mukasey requested Texas to "assist the United States in carrying out its international obligations"; that a Texas state senator has "committed to introducing legislation at the earliest opportunity when the Texas Legislature reconvenes," and that "leaders of the diplomatic and business communities have warned that Mr. Medellín's execution could have grave consequences for Americans abroad."[130] If the execution goes forward, "Texas effectively will usurp the institutional prerogative of the federal political branches—advocated by Texas in *Medellín v. Texas* and confirmed by this

---

[128] Motion to Recall and Stay the Court's Mandate in *Medellín v. Texas* at 5 (No. 08A98) (dated July 31, 2008, filed August 1, 2008).

[129] Application for Stay of Execution Pending Disposition of Motion to Recall and Stay the Mandate and Petition for Writ of Certiorari or Writ of Habeas Corpus at 1 (No. 08A99) (signed July 31, 2008, filed August 1, 2008).

[130] *Id.* at 1–2.

Court—to determine whether and how to give domestic legal effect to the treaty obligations of the Nation."[131]

George Washington University law professor Ed Swaine was quoted as saying that an execution now would "diminish the ICJ's credibility and lessen the incentive for countries to bring cases to the ICJ in the first place."[132]

In the meantime, the Texas Court of Criminal Appeals had refused to issue a stay of the execution and dismissed Medellín's latest habeas filing.[133] One judge dissented,[134] while another concurred but urged the governor to grant a reprieve so Congress could act.[135] Judge Cathy Cochran, concurring with the majority and filing the most detailed opinion, noted that while Texas authorities "clearly failed in their duty to inform this foreign national of his rights under the Vienna Convention, this foreign national equally failed in his duty to inform those authorities that he was a Mexican citizen."[136] Moreover, "there is no likelihood at all that the unknowing and inadvertent violation of the Vienna Convention actually prejudiced Medellín."[137] Perhaps most interesting, and cutting to the heart of what was really going on in this final week, Cochran concluded her opinion with this:

> Some societies may judge our death penalty barbaric. Most Texans, however, consider death a just penalty in certain rare circumstances. Many Europeans may disagree. So be it. But until and unless the citizens of this state or the courts of this nation decide that capital punishment should no longer be allowed under any circumstances at all, the jury's

---

[131] Mot. to Recall, *supra* note 128, at 4.

[132] Quoted in Dan Slater, "Texas Defies Bush, International Law; ICJ's Credibility in Jeopardy," Wall Street Journal Law Blog, August 1, 2008 (available at http://blogs.wsj.com/law/2008/08/01/texas-defies-bush-international-law-icjs-credibility-in-jeopardy/). Swaine's statement is true, but anything that reminds people that public international law is, at base, nothing more or less than political agreements written by lawyers is probably a good thing. See generally Jack L. Goldsmith and Eric A. Posner, The Limits of International Law (2005).

[133] Ex Parte Medellín, Tex. Crim. App. No. WR-50191-03, 2008 WL 2952485 (July 31, 2008).

[134] *Id.* at *9 (Meyers, J., dissenting).

[135] *Id.* at *4 (Price, J., concurring).

[136] *Id.* at *4 (Cochran, J., concurring).

[137] *Id.* at *8.

> verdict in this particular case should be honored and upheld
> because applicant received a fundamentally fair trial under
> American law.[138]

This was a plainly written differentiation of law and politics. This court could no more stop the execution in consideration of a policy debate about capital punishment than could the ICJ bind the Texas court.

After what was no doubt a sleepless weekend, on Monday morning, August 4, lawyers for the state of Texas urged the U.S. Supreme Court to allow the execution to proceed, arguing that Medellín has several times received all the review of his case that American or international law requires. In both of the state's filings, Texas said that it "acknowledges the international sensitivities" presented by *Avena*.[139] Texas also noted that Justice Stevens had commented in his concurrence to *Medellín* that it would be only a "minimal" cost to Texas to obey the ICJ.[140] Because of these considerations, the state said, "in future proceedings" involving Mexican nationals covered by *Avena* who have not had review of their cases as required by that decision, the state would not only "refrain from objecting" but "will join the defense in asking the reviewing court to address" such an inmate's claim of legal prejudice caused by a Vienna Convention violation.[141] It remains to be seen how this policy pronouncement will apply to the four other individuals named in the July 16 ICJ decision (one of whom may have an execution date set on 30 days' notice), let alone others on death row or awaiting sentencing.

The state's top legal officers contended that the Court should not postpone the execution merely because one member of Congress had introduced proposed legislation:

> Nothing in the Constitution, statute, or case law," the officials
> argued, "authorizes relief based on legislation that has been
> introduced but not enacted—especially not where Congress
> has taken no action in the over four years since *Avena*, and

---

[138] *Id.* at 8.

[139] Medellín v. Texas, 08-5573 (08A99), Brief in Opposition at 17 (August 4, 2008); 08-5574, Reply to Petition for Original Writ of Habeas Corpus at 17 (August 4, 2008).

[140] Medellín, 128 S. Ct. at 1374–75 (Stevens, J., concurring).

[141] Medellín v. Texas, 08-5573 (08A99), Brief in Opposition at 17 (August 4, 2008); 08-5574, Reply to Petition for Original Writ of Habeas Corpus at 17 (August 4, 2008).

where there is no remote, let alone reasonable, expectation that both Houses of Congress will approve the legislation. Nor does any rule of law exist to determine how much more delay is needed to further confirm that no action is indeed forthcoming.[142]

To hold otherwise, they argued,

would be to license a single member of the House of Representatives to enjoin the administration of criminal justice by a sovereign State. The Court has already held that the President of the United States, alone, cannot give domestic legal effect to *Avena* and override Texas law. A fortiori, one member of the House of Representatives cannot do so.[143]

Later that day, the Texas Board of Pardons and Paroles voted 7–0 against a reprieve, a recommendation that went to Governor Perry for a final decision on Medellín's fate. The board also rejected the lawyers' request to commute Medellín's punishment to a life sentence.

By this point, the narrative in the (non-Texas) media was overwhelmingly negative toward the way the legal endgame was playing out. "Texas Defies World Court, Bush on Execution" ran one Associated Press story that was picked up by the *Boston Globe*, ABC News, and other media.[144] Jeffrey Davidow, formerly America's senior career diplomat and one of three people ever to hold the rank of Career Ambassador, penned an op-ed in the *L.A. Times* arguing that executing Medellín would make it more difficult to protect U.S. citizens abroad.[145] This is a far cry from the headlines greeting the Supreme Court's decision in March, which were generally of the "Court to Bush: Don't Mess With Texas" variety.[146] Yet the real story

---

[142] *Id.* at 3.

[143] *Id.*

[144] Michael Graczyk, Texas Defies World Court, Bush on Execution, Associated Press, August 3, 2008 (available at various media sites, including http://abcnews.go.com/TheLaw/wireStory?id = 5506179, http://www.boston.com/news/nation/articles/2008/08/03/texas_defies_world_court_bush_on_execution/, and http://ap.google.com/article/ALeqM5gpkdpV0pGSS_ozv30DC1F1QkVd5wD92B1T1O0).

[145] Jeffrey Davidow, Protecting Them Protects Us, L.A. Times, August 4, 2008 at 15.

[146] See, e.g., Tony Mauro, Supreme Court Rules: Don't Mess With Texas, The BLT: The Blog of the Legal Times, March 25, 2008 1:36 p.m. (available at http://legaltimes.typepad.com/blt/2008/03/supreme-court-r.html).

had nothing to do with Texas (or the United States, for that matter) defying the World Court, international law, or even (elite) European opinion. Buried at the end of the AP article, a spokesman for the Texas attorney general had this to say: "The law is clear: Texas is bound not by the World Court, but by the U.S. Supreme Court, which reviewed this matter and determined that this convicted murderer's execution shall proceed."[147] Again, this is a basic legal issue; once the Supreme Court ruled, and in the absence of congressional action executing (as it were) the *Avena* decision, there is nothing for Texas to do but follow its own rules of criminal procedure.

In any event, Medellín's counsel made their last arguments on his behalf late on August 4, the eve of the scheduled execution day, in a reply to the Texas filings from earlier that day. They argued that if their client is put to death, "the world will have every reason to question the value of . . . the United States's treaty commitments."[148] The brief focused on constitutional design, painting Texas as being opposed to all branches of the federal government and throwing a wrench into the works of the American system of government. Specifically: The Supreme Court agreed that the United States has an "international obligation" (though not domestically enforceable) to provide a review of Medellín's consular rights; President Bush has attempted to comply; and Congress "has now begun to take steps to comply."[149] Yet "Texas is about to execute Mr. Medellín anyway . . . placing the United States irrevocably in breach."[150] Because Texas's governor has authority to delay the execution only another 30 days (after the parole board denied relief) and Texas's highest criminal court has decided not to block the execution, "the decision to breach the treaty has effectively been made by the District Attorney of Harris County, Texas, who, with the approval of a state trial-court judge [set the earliest execution date allowed by state law]."[151] Thus Medellín requested that the Supreme Court stay the

---

[147] Jerry Strickland, as quoted in Graczyk, *supra* at note 144.

[148] Medellín v. Texas, 08-5573, 08-5574, 08A98, 08A99, Reply to Brief in Opposition to Petition for Certiorari and to Response to Petition for Habeas Corpus, Motion to Recall and Stay Mandate, and Application for Stay of Execution, at 13 (August 4, 2008).

[149] *Id.*

[150] *Id.*

[151] *Id.* at 14.

execution "for a period of one year to allow Congress an opportunity to enact implementing legislation" to carry out U.S. obligations.[152]

Just before 10:00 p.m. (EST), the Supreme Court, by a 5–4 vote, refused to delay the execution. Each of the four dissenting justices, Stevens, Souter, Ginsburg, and Breyer, filed separate written dissents.

The majority, in a per curiam opinion, said that the chance that Congress or the Texas legislature would remedy the treaty violation was "too remote" to justify delaying the execution.[153] The majority relied in part on the fact that the Justice Department opted not to take any part in this latest round of the *Medellín* case, even though it was actively involved when the Court last ruled on it on March 25. Its silence was "no surprise" because the United States "has not wavered in its position that [Medellín] was not prejudiced by his lack of consular access."[154] Indeed, the United States had always maintained that the Texas courts were bound by the presidential memorandum, and not by ICJ decisions—and had withdrawn from the Optional Protocol.

While reaffirming that it was up to Congress to make the Vienna Convention binding domestic law, the Court noted that "Congress has not progressed beyond the bare introduction of a bill in the four years since the ICJ ruling and the four months since our ruling."[155] The Court also found it "highly unlikely as a matter of domestic or international law" that Medellín's confession was obtained illegally; and it found "insubstantial" the other arguments for why the consular rights violation invalidated the conviction and sentence.[156] Medellín's *Miranda* warnings, the Court said, gave him far more

[152] *Id.* Medellín's counsel also attached a letter that the Democratic leaders of the House Judiciary Committee wrote to Governor Perry on August 1, urging a stay of execution to give Congress—which was out of session and would remain on its annual summer recess through the Labor Day weekend—"the time needed to consider this situation and make an appropriate judgment as to the important policy matter in question." Letter from Reps. John Conyers, Jr., Jerrold Nadler, and Robert "Bobby" Scott to Gov. Rick Perry (August 1, 2008) (available at http://www.scotusblog.com/wp/wp-content/uploads/2008/08/medellin-supp-appdx.pdf).

[153] Medellín v. Texas, 06-984 (08A98), 08-5573 (08A99), 08-5574 (08A99), 2008 WL 3821478, slip op. at 1 (U.S. August 5, 2008).

[154] *Id.*, slip op. at 2.

[155] *Id.*

[156] *Id.*

protection than a Mexican consul could have—let alone what a similarly situated individual could expect in most if not all other countries—and we were beyond the point of re-litigating claims of, e.g., inadequacy of counsel.

Notably, Justice Stevens, who had provided that sixth vote supporting the Court's March ruling, here wanted to delay execution so as to invite the solicitor general to submit the government's views (in light of the looming violation of U.S. treaty obligations). "Balancing the honor of the Nation against the modest burden of a short delay to ensure that the breach is unavoidable convinces me that the application for a stay should be granted."[157]

Justice Souter said he would postpone Medellín's execution until the Court's new term begins in October to solicit the government's views and allow Congress to act—but also invoked the rule that "it is reasonable to adhere to a dissenting position [here his position in *Medellín*] throughout the Term of the Court in which it was announced."[158] Justice Ginsburg agreed.

Justice Breyer, author of the March dissent, filed the longest August opinion—three and a half pages. He again cited a multitude of factors, this time militating in favor of a stay: 1) the ICJ again asked the United States to enforce Medellín's treaty rights; 2) legislation has been introduced in Congress to provide a remedy; 3) Congress might not have understood the need to act before the Court's earlier decision; 4) permitting the execution violates international law "and breaks our treaty promises"; 5) President Bush has stressed the importance of carrying out treaty obligations here, which, in light of the president's "responsibility for foreign affairs," makes his views pertinent; and 6) the diverging views on the Court itself.[159] Breyer said the majority was wrong to suggest that the key issue was the validity of Medellín's confession. According to Breyer, the real issue is whether the United States "will carry out its international legal obligation."[160] Breyer joined his dissenting colleagues in calling for the views of the solicitor general, and noted his disappointment that

---

[157] *Id.* slip op. dissent at 1 (Stevens, J., dissenting).

[158] *Id.* at 2 (Souter, J., dissenting) (citing North Carolina v. Pearce, 395 U.S. 711, 744 (1969) (Harlan, J., concurring in part and dissenting in part)).

[159] *Id.* at 3–4 (Breyer, J., dissenting).

[160] *Id.* at 4.

"no Member of the majority has proved willing to provide a courtesy vote for a stay so that we can consider the solicitor general's views once received."[161]

Because the death warrant was to remain in effect until 1:00 a.m. (EST), Texas went ahead with the execution (which had originally been scheduled for 7:00 p.m. (EST) but was delayed at least three hours by the Court's final review). Within an hour of the Court's decision, Texas had completed its execution process. The *Houston Chronicle* reported: "Medellín was pronounced dead at [10:57 p.m. (EST)], nine minutes after receiving the fatal cocktail."[162]

Mexico's Senate had urged President Felipe Calderón to press U.S. officials to delay execution. Calderón did not respond to the Senate request. After Medellín's death, Mexico's Foreign Relations Ministry sent a note of protest to the State Department, officials saying they "were concerned for the precedent that [the execution] may create for the rights of Mexican nationals who may be detained in [the United States]."[163] At least six other Mexican nationals have been executed in Texas since 1982, when the state resumed capital punishment. Based on Texas courts' previous findings, however, it is very likely that even if *Medellín* had gone the other way, Medellín would still eventually have been executed—assuming the Supreme Court hadn't somehow ruled the death penalty unconstitutional in the interim.

As for the other gang members involved in the crime, Derrick O'Brien was executed two years ago. Peter Cantu, described as the ringleader, is awaiting his execution date. Efrain Perez and Raul Villareal had their death sentences commuted to life in prison when the Supreme Court barred executions for those who were 17 at the time of their crimes. Vernancio Medellín was 14 at the time of crime, and is serving a 40-year prison term.

---

[161] *Id.* at 5. Breyer was protesting too much; while it is considered common courtesy on the Court to provide a fifth vote for a stay of execution pending the consideration of a legitimate cert petition, it would be a far stretch to speak of a traditional courtesy vote to allow for the consideration of the government's views (especially when, as the majority explained, the government's views are easily discernible and would clearly go against Medellín's position).

[162] Allan Turner & Rosanna Ruiz, Medellín Put to Death After One Last Appeal, Houston Chronicle, August 6, 2008 at, A1.

[163] As quoted in Mexican Government Protests Texas Execution, CNN.com, (http://www.cnn.com/2008/CRIME/08/06/mexican.executed/) (August 7, 2008).

## IV. Implications

While it is unlikely that this law school exam-type fact pattern will ever present itself again—if only because a president is unlikely to both reverse his position on the binding nature of a treaty *and* try to enforce said treaty with a scant memorandum—*Medellín v. Texas* is thick with important precedent in the areas of international law and executive power.[164] Perhaps most significantly, it provides a road map of how American courts will decide treaty-based and other international law disputes in the future and draws bright lines between what the president can and cannot do in this realm.

### A. International Law

*Medellín* more or less reinforced the status quo on international law, in line with the Court's traditional deference to the political branches' powers to make and ratify treaties but asserting judicial supremacy in interpreting them. It would have been much bigger news if the Supreme Court had come out the other way, supporting the position that U.S. courts are powerless to resist World Court decisions. Helpfully for future cases, the majority opinion explained its interpretive methodology[165] and laid out four issues courts face when determining the extent to which a treaty—or the judgment of a treaty-created tribunal—is self-executing.

*First*, the Court will look to the text, in an exercise akin to statutory interpretation that also considers "as 'aids to its interpretation' the negotiating and drafting history of the treaty."[166] To not begin with, and heavily weigh, the text of a legal document one is interpreting is sheer folly, and a recipe for judicial mischief. *Second*, the Court is reluctant to subvert the "careful set of procedures that must be followed before federal law can be created under the Constitution—

---

[164] That is not to say that similarly situated criminal defendants (especially those facing capital murder charges) won't, at the last minute, plead Vienna Convention violations, just that those cases will now be unlikely to get very far in federal court (though we can expect some states to provide further hearings, as Oklahoma has for its Mexican death row inmates in the wake of *Avena* and the ICJ's July ruling). See, e.g., Larry Welborn, Judge Rejects Mexico's Bid to Halt Death Penalty Trial, Orange County Register, August 18, 2008 (available at http://www.ocregister.com/articles/motion-martinez-casas-2129411-penalty-legal).

[165] See Part II, *supra*.

[166] *Medellín*, 128 S. Ct. at 1357 (quoting Zicherman v. Korean Air Lines Co., 516 U.S. 217, 226 (1996)).

vesting that power in the political branches, subject to checks and balances."[167] It thus decidedly rejected the dissent's proposed multi-factor balancing test as providing no guidance—until a court has ruled—as to the consequences of U.S. treaty involvements. *Third*, the "postratification understanding" of signatory nations can help establish the parties' purposes in making what at base is an international contract.[168] This is one of the rare instances where it is fully appropriate to query how foreign polities look at the law; in the case of the Vienna Convention, not one member nation (out of 171) treats ICJ judgments as binding law. *Fourth*, this entire exercise is wholly different in kind from the enforcement of foreign judgments or arbitration agreements.[169] In any event, Congress enacted legislation to implement most of the treaties underlying such private enforcement mechanisms.[170]

Another key legal issue that *Medellín* teased out is that under the Optional Protocol (but also under the enforcement addenda of other treaties, and the ICJ Statute generally), only nations can bring cases before the ICJ. While nations are certainly free to bring suits on behalf of individuals (as Mexico did in *Avena*), by the normal operation of law the resulting judgments are binding only on the parties to that suit—those same national governments. To have a larger effect, national parliaments have to pass implementing legislation (preferably before the judgment but, as the proposed Avena Case Implementation Act shows, not necessarily so). It is unlikely, as both the *Medellín* majority and dissent noted, that many countries will make a habit of passing laws applicable either to individual ICJ judgments or to *all* treaties that rely on the ICJ for dispute resolution. But those countries that wish to can certainly legislate that ICJ judgments carry the same domestic weight as those of the domestic supreme court— or to negotiate terms in future treaties that move in that direction.

Still, most countries would—or should—be wary of giving up too many opportunities to review the actions of an international

---

[167] *Id.* at 1362.

[168] *Id.* at 1363 (quoting Zicherman, 516 U.S. at 226).

[169] *Id.* at 1365.

[170] For example, the famous New York Convention (formally known as the UN Convention on the Recognition and Enforcement of Foreign Arbitral Awards, June 10, 1958, 21 UST 2517, 330 UNTS 38) is executed at 9 U.S.C. § 201.

CATO SUPREME COURT REVIEW

tribunal that is by definition less accountable and less democratically legitimate than national courts. In the American context, if Congress passed a law saying that all ICJ judgments automatically become the law of the land—setting aside that such a law would be unconstitutional on its face because Article III names the Supreme Court as the nation's highest judicial body—what would happen if the ICJ ordered an unconstitutional action, or wanted to overrule a state criminal court (as it effectively did in *Medellín*)? This is a slippery slope if ever there were one.

No, under our constitutional system, it is the judiciary's duty to determine whether a treaty is self-executing, and then to define the scope and nature that execution has for purposes of domestic law. If Congress disagrees with the Court's determination that a given treaty is non-self-executing, its duty is to pass implementing or codifying legislation. The *Medellín* Court thus makes clear that the distinction between self-executing and non-self-executing treaties is very real and not at all arbitrary, and that this distinction in certain circumstances may well mean the literal difference between life and death.[171] Justice Breyer's observation that many (if not most) treaties are self-executing is irrelevant because the one at issue in this case was not.

While many commentators have warned that the *Medellín* decision will affect the treatment of Americans abroad[172]—including students, Peace Corps volunteers, servicemen, businessmen, and tourists—I for one have a hard time believing that courts in Europe, Mexico, or elsewhere change their behavior as a result of any one Supreme Court decision (beyond any general antagonism directed against

---

[171] For a sample of the rich scholarly debate about self-execution and the Supremacy Clause, see, e.g., Tim Wu, Treaties' Domains, 93 Va. L. Rev. 571 (2007); John C. Yoo, Globalism and the Constitution: Treaties, Non-Self-Execution, and the Original Understanding, 99 Colum. L. Rev. 1955 (1999); Martin S. Flaherty, Response: History Right?: Historical Scholarship, Original Understanding, and Treaties as "Supreme Law of the Land," 99 Colum. L. Rev. 2095 (1999); Curtis A. Bradley, *Breard*, Our Dualist Constitution, and the Internationalist Conception, 51 Stan. L. Rev. 529 (1999); Carlos Manuel Vazquez, The Four Doctrines of Self-Executing Treaties, 89 A.J.I.L. 695 (1995).

[172] See, e.g., Davidow, *supra* at note 145; David G. Savage, Advice of Consul, ABA Journal, June 2008 (available at http://www.abajournal.com/magazine/advice_of_consul).

the United States or President Bush). As it stands, the U.S. system provides criminal defendants with the highest level of protection— *Miranda* rights (let alone *Miranda* warnings) and the exclusionary rule, for example, are quite literally foreign to the rest of the world, not to mention the absence of habeas corpus outside the Anglo-sphere. (In many of the countries criticizing Texas, the Supreme Court, and the United States generally, Medellín would not have been able even to file anything after his first direct appeal was denied.) Moreover, as Chief Justice Roberts noted, not a single nation treats ICJ judgments regarding Vienna Convention rights as self-executing.[173] Thus, the fear of international payback for the Court's intransigence is both overblown and hypocritical, appearing to rest on little more than disagreements over capital punishment and the force of international law, and base anti-Americanism.

In the end, and notwithstanding the Court's increasing sensitivity to international law and awareness of the worldwide legal develop-ments, *Medellín* was a significant victory for national sovereignty and democratic legitimacy. The ICJ may be sophisticated and wise, but its rule can never constitute self-government as constitutionally structured—and as embodied in Texas's granting Medellín the full panoply of due process under the state's code of criminal procedure (which nobody can seriously contend failed constitutional muster).

## B. Executive Authority

Here again the case would have been bigger news if the Court had ruled against Texas and allowed the president to dictate to state courts any time he desired to put pen to paper—or at least where international affairs were concerned.[174] Instead, when enforcing treaty obligations that purport to have some sort of legal (not just political or diplomatic) component that the president seeks to enforce against the states—if this is in a sphere where such enforcement

---

[173] Medellín, 128 S. Ct. at 1363 ("[As in *Sanchez-Llamas*], the lack of any basis for supposing that any other country would treat ICJ judgments as directly enforceable as a matter of their domestic law strongly suggests that the treaty should not be so viewed in our courts."); see also *supra* at note 168 and accompanying text.

[174] Before *Medellín* was decided, one observer sketched out such a scenario in the gun control area. See David Kopel, Medellín and the Second Amendment, The Volokh Conspiracy, http://volokh.com/posts/1192051881.shtml (October 10, 2007 at 5:31 p.m.).

would not violate federalism principles—the president needs to have constitutional authority or congressional approval.

Of course, that raises a question similar to the one mentioned immediately above: Can the president make, and the Senate ratify, a treaty that grants powers to either Congress or the president that they do not have under the Constitution? For example, if the United States duly joined a treaty abolishing the death penalty, could Congress pass and the president sign a bill eliminating capital punishment from state criminal codes? As above with a theoretical treaty stripping the Supreme Court of its ability to be the final arbiter of U.S. law, the answer should be no—with the caveat that a treaty may sometimes expand the president's options within a sphere over which he already has executive authority (foreign affairs being the most obvious one).[175]

Joining high theory to *Medellín*, it is striking that Medellín's counsel argued for rather expansive executive authority over foreign affairs.[176] That was almost wholly opportunistic—particularly because the groups who supported this argument are not generally fans of robust executive authority, even as scholars who read Article II as giving plenary foreign affairs power to the president came out on the other side.[177] This case concerned the president's *domestic* affairs power, of course, albeit relating to a foreign affairs matter. Nevertheless, Medellín's position was adopted by Justice Breyer, who uncharacteristically wants to defer to the president instead of micro-managing executive branch actions with international components:

> Given the Court's comparative lack of expertise in foreign affairs; given the importance of the Nation's foreign relations;

[175] Unfortunately, the flawed case of *Missouri v. Holland*, 252 U.S. 416 (1920), makes this a surprisingly difficult question to answer. For a fascinating and detailed discussion of these issues, see Nicholas Quinn Rosenkranz, Executing the Treaty Power, 118 Harv. L. Rev. 1867 (2005).

[176] Petitioner's Brief, 2007 WL 1886212, at *34–42.

[177] And these scholars were joined by colleagues who would likely share Medellín's position on the international law issue. See, e.g., the Brief of Constitutional and International Law Scholars in Support of Respondent State of Texas (scholar amici are Erwin Chemerinsky, John Eastman, Thomas Lee, Michael Ramsey, Michael Van Alstine, Arthur Mark Weisburd, John Yoo, and Ernest Young).

given the difficulty of finding the proper constitutional balance among state and federal, executive and legislative, powers in such matters; and given the likely future importance
of this Court's efforts to do so, I would very much hesitate
before concluding that the Constitution implicitly sets forth
broad prohibitions (or permissions) in this area.[178]

Chief Justice Roberts, in his majority opinion, replies to this reasoning by saying that Justice Breyer's hypothetical scenarios are beside
the point, in that the issues here

are the far more limited ones of whether [the president]
may unilaterally create federal law by giving effect to the
judgment of the international tribunal pursuant to this non-
self-executing treaty, and, if not, whether he may rely on
other authority under the Constitution to support the action
taken in this particular case.[179]

While the president has sole authority to resolve certain international
issues—even in *Medellín*, where President Bush was fully within his
powers as chief executive to determine that the United States would
comply with *Avena*—he cannot unilaterally enact domestic law or
otherwise command other federal branches (let alone states).[180]

So what could the president have done to comply with *Avena* that
would not have run afoul of separation-of-powers principles or
federalism? Aside from moral suasion—the phone calls by Secretary
Rice and Attorney General Mukasey—several options were (and
remain) available. Texas's brief before the Court sketches three. The
president could have: 1) worked with Congress to enact a statute
providing a new federal habeas remedy; 2) concluded a treaty with
Mexico (and possibly other countries) containing a self-executing
provision requiring federal judicial review of ICJ-adjudicated Vienna
Convention violations; or 3) issued an executive order providing
for a "review and reconsideration panel" for the 51 individuals
referenced in *Avena*, perhaps composed of retired federal judges.[181]

---

[178] Medellín, 128 S. Ct. at 1391 (Breyer, J., dissenting).

[179] *Id.* at 1367 n.13.

[180] *Id.* at 1370 n.14 and 1371; *Medellín, supra,* note 83 and accompanying text.

[181] Respondent's Brief, 2007 WL 2428387, at *46–47; see also *supra*, notes 65–66 and
accompanying text.

There is room for much variation within these three options and, depending on how they played out in real life, they would not necessarily be immune from legal challenge. Still, any of the above, and possibly others, would be significantly better than the questionable course President Bush actually pursued—and the first two would at least have the backing of the full federal government.

In sum, it is now beyond dispute that the president cannot unilaterally create binding law—let alone by drafting a short memorandum that does not even rise to the level of an executive order.

## Conclusion

Endlessly fascinating for the policy wonks who spot legal issues in every twist and turn, this case was ultimately about resisting the tide of transnational global governance. While economic globalization brings opportunity and freedom to different parts of the world, what could be called "political globalization" seeks to substitute the views of elite cosmopolitan technocrats for the consent of each nation's governed.[182] The Supreme Court has, for now, put a finger in the dyke, and perhaps *Medellín*—and this term generally[183]— represents a halt in that political globalization. More likely, however, because the intricate facts of this case are sui generis, the next time something like this happens the political branches will neither be caught off-guard nor act in what can be characterized as an ad hoc manner.

Still, both the ICJ decision and the presidential memorandum were unprecedented in what they intended to do: overrule a state's lawful criminal procedures. While elite opinion around the world expressed shock that one renegade political subdivision could thwart the will of both the World Court and the president, here in the United States

---

[182] For more on this disturbing trend, see John Fonte, Global Governance vs. the Liberal Democratic Nation-State: What is the Best Regime?, Essay Commissioned by the Hudson Institute, May 14, 2008 (available at http://pcr.hudson.org/index.cfm?fuseaction = publication_details&id = 5599).

[183] Unlike the other high-profile death penalty cases over the last decade, for example, the opinion holding capital punishment for child rape to be unconstitutional, did not contain a single international citation. Compare, e.g., *Kennedy v. Louisiana*, 554 U.S. _____ , 128 S. Ct. 2641 (2008) with *Roper v. Simmons*, 543 U.S. 551 (2005) and *Atkins v. Virginia*, 536 U.S. 304 (2002).

we take our federalism seriously.[184] As a spokesman for Texas Governor Perry explained: "The world court has no standing in Texas."[185]

*Medellín* thus stands for the principle of democratic self-government. Neither a foreign tribunal nor the president can dictate to American courts, federal or state. It will be interesting to see in the future how the seemingly opposed forces of globalism and judicial supremacy interact—not least in the mind of the Court's swing vote, Justice Kennedy.

---

[184] But see, e.g., Gonzales v. Raich 545 U.S. 1 (2005); Wickard v. Filburn, 317 U.S. 111 (1942).

[185] Quoted in Reed Johnson, Amid Protests Abroad, Texas Executes Mexican, L.A. Times, August 6, 2008, at 10, and Allan Turner & Rosanna Ruiz, Texas to World Court: Executions Are Still On, Houston Chronicle, July 17, 2008, at A1.

# It's My Party—Or Is It?
# First Amendment Problems Arising from the Mixed Role of Political Parties in Elections

*Erik S. Jaffe\**

In its recently concluded October Term 2007, the Supreme Court decided two cases—*New York State Board of Elections v. López Torres* and *Washington State Grange v. Washington State Republican Party*[1]— involving the role of political parties in elections and the First Amendment limits on state regulation of election procedures. Both cases rejected First Amendment challenges to the laws at issue, reversing the decisions of the Second and Ninth Circuits, respectively. The result in each case was more a function of the posture in which the cases were presented to the Court, however, and tells us little about political parties and the First Amendment per se. Of more interest are the Court's discussion of the role of political parties and the questions left open in its decisions.

Parts I and II of this article will describe the *López Torres* and *Washington State Grange* cases, highlighting the relatively narrow grounds for decision and the broader discussions of the role of political parties in our election processes.

Part III will discuss how these two cases illustrate the First Amendment problems and confusion arising from the dual public and private roles, and excessive entanglement, of political parties in the formal election mechanisms of the states and a potential path for avoiding such problems and confusion in the future. I argue that political parties are, and should be treated as, strictly private expressive associations, and that delegating to such parties the governmental function of being a gatekeeper for ballot access is the source of

*Solo appellate attorney, Erik S. Jaffe, P.C., Washington, D.C.
[1] 552 U.S. _____ , 128 S. Ct. 791 (2008); 552 U.S. _____ , 128 S. Ct. 1184 (2008).

those problems. Separating the public function of regulating ballot access from the private function of being an association for political advocacy would significantly alleviate the tensions between those two roles and clarify the application of the First Amendment to party conduct and election processes.

## I. The Decision in *New York State Board of Elections v. López Torres*

In *López Torres*, the Court considered the constitutionality of New York State's method of electing judges to serve on the state's trial court, idiosyncratically called the New York State Supreme Court. Justices of the New York State Supreme Court are elected by judicial district in partisan elections to serve 14 year terms.[2] Over the years, the state has allowed various methods of nominating candidates for judicial office, including both direct primaries and party conventions.

Since 1921, however, state law has required political parties to select their supreme court judicial candidates by a hybrid method of electing party delegates who must then choose a party's candidates at a convention.[3] Candidates chosen at the party conventions automatically gain access to the general election ballot and are identified on that ballot as the party's nominees.[4] Independent candidates and candidates of political organizations whose candidate for governor received fewer than 50,000 votes in the previous election may gain access through a nominating petition process.[5]

---

[2] By "partisan elections" I mean an election in which recognized political parties are given a reserved spot for their nominees for various offices on the general election ballot. In such elections, each recognized party is given the power and responsibility of winnowing potential candidates from that party to a single nominee for each office, who then appears on the general election ballot. The winnowing process can take a variety of forms—including primary elections segregated by party, party conventions, or caucuses—with particular nominating processes sometimes required, and often regulated, by the state.

[3] López Torres, 128 S. Ct. at 795–96 (citing Act of May 2, 1921, ch. 479 § 45(1), 110, 1921 N.Y. Laws 1451, 1471, currently codified at N.Y. Elec. Law Ann. § 6-106, *et seq.* (West 2007)). Unless otherwise noted, all statutory citations hereafter are to sections of N.Y. Elec. Law Ann.

[4] § 7-104(5).

[5] §§ 1-104(3), 6-138, 6-142(2).

Judge Margarita López Torres and several other prospective candidates (and their supporters) challenged the procedures for nominating supreme court candidates, arguing that the convention process imposed an excessive burden on challengers seeking nominations as against candidates preferred by the party leadership. They claimed that such procedures violated the First Amendment rights of challengers and voters "to gain access to the ballot and to associate in choosing their party's candidates."[6] They argued that because single political parties tended to dominate particular judicial districts, the party nomination process effectively determined the outcome of the general election and thus they were entitled to a realistic chance to secure the party's nomination notwithstanding their lack of support from the party leadership. Respondents sought an injunction mandating a direct primary election to select party nominees for supreme court justice.

The district court granted their request for an injunction and the Second Circuit affirmed. The court of appeals held that "voters and candidates possess a First Amendment right to a 'realistic opportunity to participate in [a political party's] nominating process, and to do so free from burdens that are both severe and unnecessary.'"[7] The court reasoned that the supposed one-party rule within particular judicial districts, combined with the difficulties of fielding a competing slate of delegates against the party leadership, denied respondents such an opportunity. The court thus upheld the injunction requiring direct primary elections until such time as New York adopted some other system that complied with the standard the court announced.[8]

The Supreme Court, in an opinion by Justice Antonin Scalia for eight of the justices, reversed. Justice John Paul Stevens, joined by Justice David Souter, filed a concurring opinion. Justice Anthony Kennedy filed an opinion concurring in the judgment, which opinion was joined in part by Justice Stephen Breyer.

The crux of the Court's reasoning was straightforward: While party members may have a right to participate in some form in the

---

[6] López Torres, 128 S. Ct. at 797.

[7] *Id.* (quoting New York State Board of Elections v. López Torres, 462 F.3d 161, 187 (2d Cir. 2006)).

[8] *Id.* (citing 462 F.3d at 193–200).

selection of party-nominated candidates, and perhaps even to seek nomination without "undue state-imposed impediment," they have no First Amendment right to be nominated or to have their preferred candidate nominated.[9] Finding that the requirements for running a competing slate of delegates in the delegate primary preceding the party convention were "far from excessive," and finding ample opportunity to persuade whatever delegates were elected that they should choose a competing potential nominee at the convention, respondents' argument boiled down to the objection that "the party leadership has more widespread support than a candidate not supported by the leadership."[10]

The Court thus observed that the challengers "complain not of the state law, but of the voters' (and their elected delegates') preference for the choices of the party leadership."[11] The suggestion that challengers for nomination are entitled to a "fair shot" at success, said the Court, might be appropriate for legislative judgment, but was unmanageable as a judicially imposed rule and not required by the Constitution.[12] The Court also rejected the suggestion that the non-competitiveness of the general election in districts dominated by single parties (making the primary and the convention effectively determinative of the outcome in the general election) somehow enhanced the challengers' rights to have a direct primary. Once again, voters and potential candidates have no right to any "fair shot" at nomination or electoral success, merely a right to "an adequate opportunity to appear on the general election ballot," which was "easily" satisfied by New York's petition process.[13]

The Court's ruling that individuals have no First Amendment right to win the endorsement of a party as its nominee, nor even to a "fair shot" at winning nomination, is hardly remarkable. Political parties themselves have a First Amendment right to associate and to choose their standard-bearers for an election. But where a potential candidate's prospects for party nomination are dim due to a lack of support within the party leadership, any barrier to nomination is a

---

[9] *Id.* at 798.

[10] *Id.* at 798–99.

[11] *Id.* at 799.

[12] *Id.* at 799–800.

[13] *Id.* at 800.

function of private choice—not governmental impediment—and the First Amendment protects rather than restricts such private choices.

Of greater interest than the overall result was the Court's general discussion of state regulation of, and constitutional limits on, party nominating procedures. In the first instance, the Court recognized that a "political party has a First Amendment right to limit its membership as it wishes, and to choose a candidate-selection process that will in its view produce the nominee who best represents its political platform."[14] The Court tempered that broad statement by noting that such rights are "circumscribed, however, when the State gives the party a role in the election process."[15]

The tension between the political parties' First Amendment rights of association and the constitutional obligations and state prerogatives that come from being incorporated into state election processes, has led to limits on political parties' freedom to conduct their nomination process as they see fit. Thus, as the Court noted, it has found a political party's racial discrimination in connection with primary elections to be state action that violated the Fifteenth Amendment, and has allowed states to regulate and dictate, up to a point, the parties' nominating processes.[16] Indeed, with little argument or explanation, the Court endorsed the conclusory and questionable holding in *American Party of Texas v. White*, that it was "'too plain for argument' that a State may prescribe party use of primaries or conventions to select nominees who appear on the general-election ballot."[17]

The Court also offered an odd discussion of the nature of the First Amendment rights at issue, stating that they involved only the political parties' own rights "to structure their internal party processes and to select the candidate of the party's choosing."[18] While failing to acknowledge that it was state law, not merely private

---

[14] *Id.* at 797 (citing Democratic Party of United States v. Wisconsin ex rel. La Follette, 450 U.S. 107, 122 (1981); California Democratic Party v. Jones, 530 U.S. 567, 574–575 (2000)).

[15] *Id.* at 797.

[16] *Id.* at 798 (citing Jones, 530 U.S. at 573–77 (discussing various cases regarding constitutional and state-law restrictions on primaries, but holding that a state may not force parties to allow non-members a vote in determining party nominees)).

[17] *Id.* (quoting American Party of Texas v. White, 415 U.S. 767, 781 (1974)).

[18] *Id.* at 798.

choice, that dictated the nominating procedures, the Court noted that the parties themselves defended the state law requiring the hybrid delegate election/party convention process. The Court thus reasoned that individual party members and potential nominees claimed only a nebulous right "to have a certain degree of influence in[ ] the party."[19]

Justice Stevens, joined by Justice Souter, authored a brief concurrence noting his distaste for the deficiencies of the New York nominating process and for the broader practice of electing judges.[20]

Justice Kennedy authored an opinion concurring in the judgment, joined in part by Justice Breyer (who also had joined the majority opinion). Kennedy maintained that where the state mandates a particular process for selecting a party's nominees, the state must not design its process to impose severe burdens on First Amendment rights.[21] He noted, however, that the option of petitioning onto the general election ballot mitigated any constitutional deficiencies that might otherwise arise from New York's party nomination procedure. Although believing that such an alternative means of access to the general election ballot would not always cure deficiencies in the party nomination process, and suggesting that there was indeed an individual right "to have a voice in the selection of" a party's candidate for office, he found no unconstitutional burden on that right on the particular facts of this case.[22] Finally, like Justice Stevens, Justice Kennedy noted his concerns with New York's process for selecting judges and the need for a process that produces "both the perception and the reality of a system committed to the highest ideals of the law."[23]

## II. The Decision in *Washington State Grange v. Washington Republican Party*

In *Washington State Grange*, the Court considered a challenge by the political parties to a Washington voter initiative (Initiative 872, or I-872) that adopted a nonpartisan blanket primary in which all

---

[19] *Id.*

[20] *Id.* at 801 (Stevens, J., concurring).

[21] *Id.* (Kennedy, J, concurring in the judgment).

[22] *Id.* at 803.

[23] *Id.*

candidates for a state office (potentially including multiple candidates from the same party) petition onto a single primary ballot.[24] All voters, regardless of their party, could then vote for whichever candidate they preferred, and the top two vote-getters would move on to the general election ballot.[25] Washington's process is unusual, however, in that it requires each candidate to

> file a "declaration of candidacy" form, on which he declares his "major or minor party preference, or independent status." Wash. Rev. Code § 29A.24.030 (Supp. 2005). Each candidate and his party preference (or independent status) is in turn designated on the primary election ballot. A political party cannot prevent a candidate who is unaffiliated with, or even repugnant to, the party from designating it as his party of preference. See Wash. Admin. Code § 434-215-015 (2005).[26]

The parties themselves are given no opportunity on either the primary or general election ballot to endorse or repudiate a given candidate's party preference, or to identify any candidate as the party's nominee. It is this novel feature—the identification of party preference on the ballot—that led I-872 to be challenged by the Republican, Democratic, and Libertarian Parties as a violation of their First Amendment rights of association.[27]

---

[24] The Washington State Grange is a fraternal, social, and civic organization originally formed to represent the interests of farmers. The organization has advocated a variety of goals, and sponsored I-872. It joined the suit below as a defendant and filed its own petition for a writ of certiorari, in addition to the petition brought by the State of Washington.

[25] Wash. Admin. Code § 434-262-012 (2005).

[26] Washington State Grange, 128 S. Ct. at 1189. The party-preference feature is only applied in what Washington deems to be elections for "partisan offices." *Id.*, 128 S. Ct. at 1189 & n. 4. But a "partisan office" is defined, circularly, as "a public office for which a candidate may indicate a political party preference on his or her declaration of candidacy and have that preference appear on the primary and general election ballot in conjunction with his or her name." Wash. Rev. Code § 29A.04.110 (Supp. 2005). Despite Washington's novel definition, this article will continue to refer to Washington's system as a nonpartisan blanket primary because voting is not segregated by party and access to the general election ballot does not turn on nomination by a party.

[27] Washington State Grange, 128 S.Ct. at 1189.

Before turning to the particulars of that challenge, some background is required. Before adopting I-872, Washington used a partisan blanket primary to select nominees for state and local office. In such a primary, any voter, regardless of party, may vote for any candidate. Those candidates from each party that receive the most votes then become their party's nominee in the general election. Under that system the state gave everyone (including members of rival parties) the ability to influence who became a particular party's candidate.

In 2004, the Supreme Court in *California Democratic Party v. Jones* struck down a similar partisan blanket primary system in California. The Court held that the blanket primary was an abridgment of the parties' First Amendment rights because it forced them to associate with non-members and allowed non-members to influence—and in some cases control—who became the parties' nominee.[28] In the course of that holding, the Court also found that a nonpartisan blanket primary "was a less restrictive alternative to California's system because such a primary does not nominate candidates."[29] Following the decision in *Jones*, the Ninth Circuit struck down Washington's partisan blanket primary system.[30]

Washington adopted I-872 to replace its invalidated blanket partisan primary system with the nonpartisan variety seemingly endorsed by the Court in *Jones*. Washington voters under the new system are not choosing a *party's* nominee, so such a system generally would not infringe upon the parties' First Amendment rights. But I-872 maintained a vestige of the old system's partisan qualities by requiring each candidate to declare his or her "major or minor party preference, or independent status."[31]

Because candidates were thus allowed to affiliate themselves with the political parties, even against the parties' wishes and without opportunity on the ballot for rebuttal, the Washington State Republican Party brought a facial challenge to the law, contending "that

[28] Jones, 530 U.S. at 581.

[29] Washington State Grange, 128 S. Ct. at 1192 (describing and citing Jones, 530 U.S. at 585–86 (The nonpartisan blanket primary "has all the characteristics of the partisan blanket primary, save the constitutionally crucial one: Primary voters are not choosing a party's nominee.")).

[30] Democratic Party of Washington State v. Reed, 343 F.3d 1198, 1203 (9th Cir. 2003).

[31] Wash. Rev. Code § 29A.24.030 (Supp. 2005).

the new system violates its associational rights by usurping its right to nominate its own candidates and by forcing it to associate with candidates it does not endorse."[32]

The district court granted summary judgment in the political parties' favor and enjoined implementation of I-872, and the Ninth Circuit affirmed.[33] The court of appeals held that I-872 imposed a severe burden on the parties' First Amendment rights of association because it created an "impression of associational ties" between a candidate and his preferred party even where such party opposed the association and did not consider the candidate to be its nominee.[34] The court of appeals noted that the problem was particularly acute in light of the special attention given to ballots when used as a "vehicle[ ] for political expression."[35]

The Supreme Court, in a decision by Justice Clarence Thomas for seven Justices, reversed. Chief Justice John Roberts, joined by Justice Samuel Alito, filed a concurring opinion. Justice Scalia, joined by Justice Kennedy, dissented.

As in *López Torres*, the crux of the majority opinion was straightforward, and rested on the narrow grounds that the challengers had failed to satisfy the high standards for succeeding on a *facial* challenge.[36] Resolution of the First Amendment issues, said the Court, would depend upon a variety of matters that were currently speculative, such as: the form in which a candidate's party "preference" appeared on the ballot; whether the public was likely to be confused by the statement of preference into a false assumption of association; and whether state courts adopted any limiting constructions of the law.[37]

The Court noted that *Jones* was not dispositive of the validity of the nonpartisan blanket primary in this case because the Court "had no occasion in *Jones* to determine whether a primary system that indicates each candidate's party preference on the ballot, in effect,

[32] Washington State Grange, 128 S. Ct. at 1189.

[33] Washington State Republican Party v. Logan, 377 F. Supp.2d 907 (W.D. Wash. 2005), *aff'd*, 460 F.3d 1108 (9th Cir. 2006).

[34] Logan, 460 F.3d at 1119.

[35] *Id.* at 1121.

[36] Washington State Grange, 128 S. Ct. at 1190–91, 1195.

[37] *Id.* at 1194.

chooses the parties' nominees."[38] But the Court rejected the claim that Washington's process, by allowing candidates to express a party preference, made the winners in the primary "the *de facto* nominees of the parties they prefer, thereby violating the parties' right to choose their own standard-bearers."[39]

> [U]nlike the California primary, the I-872 primary does not, by its terms, choose parties' nominees. The essence of nomination—the choice of a party representative—does not occur under I-872. The law never refers to the candidates as nominees of any party, nor does it treat them as such. To the contrary, the election regulations specifically provide that the primary "does not serve to determine the nominees of a political party but serves to winnow the number of candidates to a final list of two for the general election." Wash. Admin. Code § 434-262-012. The top two candidates from the primary election proceed to the general election regardless of their party preferences. Whether parties nominate their own candidates outside the state-run primary is simply irrelevant. In fact, parties may now nominate candidates by whatever mechanism they choose because I-872 repealed Washington's prior regulations governing party nominations."[40]

The Court instead noted that, "[a]t bottom, respondents' objection to I-872 is that voters will be confused by candidates' party-preference designations," and that "even if voters do not assume that candidates on the general election ballot are the nominees of their parties, they will at least assume that the parties associate with, and approve of, them."[41] Such claimed confusion and mistaken association, said the Court, is not evident from the face of I-872, but turns merely on the "possibility" that voters will be confused—and thus amounts to "sheer speculation" that is insufficient to support a facial challenge.[42]

After reviewing a variety of ways in which I-872 might be implemented in order to avoid such voter confusion and misperception,

[38] *Id.* at 1192.
[39] *Id.*.
[40] *Id.* at 1192–93 (footnote omitted).
[41] *Id.* at 1193.
[42] *Id.*

the Court concluded that the availability of such methods of implementation "'is fatal to respondents' facial challenge.'"[43]

Beyond the basic holding of the case, focusing on the speculative nature of the alleged harm, the Court made a number of more general observations regarding the First Amendment rights of political parties. For example, the Court observed that while parties may no longer indicate their nominees on the ballot, this is unexceptionable:

> The First Amendment does not give political parties a right to have their nominees designated as such on the ballot. . . . Parties do not gain such a right simply because the State affords candidates the opportunity to indicate their party preference on the ballot. "Ballots serve primarily to elect candidates, not as forums for political expression."[44]

Also interesting was the Court's effort to distinguish the case before it from *Hurley v. Irish-American Gay, Lesbian and Bisexual Group of Boston, Inc.*[45] and *Boy Scouts of America v. Dale.*[46] Those cases, said the Court, involved situations in which "*actual* association threatened to distort the groups' intended messages. We are aware of no case in which the mere *impression* of association was held to place a severe burden on a group's First Amendment rights, but we need not decide that question here."[47] The Court similarly argued that I-872 did not force the political parties to engage in responsive speech, as was the case in *Pacific Gas & Electric Co. v. Public Utilities Commission of California*,[48] because "it simply provides a place on the ballot for candidates to designate their party preferences. Facilitation of speech to which a political party may choose to respond does not amount to forcing the political party to speak."[49]

Chief Justice Roberts concurred, joined by Justice Alito. Accepting the proposition that "whether voters *perceive* the candidate and the

---

[43] *Id.* at 1195.

[44] *Id.* at 1193 n. 7 (citing and quoting Timmons v. Twin Cities Area New Party, 520 U.S. 351, 362–363 (1997)).

[45] 515 U.S. 557 (1995).

[46] 530 U.S. 640 (2000).

[47] Washington State Grange, 128 S. Ct. at 1194 n. 9 (emphasis in original).

[48] 475 U.S. 1 (1986).

[49] Washington State Grange, 128 S. Ct. at 1194 n. 10.

party to be associated is relevant to the constitutional inquiry," he nonetheless observed that "individuals frequently claim to favor this or that political party; these preferences, without more, do not create an unconstitutional forced association."[50]

Responding to Justice Scalia's dissenting argument that the ballot is a unique vehicle for shaping voters' perceptions at a critical point in time, and hence that I-872 denies political parties an equivalent opportunity for counter-speech to rebut any unwanted associations with candidates, the Chief Justice argued that "because respondents brought this challenge before the State of Washington had printed ballots for use under the new primary regime, we have no idea what those ballots will look like."[51] He considered it at least possible that a ballot could be designed such that "no reasonable voter would believe that the candidates listed there are nominees or members of, or otherwise associated with, the parties the candidates claimed to 'prefer,'" and thus preferred to wait for an as-applied challenge after the new system was actually implemented.[52] Recognizing the strength of the dissenting arguments, however, he noted that "if the ballot merely lists the candidates' preferred parties next to the candidates' names, or otherwise fails clearly to convey that the parties and the candidates are not necessarily associated, the I-872 system would not survive a First Amendment challenge."[53]

As for the dissent's argument that even a unilateral statement of party preference by a candidate will affect the voters' views of a party, thereby altering the party's message without an equivalent opportunity for rebuttal by the party, the Chief Justice acknowledged that while a party ordinarily would have no "right to stop an individual from saying, 'I prefer this party,' even if the party would rather he not," this case was different because "the State controls the content of the ballot, which we have never considered a public forum."[54] Expressing skepticism that the state was particularly interested in crafting a ballot that might avoid the problems identified by the

---

[50] Id. at 1196 (Roberts, C.J., concurring) (emphasis in original).

[51] Id. at 1196–97.

[52] Id., at 1197.

[53] Id.

[54] Id.

dissent, he nonetheless thought it "important to know what the ballot actually says—both about the candidate and about the party's association with the candidate ... before deciding whether it is unconstitutional."[55] The majority and concurring opinions thus continue the Court's emerging trend of being reluctant to entertain facial challenges.

Justice Scalia, joined by Justice Kennedy, dissented.

The crux of Justice Scalia's argument was that when "the state-printed ballot for the general election causes a party to be associated with candidates who may not fully (if at all) represent its views, it undermines" both the "electorate's perception of a political party's beliefs[, which] is colored by its perception of those who support the party," and the party's defining act of selecting a candidate and "conferring upon him the party's endorsement."[56]

While recognizing that a state need not affirmatively support or favor political parties, and "is entirely free to decline running primaries for the selection of party nominees and to hold nonpartisan general elections in which party labels have no place on the ballot," he viewed I-872 as seeking "to reduce the effectiveness of that endorsement by allowing *any* candidate to use the ballot for drawing upon the goodwill that a party has developed, while preventing the party from using the ballot to reject the claimed association or to identify the genuine candidate of its choice."[57] But allowing a candidate unilaterally to express a party preference on the ballot, while "preventing the party from using the ballot to reject the claimed association or to identify the genuine candidate of its choice ... makes the ballot an instrument by which party building is impeded, permitting unrebutted associations that the party itself does not approve."[58] It is the special role of the ballot that precludes the state from mandating such selective access and limiting it to only one side of a claimed association: "[B]ecause the ballot is the only document voters are guaranteed to see, and the last thing they see before casting their vote, there is 'no means of replying' that 'would be equally effective with the voter.'"[59]

[55] *Id.*

[56] *Id.* at 1197–98 (Scalia, J., dissenting).

[57] *Id.* at 1198 (emphasis in original).

[58] *Id.* at 1199.

[59] *Id.* at 1200 (citation omitted).

Justice Scalia rejected the need to wait for an as-applied challenge, noting that even the mere statement of a party preference sufficiently associates a candidate with a party to distort the image of the party and burden its rights.[60]

Finding no compelling interest for including party preferences on the ballot, Justice Scalia rejected the state's minor interest in "'providing voters with a modicum of relevant information about the candidates.'"[61] He questioned whether that claimed interest would even satisfy the "rational basis" test because, if adherence to a particular party philosophy is indeed important to voters, it seems "irrational not to allow the party to disclaim that self-association, or to identify its own endorsed candidate."[62] Indeed, the failure also to permit "parties to disclaim on the general-election ballot the asserted association or to designate on the ballot their true nominees" meant that the law was not narrowly tailored to avoid undue intrusion on the parties' association rights.[63]

## III. First Amendment Problems from the Dual Roles of Political Parties, and Potential Solutions

The particular results in *López Torres* and *Washington State Grange*, rejecting First Amendment challenges to very different state election processes, are based on fairly narrow holdings that in themselves tell us little about political parties and the First Amendment. Some of the related reasoning and commentary in those opinions, however, are useful in that they highlight the unusual public and private roles parties play in connection with elections, and illustrate some of the problems caused by those dual roles.

*López Torres*, for example, merely rejected the novel argument that disenchanted party members have a First Amendment *right* to have the state force upon parties a particular nominating process that would supposedly enhance ordinary members' influence within the party relative to the party "bosses" and improve the challengers' chances of winning the party's nomination for office. Describing the right the challengers sought is enough to reject it.

[60] *Id.* at 1200–01.
[61] *Id.* at 1202 (quoting Petitioners' Brief, 2007 WL 1538050, at *24, 48–49).
[62] *Id.* at 1202.
[63] *Id.* at 1203.

Other aspects of the *López Torres* opinion, however, suggest a different way of looking at the First Amendment issues raised by New York's judicial election scheme. Thus, while the Court was correct in finding no First Amendment right of members to have any particular degree of influence within a party, it too readily characterized the respondents' injuries as stemming entirely from the private choices of the party leadership and voters, rather than from the New York law that mandated the nominating process at issue.

Given that freedom of association encompasses not only the right of a party to choose *who* shall be its nominee and standard-bearer in an election, but also *how* to structure its internal procedures,[64] it does not at all seem "'too plain for argument' that a State may prescribe party use of primaries or conventions to select nominees who appear on the general-election ballot."[65] Instead, the choice of what method to use in selecting a party's nominee would seem squarely within the First Amendment rights to freedom of speech and association.

Although the Court recognized the right of a party "to structure [its] internal party processes and to select the candidate of the party's choosing,"[66] it treated that right as belonging to a party as an entity, rather than to its members. And in disposing of any objection by noting that the parties themselves supported New York's law mandating conventions, the Court passed over the underlying nature of the rights at issue and missed the genuine objection that could have been raised to the law.

As for the nature of the right to structure internal party processes, those belong to the party only as a matter of convenience. The rights of a political association, of course, are derivative of the rights of its members. It is the party members themselves who have a right to decide on the internal procedures of the party. While individual

---

[64] See, e.g., Jones, 530 U.S. at 573 (Constitution protects parties' "internal processes"); Eu v. San Francisco County Democratic Central Comm., 489 U.S. 214, 224 (1989) (First Amendment protects processes by which party selects a "standard bearer"); Democratic Party of United States v. Wisconsin ex rel. La Follete, 450 U.S. 107, 122 (1981) (freedom of party to define and limit those who constitute the association).

[65] López Torres, 128 S. Ct. at 798 (quoting American Party of Texas v. White, 415 U.S. at 781.

[66] *Id.* at 798.

members or less popular factions within the party certainly do not have a right to get their way in internal deliberations on what procedures to use, they would certainly seem to have a right to an *opportunity* to influence the internal procedures. But by enacting a law that mandates a particular procedure, even one favored by the controlling faction of a political party, the state short-circuits the very deliberative processes by which a party might choose to change its nominating procedure.

The First Amendment problem in this case does not arise from the lack of greater influence over the outcome of the nominating process, but from the lack of any genuine opportunity to seek a different process within the party itself without, in the Court's words, "undue state-imposed impediment."[67] New York's law requiring a particular nominating process thus infringes on the freedom of association by short-circuiting the internal party politics that either will lead to a compromise best suited to the particular party and its members or that may prove the dispute to be intractable and hence lead to new associations.

Under this alternative view of the First Amendment rights implicated by the law in *López Torres*, the First Amendment rights of the party leadership and the party rank and file are not in tension at all, but are in fact two sides of the same coin. In choosing to associate with a party, members take the existing association as it is. If they find aspects of the association not to their liking—whether it is the leadership structure, the method of choosing candidates to support, or elements of the party platform—they are free to work within the party to change things. Failing that, they are free to accept the good along with the bad or to seek out different associations with which their views are more compatible. As the Court correctly notes in connection with the selection of a nominee, for the party itself to deny individual members a particular degree of say in party affairs does not deny them any *rights* whatsoever, but merely denies them their *preference* on a disputed matter of internal policy.[68] While the Constitution protects the right of such individuals to try to change party procedure from within, or to seek other associations more to

[67] *Id.*
[68] *Id.* at 799.

their liking, it hardly compels other similarly free members of the party to accommodate such dissenting desires.

What neither faction in an internal dispute may do, however, is use the resources and authority of the state to tilt the scales of an internal dispute—to enforce a particular solution to that dispute, or, worst of all, to shift the blame (and hence the political responsibility) for the resolution of such dispute to the state—thus short-circuiting the intra-party political process. Yet that is precisely the result of the New York law mandating a particular nominating method.

In fairness, the Court did not undertake this sort of analysis because none of the parties advocated it. Indeed, the challengers' request for an injunction ordering the state to use direct primaries was as much a violation of the principles outlined above as is existing New York law.[69] But even if the Court had considered such an argument, it still would have confronted its various cases, including *American Party of Texas*, giving states considerable leeway to dictate the nominating procedures of political parties.

Those cases, however, turn on the idea that party nomination processes have an element of state action in them—based on the incorporation of the political parties into state election machinery and the delegation of at least part of the government's gatekeeping function of controlling ballot access in partisan elections. In such a gatekeeping role, party selection of candidates to be placed on the general election ballot does seem to involve state action so as to make party nominee selection processes less than wholly private affairs. Indeed, such intertwining of party and government processes is precisely what has driven the Court to apply various constitutional limitations to the conduct of partisan primaries.[70] As described by

[69] The Cato Institute, in an amicus brief in support of no party, noted precisely that tension in the case and argued that the proper result was to strike down the New York law *and* deny the requested injunction because both were a violation of the First Amendment. See Brief of Amici Curiae the Cato Institute, Reason Foundation, and the Center for Competitive Politics, in Support of None of the Parties, in No. 06-766, New York State Board of Elections v. López Torres (May 7, 2007) (available at http://www.cato.org/pubs/legalbriefs/López Torres_amicus.pdf). (In the interest of full disclosure I should note that I authored that brief.) The parties would thus be free to use a party-boss-dominated convention to select its nominees, but would have to take internal political responsibility for that decision with the party rank and file.

[70] See Jones, 530 U.S. at 573 (discussing Smith v. Allwright, 321 U.S. 649 (1944) and Terry v. Adams, 345 U.S. 461 (1953)); López Torres, 463 F.3d at 185–86 (discussing Terry and United States v. Classic, 313 U.S. 299 (1941)).

Justice Scalia, the free association rights of political parties "are circumscribed, however, when the State gives the party a role in the election process—as New York has done here by giving certain parties the right to have their candidates appear with party endorsement on the general-election ballot."[71]

In light of such entanglement between the private functions of the parties and the public functions of the government in regulating elections and ballot access, states would indeed seem to have significant interests in regulating related party conduct as well. But appearances can be misleading in this context insofar as the states generally compel parties to play such a gatekeeping role. Asserting a state interest in regulating such gatekeeping functions thus begs the question of whether forcing private associations into governmental roles is compatible with the First Amendment, particularly where the role likewise forces them to sacrifice essential aspects of their freedom of association.

From a private-association perspective on political parties, of course, the decision to nominate a candidate for office is in fact little more than a decision formally to endorse a prospective candidate. It has no power or effect beyond its expressive and persuasive significance, and does not in and of itself have any legal consequence. An endorsement, without more, does not get a candidate on a ballot, though it certainly indicates that the candidate is likely to be able to fulfill any neutral criteria for ballot access. Where the private association perspective gets difficult is in connection with the wholly distinct state decision to use party endorsement as a proxy for its own responsibility for regulating ballot access. Giving legal effect to a mere party endorsement by converting it into the controlling factor for ballot access in effect delegates the state's power over ballot access to private associations.[72] Such delegation, in turn, is used to justify greater state regulation of those private associations

---

[71] López Torres, 128 S. Ct. at 797–98.

[72] Allowing candidate names to appear on the ballot with their party endorsement, by contrast, hardly seems relevant to whether the parties are engaged in state action and hence subject to constitutional and state-law regulation. Instead, it is more aptly viewed as the opening up of a nonpublic forum and then applying discriminatory criteria regarding whose endorsement may appear on the ballot. The proper challenge to that would come from a candidate seeking to include on the ballot an endorsement from a person or entity other than a political party.

until the distinction between public and private actors is so blurred that the First Amendment begins to lose meaning.

While a state may certainly have valid interests in seeking to free-ride on the activity of private associations in making the state's own ballot access decisions and to narrow the field to serious contenders, those interests do not justify imposing the further burden on free association of then interfering with the internal processes of such associations. To the extent that a party's nomination procedure is deemed inadequate to meet the state's interests in winnowing the field in an appropriate manner, the state is free to adopt alternative methods of regulating ballot access that do not rely on party processes (such as requiring prospective candidates to gather a certain number of signatures or percentage of the vote in the previous election). It is not free, however, to strip parties of their private character and remake them in the state's preferred image. And while a state might conceivably (though not necessarily) condition automatic ballot access on use of a favored nominating process, it cannot command the parties to play the role of gatekeeper and then use that forced role to regulate their First Amendment activities.

Even assuming that a state can legitimately force candidates to run a party gauntlet (or abandon party affiliations entirely and run as independents) in order to gain access to the general election ballot, the proposition that a party can be limited to a single slot on the ballot for each office merely justifies requiring parties to make a choice, not controlling the manner in which such a choice is made. If the state feels that party decisionmaking is too restrictive of candidate access, it is certainly free to make access to the general ballot easier and less party-dependant. That is by far a less restrictive alternative for advancing any legitimate state interests. But having forced the parties into a gatekeeper role, any dissatisfaction with how they perform that role is a self-inflicted wound that does not justify restricting party First Amendment rights in lieu of having the state directly set party-neutral ballot-access rules for the general election.[73]

[73] One, though not the only, solution, would be to have nonpartisan elections, as was almost the case in *Washington State Grange*. Political parties would, of course, remain free to endorse whichever candidates they desired—and to assist such favored candidates in getting a place on the ballot by, for example, collecting the necessary signatures to petition onto the ballot—but their decision of whom to endorse would return to the wholly private function that it should be, separate and apart from the government's requirements regarding ballot access.

Any further purported interests in preventing party splitting or minimizing factionalism not only involve harms that are—at best—speculative, but such interests are directly counter to the very core of free association. Using state power to hinder or discourage individuals from freely leaving existing associations and forming new ones (that is, party splitting) on its face runs counter to the freedom of association by coercing individuals to remain in existing associations and to forego associations with others (or with a subset of their current associates) who may have a greater congruence of views. Similarly, attempting to fight factionalism by tilting the scales in favor of existing factions more likely to achieve majority status simply misconceives the whole problem of faction. Madison's greatest concern regarding the "violence of faction" was not the proliferation of many small factions, but the "superior force of an interested majority."[74] The solution to the danger of faction was not to replace conflicting factions with a single majority faction of the public, but rather to render any potential majority faction "unable to concert and carry into effect schemes of oppression."[75] Far from being compelling, a desire to decrease or hobble the formation of smaller factions is anathema to the "republican remedy for the disease[ ]" of factionalism.[76] The proper remedy for a concern with factions is not to bind them into majorities, but rather to encourage their diversity and freedom, thereby allowing them to check each other with their conflicting efforts. The alternative of trying to suppress the phenomenon of numerous factions "by destroying the liberty which is essential to its existence," is a remedy "worse than the disease."[77]

Ultimately, a more coherent First Amendment perspective would recognize that a state's preference to delegate some of its election-related functions to private associations cannot be a valid justification for intruding into such private associations and converting them into state actors. Co-opting and controlling the field of effective political associations is no less an offense to the First Amendment than suppressing such associations directly.

---

[74] Federalist No. 10, The Federalist Papers 45 (Rossiter & Kesler eds. 1999).

[75] Id. at 49.

[76] Id. at 52.

[77] Id. at 45–46.

The decision in *Washington State Grange* thus offers an interesting counterpoint to New York's mandate of a particular party nominating process and the conflicting dual roles of political parties. As for the result in that case, it seems to be a fairly narrow holding based more on the procedural posture of the case than on any significant dispute over the rights at issue. Indeed, the Chief Justice and Justice Alito in their concurrence were quite sympathetic to the substantive views of the dissent, differing primarily on whether one could conclusively presume severe First Amendment harm from *any* ballot statement of a candidate's party preference, regardless of the form or context. While, in my estimation, Justice Scalia has the slightly better of that argument, it is hard to quibble with the Court's reticence to resolve such a claim without a concrete example before it.

Aside from the result, however, *Washington State Grange* illustrates a system in which political parties are essentially divorced from involvement in the formal election machinery, and hence can be treated as the private expressive associations they are, rather than as quasi-state actors in the context of partisan elections. Parties in Washington are now far freer to structure their affairs and advocate for their preferred candidates than they are in many other states.[78] And their lack of control over access to the ballot removes essentially all of the supposed justification for regulating them in the first place.

The problem in *Washington State Grange* was not that it went too far in removing the parties from formal involvement in the election process. Even Justice Scalia acknowledged that states may effectively exclude political parties from any formal involvement in the election process, by declining to run party primaries or to include party affiliations on nonpartisan ballots.[79] Instead, the state did not go far enough and attempted to hold on to some of the partisan nature of the process by including party preference on the ballot. That it did so in an apparent effort to dilute the content of the party label rather than to assist the parties, as seems to be the goal of ordinary partisan elections, does not change the First Amendment problems with giving parties a special role in elections and special acknowledgment on the ballot.

---

[78] See *supra* at 14–15 (quoting Washington State Grange, 128 S. Ct. at 1192).

[79] Washington State Grange, 128 S. Ct. at 1198 (Scalia, J., dissenting).

Indeed, what is troubling about Justice Scalia's opinion is that he seems to see no problem with *helping* the major parties by granting access to and labeling particular candidates as party nominees, even though he challenges the state's power to require other particular information about a candidate on the ballot.

Again, it is perhaps no surprise that such issues are not addressed in *Washington State Grange*, given that the parties themselves certainly were in no position to object to giving party affiliation a favored place on the ballot. Any challenge of that sort would have to come from an independent candidate who unsuccessfully sought to include some other information next to his name that was as meaningful as party affiliation (for example, endorsement by a prominent politician or non-party organization such as the Sierra Club or the Chamber of Commerce).

In any event, *Washington State Grange* at least shows a possible path toward segregating the expressive functions of a party from the election functions of the state, though Washington itself failed to follow that path to its end. Full separation would mean that parties have no special role in elections beyond their private expressive function—and may structure their affairs, select candidates to endorse, and advocate vigorously—without any suggestion that they are engaging in state action. They then would be treated like any other private expressive association.

The state likewise would be able to focus on its core function of running fair and efficient elections. That limited function would most readily comport with the First Amendment if the state limited itself to imposing speech-and-association-neutral requirements for ballot access (as Washington has done) and refrained from making the ballot a billboard or other type of expressive forum for particular views or pieces of information that the state seeks to inject into the election process. The state should confine itself to winnowing the field under neutral criteria and identifying the candidates in a non-confusing manner, leaving the provision of substantive information and advocacy about the candidates to the marketplace of ideas.

# District of Columbia v. Heller: The Second Amendment Is Back, Baby

## Clark Neily*

> *A well regulated Militia, being necessary to the security of a free State, the right of the people to keep and bear Arms, shall not be infringed.*
>
> U.S. Const., Amend. II

For more than 200 years, the Second Amendment was a sort of constitutional Loch Ness Monster: Despite occasional reported sightings, many people—and certainly most judges—were inclined to believe it did not really exist. But that changed dramatically on June 26, 2008, when the Supreme Court handed down *District of Columbia v. Heller,*[1] in which it unambiguously held, for the first time in history, that the Second Amendment protects an individual right to keep and bear arms.

As with any newly discovered constitutional right, the precise scope and content of the Second Amendment remain unclear and will have to be fleshed out in subsequent litigation. Within hours of the Court's announcement of the *Heller* decision (which struck down Washington, D.C.'s handgun ban), my co-counsel Alan Gura

*Senior Attorney, Institute for Justice, and co-counsel for the plaintiffs in *District of Columbia v. Heller.* I would like to thank my co-counsel Bob Levy and Alan Gura for their extraordinary work on this case and their unflagging commitment to vindicating our clients' constitutional right to have a gun in their homes for self-defense. I would also like to thank our clients, Dick Heller, Shelly Parker, Tom Palmer, Tracey Ambeau, Gillian St. Lawrence, and George Lyon, each of whom has been a sincere, passionate, and articulate champion of the Second Amendment.

[1] 554 U.S. _____, 128 S. Ct. 2783 (2008).

filed suit against Chicago's handgun ban.[2] And along with two other D.C. residents, Heller has challenged the District's new licensing rules that forbid, among other things, the registration of any semiautomatic pistol. Other lawsuits in other jurisdictions are sure to follow.

It is too soon to know what effect *Heller* will have on the vast thicket of federal, state, and local firearms regulations in America. Indeed, the Supreme Court did not even announce what standard of review it will apply in future Second Amendment cases, though it expressly ruled out its most deferential standard, the so-called rational basis test. As always, much will turn on how the Court evaluates the competing governmental and individual interests, how much deference it cedes to legislatures, and—of particular importance given the abundance of empirical data in this area—the extent to which it favors actual evidence over unsupported speculation or junk science in the resolution of future cases.

This article has five parts. First, I set the stage for the *Heller* litigation by briefly reviewing the history of Second Amendment jurisprudence and scholarship. Next, I explain how and why the *Heller* case was filed and what happened in the lower courts. Then I describe the Supreme Court proceedings, including the extraordinary outpouring of scholarship in the form of amicus briefs from across the ideological spectrum. The fourth part summarizes the majority and two dissenting opinions in *Heller*, and the fifth part offers a critique of those opinions and some thoughts about the implications of the decision and the future of Second Amendment litigation.

## I.

Until 2001, the Second Amendment was essentially a dead letter in constitutional law, at least among the federal courts. The Supreme Court had confronted it only once, in a 1939 case called *United*

---

[2] Information about that case, *McDonald v. City of Chicago*, may be found at www. chicagoguncase.com. Challenges were brought against handgun bans in several Chicago suburbs as well, which all moved to repeal those laws rather than try to defend them in court. See, e.g., Susan Kuczka & Hal Dardick, Wilmette repeals gun ban, Chicago Tribune, July 25, 2008, at W1. Chicago's Mayor Richard Daley, by contrast, has announced his intent to defend the city's handgun ban all the way to the Supreme Court if necessary. James Oliphant & Jeff Coens, Daley vows to fight for Chicago's gun ban, Chicago Tribune, June 27, 2008, at C1.

*States v. Miller.*[3] As discussed below, that decision produced a legal Rorschach test upon which nearly any interpretation of the amendment could be projected. The resulting jurisprudential vacuum was quickly filled by a series of federal circuit court decisions holding that the Second Amendment provides no meaningful protection for individual gun ownership. Legal academia, to the extent it gave the matter any attention at all, mostly echoed and supported that understanding through what came to be called the "collective rights" model. But neither the court decisions nor the academic literature advocating the collective rights model were very persuasive, and the door remained open to serious examination of the Second Amendment's true meaning, which commenced in earnest about 25 years ago.

The modern saga of the Second Amendment begins with a small-time bank robber from Oklahoma named Jackson Miller. Miller and his associate Frank Layton were arrested in 1938 for transporting an untaxed sawed-off shotgun across state lines in violation of the National Firearms Act of 1934.[4] In what may have been a deliberate test case designed to vindicate the law's constitutionality, a federal district judge in Arkansas quashed the indictment against the men on the grounds that the NFA violated the Second Amendment.[5] The government appealed directly to the Supreme Court, which overruled the lower court in a unanimous decision upholding the constitutionality of the NFA. But the Court did not hold, as later misrepresentations of *Miller* would contend, that the Second Amendment protects only a collective or militia-based right to possess firearms. Nor did the Court even hold that the sawed-off shotgun at issue fell outside the definition of constitutionally protected "arms" covered by the amendment. Instead, the Court simply found that it was "not within judicial notice" that a short-barreled shotgun "is any part of the ordinary military equipment or that its use could contribute to the common defense" and remanded the case to the

---

[3] 307 U.S. 174 (1939).

[4] Brian L. Frye, The Peculiar Story of *United States vs. Miller*, 3 N.Y.U. J. L. & Liberty 48, 58–59 (2008).

[5] *Id.* at 60, 65.

district court for further proceedings, presumably including the receipt of evidence on that point.[6]

As noted in Justice Scalia's majority opinion in *Heller*, two features of the *Miller* case are particularly significant. First, the Supreme Court only heard from the government in that case because the defendants had apparently run out of money to pay their lawyer and were not represented by counsel before the Court.[7] Second, the lead argument in the government's brief was that neither Miller nor Layton could invoke the Second Amendment because they were not in active militia service at the time of their arrest.[8] That is, of course, the collective rights theory, and despite the Court's failure to embrace it, later judges and academics would nevertheless read *Miller* as having adopted that interpretation of the Second Amendment. Indeed, until *Heller*, all but three of the twelve federal circuits endorsed some version of the collective rights model.[9] State appellate courts were more evenly split, with about ten cases on either side of the individual rights versus collective rights divide.[10]

---

[6] Miller, 307 U.S. at 178, 183. Somewhat ironically, Mr. Miller was shot to death, apparently by fellow criminals, before his case could proceed any further in the district court. See Frye, *supra* note 4 at 68–69. His co-defendant Frank Layton pleaded guilty to the NFA charge and received five years in prison, thus terminating the Miller litigation. *Id.* at 69.

[7] As explained in a suitably brief telegram from their former attorney to the Clerk of the Supreme Court, "'Suggest case be submitted on [government's] brief. Unable to obtain any money from clients to be present and argue case.'" *Id.* at 67.

[8] Parker v. District of Columbia, 478 F.3d 370, 393 (D.C. Cir. 2007); see also Heller, 128 S. Ct. at 2814.

[9] Cases v. United States, 131 F.2d 916, 921-23 (1st Cir.1942); United States v. Rybar, 103 F.3d 273, 286 (3d Cir. 1996); Love v. Pepersack, 47 F.3d 120, 124 (4th Cir. 1995); United States v. Warin, 530 F.2d 103, 106 (6th Cir. 1976); Gillespie v. City of Indianapolis, 185 F.3d 693, 710 (7th Cir. 1999); United States v. Hale, 978 F.2d 1016, 1019–20 (8th Cir. 1992); Silveira v. Lockyer, 312 F.3d 1052, 1086 (9th Cir. 2003); United States v. Oakes, 564 F.2d 384, 387 (10th Cir. 1977); United States v. Wright, 117 F.3d 1265, 1273–74 (11th Cir. 1997). The Second Circuit declined to address the collective-rights versus individual-rights dispute and instead held that whatever its content, the right may not be invoked against state governments. Bach v. Pataki, 408 F.3d 75, 84–85 (2d Cir. 2005). As discussed below, the Fifth Circuit was the first to adopt the individual rights view. United States v. Emerson, 270 F.3d 203 (5th Cir. 2001).

[10] See Parker, 478 F.3d at 381 n.6 (collecting cases); see also Brief in Response to Petition for Certiorari in District of Columbia v. Heller at 15–16 (identifying several more individual rights cases) (available at http://www.gurapossessky.com/news/parker/documents/petition_response.pdf).

Meanwhile, historical and legal scholarship, such as it was, favored the collective rights model during that era. Writing in a 2000 symposium issue of the *Chicago Kent Law Review* promoting the collective rights model, Professor Robert Spitzer describes an exhaustive literature survey from which he concluded that "a total of eleven articles on the Second Amendment appeared in law journals from 1912 to 1959," all of which endorsed some version of the collective rights model.[11] But that would change.

As described by leading collective rights proponent Carl Bogus in the same symposium issue, the period 1970 to 1989 saw a rough parity in the law review literature, with 27 articles supporting the individual rights model and 25 supporting the collective right view.[12] Then came an unmistakable shift. As more and more scholars looked more and more carefully at the Second Amendment, a growing majority concluded that the Second Amendment does protect an individual right to keep and bear arms outside the context of military service. So complete was this reversal that the individual rights interpretation soon came to be known as the "Standard Model."[13]

Many people contributed to the resurgence of the individual rights interpretation, including Stephen Halbrook, Dave Kopel, Joyce Lee Malcom, and Randy Barnett, to name just a few. But most agree that the seminal work was Don Kates's "Handgun Prohibition and the Original Meaning of the Second Amendment," which appeared in the *Michigan Law Review* in 1983.[14] Acknowledging that the individual rights model was then endorsed "by only a minority of legal scholars," Kates provided a comprehensive and devastating critique of what he called the "exclusively state's right" interpretation of the Second Amendment. There followed an outpouring of new scholarship supporting the individual rights model and thoroughly undermining the historical, linguistic, and structural premises of the various militia-centric interpretations that had gained largely uncritical acceptance since *Miller* was decided in 1939.

---

[11] Robert J. Spitzer, Lost and Found: Researching the Second Amendment, 76 Chi.-Kent L. Rev. 349, 366 (2000).

[12] Carl T. Bogus, Fresh Looks: The History and Politics of Second Amendment Scholarship: A Primer, 76 Chi.-Kent L. Rev. 3, 8 (2000).

[13] See, e.g., Glenn H. Reynolds, A Critical Guide to the Second Amendment, 62 Tenn. L. Rev. 461, 463 (1995).

[14] 82 Mich. L. Rev. 204 (1983).

Particularly damaging to the collective rights camp was the perceived defection of several high-profile liberal academics, whose stature and lack of personal or professional bias towards gun ownership made them difficult to dismiss as mere shills for the National Rifle Association.[15] The two most prominent examples are University of Texas law professor Sanford Levinson and Harvard's Laurence Tribe. Levinson created a stir with his 1989 essay in the *Yale Law Journal* titled "The Embarrassing Second Amendment,"[16] where he candidly surmised that he could not

> help but suspect that the best explanation for the absence of the Second Amendment from the legal consciousness of the elite bar, including that component found in the legal academy, is derived from a mixture of sheer opposition to the idea of private ownership of guns and the perhaps subconscious fear that altogether plausible, perhaps even "winning," interpretations of the Second Amendment would present real hurdles to those of us supporting prohibitory regulation.[17]

Ten years later, Professor Tribe released the third edition of his influential treatise on American constitutional law in which he acknowledged, for the first time, that the Second Amendment protects "a right (admittedly of uncertain scope) on the part of individuals to possess and use firearms in the defense of themselves and their homes."[18] Others followed, including Yale's Akhil Amar and Duke's (now William and Mary's) William Van Alstyne.

The resurgence of academic interest in the Second Amendment produced a body of scholarship that could neither be ignored nor dismissed by opponents of the individual rights model—or, it turns out, by the federal courts. Remarkably, despite the rejection by nine federal circuit courts of the proposition that the Second Amendment protects an individual right to keep and bear arms, none of those decisions contained any serious analysis of the amendment itself.

---

[15] See, e.g., Bogus, *supra* note 12 at 9–10.

[16] 99 Yale L. J. 637 (1989).

[17] *Id.* at 642.

[18] 1 Laurence H. Tribe, American Constitutional Law 902 n. 211 (3d ed. 2000).

In 2001, the Fifth Circuit became the first federal appellate court to undertake that analysis, in *United States v. Emerson.*[19]

The case arose when Dr. Timothy Joe Emerson was charged with violating a federal law that forbids persons under a domestic restraining order from possessing firearms. He challenged the prosecution on several grounds, including that it violated his rights under the Second Amendment, at least in the absence of any express judicial finding that he posed a danger to his estranged wife.[20] In a thorough, scholarly decision, Judge Will Garwood conducted an exhaustive analysis of the Second Amendment and concluded that it "protects individual Americans in their right to keep and bear arms whether or not they are a member of a select militia or performing active military service or training."[21]

Turning to the specific facts of the case, the panel expressed "concern[]" about the lack of express findings in the restraining order upon which Emerson's prosecution was based,[22] but ultimately construed both the federal and state laws at issue as having implicitly required a specific showing of likely future harm before the restraining order could issue.[23] The court thus concluded that while the prosecution implicated Emerson's Second Amendment right to own a firearm, it did not violate that right under the particular facts of his case.[24]

Although there is some question whether the Fifth Circuit's Second Amendment analysis was mere dicta, as Judge Robert Parker argued in his special concurrence,[25] the effects of the decision were swift and dramatic. Among other things, the U.S. Department of Justice, under Attorney General John Ashcroft, reversed its earlier position and acknowledged in its brief opposing Emerson's petition for certiorari that the Second Amendment protects an individual right to "possess and bear" firearms, subject to "reasonable

---

[19] 270 F.3d 203 (5th Cir. 2001).

[20] *Id.* at 261.

[21] *Id.* at 260.

[22] *Id.* at 261.

[23] *Id.* at 262–64.

[24] *Id.* at 265.

[25] See, e.g., *id.* at 272–74 (Parker, J., specially concurring).

restrictions" designed to prevent possession by "unfit persons."[26] But there was one very specific reaction to *Emerson* that would ultimately give rise to the *Heller* case: Criminal defense attorneys throughout the country began asserting Second Amendment defenses to gun charges.[27]

## II.

The idea to file what would become the *Heller* case originated with my colleague Steve Simpson and me and solidified when we presented it to our friend and colleague Bob Levy. Steve and I are attorneys at the Institute for Justice, a libertarian public interest law firm based in Arlington, Virginia, that litigates to promote property rights, economic liberty, free speech, and school choice. Although neither of us had ever done any Second Amendment work, we stayed generally abreast of developments in that area. Like many other Americans, we were delighted by the *Emerson* decision. But as public interest lawyers, we were also concerned.

By creating a split of authority among federal courts over the proper interpretation of the Second Amendment, *Emerson* dramatically increased the likelihood of the Supreme Court accepting a case to review the issue and perhaps clarify its murky *Miller* decision. DOJ's change in policy increased those odds still further, and the fact that criminal defense attorneys were now routinely asserting Second Amendment defenses to gun charges added elements of urgency and uncertainty. In short, we believed it was only a matter of time before the Supreme Court accepted a Second Amendment case, and it seemed clear that the odds of a favorable outcome would be better if the issue went up on behalf of law-abiding citizens instead of an accused criminal.

At the time, Washington, D.C., had the most draconian gun laws in the nation. Besides banning handguns outright, D.C. law required even lawfully owned shotguns and rifles to be unloaded and either

---

[26] See Opp'n to Pet. for Cert. in United States v. Emerson, No. 01-8780, at 19 n.3 (available at www.usdoj.gov/osg/briefs/2001/0responses/2001-8780.resp.pdf).

[27] See, e.g., Silveira v. Lockyer, 312 F.3d 1052, 1065 (9th Cir. 2002) (noting that Second Amendment defenses have been raised by criminal defendants throughout the nation as a result of the Justice Department's new position on the amendment) (citing Adam Liptak, Revised View of Second Amendment Is Cited As Defense in Gun Cases, N.Y. Times, July 23, 2002, at A1).

bound by a trigger lock or disassembled at all times.[28] Steve and I knew about those laws, and we knew the D.C. Circuit was one of the few federal appellate courts that had not yet interpreted the Second Amendment. We began to think seriously about what it would take to challenge D.C.'s functional firearms ban. One of the first people we approached was Bob Levy, a former entrepreneur, senior fellow in constitutional studies at the Cato Institute, and member of the Institute for Justice's board of directors. Bob and I became friends in 1994 while we were both clerking for Judge Royce Lamberth of the D.C. District Court. Bob immediately agreed to back the case, both financially and personally, and that was the watershed moment.

Steve's IJ-related duties prevented him from taking an active role in the actual litigation, but IJ's president Chip Mellor agreed to let me work on the case on my own time so long as I maintained a sufficiently low profile to avoid giving the impression that it was an Institute for Justice case.[29] Bob enlisted his Cato colleague Gene Healy, and the three of us began searching for potential clients. Before long, we received phone calls from various interested parties and from people who knew people who might be interested. We spent considerable time in the summer of 2002 interviewing potential clients and looking for people with the sincerity, character, and commitment to stay the course.

The lead plaintiff was an African-American woman of strong principles and iron will named Shelly Parker, who had tried to rid her neighborhood of drug dealers through community activism. For her efforts, Parker was labeled a "troublemaker" by the drug dealers, who began threatening her and even threw rocks through the windows of her house and car to make sure she got the message. Parker joined the lawsuit because she wanted to be able to keep a pistol at home to defend herself from those criminals, one of whom came to

---

[28] D.C. Code § 7-2502.02(a)(4) (forbidding registration of handguns); § 7-2507.02 (trigger lock requirement) (1981) (amended 2008).

[29] While the Institute for Justice litigates constitutional cases to promote individual liberty, the Second Amendment is not one of its core mission areas. In the Supreme Court, IJ filed an amicus brief supporting Heller and addressing the history and relevance of the Fourteenth Amendment as it relates to the right to keep and bear arms.

her front door shortly after the lawsuit was filed and tried to force his way inside yelling, "Bitch, I'll kill you, I live on this block too."[30]

Dick Heller was working as a security guard at the Federal Judicial Center in Washington, D.C. when we first spoke with him. D.C. law allows privately employed "special police officers" to carry pistols on the job but generally forbids them from taking their weapons home at night. Heller found it outrageous that the District allowed him to carry a pistol to protect the lives of government officials during the day, but forbade him from taking that same weapon home at night to defend his own life. On the advice of a friend, Heller went down to the Municipal Police Department in July 2002 and attempted to register a .22 caliber revolver that he kept at a location outside of D.C. The application was summarily rejected.

The remaining plaintiffs each had their own reasons for challenging D.C.'s gun ban. For example, Tom Palmer, who is Vice President for International Programs at the Cato Institute, believes he saved his own life years before in another state by brandishing a pistol at a gang of homophobes who assaulted him and a companion for being gay. Tracey Ambeau and Gillian St. Lawrence both wanted access to a functional firearm to protect themselves when their husbands were away, and St. Lawrence actually owned a shotgun for that purpose. But D.C. law prohibited her from ever loading it, even in self-defense.[31] Finally, George Lyon is a lawyer who lives and works in Washington, D.C. and believes he has the right to keep a pistol at home to defend himself and his family.

As word spread of our plan to challenge D.C.'s gun ban, we were somewhat surprised at the amount of pushback we received from people within the conservative and libertarian movement. That response was understandable to an extent. After all, there were not five clear votes on the Court to embrace a robust individual rights interpretation of the Second Amendment, and there was a very real risk that a majority of justices would either reject that model outright or render it meaningless by characterizing the right as non-fundamental. On the other hand, none of the skeptics we spoke with had a persuasive response to our concern that a criminal case was likely

---

[30] The biographical information about each of the six clients is taken from the declarations filed on their behalf in the district court proceedings. Those declarations are available, along with all of the other relevant pleadings in the Parker/Heller litigation at www.dcguncase.com/blog/case-filings.

[31] D.C. Code § 7-2507.02 (1983) (amended 2008).

to get to the Supreme Court first if no one seized the opportunity to bring a civil challenge.

The remaining member of the *Heller* team was Alan Gura, whom Bob hired to lead the litigation when it became clear that I would be unable to do so while carrying a full workload of IJ cases. A graduate of the Georgetown Law Center, Alan ran a successful litigation practice from his office in Alexandria, Virginia. Alan had a diverse employment history, having served as counsel to the Senate Judiciary Committee, an associate at Sidley Austin, and as a deputy attorney general for the state of California. Most important, he had a reputation as a smart, aggressive litigator who was interested in and knowledgeable about the Second Amendment. He signed on immediately.

Styled *Parker v. District of Columbia*, the complaint was filed in the U.S. District Court for the District of Columbia on February 10, 2003, and assigned to Judge Emmet Sullivan. It presented a single claim: that D.C.'s gun ban violated our clients' Second Amendment right to keep functional firearms in their homes. The District's lawyers immediately moved to dismiss the complaint on the ground that the Second Amendment does not protect an individual right, and we filed a summary judgment motion arguing that it does.

Two months after we filed the *Parker* case, a separate group of plaintiffs filed another federal court challenge to D.C.'s gun ban. The new challenge was called the "Seegars" case, after its lead plaintiff Sandra Seegars.[32] Represented by veteran Second Amendment advocate Stephen Halbrook, the *Seegars* plaintiffs drew a different judge, Reggie Walton, and Halbrook immediately moved to consolidate the two cases. We opposed that motion because we did not believe it was in our clients' best interests for the two cases to proceed as one. Of particular concern to us was the fact that the *Seegars* plaintiffs had named Attorney General John Ashcroft as a defendant, which meant the Department of Justice, with its greater resources and generally more sophisticated legal acumen, would help defend the case. Although the consolidation effort was denied and the cases proceeded on different tracks before their respective judges, our concerns about picking what we believed was an unnecessary fight with DOJ were soon borne out.

The only argument raised by the District's lawyers in their motion to dismiss the *Parker* case was that the Second Amendment protects

---

[32] Seegars v. Ashcroft, 297 F. Supp.2d 201 (D.D.C. 2004).

only a collective, not an individual, right to keep and bear arms. But the DOJ lawyers in *Seegars* raised a new defense that would very nearly derail both cases: standing.

In order to have standing to bring a federal lawsuit, a plaintiff must allege a concrete injury caused by the defendant that is redressable by the court. The point of standing doctrine is to ensure that courts only resolve actual cases and controversies and do not become embroiled in abstract policy disputes where their rulings would amount to mere advisory opinions. When misapplied, however, it can amount to little more than a "get out of court free" card for the government, which is precisely what happened to the *Seegars* plaintiffs and why *Parker* became *Heller*.

Although *Seegars* was filed two months after *Parker*, it proceeded more rapidly through the district court. After holding a hearing in October 2003 on D.C.'s and DOJ's motions to dismiss, Judge Walton found that none of the five *Seegars* plaintiffs had standing to challenge D.C.'s handgun ban.[33]

The week after the *Seegars* argument before Judge Walton, Judge Sullivan held a hearing in the *Parker* case to resolve the District's motion to dismiss and the plaintiffs' motion for summary judgment. He began the hearing by noting that neither the District nor its amici had raised the issue of standing in their briefs, prompting this exchange:

| | |
|---|---|
| The Court: | You didn't raise [standing] as a basis for your motion to dismiss. |
| D.C.'s Counsel: | No, we did not . . . . |
| The Court: | When were you planning to raise it? Had I not raised it, were you going to raise it today? |
| D.C.'s Counsel: | No, I was not planning on raising it today. |
| The Court: | When were you going to raise it? On appeal?[34] |

---

[33] Judge Walton found that one of the *Seegars* plaintiffs, Gardine Hailes, had standing to challenge the trigger lock requirement for her lawfully registered shotgun, but he dismissed that claim on the grounds that the Second Amendment neither protects an individual right to possess firearms nor applies to the District of Columbia in any event. Seegars, 297 F. Supp.2d at 235–39.

[34] This exchange is quoted at greater length, with citations to the hearing transcript, on pages 12–14 of the plaintiffs' Motion to Issue Briefing Schedule and Set Oral Argument on the Merits, available on the "Case Filings" page of www. dcguncase.com.

After a similar colloquy with counsel for one of D.C.'s amici, Judge Sullivan said he found it "mystifying" that everyone on that side of the case agreed that the plaintiffs lacked standing to pursue their Second Amendment claims but that none of them had raised it in their briefs. After requesting more briefing on the standing issue, Judge Sullivan dismissed the case not for lack of standing but on the substantive ground that the Second Amendment does not protect an individual right to keep and bear arms.[35]

Both *Seegars* and *Parker* went up on appeal to the D.C. Circuit around the same time, with *Seegars* slightly in the lead. The District successfully moved to stay proceedings in *Parker* until the *Seegars* appeal was finally resolved, as a result of which *Parker* ground to a halt for nearly two years. Meanwhile, things went from bad to worse for the *Seegars* plaintiffs.

Despite Supreme Court precedent clearly providing that would-be plaintiffs need only show a credible threat of prosecution under the law they wish to challenge, the D.C. Circuit applied a much narrower version of standing doctrine in *Seegars* that required Second Amendment plaintiffs to show they had been personally threatened with prosecution or otherwise singled out in some way by the government.[36] Of course, that rule has the perverse effect of requiring anyone who wishes to challenge a given law to first break it and then notify government officials so they can receive the requisite threat of prosecution. Notwithstanding two judges' stated belief that the standing rule applied in *Seegars* departed from Supreme Court precedent,[37] the D.C. Circuit declined to reconsider the ruling en banc,[38] and the Supreme Court denied certiorari. *Seegars* was over.

The District immediately filed a motion for summary affirmance in *Parker*, arguing that because none of the *Seegars* plaintiffs were found to have standing, none of the *Parker* plaintiffs did either. The D.C. Circuit rejected that motion and directed the parties to submit briefing on both standing and the merits of the Second Amendment claim. The court heard oral argument on December 12, 2006.

[35] Parker v. District of Columbia, 311 F. Supp.2d 103 (D.D.C. 2004).

[36] Seegars v. Gonzales, 396 F.3d 1248, 1252–56 (D.C. Cir. 2005).

[37] 413 F.3d 1, 2–3 (D.C. Cir. 2005) (Sentelle, J., dissenting from the denial of rehearing en banc and statement of Williams, J., calling for rehearing en banc).

[38] *Id.* at 1.

In the briefs and at oral argument, Alan hammered home the point that unlike any of the *Seegars* plaintiffs, one of our clients, Dick Heller, had actually attempted to register a handgun and had his application denied. It worked. As Senior Circuit Judge Silberman wrote in his majority decision, the D.C. Circuit has "consistently treated a license or permit denial pursuant to a state or federal administrative scheme as an Article III injury."[39] Accordingly, Dick Heller's act of filling out a perfectly meaningless application whose denial was a foregone conclusion under D.C. law meant he had standing to challenge D.C.'s gun ban, while the other five *Parker* plaintiffs did not.[40]

Judge Silberman's opinion striking down the District's functional firearms ban was an intellectual tour de force. After summarizing the history of the struggle between the individual and collective rights interpretations of the Second Amendment, Silberman undertook a close textual and historical analysis in which he systematically engaged and rejected each of the District's arguments against the individual rights position. He concluded that the Second Amendment protects a right to keep and bear arms that predated the Constitution and is not "contingent upon [a citizen's] continued or intermittent enrollment in the militia."[41] Finding D.C.'s functional firearms ban inconsistent with that right, Judge Silberman (joined by Judge Griffith, over Judge Henderson's dissent) remanded the case to the district court with instructions to enter summary judgment for Mr. Heller.[42]

No federal court of appeals had ever struck down a gun control law on Second Amendment grounds before, and with the denial of the District's petition for rehearing en banc, the stage was set for a momentous decision by the city: whether to appeal the decision to the Supreme Court. The stakes were enormous, and there were conflicting considerations. On the one hand, it was clearly galling

---

[39] Parker v. District of Columbia, 478 F.3d 370, 376 (D.C. Cir. 2007).

[40] *Id.* 375–76. Cf. Seegars, 413 F.3d at 2 (statement of Williams, J.) (observing that D.C. law "plainly, unequivocally" forbids the issuance of pistol permits and explaining that "it is mysterious to me how plodding through the charade of seeking permits would render the threat of prosecution . . . one iota more imminent").

[41] Parker, 478 F.3d at 395.

[42] *Id.* at 401.

to Mayor Fenty and many D.C. Council members to have the center-piece of the District's zero-tolerance gun policy swept aside by the federal courts. And while there is no credible evidence that the policy did anything to reduce crime or prevent gun-related deaths in D.C., the regulations served as a powerful symbol of the District's attitude towards individual gun ownership and its stance in the culture clash engendered by that issue. On the other hand, a loss in the D.C. Circuit could be contained because, other than regarding the federal government (which was not Mayor Fenty's concern), the effects of the decision would be limited to Washington, D.C. But a loss in the Supreme Court could have national implications.

On July 16, 2007, Mayor Fenty announced that the District of Columbia would seek review of the *Heller* decision in the Supreme Court.

### III.

In hindsight, it seems almost inevitable that the Supreme Court would agree to review *Heller*, but it certainly did not appear that way at the time. Many knowledgeable observers expressed doubt about the Court's willingness to involve itself in such an emotionally and politically charged issue, especially in an election year. Nevertheless, the case captured the popular imagination and there appeared to be a public consensus that it was finally time for the Supreme Court to clarify the Second Amendment's meaning one way or the other.

Perhaps reflecting that sense of inevitability was the District's decision to devote the bulk of its cert petition to explaining not why the Supreme Court should take the case, but instead why the D.C. Circuit's decision was wrong. Normally, arguing the merits of one's case in a cert petition is considered a classic rookie blunder, but D.C.'s legal team, which by this time included veteran Supreme Court litigators Walter Dellinger, Alan Morrison, and Tom Goldstein, certainly knew what it was doing. They might simply have assumed that in a case of such magnitude, with such clearly drawn battle lines, the Court's decision whether to grant certiorari was unlikely to be influenced significantly by the parties themselves, and therefore the most effective tactic would be to preview the District's substantive arguments and try to set the terms of the debate from the beginning.

That is certainly the impression one gets from the District's framing of the question presented, which asked: "Whether the Second Amendment forbids the District of Columbia from banning private possession of handguns while allowing possession of rifles and shotguns." Thus, from the District's (new) perspective, this case was not mainly about individual versus collective rights or banning the possession of all functional firearms within the home, but simply whether the government may ban a particular class of firearm that it considers uniquely dangerous and unsuitable for civilian use in urban environments so long as it leaves people with reasonable alternatives. It was a clever makeover.

Of course, we framed the issue quite differently, asking: "Whether the Second Amendment guarantees law-abiding adult individuals a right to keep ordinary, functional firearms, including handguns, in their homes." And despite having prevailed below, we supported the District's request for Supreme Court review and devoted our response, as the District had with its petition, to setting the terms of the debate in the event of a cert grant.[43]

On November 20, 2007, the Supreme Court announced that it would hear the case. As framed by the Supreme Court, the question presented was whether the challenged provisions of the D.C. Code, including its handgun ban and trigger lock requirements, "violate the Second Amendment rights of individuals who are not affiliated with any state-regulated militia, but who wish to keep handguns and other firearms for private use in their homes?"[44] Against long odds, we had succeeded in our goal of presenting a carefully crafted, well-framed Second Amendment case to the Supreme Court before a criminal case got there first.

Although there is much to tell about the preparation, strategy, and work that went into the presentation of Heller's case to the Supreme Court, of perhaps greater interest to most readers is the extraordinary outpouring of Second Amendment scholarship that attended this case in the form of amicus briefs filed with the Court.

---

[43] We also filed a Conditional Cross-Petition for a Writ of Certiorari on behalf of the five plaintiffs whom the D.C. Circuit ruled did not have standing to challenge D.C.'s gun ban. The District opposed that cross-petition, and the Supreme Court held it in abeyance until after it announced the Heller decision in June 2008, then dismissed it without explanation.

[44] District of Columbia v. Heller, 128 S. Ct. 645 (2007) (grant of certiorari).

A total of 68 amicus briefs were filed: 19 for the District, 48 for Heller, and one by the United States purporting to take neither side. Besides their sheer number (apparently a record[45]), the briefs were notable both for their quality and for the remarkable array of people, organizations, and perspectives they represented. While there is not space to give all of the briefs their proper due, a few bear special mention.

From a purely symbolic standpoint, the two most remarkable amicus briefs had to be the ones filed on behalf of a majority of members of the U.S. Congress and on behalf of 31 states. The "Congress brief" was prepared by Stephen Halbrook, and it was submitted on behalf of 55 senators, 250 representatives, and Dick Cheney in his capacity as president of the Senate. The "States Brief" was headed up by then-Texas Solicitor General Ted Cruz, a veteran Supreme Court litigator who worked indefatigably to persuade other states to join the brief. Both briefs are extraordinary in that they were filed on behalf of government officials who would normally be quite reluctant to cede power to another branch of government. Thus, while it is one thing for politicians to acknowledge limits on their power in theory, it is quite another for them to urge the Supreme Court to impose concrete, enforceable limits on that power. And yet, that is precisely what the Congress and States briefs did in *Heller*.

Other briefs remarkable as much for their symbolism as their substance were those submitted by the Congress of Racial Equality (CORE), GeorgiaCarry.org, and the Pink Pistols, a gay and lesbian firearms advocacy group. Together, the CORE and GeorgiaCarry briefs showed that "[t]he history of gun control in America has been one of discrimination, disenfranchisement, and oppression of racial and ethnic minorities, immigrants, and other 'undesirable' groups."[46] Extending and updating that history of discrimination, the Pink Pistols brief not only provided disturbing statistics about gays' and lesbians' heightened risk of and greater vulnerability to violent

---

[45] According to the editor of this *Review*, the Michigan affirmative action cases, Gratz v. Bollinger, 539 U.S. 244 (2003), and Grutter v. Bollinger, 539 U.S. 306 (2003), together generated 104 amicus briefs, but neither of those cases, which were consolidated for argument, garnered more briefs than *Heller* did alone. See Ilya Shapiro, "Friends of the Second Amendment: A Walk Through the *Amicus* Briefs in *D.C. v. Heller*," 20 J. Firearms & Pub. Policy _____ (Sept. 2008).

[46] Brief of *Amicus Curiae* Congress of Racial Equality at 2.

assault because of their sexual orientation, but also showed how the District's militia-centric conception would "eradicate any Second Amendment right" for gays and lesbians on account of the federal government's "Don't Ask, Don't Tell" policy.[47]

Among the most persuasive were those written by Professor Nelson Lund for the Second Amendment Foundation and Professors David Hardy and Joe Olson on behalf of Academics for the Second Amendment. Those briefs exposed what is arguably the deepest and most fundamental problem with D.C.'s theory of the case: that no one has ever devised a militia-centric interpretation of the Second Amendment that can be squared with the historical record and that does not lead to absurd results.

As explained in the Academics for the Second Amendment brief, Madison and other Federalists who agreed to add a bill of rights to the Constitution adamantly opposed any attempt to revisit the issue of how power over the militia was to be allocated between the federal and state governments, even though this was among the principal concerns of the Anti-Federalists whom the proposed bill of rights was intended to mollify. And yet that is precisely what militia-centric interpretations—including the District's—ultimately contend: that the Second Amendment represents a devolution of militia control from the federal government to the states. By contrast, Madison and the other Federalists had no qualms about disclaiming any power on the part of the federal government to disarm citizens, because they did not think the government had that power in the first place. As the Academics' brief explains: "In 1789, for Congress to renounce any intent to disarm Americans would be no real loss; the same cannot be said of reopening the fight over control of the militia."[48]

Given the centrality of history to both Justice Scalia's and Justice Stevens's opinions, another key amicus brief was the one filed by the Cato Institute and historian Joyce Lee Malcolm.[49] Professor Malcolm's book *To Keep and Bear Arms: The Origin of an English-American Right* has been a key resource in the debate over the

---

[47] Brief of Pink Pistols and Gays and Lesbians for Individual Liberty as Amici Curiae in Support of Respondent at 2, 28–34.

[48] Brief of Amicus Curiae Academics for the Second Amendment in Support of the Respondent at 2.

[49] Brief of the Cato Institute and Historian Joyce Lee Malcolm as Amici Curiae in Support of Respondent.

meaning of the Second Amendment because it documents the right of armed self-defense in England and explains how that right influenced the Framers' conception of the natural right to arms they codified in the Second Amendment. The Cato-Malcolm brief describes how various English monarchs sought to limit their subjects' right to own weapons and demonstrates that the Framers were both well aware of that history and determined not to repeat it in America. Of particular importance to the debate between Scalia and Stevens over the *scope* of the right, the Cato-Malcolm brief thoroughly debunks the notion that the English right to arms was in any way limited to or dependent upon militia service.[50]

Finally, there is the amicus brief submitted by Solicitor General Paul Clement on behalf of the United States. Like most Republicans, President Bush identified himself as an ardent supporter of the Second Amendment who understood it to protect an individual right to keep and bear arms. Assuming that is true, the brief filed on behalf of his administration was a huge disappointment, and one that speaks volumes about the difference between *saying* that one supports a particular constitutional right and actually meaning it.

The essence of the solicitor general's brief was this: While the Second Amendment does protect an individual right to keep and bear arms, that right is subject to reasonable regulation, the legitimate scope of which will depend on the "practical impact" on citizens' ability to possess firearms for lawful purposes and the strength of the government's law enforcement interests.[51] To the casual observer, that might seem like an appropriate framework. But the more worldly reader quickly identifies the serpent in the garden: the word "reasonable," which appears in the solicitor general's brief nearly a dozen times. "Reasonable" can be a slippery and dangerous term in constitutional litigation, one that can easily be used to drain a right of all meaningful content while pretending to embrace it. That risk is vividly illustrated by the solicitor general's brief, which, though it purported to invoke a heightened standard of review, nevertheless argued that the case should be remanded to the lower courts to determine whether the most sweeping imposition on gun

---

[50] See *id*. at 4–12.

[51] Brief for the United States as *Amicus Curiae* at 8, 20–27.

ownership in America since the British disarmed the colonists at Boston was "reasonable."[52]

Merits briefing by the parties continued through March 2008, and the Court heard oral argument on March 18. Preparation on our side was intense. Besides devouring seemingly everything written about the history of the Second Amendment, Alan participated in five separate moot courts, which were attended by some of the leading Supreme Court practitioners, academics, and Second Amendment experts in the country. Critical issues were identified, potential weaknesses examined, themes honed, and strategic decisions made. Among other things, a consensus emerged that a protracted discussion regarding the proper standard of review should be avoided if possible. While we had argued for strict scrutiny in our merits brief, there was general agreement that the best approach during the argument itself would be to say that under any appropriately robust standard of review a complete ban on all functional firearms in the home—or even just handguns—was unconstitutional. The key, as always, was to stake out no more territory than absolutely necessary to win the case.

*Heller* was the only case set for argument on March 18, and the justices were engaged, focused, and well prepared. The questioning from the bench was lively, as one would expect given the magnitude and the novelty of the issue, and the Chief Justice extended the argument time accordingly. There is little point in recounting the back-and-forth between the justices and the three advocates—Walter Dellinger for the District, Solicitor General Paul Clement for the United States, and Alan Gura for Heller—other than to repeat here what others have recognized: Alan's performance, particularly for a first-time advocate in the Supreme Court, was outstanding.

## IV.

The Supreme Court handed down its *Heller* decision on Thursday, June 26, 2008. Writing for a 5–4 majority that included Chief Justice John Roberts and Justices Anthony Kennedy, Clarence Thomas, and Samuel Alito, Justice Antonin Scalia conducted an exhaustive analysis of the Second Amendment's text, history, and purpose that spanned some 64 pages in the slip opinion. Concluding that the

---

[52] *Id.* at 27–32.

Second Amendment protects an individual right to possess a firearm unrelated to militia service, the Court struck down D.C.'s handgun ban and trigger lock requirement. Justice John Paul Stevens authored a dissent in which Justices David Souter, Ruth Bader Ginsburg, and Stephen Breyer joined, and Justice Breyer authored a dissent in which Justices Stevens, Souter, and Ginsburg joined. Justice Stevens adopted a version of the militia-centric collective rights model, while Justice Breyer argued that even if the Second Amendment does protect a non-military individual right—which he denied for the reasons stated by Justice Stevens—the District's regulation of firearms represented an appropriate balancing of the competing interests at stake and was thus immune from constitutional challenge.

Anyone with enough interest in the Second Amendment to read a law review article about it has probably already read—and certainly should read—the majority and dissenting opinions in *Heller*. Accordingly, I will provide only a brief summary of the three opinions before moving on to the final part of this article, in which I offer some thoughts about those opinions and the likely future of Second Amendment litigation in the wake of *Heller*.

Justice Scalia's majority decision is everything a Second Amendment supporter could realistically have hoped for. The reasoning is meticulous, precise, and well supported. And while the majority concedes a fairly broad scope of government authority to regulate gun ownership—disarming felons and outlawing "dangerous and unusual weapons," for example[53]—there is simply no plausible basis to expect that the Court would ever have done otherwise (and might well have done worse had the issue arrived in a less favorable setting).

Beginning with the text of the Second Amendment, Justice Scalia first demonstrates that "the people" whose right to keep and bear arms is not to be infringed refers to "all members of the political community, not an unspecified subset," such as those engaged in active militia service.[54] Next he dispatches the argument that the terms "bear arms" or "keep and bear arms" had an exclusively military connotation at the time of ratification. Putting those points together and examining them against the backdrop of the history

[53] Heller, 128 S. Ct. at 2816–17.
[54] *Id.* at 2790–91 (2008).

relevant to the Framers—including particularly the disarmament of political dissidents by the Stuart kings in 17th-century England— Justice Scalia concludes the Second Amendment codified a widely recognized, pre-existing right of individuals "to possess and carry weapons in case of confrontation."[55]

Examining the prefatory clause next, Justice Scalia describes the political tensions that gave rise to the Second Amendment and argues persuasively that while maintaining a well-regulated militia happens to be the specific reason mentioned in the text of the amendment for prohibiting the government from infringing the people's right to keep and bear arms, it was certainly not "the only reason Americans valued the ancient right; most undoubtedly thought it even more important for self-defense and hunting."[56] He then shows that the drafting history of the Second Amendment is inconclusive at best, with at least as many clues pointing towards an individual rights interpretation as otherwise.

Among the most devastating points in Justice Scalia's opinion— and one for which the collective rights camp has never had much of a response—is the raft of historical evidence showing that all the major commentators from the time of ratification through the early 20th century understood the Second Amendment as protecting an individual, not a collective or militia-centric, right to arms. As Stephen Halbrook has quipped, "if anyone entertained [the collective rights] notion in the period during which the Constitution and Bill of Rights were debated and ratified, it remains one of the most closely guarded secrets of the eighteenth century, for no known writing surviving from the period between 1787 and 1791 states such a thesis."[57]

Next, Justice Scalia critiques Justice Stevens's reading of *Miller* and shows that Stevens, like many commentators and courts before him, dramatically overstates *Miller*'s holding in order to find within it the militia-centric interpretation he favors.[58]

[55] *Id.* at 2797.

[56] *Id.* at 2801.

[57] Stephen P. Halbrook, That Every Man May Be Armed: The Evolution of a Constitutional Right 83 (1984).

[58] Heller, 128 S. Ct. at 2814–16.

Turning to the specific laws at issue, Justice Scalia notes that D.C.'s handgun ban outlaws the class of weapons "overwhelmingly chosen by American society" for lawful self-defense, while the District's trigger lock requirement requires that even lawfully owned firearms be kept inoperable at all times with no exception for self-defense.[59] Without announcing a specific standard of review, Scalia simply declares the trigger lock requirement unconstitutional on its face and says of the handgun ban that "[u]nder any of the standards of scrutiny that we have applied to enumerated constitutional rights, banning from the home the most preferred firearm in the nation to 'keep' and use for protection would fail constitutional muster."[60]

Not surprisingly, I find much to disagree with in the dissenting opinions of Justice Stevens and Justice Breyer. While I will preview some of those disagreements in the summaries that follow, my main critiques come in the next section. As noted above, all four dissenting Justices—Stevens, Souter, Ginsburg, and Breyer—signed on to each of the two dissenting opinions, which, taken together, constitute arguments in the alternative for why the Second Amendment's right to keep and bear arms should not receive the same protection as some of those justices' more preferred rights like free speech, intimate association, and abortion.

Justice Stevens begins with a rather extraordinary assertion about the nature of the right protected by the Second Amendment, the implications of which he never explores. According to Justice Stevens, "[t]he Second Amendment plainly does ... encompass the right to use weapons for certain military purposes."[61] Consider what that would mean if it were true. Military operations are necessarily run by the government. They involve troops—sometimes conscripted troops—serving under the command of officers whose lawful orders must be obeyed on pain of death (in some cases), and whose discretion about how to conduct combat operations—including specifically how to arm and deploy their soldiers—is virtually unbounded. The notion that soldiers have a *constitutionally enforceable right* "to use weapons for certain military purposes" in that setting

---

[59] *Id.* at 2817–19.

[60] *Id.* at 2817–18 (internal quotations and citation omitted).

[61] *Id.* at 2822 (Stevens, J., dissenting).

is mind-boggling. Just try to imagine a scenario in which the courts might actually enforce such an oddly conceived right on behalf of an aggrieved citizen. Inconceivable.

Justice Stevens's dissent strikes another false note when he describes the *Miller* decision as having upheld a conviction under the National Firearms Act.[62] In fact, *Miller* arrived at the Supreme Court in a much different procedural posture: The indictment against Miller and Layton had been quashed, as specifically noted in the first paragraph of the Court's opinion, so there was no conviction to uphold.[63]

Moving beyond these initial hiccups, Justice Stevens begins his analysis, like Justice Scalia, with the text of the amendment itself. Unlike Scalia, however, Stevens starts with the prefatory clause, in which he finds a "single-minded focus" on the Framers' part to protect "military uses of firearms."[64] He then imports that assumption into his interpretation "the people" in the operative clause, which refers "back to the object announced in the Amendment's preamble," namely, protecting "the collective action of individuals having a duty to serve in the militia." But the ultimate purpose of the Second Amendment, says Stevens, "was to protect the States' share of the divided sovereignty" over control of militia forces.[65] Finally, he analyzes the phrase "keep and bear arms" and concludes that it is essentially a term of art with an exclusively military connotation.

Justice Stevens then turns to the ratification history, in which he discerns two relevant themes: First, a widespread fear of the standing army the Constitution empowered the federal government to create; and second, a recognition "of the dangers inherent in relying on inadequately trained militia members as a primary means of providing for the common defense."[66] Stevens concludes that a compromise was reached to address those twin concerns under which Congress would retain the authority to maintain a standing army *and* have

[62] *Id.* at 2822–23. Justice Scalia makes the same mistake about Miller, but he does so in the midst of critiquing Justice Stevens's interpretation of the case. *Id.*, slip op. at 49, 128 S. Ct. at 2814 (Scalia, J.).

[63] Miller, 307 U.S. at 177.

[64] Heller, 128 S. Ct. at 2826 (Stevens, J., dissenting).

[65] *Id.* at 2827.

[66] *Id.* at 2831–32.

considerable control over state militias, including the power to organize, arm, discipline, and call them up for service. Meanwhile, the
states retained the limited powers (which Stevens dubiously refers
to as a "significant reservation") to appoint militia officers and to
train their militias "in accordance with the discipline prescribed
by Congress."[67] But the concern remained that Congress had not
specifically been prohibited from disarming the militia, and this,
according to Stevens, was the oversight the Second Amendment
was designed to correct.[68] But it is difficult to reconcile that assertion
with the fact that Madison and the first Senate both considered—
and rejected—language that would have unambiguously addressed
that precise concern.[69] Stevens's failure to engage that point, which
was made in several of the briefs, further diminishes the persuasive-
ness of his argument.

Justice Stevens next confronts the majority's historical arguments
in what amounts to a series of vignettes discussing the English Bill
of Rights, Blackstone's *Commentaries*, post-enactment commentaries,
and post-Civil War legislative history—all of which contradict, to
one degree or another, any militia-centric reading of the Second
Amendment. He then returns to *Miller*, where he fails to address
the fact that the government's brief in that case actually led with
the very militia-centric theory he espouses.[70] As Justice Scalia points
out, if the *Miller* Court had truly meant to embrace that interpretation, "it would have been odd to examine the character of the weapon
rather than simply note that the two crooks were not militiamen."[71]

Justice Stevens concludes with a warning that D.C.'s gun laws
may be "the first of an unknown number of dominoes to be knocked
off the table" of firearms regulation and worries that the decision

[67] *Id.* at 2832.

[68] *Id.* at 2833.

[69] See, e.g., Brief of Amicus Curiae Academics for the Second Amendment in Support
of the Respondent at 6–9 (describing Madison's and the First Senate's rejection of a
proposed amendment stating "'[t]hat each state respectively shall have the power
to provide for organizing, arming, and disciplining its own militia, whensoever
Congress shall omit or neglect to provide for the same'").

[70] Parker, 478 F.3d at 393 (noting that the brief submitted to the Supreme Court by
the government in *Miller* argued that the Second Amendment right only exists where
the arms in question "are borne in the militia or some other military organization. . . .")
(internal quotations and citations omitted).

[71] Heller, 128 S. Ct. at 2814.

to enforce individual rights under the Second Amendment may "increase the labor of federal judges to the 'breaking point.'"[72] Of course, those concerns apply equally to the enforcement of virtually any constitutional right; why the Second Amendment should be singled out to carry that baggage is unclear.

Justice Breyer begins his dissent by expressing his agreement with Justice Stevens's militia-centric interpretation of the Second Amendment. He then argues that even if the amendment does protect a non-military individual right to keep and bear arms, restrictions should be evaluated under a balancing test that asks whether they "*disproportionately* burden Amendment-protected interests."[73] Applying that proposed test to D.C.'s handgun ban and trigger lock requirement, he concludes that neither restriction impermissibly interferes with citizens' Second Amendment rights.

Justice Breyer starts with four propositions to which he believes the entire Court subscribes: (1) the Second Amendment protects an individual right that may be "separately enforced by each person upon whom it is conferred"; (2) the amendment was adopted "'[w]ith obvious purpose'" to ensure the effectiveness of militia forces; (3) the amendment must be interpreted with that end in view; and (4) the right protected by the Second Amendment is not absolute.[74] The first point seems tendentious because the "individual right" the dissenting justices have in mind is one that can only be exercised (they never explain just how) in the context of *government-directed* military service. The second and third points seem trivial since no one disputes that *a* purpose of the Second Amendment is to promote militia effectiveness—the question is whether it serves other purposes as well. The fourth point likewise states a mere truism that applies to all constitutional rights. One might just as well note that the entire Court subscribes to the proposition that the Second Amendment contains both nouns and verbs.

Seeking to establish a parallel between the District's functional firearms ban and Founding-era practices, Justice Breyer points out that Boston, Philadelphia, and New York City "all restricted the

---

[72] *Id.* at 2846–47 (Stevens, J., dissenting).

[73] *Id.* at 2865 (Breyer, J., dissenting) (emphasis in original).

[74] *Id.* at 2848.

firing of guns within city limits to at least some degree" and regulated the storage of gunpowder.[75] Having thus established the existence of at least some Founding-era impositions on armed self-defense, Breyer concludes that the question is essentially one of degree: What restrictions are reasonable for the legislature to adopt in light of the goals it seeks to achieve? Breyer believes this will inevitably be an interest-balancing analysis, one that he would adopt explicitly. The question, he says, is whether the challenged restriction burdens the protected interest in a way that is "out of proportion to the statute's salutary effects," with due consideration being given to the existence of "any clearly superior less restrictive alternative."[76] And while Breyer disclaims any explicit presumption of constitutionality or unconstitutionality,[77] his repeated invocation of "deference" to and "judicial confidence" in the reasonableness of legislatures makes clear which way the playing field is tilted.

Having articulated his proposed test, Justice Breyer applies it to the facts of the case, comparing the empirical data offered by the parties and various amici for and against D.C.'s gun ban, and concluding that it amounts to a wash at best.[78] After dispensing with the trigger lock requirement by inferring a self-defense exception, Breyer considers the avowed purposes of the District's handgun ban. Finding that one of those purposes is to "reduce significantly the number of handguns in the District," he concludes, ineluctably, that "there is no plausible way to achieve that objective other than to ban the guns."[79] Breyer concludes his analysis by asking whether the District's ban "disproportionately" burdens any Second Amendment-protected interests and finds that it does not.[80]

## V.

The majority and two dissenting opinions in *Heller* have already proved a rich source of material for scholarship, debate, and reflection. They have provoked fascinating—and hopefully fruitful—discussions about the nature of originalism, its limits, and the extent

[75] *Id.* at 2848–49.
[76] *Id.* at 2852.
[77] *Id.*
[78] *Id.* at 2860.
[79] *Id.* at 2864.
[80] *Id.* at 2865–68.

to which other interpretive methodologies should supplement or perhaps even supplant it. From the standpoint of a libertarian constitutional litigator, I find two things especially interesting about the *Heller* opinions: First what they suggest about the Court's current conception of liberty, and second, the ease with which even enumerated rights may be drained of all meaning through application of ostensibly even-handed constitutional balancing tests.

A well-known thought experiment has us travel back in our minds to the period between the adoption of the Constitution in 1789 and the ratification of the Bill of Rights in 1791. Did citizens during that time have only the handful of rights specifically mentioned in the unamended Constitution, such as habeas corpus? Most people reject that view, and correctly so. The Framers believed in natural rights— the "unalienable rights" famously invoked in the Declaration of Independence—and government can neither create nor abrogate those rights. The notion that the federal government in 1790 could ban books, outlaw newspapers, or seize private property at will simply because those things were not specifically enumerated as rights is, by most lights, absurd.

So did citizens have a right to own guns in 1790, even though the Constitution did not yet address that subject? The answer is plainly yes, as the Supreme Court recognized in an 1876 case where it explained that the right to keep and bear arms "is not a right granted by the Constitution. Neither is it in any manner dependent upon that instrument for its existence."[81] The notion that the Second Amendment was intended to circumscribe—rather than merely codify—that preexisting right seems obviously preposterous, which presents a real conundrum for those seeking to drain the amendment of any meaningful content.

The only solution to that problem is the one Justice Stevens attempts in his dissent, which is to characterize the *natural* right to keep and bear arms—that is, the one that predated the ratification of the Second Amendment—as being limited to military uses only. But as Justice Stevens's opinion demonstrates, there is no sound historical basis for that limited conception, which is really just an artifact of the Court's rather offhanded treatment of the Second Amendment in *Miller*. The idea that colonial-era Americans seriously

---

[81] United States v. Cruikshank, 92 U.S. 542, 553 (1876).

believed they had a right to own guns for one lawful purpose (partici-pating in militia service), but not for other lawful purposes (shooting game, resisting highwaymen, target practice) is not only ahistorical, but idiosyncratic as well.

For example, while some have argued that the First Amendment's free speech provisions were only intended to cover political speech, that view has been thoroughly rejected by the Supreme Court, espe-cially the more liberal justices—much to their credit. Nevertheless, one could certainly troll through Founding-era history and cobble together an argument at least as persuasive as the one in Justice Stevens's *Heller* dissent for why the preexisting natural right to freedom of speech and the press was limited to specifically political, democracy-promoting purposes. An even easier mark would be the right to "intimate sexual conduct" approved by all four of the dissenting *Heller* justices in *Lawrence v. Texas*.[82] As between the right to own guns and the right to have sex, it seems far more likely that Founding-era Americans would have viewed the latter as applying to some purposes (procreation, marital intimacy) but not others (employment, entertainment).

It appears the dissenting justices' only basis for construing the natural right to arms narrowly when they construe other natural rights like speech and sex quite broadly is the 13-word preamble to the Second Amendment containing the word "Militia." In other words, the *Heller* dissenters departed from their traditionally expan-sive conception of liberty because they find in the Second Amend-ment's militia clause evidence of a national consensus among Found-ing-era Americans that the natural right to keep and bear arms was a strictly limited one—indeed a "right" that exists *only* in the context of government-controlled military service.

But the evidence against that position—which includes the English Bill of Rights, Blackstone's *Commentaries*, contemporaneous writ-ings of influential thinkers, and the utterly commonplace status of guns in colonial America—is simply too overwhelming to be swept aside by such a thin reed. And perhaps that accounts for Justice Breyer's rather unusual "in the alternative" dissent, to which I now turn.

---

[82] 539 U.S. 558 (2003).

Reading Justice Breyer's dissent—which he begins by affirming his agreement with Justice Stevens's militia-centric analysis but then explains why D.C.'s handgun ban would not violate an individual-rights model of the Second Amendment either—I could not help but think of Groucho Marx's famous line where he says, "Those are my principles, and if you don't like them . . . well, I have others." The fact that the same four justices signed on to both dissenting opinions seems odd, even troubling, particularly in such a momentous context. Can it really be that Justice Stevens's and Justice Breyer's much different takes on the Second Amendment are both correct? Is one more correct than the other?

It is one thing for lawyers to argue alternative theories—after all, our assigned role is simply to win cases however we can, consistent with our various ethical duties, including candor towards the tribunal. But the same is not true of judges, and certainly not U.S. Supreme Court justices; in our system they are charged with saying what the Constitution *means*. There is something unsettling about the spectacle of four justices confronting an essentially blank constitutional slate regarding what many consider to be the quintessentially American right and saying, in effect, "Maybe it means this, or maybe it means that; but either way it doesn't mean very much."

All of this lends a distinctly preordained feeling to the whole enterprise, which is only reinforced by Justice Breyer's deference-heavy interest-balancing test. Under the framework he proposes, the constitutionality of gun laws would be evaluated by determining whether a particular restriction "burdens a protected interest in a way or to an extent that is out of proportion to the statute's salutary effects," with due consideration being given to the existence of "any clearly superior less restrictive alternatives."[83]

There are many reasons to be wary of such a test, starting with the fact that scientific-looking "support" may be ginned up for literally any social policy. For example, consider the debate over teaching creationism in public schools. When the Supreme Court ruled that out-of-bounds, creationism came back as "intelligent design," complete with its own set of purportedly scientific underpinnings. One suspects that Justice Breyer would be much more skeptical of empirical claims from the Discovery Institute than he appears to have

[83] Heller, 128 S. Ct. at 2852 (Breyer, J., dissenting).

been in reviewing the data—one cannot call it evidence—offered to support D.C.'s gun ban. But after reviewing each side's empirical submissions, Breyer concludes that "[t]he upshot is a set of studies and counterstudies that, at most, could leave a judge uncertain about the proper policy conclusion."[84] Unlike with most other enumerated rights, however, with the Second Amendment, Umpire Breyer says the tie goes to the government.

Another problem with Justice Breyer's proposed interest-balancing test is that it apparently does not consider the effect of challenged restrictions on particular individuals, which it ought to do if the concept of "balancing" is to make any sense at all. Thus, Breyer rather casually dismisses the hardship of being prevented from having a loaded handgun in one's home for self-defense, but does so in the abstract. But imagine a person could show that: (a) she is at unusual risk of a violent confrontation—say, because she lives in an under-policed high-crime area where a serial rapist has been preying on victims[85]; and (b) she is unable due to her stature or other physical limitations to wield a shotgun or rifle effectively within the confines of her small apartment. It seems quite clear that D.C.'s handgun ban would interfere much more seriously with that person's constitutional interests in self-defense than, say, with that of a person living in a gated community patrolled by armed security guards. But based on the way he applies it in his *Heller* dissent, there appears to be no room in Breyer's calculus for such fine-tuning.

Finally, the "clearly superior least restrictive alternative" adds no real teeth to Justice Breyer's test, particularly the way he applies it in his opinion. Thus, as Breyer himself acknowledges, the District's crime rate soared in the years following enactment of the handgun ban,[86] and so did its murder rate, which in 2006 was more than five times higher than the national average and more than double the rate in comparably sized cities.[87] Assuming Breyer is correct that the handgun ban's "basic purpose" was to save lives,[88] those numbers

[84] *Id.*, 128 S. Ct. at 2860.

[85] See, e.g., Aaron Davis, *Serial Rape Suspect's Trail Of Clues Leads to Violent End*, Washington Post, July 28, 2008, at A1.

[86] Heller, 128 S. Ct. at 2858–59 (Breyer, J., dissenting).

[87] Brief of Criminologists, Social Scientists, Other Distinguished Scholars and the Claremont Institute as Amici Curiae in Support of Respondent at 7.

[88] Heller, 128 S. Ct. at 2854 (Breyer, J., dissenting).

suggest it failed to do so. Justice Breyer has a ready answer for that, namely the principle that *"after it* doesn't mean *because of it."*[89]

But that sort of epistemological agnosticism, which also shows up in Justice Breyer's refusal to evaluate the quality of the competing studies offered for and against the gun ban, makes it hard to imagine any litigant ever establishing that some alternative regulation would have been "clearly superior" to any given restriction. In other words, D.C.'s gun ban appears to have done nothing to promote the legislative goal of saving lives; if so, then it would seem that *any* alternative—comprehensive registration requirements together with zealous enforcement against illegal pistol possession, for example—would be superior to the District's feckless handgun ban.

And that takes us to the implications of the *Heller* decision, which I think will be fairly modest in terms of their impact on existing gun laws, but hopefully more significant from a symbolic standpoint. Perhaps the most immediate effect of *Heller* will be on D.C.'s recalcitrant effort to maintain as many of its draconian restrictions on gun ownership as possible. Thus, despite the Court's clear recognition of handguns' utility for lawful self-defense, D.C. has announced that it intends to enforce its absurd statutory definition of prohibited "machine gun" as including any firearm that can shoot "[s]emiautomatically, more than 12 shots without manual reloading"—which means essentially all semiautomatics.[90] The new lawsuit filed by Heller and others challenges not only that provision but also certain administrative features of the registration process that seem unduly burdensome and more plausibly intended to discourage citizens from exercising their newfound right to own firearms than to address any genuine law enforcement or public safety concerns.

In the wake of *Heller*, Chicago appears to be the only jurisdiction in America that completely bans handguns (now that its suburbs have repealed their handgun bans in response to suits filed by the NRA in the wake of *Heller*), and the only defense it has now for that law is the argument that the Second Amendment right to keep and bear arms should not be applied against state and local governments—the way nearly every other provision of the Bill of Rights

---

[89] *Id.*, at 2859 (emphasis in original).

[90] D.C. Code § 7-2501.01(10) (1981); see also § 7-2502.02(a)(2) (forbidding registration of any statutorily defined "machine gun") (1983).

has been. Most commentators consider that a losing argument, in part because the Fourteenth Amendment's ratification history shows quite clearly that that is precisely what it was intended to do.

Even assuming that the Second Amendment is incorporated against the states through the Fourteenth, relatively few kinds of firearms restrictions are likely to fall. Certainly reasonable licensing and registration procedures will remain viable, but not so-called discretionary permitting systems like those in New York and California where the decision whether to issue someone a concealed-carry permit is left to the utterly arbitrary authority of local officials. Arbitrary, unreviewable government discretion over the enjoyment of a right has always been anathema in American constitutional law, and so I predict it will be with the Second Amendment.

As I said, while the practical effects of *Heller* will likely be fairly modest, its symbolic value is tremendous. America went over 200 years without knowing whether a key provision of the Bill of Rights actually meant anything. We came within one vote of being told that it did not, notwithstanding what amounts to a national consensus that the Second Amendment means what it says: The right of *the people* to keep and bear arms shall not be infringed. Taking rights seriously, including rights we might not favor personally, is good medicine for the body politic, and *Heller* was an excellent dose.

# Judicial Supremacy and Federalism: A Closer Look at *Danforth* and *Moore*

*Edward J. Loya Jr.**

## I. Introduction

Following the close of the Supreme Court's most recent term, Seattle University law professor Andrew Siegel wrote:

> To a degree that current political and judicial rhetoric masks, all of the current Justices share a conception of the judicial role that gives Courts the right and the obligation to independently assess the meaning of ambiguous constitutional rights guarantees and then follow their own best judgment, letting the chips fall where they may. The Justices have differed in their vision of the society that the Constitution's rights provisions are designed to protect, not on their vision of the judicial role.[1]

Siegel went on to suggest that this shared vision of the Court's role will eventually show that "the gap between the reality of constitutional law (in which two groups of judges committed to a broad judicial role battle over the substance of the rights to be jealously protected) and the rhetoric of constitutional politics (in which liberal 'activists' battle conservatives committed to 'judicial restraint') has grown untenable."[2] These observations may sound like high-minded academic talk to be appreciated only by tenured professors, but they accurately describe a fundamental (and very real) shift in the Court's understanding of its constitutional role.

---

*At the time this *Review* goes to press, I am due to assume a new position as a trial attorney in the Criminal Division at the U.S. Department of Justice. I would like to thank Andrew Coan for his comments on a later draft. All views expressed herein should be attributed to me alone.

[1] A Shared Vision of the Judicial Role, ProfsBlawg, http://prawfsblawg.blogs.com, (June 26, 2008, 2:28 p.m.).

[2] *Id.*

The doctrine of "judicial supremacy" is nothing new. James Madison was skeptical about the Supreme Court's role as the ultimate arbiter of matters of federal constitutional interpretation, stating initially that judicial supremacy "was never intended and can never be proper."[3] By 1785, however, he came to understand, if not fully embrace, the notion that

> [i]t is the Judicial department in which questions of constitutionality, as well as of legality, generally find their ultimate discussion and operative decision: and the public deference to and confidence in the judgment of the body are peculiarly inspired by the qualities implied in its members; by the gravity and deliberation of their proceedings; and by the advantage their plurality gives over the unity of the Executive department, and their fewness over the multitudinous composition of the Legislative department.[4]

*Marbury v. Madison*, with its pronouncement that "[i]t is emphatically the province and duty of the judicial department to say what the law is,"[5] was a significant step for the Court. But it was not until the landmark decision in *Cooper v. Aaron*[6]—in which the Court asserted its interpretive supremacy as against the state of Arkansas— that the Court made major strides toward establishing itself as the Constitution's ultimate interpreter. *Cooper* presented a claim by the Arkansas governor and legislature that state officials had no duty to obey federal court orders attempting to implement the Court's decision in *Brown v. Board of Education*.[7] Explaining that Arkansas officials were bound by its federal constitutional decisions, the Court stated that "[*Marbury*] declared the basic principle that the federal judiciary is supreme in the exposition of the law of the Constitution, and that principle has ever since been respected by this Court and

---

[3] See Larry D. Kramer, The Supreme Court 2000 Term Foreword: We the Court, 115 Harv. L. Rev. 4, 90 (2001) (quoting Madison's Observations on Jefferson's Draft of a Constitution for Virginia, in 6 The Papers of Thomas Jefferson 315 (Julian P. Boyd ed., 1952)).

[4] *Id.* at 90 (quoting Letter from James Madison to Caleb Wallace (Aug. 23, 1785), in 8 Papers of Madison 349, 349–50 (Philadelphia, J.B. Lippincott & Co. 1865)).

[5] 5 U.S. (1 Cranch) 137, 177 (1803).

[6] 358 U.S. 1 (1958).

[7] 347 U.S. 483 (1954).

country as a permanent and indispensable feature of our constitutional system."[8]

Since *Cooper*, the Court has repeatedly asserted its interpretive supremacy vis-à-vis the other federal branches.[9] The Court's increasing willingness to assert itself as the ultimate authority on constitutional concerns has been the focus of modern constitutional law scholarship,[10] and this fundamental shift in the Court's perception of its constitutional role has been criticized at different times by the right[11] and

---

[8] Cooper, 358 U.S. at 18.

[9] See, e.g., Rachel E. Barkow, More Supreme than Court? The Fall of the Political Question Doctrine and the Rise of Judicial Supremacy, 102 Colum. L. Rev. 237, 241 (2002) ("The seeds for this vision of the Supreme Court's [one-sided supremacy] can be found in *Cooper v. Aaron* and its proclamation that the Court is 'supreme in the exposition of the law of the Constitution.'"); (internal citation omitted) but see Michael Stokes Paulsen, Nixon Now: The Courts and The Presidency After Twenty-Five Years, 83 Minn. L. Rev. 1337, 1346 (1999) ("*Cooper v. Aaron*'s assertion of judicial supremacy (1958) was directed at the power of states, and can be read as an assertion of federal supremacy, not judicial supremacy.").

[10] See Larry D. Kramer, The People Themselves: Popular Constitutionalism and Judicial Review (2004); Mark Tushnet, Taking the Constitution Away from the Courts (1999); Adrian Vermeule, Judicial Review and Institutional Choice, 43 Wm. & Mary L. Rev. 1557 (2002); Barry Friedman, The Politics of Judicial Review, 84 Tex. L. Rev. 257 (2005).

[11] In his famous 1986 speech, Attorney General Edwin Meese III stated:

Once we understand the distinction between constitutional law and the Constitution, once we see that constitutional decisions need not be seen as the last words in constitutional construction, once we comprehend that these decisions do not necessarily determine future public policy, once we see all of this, we can grasp a correlative point: constitutional interpretation is not the business of the Court only, but also properly the business of all branches of government.

The Supreme Court, then, is not the only interpreter of the Constitution. Each of the three coordinate branches of government created and empowered by the Constitution—the executive and legislative no less than the judicial—has a duty to interpret the Constitution in the performance of its official functions. In fact, every official takes an oath precisely to that effect.

Edwin Meese III, The Law of the Constitution, 61 Tul. L. Rev. 979, 985–86 (1987); see also Gary Lawson & Christopher D. Moore, The Executive Power of Constitutional Interpretation, 81 Iowa L. Rev. 1267 (1996).

by the left.[12] Yet it is difficult to deny that a shift has taken place in the last several decades.[13]

Siegel anticipates a time when the old labels of "judicial activism" and "judicial restraint" will no longer adequately describe the justices' approach to constitutional decisionmaking, but this has been the reality for many justices for quite some time. Like their liberal colleagues, conservative justices have shown themselves to be judicial supremacists but to different effect. Stanford Law School Dean Larry Kramer pointed out as early as 2001 that far from relinquishing its interpretive supremacy, the Rehnquist Court showed itself to be "able and willing to be as activist in the domains it care[d] about as the liberal Court had been in protecting individual rights."[14] Indeed, the Rehnquist Court's harnessing of interpretive superiority to promote a federalism agenda has been well-documented.[15] Thus,

[12] See, e.g., Jack M. Balkin, Understanding the Constitutional Revolution, 87 Va. L. Rev. 1045, 1051 (2001) (discussing Bush v. Gore, 531 U.S. 98 (2000), in the context of "a fundamental shift in constitutional thought and constitutional doctrine" toward judicial supremacy).

[13] New York University law professor Rachel Barkow describes the shift as follows:
    In the past few decades, however, the Supreme Court has become increasingly blind to its limitations as an institution—and, concomitantly, to the strengths of the political branches—and has focused on Marbury's grand proclamation of its power without taking that statement in context. The modern Supreme Court—beginning with the Warren Court, continuing through the Burger Court, and exponentially gaining strength with the Rehnquist Court— acknowledges few limits on its power to say what the law is.
Barkow, *supra* note 9, at 301–02.

[14] Kramer, Foreword, *supra* note 3, at 130; see also *id.* at 129.

[15] See, e.g., United States v. Lopez, 514 U.S. 549, 551 (1995) (invalidating the Gun Free Zones Act on the ground that it exceeded congressional power and invaded the state's regulatory domain); Printz v. United States, 521 U.S. 898, 935 (1997) (invalidating provisions of the Brady Act requiring state and local government officials to execute a federal regulatory program); City of Boerne v. Flores, 521 U.S. 507, 536 (1997) (holding obligations on state and local governments in the Religious Freedom Restoration Act unconstitutional, largely on separation-of-powers grounds); United States v. Morrison, 529 U.S. 598, 602 (2000) (invalidating portions of the Violence Against Women Act as an attempted exercise of legislative power reserved to the states). See Richard H. Fallon, Jr., The "Conservative" Paths of the Rehnquist Court's Federalism Decisions, 69 U. Chi. L. Rev. 429 n.2 (2002); see also Neal Devins, Congress, The Supreme Court, and Enemy Combatants: How Lawmakers Buoyed Judicial Supremacy by Placing Limits on Federal Court Jurisdiction, 91 Minn. L. Rev. 1562, 1584 (2007) (discussing the Rehnquist Court's federalism decisions).

we are right to ask ourselves not whether the Chief Justice and his conservative colleagues will follow the Rehnquist Court's brand of federalism-based judicial supremacy, but when.[16]

To be sure, one should be careful about trying to extrapolate too much from one or two isolated cases.[17] But while Chief Justice John Roberts's ability to push the Court in a more conservative direction has not been fully revealed, the Court's recent decisions are not as inconclusive as some may think. *Danforth v. Minnesota*[18] and *Virginia v. Moore*[19] provide important insight. When taken individually, each case is hardly a groundbreaking constitutional decision. When studied together, however, the cases suggest the sort of impact the Chief's leadership may have on the Court. Moreover, the two cases suggest that Chief Justice Roberts is, like his predecessor and former boss, committed to a judicial supremacy that not only asserts the Court's interpretive primacy in matters of federal constitutional law, but also respects the role of states to provide greater protection in the context of individual rights than does the federal Constitution.

Both *Danforth* and *Moore* involved issues relating to federal criminal procedure that required the Court to consider the relationship between federal and state law in protecting the rights of criminal defendants. *Danforth* was handed down on February 20, 2008. Joined by Justice Anthony Kennedy, Chief Justice Roberts dissented from Justice John Paul Stevens's opinion permitting state courts to give newly established federal rules of criminal procedure broader retroactive effect than that given by the U.S. Supreme Court. Invoking *Marbury*, the Chief Justice understood *Danforth* as implicating the Court's fundamental authority to say what federal law is. He believed that the majority's decision ran afoul of "[the Court's] role under the Constitution as the final arbiter of federal law, both as to its meaning and its reach, and the accompanying duty to ensure

---

[16] See Siegel, *supra* note 1 (discussing the Court's decision in *District of Columbia v. Heller*, 128 S.Ct. 2783 (2008), as evidence of the Court's shared commitment to judicial supremacy).

[17] As Dahlia Lithwick wisely suggested, "I think you have to be very, very careful when you're talking about a handful of cases." See Panel II, Scholars & Scribes Review the Rulings: The Supreme Court's 2007–2008 Term, The Heritage Foundation, July 8, 2008 (available at http://www.heritage.org/Press/Events/ev070808a.cfm).

[18] 552 U.S. \_\_\_\_, 128 S.Ct. 1029 (2008).

[19] 553 U.S. \_\_\_\_, 128 S.Ct. 1598 (2008).

the uniformity of that federal law."[20] The Chief Justice's dissent articulated a bold federalism to the other members of the Court— one that jealously guards the Court's interpretive supremacy on federal constitutional matters and exercises that authority to maintain a separation and balance between federal and state law.

Decided on the heels of *Danforth*, *Moore* was issued on April 23, 2008. The near unanimity of the Court's decision (Justice Ruth Bader Ginsburg concurred in the result) suggests that the Chief Justice's views regarding the Court's constitutional role were more convincing the second time around. In *Moore*, the Court emphatically rejected the notion that state law arrest standards could define the scope of the Fourth Amendment. In an opinion authored by Justice Antonin Scalia, the Court held that an arrest based on probable cause but in violation of state law, did not violate the Fourth Amendment. Applying an analytical framework that is remarkably similar to the Chief Justice's *Danforth* dissent, Scalia explained that the Supreme Court's constitutional decisions (not decisions by state courts or legislatures) define Fourth Amendment protections, and that the need for easily administrable rules and uniformity in federal law counseled against incorporating state laws into the Fourth Amendment.

In this article, I will analyze the Court's decisions in *Danforth* and *Moore*. I will show that although the individual members of the Roberts Court may disagree about whether a particular case raises a federal constitutional question, most of the justices favor exclusive federal judicial authority over the interpretation of federal law when it is clear that a federal question is presented.

## II. The *Danforth* Decision

### A. *Background*

The issue in *Danforth* was whether state courts can give broader retroactive effect to "new" rules of federal criminal procedure than is required by the Supreme Court.

In 1996, Stephen Danforth was convicted in Minnesota state court of first-degree criminal sexual conduct with a minor.[21] During trial, the government did not call the six-year-old victim to testify but

---

[20] Danforth, 128 S.Ct. at 1058.

[21] See Minn. Stat. § 609.342, subd. 1(a) (1994).

instead showed the jury a videotaped interview of the child. Danforth appealed his conviction on the ground that the admission of the videotape violated his confrontation right under the Sixth Amendment. Applying the rule of admissibility set forth in *Ohio v. Roberts*,[22] the Minnesota Court of Appeals concluded that the tape "was sufficiently reliable to be admitted into evidence," and affirmed the conviction.[23] The Minnesota Supreme Court denied review and Danforth's time for filing for a writ of certiorari eventually elapsed.

After Danforth's conviction had become final, the U.S. Supreme Court decided *Crawford v. Washington*,[24] in which it established a "new rule" for evaluating the reliability of testimonial statements in criminal trials. The decision held that "[w]here testimonial statements are at issue, the only indicium of reliability sufficient to satisfy the constitutional demands is the one the Constitution actually prescribes: confrontation."[25] Contending that he was entitled to a new trial because the admission of the taped interview violated the *Crawford* rule, Danforth filed a state post-conviction petition.

Applying the retroactivity standard set forth in *Teague v. Lane*,[26] the Minnesota trial and appellate courts concluded that *Crawford* did not apply to Danforth's case. The Minnesota supreme court affirmed the appellate court's decision. It rejected Danforth's contention that the lower courts erred in determining that the holding in *Crawford* did not apply retroactively and that Minnesota courts could not give broader retroactive effect to the *Crawford* rule than that required by the U.S. Supreme Court. The Minnesota supreme court recognized that some states have held that *Teague* does not apply to state court proceedings,[27] but concluded that it was not free to give a U.S. Supreme Court decision broader retroactive application than that given by the Court itself.[28]

### B. The Court's Precedent

The Court's precedent did not require state courts to apply the *Crawford* holding to cases that were final when *Crawford* was

---

[22] 448 U.S. 56 (1980).

[23] See State v. Danforth, 573 N.W.2d 369, 375 (Minn. Ct. App. 1999).

[24] 541 U.S. 36 (2004).

[25] *Id*. at 68–69.

[26] 489 U.S. 288 (1989).

[27] Danforth, 128 S.Ct. at 1034 n.3 (listing state court decisions).

[28] Danforth v. State, 718 N.W.2d at 456 (Minn. 2006).

decided.[29] But it was not clear whether federal law prohibited them from doing so.

As the Court explained in *Danforth*, the term "retroactivity" is somewhat confusing. Because the source of the "new" rule is the Constitution (not some sort of judicial power to create new rules of law), a determination that a new rule is "non-retroactive" does not imply that the rule was not in existence before the decision in which the new rule was announced. Rather, what the Court is "actually determining when [it] assess[es] the 'retroactivity' of a new rule is not the temporal scope of a newly announced right, but whether a violation of the right that occurred prior to the announcement of the new rule will entitle a criminal defendant to the relief sought."[30]

The Court first addressed the issue of retroactivity in *Linkletter v. Walker*.[31] The issue in that case was whether the exclusionary rule announced in *Mapp v. Ohio*[32] should be given retroactive effect. The Court adopted a practical approach that required courts to make a case-by-case determination each time a new rule was announced. This approach required examination of the purpose of the rule, the reliance of the states on the prior law, and the effect retroactive application would have on the administration of justice.[33] Applying that standard, the Court concluded that the *Mapp* rule would not be applied to convictions that were final before the date of the *Mapp* decision.[34]

Because the *Linkletter* standard produced divergent results, the Court eventually rejected application of *Linkletter* to cases pending on direct review.[35] In *Teague*, Justice Sandra Day O'Connor articulated a general rule of non-retroactivity for cases on collateral review, stating that "[u]nless they fall within an exception to the general rule, new constitutional rules of criminal procedure will not be applicable to those cases which have become final before the new rules

---

[29] Danforth, 128 S.Ct. at 1034.

[30] Danforth, 128 S.Ct. at 1035.

[31] 381 U.S. 618 (1965).

[32] 367 U.S. 643 (1961).

[33] Linkletter, 381 U.S. at 629.

[34] *Id.* at 636–40.

[35] See Griffith v. Kentucky, 479 U.S. 314 (1987).

are announced."[36] *Linkletter* and *Teague* dealt with the standard for determining what constitutional violations may be remedied on federal habeas, but they had no occasion to address whether states can provide remedies for federal constitutional violations in their own post-conviction proceedings.

Some of the Court's decisions, however, suggested that states were precluded from applying retroactivity rules different from those announced by the U.S. Supreme Court. In *Michigan v. Payne*,[37] for instance, the Court considered the retroactivity of the rule against "vindictive" resentencing that had been announced in *North Carolina v. Pearce*.[38] The Michigan supreme court had applied *Pearce* to the appeal "pending clarification" by the U.S. Supreme Court concerning whether *Pearce* applied to resentencing proceedings that occurred before *Pearce* had been decided. Applying the *Linkletter* standard for retroactivity, the Court held that *Pearce* did not apply retroactively, reversed the judgment of the Michigan supreme court, and remanded for further proceedings.

Against this background, the Court decided *Danforth*.[39]

## C. *Justice Stevens's Opinion*

Justice Stevens's majority opinion began by recognizing that "[n]either *Linkletter* nor *Teague* explicitly or implicitly constrained the authority of the States to provide remedies for a broader range of constitutional violations than are redressable on federal habeas."[40] "A close reading of the *Teague* opinion," Stevens wrote, "makes clear that the rule it established was tailored to the unique context of federal habeas and therefore had no bearing on whether States could provide broader relief in their own postconviction proceedings than required by that opinion."[41]

---

[36] Teague, 489 U.S. at 310. The exceptions included rules that render types of primary conduct "beyond the power of the criminal law-making authority to proscribe" and "watershed" rules that "implicate the fundamental fairness of the trial." *Id.* at 311–12.

[37] 412 U.S. 47 (1973).

[38] 395 U.S. 711 (1969).

[39] For a more thorough discussion of *Teague*, see 7 Wayne R. LaFave, et al., Criminal Procedure § 28.6, at 241–62 (3d ed. 2007).

[40] Danforth, 128 S.Ct. at 1038.

[41] *Id.* at 1039.

The Court made three observations concerning Justice O'Connor's discussion in *Teague*. First, it pointed out that "not a word . . . asserts or even intimates that her definition of the class eligible for relief under a new rule should inhibit the authority of any state agency or state court to extend the benefit of a new rule to a broader class than she defined."[42] Second, it narrowed the grounds on which *Teague* was decided, stating that "*Teague*'s general rule of nonretroactivity was an exercise of this Court's power to interpret the federal habeas statute."[43] It then reasoned that "[s]ince *Teague* is based on statutory authority that extends only to federal courts applying a federal statute, it cannot be read as imposing a binding obligation on state courts."[44] Finally, it limited the scope of the decision, observing that "the [*Teague*] rule was meant to apply only to federal courts considering habeas corpus petitions challenging state-court criminal convictions."[45] Discussing Justice O'Connor's concern for comity and finality of state convictions, Stevens stated that those considerations are "unique to *federal* habeas review of state convictions."[46] If anything, he reasoned, "comity militate[s] in favor of allowing state courts to grant habeas relief to a broader class of individuals than is required by *Teague*" and "[finality of state convictions] is a matter that States should be free to evaluate, and weigh the importance of, when prisoners held in state custody are seeking a remedy for a violation of federal rights by their lower courts."[47] Stevens concluded:

> In sum, the *Teague* decision limits the kinds of constitutional violations that will entitle an individual to relief on federal habeas, but does not in any way limit the authority of a state court, when reviewing its own state criminal convictions, to provide a remedy for a violation that is deemed "nonretroactive" under *Teague*.[48]

[42] *Id.*

[43] *Id.* at 1039–40.

[44] *Id.* at 1040.

[45] *Id.*

[46] *Id.* at 1041 (emphasis in original).

[47] *Id.*

[48] *Id.* at 1042. As for the Court's civil retroactivity decisions such as *Payne*, the majority determined that they supported the conclusion that states can decide what remedy to provide its citizens for violations of the U.S. Constitution. It recognized that "[a]t first blush" *Payne* appears to suggest that states may not give new rules broader retroactive effect than that given by the Court. It pointed out, however, that

Justice Stevens ended his opinion by emphasizing that the Court's retroactivity decisions are primarily concerned with "the availability or nonavailability of remedies," not "whether a constitutional violation occurred."[49] As he put it, "[a] decision by this Court that a new rule does not apply retroactively under *Teague* does not imply that there was no right and thus no violation of that right at the time of trial—only that no remedy will be provided in federal habeas court."[50]

### D. *Chief Justice Roberts's Dissent*

Chief Justice Roberts saw the matter differently. He did not see retroactivity as a "remedial question," but rather as an issue involving "the nature of the substantive federal rule at issue."[51] It was his belief that, at bottom, *Danforth* presented a federal question that motivated his dissent.

In the Chief Justice's view, the case implicated a fundamental feature of our constitutional system: the Court's supreme authority to interpret the Constitution. He stated:

> [T]he question whether a particular ruling is retroactive is itself a question of federal law. It is basic that when it comes

(1) "[t]he Michigan Court did not purport to make a definitive ruling on the retroactivity of *Pearce*" or "to apply a broader state rule of retroactivity than required by federal law"; (2) *Payne* "remanded for further proceedings after providing the clarification that the Michigan Court sought"; and (3) "not a word in [the] *Payne* opinion suggests that the Court intended to prohibit state courts from applying new constitutional standards in a broader range of cases than [the Court] require[s]." *Id.* at 1042–43.

[49] *Id.* at 1047.

[50] *Id.*

[51] *Id.* at 1054. Understanding the difference between the way the majority and the dissent conceptualized the case is crucial. If one understands *Teague* as establishing a "choice of law" rule rather than a limit on the habeas remedy, then one is likely to agree with Chief Justice Roberts's view that *Danforth* implicates the Court's supreme authority to interpret federal law. See James S. Liebman and William F. Ryan, "Some Effectual Power": The Quantity and Quality of Decisionmaking Required of Article III Courts, 98 Colum. L. Rev. 696, 837–43, 855–57 (1998). But if one understands *Teague* as concerned primarily with establishing a limit on the habeas remedy, then one is likely to agree with Justice Stevens's view that states can use their own laws to overprotect beyond the Constitution. See Kent S. Scheidegger, Habeas Corpus, Relitigation, and the Legislative Power, 98 Colum. L. Rev. 888, 922–25 (1998). See also Kent Scheidegger, Retroactivity, Remedies, and AEDPA, Crime and Consequences, http://www.crimeandconsequences.com/2008/02/retroactivity_remedies_and_aed.html (February 20, 2008, 9:13 a.m.).

> to any such question of federal law, it is "the province and
> duty" of this Court "to say what the law is." *Marbury v.
> Madison*, 1 Cranch 137, 177, 2 L.Ed. 60 (1803). State courts
> are the final arbiters of their own state law; this Court is the
> final arbiter of federal law. State courts are therefore bound
> by our rulings on whether our cases construing federal law
> are retroactive.[52]

The Chief Justice explained that the majority's decision was based on a misunderstanding of precedent. He recognized that the Court's retroactivity decisions were silent regarding the states' power to give broader retroactive effect than the Supreme Court. But he pointed out, "[b]ecause the question of retroactivity was so tied up with the nature and purpose of the underlying federal constitutional right, it would have been surprising if any of our cases had suggested that States were free to apply new rules of federal constitutional law retroactively even when we would not."[53]

The Chief's dissent was not motivated by an empty faith in the Court's role as the ultimate court in the land. Instead, it was guided by a basic understanding that it was the Court's duty to ensure uniformity—and therefore fairness—in matters of constitutional interpretation. Early in the dissent, he made the point:

> The majority contravenes [*Marbury's*] bedrock propositions.
> The end result is startling: Of two criminal defendants, each
> of whom committed the same crime, at the same time, whose
> convictions became final on the same day, and each of whom
> raised an identical claim at the same time under the Federal
> Constitution, one may be executed while the other is set
> free—the first despite being correct on his claim, and the
> second because of it. That result is contrary to the Supremacy
> Clause and the Framers' decision to vest in "one supreme
> Court" the responsibility and authority to ensure the unifor-
> mity of federal law. Because the Constitution requires us

---

[52] Danforth, 128 S.Ct. at 1047.

[53] *Id.* at 1049; see also *id.* at 1049–50 (Because "[the Court's] early retroactivity cases nowhere suggested that the retroactivity of new federal constitutional rules of criminal procedure was anything other than a matter of federal law," it was not surprising "that when [the Court] held that a particular right would not apply retroactively, the language in [its] opinions did not indicate that [the] decisions were optional.").

to be more jealous of that responsibility and authority, I
respectfully dissent.[54]

As he saw it, the Court's obligation to reduce "the inequity of hap-
hazard retroactivity standards" and "disuniformity in the application of federal law" is "the very interest that animates the Supremacy
Clause and [the Court's] role as the 'one supreme Court' charged
with enforcing it."[55]

Chief Justice Roberts's dissent defended the Court's interpretive
authority to define federal constitutional protections, but it also
recognized that under their own laws states may provide greater
protections than those afforded by the Constitution. Indeed, the
dissent suggests that it is the Court's failure to assert its supremacy
on matters of federal law that ultimately disrupts the balance
between federal and state governments:

> States are free to announce their own state-law rules of crimi-
> nal procedure, and to apply them retroactively in whatever
> manner they like. That is fully consistent with the principle
> that "a single sovereign's law should be applied equally to
> all." But the Court's opinion invites just the sort of disunifor-
> mity in federal law that the Supremacy Clause was meant
> to prevent. The same determination of a federal constitutional
> violation at the same stage in the criminal process can result
> in freedom in one State and loss of liberty or life in a neighbor-
> ing State. The Court's opinion allows "a single sovereign's
> law"—the Federal Constitution, as interpreted by this
> Court—to be applied differently in every one of the sev-
> eral States.[56]

Thus, Chief Justice Roberts championed a federalism-based
approach to the *Danforth* case that advocated on behalf of the Court's

[54] *Id.* at 1047–48.

[55] *Id.* at 1053; see also *id.* at 1058 ("This dissent is compelled not simply by disagreement over how to read [the Court's retroactivity cases], but by the fundamental issues
at stake—our role under the Constitution as the final arbiter of federal law, both as
to its meaning and its reach, and the accompanying duty to ensure the uniformity
of that federal law.")

[56] *Id.* at 1053–54; see also *id.* at 1049 ("Our precedents made clear that States could
give greater substantive protection under their own laws than was available under
federal law, and could give whatever retroactive effect to *those* laws they wished.")

interpretive supremacy on federal constitutional questions and signaled to the states that they should feel free to provide greater substantive and remedial protections under their own laws.[57] The Chief may have been unable to convince his colleagues in *Danforth*, but *Moore* presented a second opportunity for the Court to follow this approach.

## III. The *Moore* Decision

### A. Background

The issue presented in *Moore* was whether a search incident to an arrest based on probable cause, but in violation of a state law prohibiting arrest, violated the Fourth Amendment.

Under Virginia law, driving on a suspended license is a misdemeanor offense, punishable by a year in jail and a $2,500 fine.[58] The statute requires an officer to issue a summons and notice to appear in court, but with several exceptions.[59] An arrest is permitted if (1) the offender fails or refuses to discontinue the offense; (2) the officer believes that the offender is likely to disregard the summons; (3)

---

[57] To some, the majority's decision was itself a federalist victory. George Mason University law professor Ilya Somin perceives Justice Stevens's opinion as affirming the basic federalist principle that state courts can overprotect individual rights beyond what the federal Constitution allows. He writes, "The Supreme Court should establish a floor for remedies below which states cannot fall. But there is no reason for it to also mandate a ceiling." Ilya Somin, A Floor, Not a Ceiling: Federalism and Remedies for Violations of Constitutional Rights in *Danforth v. Minnesota*, 102 Nw. U.L. Rev. Colloquy 365, 371–73 (2008) (contending that the majority's decision is defensible on policy-based grounds). Like the majority's decision, however, Somin's position is acceptable only if one understands *Danforth* as presenting a remedial question that is entirely removed from the Court's interpretive supremacy over federal law. As Columbia law professor Michael Dorf points out, "*Danforth* was no ordinary application of the floor-but-not-a-ceiling principle, because the question in the case was not whether Minnesota could interpret its own *state* law more broadly than federal law. Everyone accepts that it (like every other state) can. The question in *Danforth* was whether Minnesota could overprotect *federal* law. Perhaps surprisingly, the Supreme Court said yes." Michael C. Dorf, Did Justice Stevens Pull a Fast One? The Hidden Logic of a Recent Retroactivity Case in the Supreme Court, FindLaw, http://writ.news.findlaw.com/dorf/20080225.html (February 25, 2008). Moreover, the same policy-based justifications endorsed by Somin apply when states experiment with substantive rights and remedies under their own law; states need not manipulate federal law to achieve those policy preferences.

[58] Va. Code Ann. §§ 18.2-11, 18.2-272, 46.2-307(c) (2004).

[59] *Id.* § 19.2-74.

the officer reasonably believes the offender is likely to harm himself or others; or (4) prior approval to arrest has been granted by order of the state court.[60]

The case involved a stop of David Lee Moore for violating the Virginia law. Even though none of the exceptions for making an arrest applied, the officers decided to arrest Moore for the offense instead of issuing a summons. After arresting him, the officers took Moore to his hotel room, where they searched him and found crack cocaine on his person. Moore was charged with possession with intent to distribute cocaine. Following the trial court's denial of his motion to suppress the fruits of the search under the Fourth Amendment, he was convicted and sentenced to five years' imprisonment.

The case reached the Virginia supreme court. The court rejected the government's contention that the search fell within the search-incident-to-arrest exception. It emphasized that the exception does not apply when state law prohibits an officer from conducting an arrest for that particular offense.[61] Because Virginia law required the officer to issue a summons under the circumstances and officers are not permitted to conduct an arrest incident to the issuance of a citation, the court unanimously held that the officers' conduct violated the Fourth Amendment.[62]

## B. *The Court's Precedent*

The Fourth Amendment protects individuals from "unreasonable searches and seizures" and thus generally prohibits warrantless searches. A long-standing exception, however, is that an officer may conduct a search incident to a lawful arrest.

The Court established the search-incident-to-arrest exception in *United States v. Robinson*, where it held that such a search was justifiable for two reasons: the need to disarm the suspect and the need to preserve evidence for later use at trial.[63] The Court eventually limited the exception in *Knowles v. Iowa*,[64] in which it held that the exception did not encompass a search in conjunction with the mere

---

[60] *Id.*

[61] Moore v. Commonwealth, 636 S.E.2d 395, 397–400 (Va. 2006).

[62] *Id.* at 400.

[63] 414 U.S. 218, 234 (1973).

[64] 525 U.S. 113 (1998).

issuance of a citation. The Court reasoned that the *Robinson* justification of self-defense and evidence-gathering did not apply in that situation. The Court then clarified an officer's ability to conduct an arrest in the case of *Atwater v. City of Lago Vista.*[65] It concluded that an officer who has probable cause to believe that a suspect has committed a minor offense (in that case, a misdemeanor seat belt violation) may conduct a warrantless arrest without violating the Fourth Amendment. Taken together, the Court's decisions made it clear that an officer may conduct a search incident to an arrest for even a very minor offense. But they did not address the interesting twist presented in the *Moore* case—that is, the constitutionality of a search incident to an arrest that was itself in violation of state law.

Nor did those cases explain the significance of state law in defining Fourth Amendment protections. Two competing lines of cases provided insight into how the Court was likely to approach the issue. *United States v. Di Re*[66] is representative of the cases that suggest that state-law arrest provisions should be used to determine whether an arrest and attendant search violated the Fourth Amendment. In *Di Re*, the Court held that an arrest of a suspect for a federal offense and subsequent search "were beyond the lawful authority of those who executed them," because the arrest was made in violation of a state-law arrest provision.[67] The Court reasoned that in the absence of a federal statute governing arrests, state-law standards determine the lawfulness of the arrest.[68]

Other decisions suggested that Fourth Amendment protections should not track state law standards. In *Cooper v. California*, the Court held that the officers' search of an impounded vehicle was constitutional, even though, as a matter of state law, the officers

---

[65] In a 5–4 decision, the Court held that the Fourth Amendment, as it was originally understood, did not forbid "arrest without a warrant for misdemeanors not amounting to or involving breach of the peace." 532 U.S. 318, 340 (2001).

[66] 332 U.S. 581 (1948).

[67] *Id.* at 595.

[68] The Court added, however, that this rule should apply in all situations "except in those cases where Congress has enacted a federal rule." *Id.* at 590. As discussed below, Justice Scalia understood this language to mean that *Di Re* was not decided on constitutional grounds, but rather on the Court's supervisory powers in federal criminal proceedings.

were not permitted to conduct the search.[69] The Court explained, "Just as a search authorized by state law may be an unreasonable one under that amendment, so may a search not expressly authorized by state law be justified as a constitutionally reasonable one."[70] The Court pointed out that, when appropriate, states can choose to provide greater protection than the federal Constitution: "Our holding, of course, does not affect the State's power to impose higher standards on searches and seizures than required by the Federal Constitution if it chooses to do so."[71]

In *California v. Greenwood*, the Court held that a person does not have a privacy expectation in garbage left for collection outside the curtilage of a home, even though California law prohibited warrantless searches of garbage placed there.[72] The Court rejected the notion that the Fourth Amendment should be used to vindicate state law violations, explaining that

> Individual States may surely construe their own constitutions as imposing more stringent constraints on police conduct than does the Federal Constitution. We have never intimated, however, that whether or not a search is reasonable within the meaning of the Fourth Amendment depends on the law of the particular State in which the search occurs.[73]

Finally, in *Whren v. United States*, the Court held that a stop of a motorist based on probable cause that he had committed a traffic violation did not violate the Fourth Amendment, despite state regulations limiting the arrest authority of plainclothes officers in unmarked vehicles.[74] The Court reasoned that Fourth Amendment protections should not "vary from place to place and from time to time" with "police enforcement practices," or "turn upon such trivialities."[75]

Thus, *Moore* placed state law prerogatives at the heart of the controversy. The basic question was whether the Court would allow

[69] 386 U.S. 58 (1967).

[70] *Id.* at 61.

[71] *Id.* at 62.

[72] 486 U.S. 35 (1988).

[73] *Id.* at 43.

[74] 517 U.S. 806 (1996).

[75] *Id.* at 815.

states to define the scope of Fourth Amendment protections.[76] As in *Danforth*, *Moore* implicated the Court's ultimate authority to define the scope of the Constitution and its related duty to ensure uniformity in the administration of federal law.[77]

## C. Justice Scalia's Opinion

In a near unanimous opinion authored by Justice Scalia, the Court held that an officer does not violate the Fourth Amendment by making an arrest based on probable cause but prohibited under state law.[78] Justice Scalia began by analyzing whether there was any historical indication that the ratifiers of the Fourth Amendment had intended it "as a redundant guarantee of whatever limits on search and seizure legislatures might have enacted."[79] Because the Court could find no case law, commentaries, or statutes suggesting that the Fourth Amendment was meant to incorporate subsequently enacted state laws—indeed, it determined that the evidence suggested "if anything, that Founding-era citizens were skeptical of using rules for search and seizure set by government actors as the index of

[76] Moore's amici focused instead on the potential for abuse of police arrest power. The American Civil Liberties Union, for instance, argued that reversal of the Virginia decision would permit officers to conduct arrests for minor offenses as pretexts for evidence-gathering searches. See Brief of Amicus American Civil Liberties Union in Support of Respondent at 21–26, Virginia v. Moore, 128 S.Ct. 1598 (2007). Noticeably absent from the ACLU's brief was then-Justice Janice Rogers Brown's impassioned dissent in People v. McKay, 27 Cal. 4th 601 (Cal. 2002). There, she boldly criticized the California Supreme Court's decision to uphold a search under similar circumstances. As she understood it, equipping "rummagers" with discretion to conduct a full-blown arrest perpetuates racially discriminatory police practices. See McKay, 27 Cal. 4th at 631 (Brown, J., dissenting).

[77] After *Moore* had been briefed but before oral argument, I wrote that the Court's precedent made this an easy case to decide and that, after all, state legislatures (not courts applying the Fourth Amendment) are in a better position to craft remedies for violations of state arrest provisions. See Edward J. Loya, Jr., Fourth Amendment Protections Should Not Be [Strengthened] by State Laws, Los Angeles Daily Journal, Jan. 3, 2008. George Washington University law professor Orin Kerr's posts on the *Di Re* case, however, made it clear that this was not an open-and-shut case. See Kerr, *infra* note 87.

[78] Moore, 128 S.Ct. at 1607 ("We conclude that warrantless arrests for crimes committed in the presence of an arresting officer are reasonable under the Constitution, and that while States are free to regulate such arrests however they desire, state restrictions do not alter the Fourth Amendment's protections.").

[79] Moore, 128 S.Ct. at 1602.

reasonableness'"[80]—the Court concluded there was no clear answer that existed in 1791 and that had been adhered to ever since.[81]

Turning to the traditional reasonableness analysis, Scalia explained, "we have said [in a long line of cases] that when an officer has probable cause to believe a person committed even a minor crime in his presence, the balancing of private and public interests is not in doubt."[82] In such a situation, the answer is clear: "The arrest is constitutionally reasonable."[83] Moreover, Scalia concluded that its precedent "counsel[ed] against changing this calculus when a State chooses to protect privacy beyond the level that the Fourth Amendment requires."[84] Pointing to *Cooper, Greenwood*, and *Whren*, he stated that it has consistently treated "additional protections [under state law] exclusively as matters of state law."[85]

Justice Scalia's opinion recognized that earlier decisions beginning with *Di Re* excluded evidence obtained in violation of state law, but distinguished them on the ground that "those decisions rested on [the Supreme Court's] supervisory power over the federal courts, rather than the Constitution."[86] Scalia explained that the rule in *Di Re* requiring an arrest for a federal offense to be judged according to state-law standards in the absence of an applicable statute was "plainly not a rule derived from the Constitution," because the Court made it clear that Congress could change it by statute. He rejected the notion that state law provisions providing greater protection should be incorporated into the Fourth Amendment:

[80] *Id*. at 1603. The Court recognized that perhaps no such constitutional claims were raised because "actions taken in violation of state law could not qualify as state action subject to Fourth Amendment constraints." *Id*. at 1604 (citing Thomas Y. Davies, Recovering the Original Fourth Amendment, 98 Mich. L. Rev. 547, 660–63 (1999)).

[81] Moore, 128 S.Ct. at 1604. In her concurring opinion, Justice Ginsburg found more support for *Moore's* historical analysis than did the majority. She stated, "Under the common law prevailing at the end of the 19th century, it appears that arrests for minor misdemeanors, typically involving no breach of the peace, depended on statutory authorization." *Id*. at 1609.

[82] *Id*.

[83] *Id*.

[84] *Id*.

[85] *Id*.

[86] *Id*. at 1605.

> Neither *Di Re* nor the cases following it held that violations
> of state arrest law are also violations of the Fourth Amend-
> ment, and our more recent decisions [in *Cooper, Greenwood,*
> and *Whren*] have indicated that when States go above the
> Fourth Amendment minimum, the Constitution's protec-
> tions concerning search and seizure remain the same.[87]

With the arrest being constitutional, and in this sense "lawful," he
determined that the search that followed fell within the search-
incident-to-arrest exception.

Justice Scalia summed up the opinion: "We reaffirm against a
novel challenge what we have signaled for more than a half century.
When officers have probable cause to believe that a person has
committed a crime in their presence, the Fourth Amendment permits
them to make an arrest, and to search the suspect in order to safeguard evidence and ensure their own safety."[88]

### D. The Significance of the Moore Decision

The majority's opinion in *Moore* resonates with Chief Justice Roberts's views in *Danforth* on judicial supremacy and the need for
uniformity in the administration of federal law. Of course, the extent
of the Chief Justice's influence on the other members of the Court
is difficult to discern, particularly in a case in which he did not write
the majority opinion. But the tone, near unanimity, and concerns in
the *Moore* opinion suggest that the Chief Justice's dissent in *Danforth*
influenced the way the justices approached the case.[89] Justice Scalia's

[87] *Id.* The Court's quick work with *Di Re* was no doubt surprising to many. Before
*Moore* had been handed down, law professor Orin Kerr wrote several thoughtful
posts on the significance of the case. He contended that "the *Di Re* precedent pretty
much answers *Virginia v. Moore,*" Orin Kerr, Why the Defendant Should Win in
*Virginia v. Moore,* The Volokh Conspiracy, http://volokh.com/posts/1199753815.
shtml (Jan. 7, 2008), and that *Di Re* was not a supervisory-power decision, see Orin
Kerr, Why *United States v. Di Re* Clearly Was *Not* a Case on the Federal Supervisory
Power, The Volokh Conspiracy, http://volokh.com/posts/1199922681.shtml (Jan.
10, 2008).

[88] Moore, 128 S.Ct. at 1608.

[89] This is not to suggest, of course, that the Chief Justice is the first member of the
Court to advocate in favor of the Court's primacy in federal constitutional interpretation, or that the Chief Justice is the leading proponent of the use of judicial supremacy
to further the Court's federalism jurisprudence. Indeed, the reader will note that
much of the Chief Justice's rhetoric is reminiscent of Justice Kennedy's majority
opinion in *City of Boerne v. Flores,* 521 U.S. 507 (1997). I am less concerned, however,
with establishing the Chief Justice as the leading conservative proponent of judicial
supremacy as I am with showing that this doctrine was an important concern for a
majority of justices in both cases.

opinion makes it clear that the Court will exercise its interpretive supremacy to establish administrable and uniform constitutional rules that have the same meaning in every state. It also demonstrates the Court's respect for state law regimes that provide greater protection for individual rights beyond what is required by the Constitution by leaving it to the states to remedy state-law violations under their own laws.

1. The Court's Interpretive Supremacy

*Moore* is remarkable for its lack of deference to the states in matters of *federal* constitutional interpretation. The decision emphatically rejects the idea that the scope of the Fourth Amendment should depend on the intricacies of state law violations.

In the context of the Fourth Amendment, the need for easily administrable rules is particularly important. In *Atwater*, the Court had previously rejected the defendant's contention that the Court should adopt a modern arrest rule forbidding an arrest "when conviction could not ultimately carry any jail time and when the government shows no compelling need for immediate detention."[90] The Court concluded that the rule permitting an arrest based on probable cause should extend even to minor misdemeanors, such as an arrest for a misdemeanor seat belt violation, because of the need for clear rules capable of being applied in the spur of the moment.[91] The Court explained that the constitutionality of an arrest should not turn on judgments concerning whether an offense was "jailable" or "fine-only," or whether there was a "risk of immediate repetition," because "an officer on the street might not be able to tell" and this predicament might deter officers from making legitimate arrests.[92]

[90] Atwater, 532 U.S. at 346.

[91] *Id*. at 347–50.

[92] *Id*. at 348–350. *Atwater*'s principal contention was that the Fourth Amendment incorporated common law arrest restrictions that forbade warrantless arrest for misdemeanor offenses that do not involve a "breach of the peace." *Id*. at 326–27. See also Brief of Amicus Cato Institute in Support of Petitioners at 5, Atwater v. City of Lago Vista, 532 U.S. 315 (2001) ("Typically, the Fourth Amendment assures protection of the common liberties of citizens that were guaranteed at the time of the Founding. In this case, the common law could not be more clear or straightforward: warrantless arrests for minor offenses are prohibited unless they involve a breach of the peace."). The *Atwater* majority's discussion of Framing-era common law protections has been severely criticized. See Thomas Y. Davies, The Fictional Character of Law-and-Order Originalism: A Case Study of the Distortions and Evasions of Framing-Era Arrest Doctrine in *Atwater v. Lago Vista*, 37 Wake Forrest L. Rev. 239 (2002). But since the

Justice Scalia concluded that "[i]ncorporating state-law arrest limitations into the Constitution would produce a constitutional regime no less vague and unpredictable than the one we rejected in *Atwater*. The constitutional standard would be only as easy to apply as the underlying state law, and state law can be complicated indeed."[93]

Virginia's amici emphasized the need for uniformity in Fourth Amendment protections. In particular, the brief filed by the Office of the Solicitor General warned that constitutionalizing state-law restrictions would "balkanize" Fourth Amendment protections.[94] As the solicitor general explained, protections under the Fourth Amendment would vary from state to state. While the Fourth Amendment would protect individuals in Virginia, New Mexico, and Massachusetts, where states generally prohibit warrantless arrests for driving on a suspended license, individuals in Arizona, Washington, and Maine would not be protected, because those states permit warrantless arrests for that offense.[95] In other words, citizens in some states would be entitled to greater protections under the Federal constitution than citizens in other states.[96] Fourth Amendment protections would also vary within the same state. Because Virginia law permits warrantless arrests for driving on a suspended license in jurisdictions where a state court has granted approval, an arrest in such jurisdictions would not violate the Fourth Amendment even though individuals would be protected in the rest of the state.[97] Finally, Fourth Amendment protections would vary over time as states established non-arrestable offenses.[98]

---

Court had already held in *Atwater* that the Fourth Amendment permits warrantless arrest for non-felony offenses that do not constitute breach of the peace, it was easier for it to conclude in *Moore* that the Fourth Amendment does not protect against the small subset of misdemeanor arrests for which "the State ha[d] already acted to constrain officers' discretion and prevent abuse." 128 S.Ct. at 1607.

[93] Moore, 128 S.Ct. at 1606–07.

[94] Brief of Amicus Curiae the Office of U.S. Solicitor General in Support of Appellee at 13, Virginia v. Moore, 128 S.Ct. 1598 (2007).

[95] *Id.* at 14–15.

[96] See Brief of Eighteen States and Puerto Rico in Support of Appellee at 23, Virginia v. Moore, 128 S.Ct. 1598 (2007).

[97] See Brief of U.S. Solicitor General, *supra* note 94, at 15.

[98] *Id.* The solicitor general suggested that another oddity in constitutionalizing state-law restrictions is that it would put courts in the awkward position of using the federal Constitution to tell state officials how to conform their conduct to their own laws. *Id.* at 20.

Obviously aware of these concerns, Justice Scalia stated that "linking Fourth Amendment protections to state law would cause them to 'vary from place to place and from time to time.'"[99] He pointed out yet another disturbing scenario, stating: "Even at the same place and time, the Fourth Amendment's protections might vary if federal officers were not subject to the same statutory constraints as state officers."[100] The Court would not sanction such an odd result. As Scalia put it, "It would be strange to construe a constitutional provision that did not apply to the States at all when it was adopted to now restrict state officers more than federal officers, solely because the States have passed search-and-seizure laws that are the prerogative of independent sovereigns."[101]

From a federalism standpoint, *Moore* could not have been written more persuasively had Chief Justice Roberts penned it himself. The decision is striking for its refusal to defer to the states in matters of federal constitutional interpretation. In this sense, it is a strong defense of a constitutional system in which federal and state governments separate and share responsibilities to protect individual rights.

### 2. The State's Role in Providing Greater Protection

The analytical framework articulated in Chief Justice Roberts's dissent, and applied in *Moore*, considers federal constitutional rights as distinct from and independent of state policies that may provide increased protections. The benefit of this framework is that it respects the state's interest in protecting individual rights under state law by leaving it to them to implement remedies for violations of their own laws.

Justice Scalia rejected Moore's contention that the Fourth Amendment should be used to remedy state law violations because a state that has enacted a policy prohibiting an arrest for a particular offense has no interest in such an arrest. He found that a state retains an interest in the arrest "because arrest will still ensure a suspect's appearance at trial, prevent him from continuing his offense, and enable officers to investigate the incident more thoroughly."[102] Scalia explained:

---

[99] Moore, 128 S.Ct. at 1607 (quoting Whren, 517 U.S. at 815).

[100] Moore, 128 S.Ct. at 1607.

[101] *Id.*

[102] *Id.* at 1605.

> State arrest restrictions are more accurately characterized as
> showing that the State values its interests in forgoing arrests
> more highly than its interests in making them . . . or as show-
> ing that the State places a higher premium on privacy than
> the Fourth Amendment requires. A State is free to prefer
> one search-and-seizure policy among the range of constitu-
> tionally permissible options, but its choice of a more restric-
> tive option does not render the less restrictive ones unreason-
> able, and hence unconstitutional.[103]

The Court's underlying concern, however, was the possibility that
using the Fourth Amendment to remedy state law violations would
usurp a state's authority to create remedies for violations of its own
laws and thus upset the balance between federal and state authority.
Justice Scalia stated that application of the federal exclusionary rule
to remedy state law arrest violations "would often frustrate rather
than further state policy."[104] He observed that many states like Virginia do not normally exclude from criminal trials evidence obtained
in violation of state arrest laws;[105] and that, if the Fourth Amendment
were used to remedy violations of state arrest law, "States unwilling
to lose control over the remedy would have to abandon restrictions
on arrests altogether."[106] As Scalia understood it, "This is an odd
consequence of a provision designed to protect against searches and
seizures."[107]

[103] *Id.* at 1605–06.

[104] *Id.* at 1606.

[105] See, e.g., Moore v. Commonwealth, 45 Va. App. 146, 161 (Va. App. 2005) (Annun-
ziata, J., dissenting).

[106] Moore, 128 S.Ct. at 1606.

[107] *Id.* Louisville University law professor Luke Milligan writes that the Court's
decision not to incorporate state-law violations into the Fourth Amendment creates
a "tax-free zone" for states to develop their own search-and-seizure law. He explains:

> The Fourth Amendment provides an absolute floor on search and seizure
> rights. All observers, no matter their judicial philosophy, envision that the
> states, which are well-positioned to gauge the particular privacy and enforce-
> ment interests of their citizens, are free to enact extra-constitutional regula-
> tions to protect privacy rights beyond those guaranteed by the Fourth
> Amendment.

> Extra-constitutional regulations are more likely to be enacted, all things
> being equal, by legislatures with unfettered authority to select remedies (e.g.,
> exclusion, civil liability, administrative sanctions, or, for that matter, no
> remedy at all). If the Court had, as Moore [advocated], pegged the "search
> incident" doctrine to state law rather than constitutional law, the Fourth
> Amendment (which is bound to the costly remedy of exclusion) would

Justice Ginsburg agreed on this point. She observed that "[t]he Fourth Amendment, today's decision holds, does not put States to an all-or-nothing choice in this regard. A State may accord protection against arrest beyond what the Fourth Amendment requires, yet restrict the remedies available when police deny to persons they apprehend the extra protection state law orders."[108]

Chief Justice Roberts expressed a similar sensitivity to the integrity of state law schemes that provide increased protections. His lodestar was the basic federalist principle that just as the Supreme Court cannot subvert a state's decision to give retroactive effect to its own laws, a state should not be able to provide broader retroactive effect to a federal right than the Court has provided. He explained the point this way:

> Principles of federalism protect the prerogative of States to extend greater rights under their own laws than are available under federal law. The question here, however, is the availability of protection under the Federal Constitution—specifically, the Confrontation Clause of the Sixth Amendment. It is no intrusion on the prerogatives of the States to recognize that it is for this Court to decide such a question of federal law, and that our decision is binding on the States under the Supremacy Clause.
>
> Consider the flip side of the question before us today: If a State interprets its own constitution to provide protection beyond that available under the Federal Constitution, and has ruled that this interpretation is not retroactive, no one would suppose that a federal court could hold otherwise, and grant relief under state law that a state court would refuse to grant. The result should be the same when a state court is asked to give retroactive effect to a right under the Federal Constitution that this Court has held is not retroactive.[109]

effectively impose an "exclusion tax" on those well-meaning legislatures that opt to enact extra-constitutional search and seizure regulations.
Luke M. Milligan, Virginia v. Moore: A Tax-Free Zone for the Development of Search and Seizure Law, University of Louisville Law Faculty Blog, http://www.law.louisville.edu/node/1788 (April 24, 2008).

[108] Moore, 128 S.Ct. at 1609.

[109] Danforth, 128 S.Ct. at 1057.

Thus, Chief Justice Roberts and Justice Scalia took the position that our federalist form of government requires federal and state courts to respect the separation of federal and state law.

## IV. Conclusion

Legal commentators frequently criticize both judicial supremacy and federalism—and especially federalism-based judicial supremacy. They criticize judicial supremacy as an attempt by the nine members of the Court to overrule the political will of the people themselves.[110] They criticize federalism as shorthand for a system dedicated to the elimination of rights.[111] And decisions resembling a federalism-based judicial supremacy are perceived as phony attempts to recapture the "real" Constitution.[112] *Danforth* and *Moore* offer an opportunity to rethink these ideas.

In *Danforth*, Chief Justice Roberts was not concerned with overruling state law prerogatives, defining the rights criminal defendants deserve, or pursuing a quest for original meaning. Rather, he was preoccupied solely with the rights afforded under the U.S. Constitution and the Court's authority to determine how those rights are applied. Moreover, he explained that the Court's interpretive supremacy in federal constitutional matters carries with it the related duty to ensure uniformity (and as I understand it, fairness) in the administration of federal law. To illustrate the importance of the question presented in the case, he posed the possibility that "[o]f two criminal defendants, each of whom committed the same crime,

---

[110] See, e.g., Robert H. Bork, The Tempting of America 130 (Free Press 1997) ("What is worrisome is that so many of the Court's increased number of declarations of unconstitutionality are not even plausibly related to the actual Constitution. This means that we are increasingly governed not by law or elected representatives but by an unelected, unrepresentative, unaccountable committee of lawyers applying no will but their own."). See also Tushnet, *supra* note 10, at 8 (describing the *Dred Scott* decision as an instance in which the Court asserted its judicial supremacy "to take contention over slavery off the national political agenda in the 1850's").

[111] See Mitchell F. Crusto, The Supreme Court's "New" Federalism: An Anti-Rights Agenda?, 16 Ga. St. U.L. Rev. 517, 520 (2000) ("Federalism that promotes states' rights arguably promotes democracy, which is by definition majority rule. However, majority rule can lead to oppression of minority interests and individual rights. Many of those rights are constitutionally protected. Hence, federalism encroaches upon constitutionally-protected rights.").

[112] See Larry D. Kramer, Putting the Politics Back Into the Political Safeguards of Federalism, 100 Colum. L. Rev. 215, 291 (2000).

at the same time, whose convictions became final on the same day, and each of whom raised an identical claim at the same time under the Federal Constitution, one may be executed while the other is set free—the first despite being correct on his claim, and the second because of it."[113] Understandably, he saw that as an outcome in which federal law should have no part.

*Moore* presented a second chance for the Court to apply the federalist framework that the Chief Justice had articulated in *Danforth*. The Court rejected the idea that state legislatures could define the scope of the Fourth Amendment. In doing so it did away with the possibility that Fourth Amendment protections might vary from state to state, within the same state, over time, or depending on whether the arrest involved a federal or state officer. And it put it to the state legislatures to decide for their own citizens what protections should apply when a state-law violation occurs. In this sense *Moore* affirms what should have been obvious in both cases: We have one Constitution but many state laws; and while states can create and administer greater protections than those provided in that Constitution, the application of the Constitution should remain the same in every state.

[113] Danforth, 128 S.Ct. at 1047–48.

# Chamber of Commerce v. Brown: Protecting Free Debate on Unionization

*William J. Kilberg and Jennifer J. Schulp**

## Introduction

Congress enacted the National Labor Relations Act in 1935 to provide uniform federal regulation of the relationship between labor unions and management.[1] As originally enacted, the NLRA strictly regulated employer conduct, but did not impose the same level of regulation (or similar prohibitions) on unions themselves. Just over a decade later, Congress amended the NLRA to respond to the growing imbalance of power that favored unions by setting limits on certain union conduct. The Taft-Hartley Act amendments to the NLRA also sought to level the field by expressly guaranteeing the rights of employers to engage in non-coercive speech regarding unionization. Section 8(c) of the NLRA embodies this protection, providing that

> [t]he expressing of any views, argument, or opinion, or the dissemination thereof, whether in written, printed, graphic or visual form, shall not constitute an unfair labor practice under any of the provisions of this subchapter, if such expression contains no threat of reprisal or force or promise of benefit.[2]

Quite simply, section 8(c) gets it right.

This term, the Supreme Court found that the NLRA's protection of free debate in the context of union organization, articulated in

*William J. Kilberg is a partner and Jennifer J. Schulp an associate at Gibson, Dunn & Crutcher LLP in Washington, D.C. Kilberg was U.S. Solicitor of Labor from 1973 to 1977. The authors thank Mark Perry for his review of this article.

[1] 29 U.S.C. §§ 151–69.

[2] 29 U.S.C. § 158(c).

part by section 8(c), preempts state regulation that purports to prohibit the expenditure of state funds by certain employers on speech "to assist, promote, or deter union organizing."[3] The Court struck down California's Assembly Bill (AB) 1889, which restricted the speech of recipients of state funds, because the NLRA preempts state regulation that interferes with Congress's intention that certain activities be left unregulated and instead controlled by the free play of economic forces. The decision reinforces the NLRA's preemptive power over state regulation of employer speech and highlights Congress's aim in protecting free debate on the issue of unionization.

Legislation like AB 1889 has been gaining popularity in recent years, as unions have increased their efforts to curtail employer speech and its effects on employees' decisions to unionize, particularly on the state and local levels. Such legislation, however, is now likely foreclosed by the Supreme Court's decision in *Chamber of Commerce v. Brown*, and unions may turn their attention to alternate means of easing the path to unionization. Ultimately, though, despite union outcry over declining rates of unionization, the balance struck by the NLRA is the right one—protecting the freedom of both unions and employers to speak will provide employees with more, and competing, information regarding the consequences of unionization (both positive and negative). This free debate ought to remain an integral part of any federal framework regulating employer/ union relations.

## I. California Assembly Bill 1889 Litigation

### A. Assembly Bill 1889

On September 28, 2000, California Governor Gray Davis signed AB 1889, which prohibits certain employers from using funds received from the state "to assist, promote, or deter union organizing."[4] This provision was passed over the hard-fought opposition of employer groups and with the strong support of unions. Unions asserted that employer suppression of organizing campaigns had grown into a multi-million dollar business and that the law would ensure that state resources would no longer be used by employers

---

[3] Chamber of Commerce v. Brown, 522 U.S. _____ , 128 S. Ct. 2408 (2008) ("Chamber v. Brown").

[4] See Cal. Gov't. Code Ann. §§ 16645–16649.

for such a purpose.[5] Although the bill was anticipated to impact employers in a wide range of industries, the main target of AB 1889 was the healthcare sector, in which many employers received state funds through the state's MediCal program.[6] Employers vocally opposed the measure as, among other things, infringing upon their constitutional right to free speech, specifically protected by section 8(c) of the NLRA, by intending to eliminate employer opposition during union organizing drives.[7] Some employer groups predicted that AB 1889 would have a negative impact on business performance, particularly because of the bill's recordkeeping requirements.[8] The bill passed the California General Assembly in September 2000 on a strict party line vote.

AB 1889's preamble clearly lays out that the bill is intended to further California's general policy objectives:

> It is the policy of the state not to interfere with an employee's choice about whether to join or to be represented by a labor union. For this reason, the state should not subsidize efforts by an employer to assist, promote, or deter union organizing. It is the intent of the Legislature in enacting this act to prohibit an employer from using state funds and facilities for the purpose of influencing employees to support or oppose unionization and to prohibit an employer from seeking to influence employees to support or oppose unionization while those employees are performing on a state contract.[9]

To achieve those policy objectives, AB 1889 prohibits several classes of employers that receive state funds from using the funds "to assist, promote, or deter union organizing."[10] The statute defines the prohibition on the use of funds in neutral terms: "Assist, promote, or deter union organizing" means "any attempt by an employer to influence the decision of its employees in this state or

---

[5] See John Logan, Innovations in State and Local Labor Legislation: Neutrality Laws and Labor Peace Agreements in California, University of California Institute for Labor and Employment, The State of California Labor 2003, 159–162 (2003).

[6] *Id.* at 160.

[7] *Id.* at 162–166.

[8] *Id.* at 164.

[9] 2000 Cal. Stats. ch. 872, § 1.

[10] See Cal. Gov't. Code Ann. §§ 16645–16649.

those of its subcontractors regarding . . . [w]hether to support or oppose a labor organization that represents or seeks to represent those employees [or] [w]hether to become a member of any labor organization."[11] But it is clear that the bill's effect was intended to limit anti-union speech. In particular, AB 1889 expressly exempts from its funding restrictions "activit[ies] performed" or "expense[s] incurred" in connection with "[a]llowing a labor organization or its representatives access to the employer's facilities or property," and "[n]egotiating, entering into, or carrying out a voluntary recognition agreement with a labor organization."[12]

AB 1889 enacted numerous recordkeeping-type provisions to ensure that covered employers did not use state funds in a manner prohibited by statute. Covered employers must certify that no state funds will be used for prohibited expenditures and must also maintain and provide upon request "records sufficient to show that no state funds were used for those expenditures."[13] Although records are not required to be maintained in any particular form, the statute provides that if state funds are commingled with other funds, "any expenditures to assist, promote, or deter union organizing shall be allocated between state funds and other funds on a pro rata basis."[14] In other words, if an employer commingles funds and makes any prohibited expenditure, that employer could be found to have violated the statute.

The law also provides for dual enforcement, allowing a civil action either by the state attorney general or by any private taxpayer.[15] Penalties for violations are harsh: An out-of-compliance employer is liable to the state for the funds expended in violation of the statute plus a civil penalty equal to twice the amount of those funds, and prevailing plaintiffs are entitled to reasonable attorney's fees and costs.[16]

Shortly after AB 1889 became effective in January 2001, labor unions began to add allegations to their organizing drives that

---

[11] Id. at § 16645(a).

[12] Id. at §§ 16647(b), (d).

[13] Id. at §§ 16645.2(c), 16645.7(b)–(c).

[14] Id. at § 16646(b).

[15] Id. at § 16645.8(a).

[16] Id. at §§ 16645.2(d), 16645.7(d), 16645.8(a), 16645.8(d).

employers were using public funds to oppose organization. Unions both filed complaints with the California attorney general—including 24 requests for investigation through December 2002—and initiated private civil litigation.[17] The complaints alleged violations for a variety of prohibited activities, including: hiring consultants and law firms to direct anti-union campaigns; running anti-union orientation and training sessions for supervisors; paying supervisors and managers to conduct group and individual captive meetings; paying employees to attend anti-union meetings; creating and distributing anti-union literature; and mounting elaborate public campaigns against unionization.[18]

Employers' active opposition to AB 1889 was based in large part on the potential for unions to use the legislation as leverage in conducting organizing drives. Unions' active attempts to enforce the law once it was enacted only confirmed the business community's predictions. It was no surprise, then, that AB 1889 soon became the subject of litigation.[19]

## B. Lower Court Litigation

### 1. District Court Litigation

In April 2002, several organizations composed of members that do business with the state of California and several health care industry employers brought an action in the U.S. District Court for the Central District of California against the California Department of Health Services and several state officials, including Attorney General Bill Lockyer, to enjoin the enforcement of AB 1889. The American Federation of Labor and Congress of Industrial Organizations and California Labor Federation intervened to defend the statute's validity.

---

[17] See Logan, *supra* note 5, at 171 (2003) (collecting complaints); see also Chamber of Commerce v. Lockyer, 422 F.3d 973, 980–82 (9th Cir. 2003), vacated by 463 F.3d 1076 (9th Cir. 2006) (en banc).

[18] See Logan, *supra* note 5, at 171 (collecting and describing complaints).

[19] In fact, AB 1889 was the subject of litigation prior to its implementation. In late 2000, several business organizations (including the California Healthcare Association) filed a declaratory and injunctive relief action in federal district court challenging AB 1889's constitutionality. *California Chamber of Commerce v. California*, No. 8:00-cv-01190-GLT-AN (C.D. Cal. 2000). The district court denied plaintiffs' motion for a preliminary injunction, and plaintiffs subsequently voluntarily dismissed their suit.

Plaintiffs sought declaratory and injunctive relief, and filed a motion for summary judgment on the grounds that AB 1889 is unconstitutional under the federal and California Constitutions, and preempted by the NLRA, the Labor Management Reporting and Disclosure Act, and the Medicare Act.[20] The defendants and intervenors contended that the plaintiffs lacked standing to sue, and that their claims were barred by the Eleventh Amendment and abstention doctrines.

The district court found that at least one plaintiff—the U.S. Chamber of Commerce—had standing to challenge certain provisions of AB 1889, and allowed all properly named plaintiffs to challenge the provisions that governed the recipients of state funds grants, employers conducting business on state property, and private employers receiving state funds in excess of $10,000.[21] The court rejected the defendants' Eleventh Amendment and abstention doctrine defenses.

The court did not reach plaintiffs' federal and state constitutional arguments or their arguments with respect to preemption by the Labor Management Reporting and Disclosure Act and the Medicare Act because it found that "AB 1889 is preempted by the National Labor Relations Act."[22] It accordingly granted plaintiffs' summary judgment motion as to the provisions for which they demonstrated standing, sections 16645.2 and 16645.7, which bar private employers who are recipients of state grants and state program funds in excess of $10,000, respectively, from using the funds to "assist, promote, or deter union organizing."

In short, the district court found that AB 1889 was not enacted in the state's capacity as a market participant, but rather as a traditional exercise of regulatory power. Thus it is preempted because it "regulates employer speech about union organizing under specified circumstances, even though Congress intended free debate" under section 8(c) of the NLRA.[23]

---

[20] See Chamber of Commerce v. Lockyer, 225 F. Supp. 2d 1199, 1201 (C.D. Cal. 2002) ("Chamber I").

[21] *Id.* at 1203.

[22] *Id.* at 1204.

[23] *Id.* at 1205.

### 2. Ninth Circuit Litigation—Initial Panel

Defendants appealed the district court's grant of summary judgment to the Ninth Circuit, and on April 20, 2004 a unanimous panel of the Ninth Circuit affirmed the district court.[24] The panel found that "California—acting as a regulator, not a proprietor in imposing these restrictions—has acted in such a way as to undermine federal labor policy by altering Congress' design for the collective bargaining process."[25] The panel's decision rested on the preemption doctrine established by the *Machinists* case.[26] A state statute is preempted by the NLRA under the *Machinists* doctrine when Congress intended to leave an area "to be controlled by the free play of economic forces."[27]

The two provisions at issue barring private employers who receive state grants and private employers who receive state funds in excess of $10,000 from using state funds to "assist, promote, or deter union organizing," the panel concluded, were not passed in the state's proprietary capacity—"the statute on its face does not purport to reflect California's interest in the efficient procurement of goods and services" and "there is no question but that sections 16645.2 and 16645.7 are designed to have a broad social impact, by altering the ability of a wide range of recipients of state money to advocate about union issues."[28]

The panel found AB 1889 preempted under the *Machinists* doctrine because "the California statute, on its face, directly regulates the union organizing process itself and imposes substantial compliance costs and litigation risk on employers who participate in that process, it interferes with an area Congress intended to leave free of state regulation."[29] The panel concluded that the statute "has both the explicit purpose and the substantive effect of interfering with the NLRA system for organizing labor unions" and "will alter the NLRA process of collective bargaining and union organization, because an

[24] Chamber of Commerce v. Lockyer, 364 F.3d 1154 (9th Cir. 2004) ("Chamber II").

[25] *Id.* at 1159.

[26] Lodge 76, International Association of Machinists & Aerospace Workers v. Wisconsin Employment Relations Comm'n, 427 U.S. 132 (1976).

[27] *Id.* at 140.

[28] Chamber II, 364 F.3d at 1163.

[29] *Id.* at 1165.

employer who decides against neutrality will incur both compliance costs and litigation risk."[30]

The panel explained that First Amendment jurisprudence, which allows the government in some circumstances to limit the use of governmental funds to subsidize speech or conduct, is not properly applied when analyzing whether a state statute is preempted by the NLRA: "First Amendment concepts cannot be imported wholesale in construing the NLRA for the purpose of preemption analysis—especially when to apply constitutional analysis mechanically would substantially alter the balance of forces established by Congress under the statute."[31] "[T]he balance between employer and employee expression established by the NLRA differs substantially from the standard First Amendment balancing of speech interests," the panel found, and in any event, "state regulation is not automatically immune from First Amendment concern simply because that regulation comes in the form of a subsidy rather than a prohibition."[32]

### 3. Ninth Circuit Litigation—Panel Rehearing

The panel granted defendants' petition for rehearing and again affirmed the district court's grant of summary judgment to the plaintiffs.[33] Over Judge Raymond Fisher's dissent, the panel majority's decision on rehearing rested on slightly different grounds than its vacated opinion, concluding that "the California statute chills employers from exercising their free speech rights that are explicitly protected by Congress under the National Labor Relations Act," and "the California statute interferes with the National Labor Relations Act's extension of exclusive jurisdiction to the National Labor Relations Board for the adoption and enforcement of representation election rules."[34]

The majority elaborated on the effects of the statute, describing AB 1889 as requiring "burdensome and detailed record-keeping" and carrying "a false air of evenhandedness."[35] It also articulated how the statute reaches beyond the state funds it purports to restrict

[30] *Id.* at 1168.

[31] *Id.* at 1170.

[32] *Id.* at 1170, 1171 n.8.

[33] Chamber of Commerce v. Lockyer, 422 F.3d 973 (9th Cir. 2005) ("Chamber III").

[34] *Id.* at 976.

[35] *Id.* at 978.

to an employer's private resources. Central to that analysis is the characterization of some funds paid to state contractors as "profits," which belong to the employer. AB 1889, the panel majority explained, "commandeers employers' *own* money" by prohibiting the use of profits from state contracts "to discuss the advantages and disadvantages of union organizing efforts with employees."[36] And it pointed to union actions taken under the statute "to gain a special advantage in labor disputes, and thereby alter the balance of power between unions and employers."[37]

On rehearing, the panel majority concluded, as it had before, that the California statute was preempted under the *Machinists* doctrine, but it also concluded that AB 1889 was preempted under the related doctrine set forth in *San Diego Building Trades Council v. Garmon.*[38] *Garmon* preemption functions to prevent state laws from interfering with the National Labor Relations Board's "administration of the labor policy."[39] Because "[t]he California statute stifles employers' speech rights which are granted by federal law," the panel majority stated, it "impedes the ability of the National Labor Relations Board to uphold its election speech rules and administer free and fair elections."[40] Central to this analysis, the panel majority concluded that "the same partisan employer speech" regulated by AB 1889 was "committed to the jurisdiction of the National Labor Relations Board" by Congress.[41] AB 1889 was therefore preempted because it "discourages employer speech, which works at cross-purposes with the relaxed election speech rules as established by the NLRB."[42]

Judge Fisher disagreed. In his view, because AB 1889 allowed "employers to spend their *own* funds, in whatever manner they please, to advocate for or against unionization," "California is not actually regulating the speech at issue."[43] Accordingly, neither *Garmon* nor *Machinists* preemption applies.

---

[36] *Id.* at 980.

[37] *Id.* at 982.

[38] 359 U.S. 236 (1959).

[39] Garmon, 359 U.S. at 242.

[40] Chamber III, 422 F.3d at 985.

[41] *Id.* at 987.

[42] *Id.*

[43] *Id.* at 995.

### 4. Ninth Circuit Litigation—En Banc

Citing Judge Fisher's position, defendants sought and were granted rehearing en banc by the Ninth Circuit. The en banc court reversed the district court's grant of summary judgment and held that AB 1889 was not preempted under either *Machinists* or *Garmon* and does not impinge on an employer's First Amendment right to express views on union organization.[44]

Judge Fisher, now writing for a 12-member majority, framed the question as "whether a state's exercise of its sovereign power to control the use of its funds conflicts with national labor policy as expressed in the National Labor Relations Act."[45] Although the en banc majority agreed with the district court and both panel opinions that "California has acted as a regulator in enacting sections 16645.2 and 16645.7 and that the market participant exception does not apply," it found that these provisions were not preempted by *Machinists* or *Garmon*.[46]

The en banc majority concluded that "AB 1889's restrictions on the use of grant and program funds do not interfere with an employer's ability to engage in 'self-help' in the sense protected by *Machinists*" and "[i]n restricting the *use* of state funds, California has not made employer neutrality or the substantive terms of employment between employer and employee a condition for the *receipt* of state funds."[47]

The en banc majority also concluded that section 8(c) does not grant any speech rights to employers.[48] *Garmon* preemption was thus inapplicable because "California's refusal to subsidize employer speech for or against unionization does not regulate an activity that is actually protected or actually prohibited by the NLRA."[49]

Interestingly, the en banc majority discussed, for the first time in the litigation, arguments that AB 1889 violates the First Amendment. Although the panel decisions had addressed the parties' arguments

---

[44] Chamber of Commerce v. Lockyer, 463 F.3d 1076, 1080 (9th Cir. 2006) (en banc) ("Chamber IV").

[45] *Id.*

[46] *Id.* at 1082, 1085.

[47] *Id.* at 1087–88.

[48] *Id.* at 1091.

[49] *Id.* at 1092.

analogizing the NLRA's protections to the First Amendment, the en banc majority made it a point to reach the First Amendment argument and specifically held that AB 1889 did not run afoul of the First Amendment: "Because an employer retains the freedom to raise and spend its own funds however it wishes—so long as it does not *use* state grant and program funds on union-related advocacy—AB 1889 does not infringe employers' First Amendment right to express whatever view they wish on organizing."[50]

Judge Robert Beezer, joined by Judges Andrew Kleinfeld and Consuelo Callahan, dissented, finding that AB 1889 both is preempted by the NLRA and violates the First Amendment.[51] The dissent began by addressing the First Amendment, explaining that "[a] statutory blanket prohibition on employers advocating for or against unions would blatantly violate the First Amendment as the state has no legitimate interest in prohibiting employers from speaking on union issues."[52] The state's legitimate interest "in the funds it pays for the contracted goods and services is at an end" once the state has chosen to award the contract.[53]

The dissenters instead found AB 1889 preempted under the *Machinists* doctrine because it "directly regulates the union organizing process itself," "imposes substantial compliance costs and litigation risks on employers who participate in that process using the statutorily protected self-help mechanisms," and accordingly, "interferes with an area Congress intended to leave free of state regulation."[54] The dissent would have also held the statute to be preempted under *Garmon* because AB 1889 displaced section 8(c)'s speech protections and consequently usurps the ability of the NLRB to administer elections that "foster fair and free employee choice."[55]

## C. Supreme Court Decision

In the fall of 2007, the Supreme Court granted certiorari on the question of whether federal labor law preempts AB 1889. The Court heard oral argument in March 2008 and released its opinion on June

[50] *Id.* at 1096.
[51] *Id.* at 1098.
[52] *Id.* at 1099.
[53] *Id.*
[54] *Id.* at 1105.
[55] *Id.* at 1108.

19, 2008—more than six years after the litigation began.[56] Justice John Paul Stevens wrote for the seven-justice majority, holding that AB 1889 is preempted by the NLRA under the *Machinists* doctrine. Justice Stephen Breyer, joined by Justice Ruth Bader Ginsburg, dissented.

The Court held that sections "16645.2 and 16645.7 are preempted under *Machinists* because they regulate within 'a zone protected and reserved for market freedom.'"[57] Although NLRA section 8(c), added by the Taft-Hartley amendments, "forcefully buttresses the pre-emption analysis in this case," protection of free debate is not limited to section 8(c), the Court explained:

> In the case of noncoercive speech . . . the protection is both implicit and explicit. Sections 8(a) and 8(b) demonstrate that when Congress sought to put limits on advocacy for or against union organization, it has expressly set forth the mechanisms for doing so. Moreover, the amendment to § 7 calls attention to the right of employees to refuse to join unions, which implies an underlying right to receive information opposing unionization.[58]

The Court found that the "policy judgment" made by AB 1889— "that partisan employer speech necessarily 'interfere[s] with an employee's choice about whether to join or to be represented by a labor union'"—was renounced by Congress in the Taft-Hartley Act. Thus, "[t]o the extent §§ 16645.2 and 16645.7 actually further the express goal of AB 1889, the provisions are unequivocally pre-empted."[59]

The Court specifically declined to address the validity of AB 1889 under the First Amendment, explaining that the question "is not whether AB 1889 violates the First Amendment, but whether it 'stands as an obstacle to the accomplishment and execution of the

---

[56] Chamber v. Brown, 128 S. Ct. 2408 (2008). Edmund (Jerry) Brown replaced Bill Lockyer as California's attorney general and was substituted as a defendant in the litigation.

[57] 128 S. Ct. at 2412 (quoting Bldg. & Constr. Trades Council v. Associated Builders & Contractors of Mass./R.I., Inc., 507 U.S. 218, 227 (1993)).

[58] *Id.* at 2414.

[59] *Id.* at 2414.

full purposes and objectives' of the NLRA."[60] Under the NLRA, California "plainly could not directly regulate noncoercive speech about unionization by means of an express prohibition [and] may not indirectly regulate such conduct by imposing spending restrictions on the use of state funds."[61] Moreover, by coupling its "use" restriction with "compliance costs and litigations risks that are calculated to make union-related advocacy prohibitively expensive for employers that receive state funds," "AB 1889 effectively reaches beyond 'the use of funds over which California maintains a sovereign interest.'"[62] Justice Stevens also stated that "Congress has clearly denied [the NLRB] the authority to regulate the broader category of noncoercive speech encompassed by AB 1889." And this protection extends to speech that goes beyond the "narrow zone of speech to ensure free and fair elections under the aegis of § 9 of the NLRA."[63]

The Court distinguished the few federal statutes that restrict the use of federal funds for union-related speech: "We are not persuaded that these few isolated restrictions, plucked from the multitude of federal spending programs, were either intended to alter or did in fact alter the 'wider contours of federal labor policy.'"[64] Importantly, "the mere fact that Congress has imposed targeted federal restrictions on union-related advocacy in certain limited contexts does not invite the States to override federal labor policy in other settings."[65] The Court recognized, however, that "[h]ad Congress enacted a federal version of AB 1889 that applied analogous spending restrictions to *all* federal grants or expenditures, the preemption question would be closer."[66]

Justice Breyer disagreed with the majority's holding that AB 1889 is preempted under the *Machinists* doctrine, explaining that "a State's refusal to pay for labor-related speech does not *impermissibly* discourage that activity."[67] In fact, the federal statutes imposing restrictions

---

[60] *Id.* at 2417 (quoting Livadas v. Bradshaw, 512 U.S. 107, 120 (1994)).

[61] *Id.* at 2415.

[62] *Id.* at 2416.

[63] *Id.* at 2417.

[64] *Id.* at 2418 (quoting Metro. Life Ins. Co. v. Massachusetts, 471 U.S. 724, 753 (1985)).

[65] *Id.* at 2418.

[66] *Id.* (emphasis in original).

[67] *Id.* at 2420 (emphasis in original).

on the use of federal funds are evidence of Congress's intent to permit states to enact similar legislation:

> Could Congress have thought that the NLRA would prevent the States from enacting the very same kinds of laws that Congress itself has enacted? Far more likely, Congress thought that directing government funds away from labor-related activity was *consistent*, not *inconsistent*, with the policy of 'encourag[ing] free debate' embedded in its labor statutes.[68]

Justice Breyer did not foreclose, however, the possibility that the effects of AB 1889 would lead to the statute's preemption. Breyer recognized that "should the compliance provisions, as a practical matter, unreasonably discourage expenditure of *nonstate* funds, the NLRA may well pre-empt California's statute," and would have remanded the case for further development of the record.[69]

## II. Effect of Supreme Court's Decision on Efforts to Restrict Employer Speech

The Supreme Court's decision in *Chamber of Commerce v. Brown* stands as a significant obstacle to labor-backed state and local initiatives to curtail noncoercive employer speech. At the very least, Justice Stevens's opinion forecloses the ability of states and localities to regulate the use of government funds when such a restriction is coupled with "compliance costs and litigation risks" that make union-related advocacy prohibitively expensive for state-funded employers.[70] The Court's opinion arguably reaches farther, and could be read to prohibit all state regulation that "indirectly regulate[s] [employer speech] by imposing spending restrictions on the use of state funds."[71]

Because legislation similar to AB 1889 has been gaining popularity in recent years as a means of easing the path to unionization by stifling speech in opposition, the Supreme Court's decision will likely

---

[68] *Id.* at 2420 (emphasis in original).

[69] *Id.* at 2421. Ironically, had the case gone the other way—perhaps if the California law had been more narrowly drawn—it would have become part of the growing narrative about the Roberts Court's reticence to uphold facial challenges.

[70] *Id.* at 2416.

[71] *Id.* at 2415.

have a noticeable effect on the legislative strategies labor unions and their supporters follow in the near term. The remainder of this article examines the viability of legislation that aims to restrict noncoercive employer speech, and predicts alternate methods that union supporters might propose to either limit employer speech itself or to limit the effect of employer speech on employees' decisions to unionize.

Ultimately, the balance struck by the NLRA section 8(c)—which protects free debate on unionization by both unions and employers— is the correct one. Despite concerns expressed about declining private sector unionization rates, by protecting the rights of all parties to speak, section 8(c) preserves the general principle that underlies both our democratic system and our economic markets: A free exchange of ideas is the best mechanism for decisionmaking. Limiting noncoercive employer speech deprives employees of valuable information about the consequences (both positive and negative) of unionization, and presuming that union speech alone will adequately inform the employee decisionmaker does not reflect the realities of the unionization process, as Congress recognized in enacting the Taft-Hartley Act.

*A. The Importance of Employer Speech*

The Taft-Hartley Act amendments were passed as a response to the NLRA's original focus on encouraging union organization.[72] They shifted the emphasis to a more balanced statutory scheme that protects the rights of workers to join or not join a union, and added restrictions on unions, while also guaranteeing certain freedoms of speech and conduct to employers and individual employees.[73]

Specifically, the Taft-Hartley amendments guaranteeing employer free speech were in response to several decisions by the NLRB, finding that the NLRA required "complete neutrality" on the part of employers.[74] These NLRB decisions continued despite admonishment from the courts of appeals applying the Supreme Court's jurisprudence in *Thomas v. Collins*[75] and *NLRB v. Virginia Elec. &*

---

[72] See 1 Developing Labor Law 41 (John E. Higgins, Jr. ed., 5th ed., 2006).

[73] *Id.*

[74] See Matter of Am. Tube Bending Co., Inc., 44 N.L.R.B. 121, 129 (1942) (finding that an employer committed an unfair labor practice on the basis of a finding that the employer acted with the purpose "to influence the result of the election"); Matter of Clark Bros. Co., Inc., 70 N.L.R.B. 802, 803 (1946) (finding an unfair labor practice where the company "injected itself into the then pending run-off election").

[75] 323 U.S. 516, 537–38 (1945).

*Power Co.*[76], which made clear that employers' speech is protected under the First Amendment.

Accordingly, the Taft-Hartley Act was understood to "guarantee[] to employees, to employers, and to their respective representatives, the full exercise of the right of free speech."[77] Opponents took issue with the evidentiary rule laid out in section 8(c):

> [T]hese provisions go far beyond mere protection of an admitted constitutional right. By saying that statements are not to be considered as evidence, they insist that the Board and the courts close their eyes to the plain implications of speech and disregard clear and probative evidence. In no field of the law are a man's statements excluded as evidence of an illegal intention.[78]

Still, even those opposed to the general tenor of the Taft-Hartley Act did not take issue with its basic premise of free speech rights. For example, Representative John F. Kennedy, an opponent of many aspects of Taft-Hartley, explained that "[t]here should be a readjustment of the collective-bargaining processes so that collective bargaining will be really free and equal and in good faith on both sides. To

---

[76] 314 U.S. 469, 477 (1941).

[77] H.R. Rep. No. 245, 80th Cong., 1st Sess., on H.R. 3020 at 6 (April 11, 1947). Reprinted in 1 Legislative History of the Labor Management Relations Act, 1947 (National Labor Relations Board, 1985). See also House Conference Report No. 510 on H.R. 3020 at 45:

> Both the House bill and the Senate amendment contained provisions designed to protect the right of both employees and labor organizations to free speech. The conference agreement adopts the provisions of the House bill in this respect with one change derived from the Senate amendment. It is provided that expressing any views, argument, or opinion or the dissemination thereof, whether in written, printed, graphic, or visual form, is not to constitute or be evidence of an unfair labor practice if such expression contains no threat of force or reprisal or promise of benefit. The practice which the Board has had in the past of using speeches and publications of employers concerning labor organizations and collective bargaining arrangements as evidence, no matter how irrelevant or immaterial, that some later act of the employer had an illegal purpose gave rise to the necessity for this change in the law. The purpose is to protect the right of free speech when what the employer says or writes is not of a threatening nature or does not promise a prohibited favorable discrimination.

[78] House Minority Report No. 245 on H.R. 3020 at 84–85.

this end, employers must be guaranteed the same rights of freedom of expression now given to unions."[79]

Organized labor was steadfastly opposed to the passage of the Taft-Hartley amendments and after its passage, publicized "its opposition to what it called the 'slave labor law.'"[80] Although more than 60 years have passed since its enactment, and efforts of unions to repeal it have not been successful, many of the same objectives motivate organized labor today in seeking to rebalance the scale between management and labor.

## B. State and Local Efforts to Curtail Employer Speech

Opponents of the federal labor law regime contend that to cope with the purportedly outdated and ossified NLRA, state and local governments have increasingly had to engage in labor regulation.[81] Whether to combat what they view as a frozen employer-friendly federal regime, or because local efforts allow unions to efficiently expend resources on legislative change, unions have focused their attention, to a great degree, on state and local government initiatives, rather than seeking legislative change on the national level.

Although the Supreme Court's decision in *Chamber of Commerce v. Brown* makes clear the strength of the NLRA's preemptive power, particularly under the *Machinists* doctrine, federal labor law does not preclude all state and local regulation. For example, state laws may set minimal employment standards that are not inconsistent with the general legislative goals of the NLRA (such as minimum wage laws).[82] Where state or local legislation does conflict with the goals of the NLRA, that regulation runs a high risk of preemption.

Although the target of AB 1889 appears to have been the health care industry, the statute was not narrowly tailored either to restrict the use of state funds to affect unionization in any particular economic sector or to prohibit a narrow class of actions undertaken on

---

[79] House Supplemental Minority Report No. 245, Supplemental Minority Report By Hon. John F. Kennedy at 114.

[80] 1 Developing Labor Law at 47.

[81] See, e.g., Benjamin I. Sachs, Labor Law Renewal, 1 Harv. L. & Pol'y Rev. 375, 394 (2007).

[82] See Metro. Life Ins. Co. v. Mass., 471 U.S. 724, 757 (1985).

the employer's behalf.[83] Indeed, AB 1889 was limited only by the relatively loose definition of "employers" covered under the act, which amounted to essentially any employer who received a comparatively small amount of funding from the state in a given year.[84]

Although legislation of this general type has achieved some success in recent years, California's statute is among the most (if not *the* most) broad of these laws. Obviously, regulations styled after AB 1889 are unlikely to survive a preemption challenge under the plain holding of *Chamber of Commerce v. Brown*. State and local efforts to impose a similar restriction are also unlikely to survive a preemption challenge, but the form of the regulation at issue may play a role in structuring defenses to future challenges to such regulation.

At least one union representative has indicated support for a reading that such regulation can survive in substance if the enforcement provisions are less burdensome than those of AB 1889: Stephen Berzon, a lawyer for the AFL-CIO and its California affiliate and husband of Ninth Circuit Judge Marsha Berzon, has said that "the ruling may leave room for a more limited law that restricts the use of state funds but omits some of the enforcement provisions in California's law."[85] Mr. Berzon's understanding likely rests on Justice Breyer's dissent (and Judge Fisher's), in which a crucial factor to the rejection of preemption was the level of intrusiveness of the regulation on the employer's ability to use its own funds to speak on union issues.[86] Breyer's criticism that the majority acted with an inadequate record implies that, at the very least, he viewed the determination on burden to be a critical component of the Court's ultimate finding of preemption.

Justice Stevens's opinion, however, clearly endorses a broad reading of Taft-Hartley's speech protections and does not leave much

[83] Logan, *supra* note 5, at 160.

[84] See Cal. Gov't. Code Ann. §§ 16645.2, 16645.7.

[85] Bob Egelko, State Funds Can Be Used Against Unions, San Francisco Chronicle, B4 (June 20, 2008).

[86] See, e.g., Chamber v. Brown, 128 S. Ct. at 2421 (Breyer, J., dissenting); Chamber III, 422 F.3d 973, 1004 ("In certain respects, I share the majority's concerns. Some of the statute's enforcement provisions appear to have an impermissibly intrusive effect on the NLRA's balance of private actions between employer and employee, by exposing employers to the risk of significant litigation costs and punitive sanctions if they support or oppose unionization, even without using state funds.").

room for this suggested balancing approach. Given the uncertainty as to whether legislation can be drafted to fit the contours between too burdensome and not burdensome—if there is any space to be found—it seems that support for California-style provisions will wane as unions and legislatures weigh the potential risks and expenses in defending these types of proposals against political and legal attack.

### 1. Limited By Activity Prohibited

One alternative to the AB 1889-type statute is legislation defining with more specificity the actions that an employer may not fund with state monies. New York, for example, proscribes the use of state money for three specific actions: (1) training managers, supervisors, or other administrative personnel on methods to encourage or discourage unionization; (2) hiring or paying attorneys, consultants, or other contractors to encourage or discourage unionization; and (3) hiring employees or paying the salary and other compensation of employees whose principal job duties are to encourage or discourage unionization.[87] Massachusetts has also passed a similarly limited regulation.[88]

Although this type of regulation is narrower than AB 1889, it is likely to be found to similarly limit the protection for an employer's exercise of speech. The New York law has already been found by one court to have been preempted by the NLRA under the *Machinists* doctrine.[89] Although the Second Circuit reversed the district court's grant of summary judgment, finding that material issues of fact regarding the effect of the regulation remained for the district court to resolve on remand, it did not preclude the district court's ultimate finding of either *Machinists* or *Garmon* preemption.

Moreover, nothing in the Court's decision in *Chamber of Commerce v. Brown* suggests that a relevant factor to consider in the preemption

---

[87] N.Y. Lab. Law. § 211-a. See also Debra Charish, Union Neutrality or Employer Gag Law? Exploring NLRA Preemption of New York Labor Law Section 211-a, 14 J.L. & Pol'y 799–803 (2006) (describing legislative history and amendment of § 211-a and noting that the law in its original form was targeted solely at "employers who actively discouraged unionization as a part of employee training").

[88] See Mass. Gen. L. 7 § 56.

[89] See Healthcare Ass'n of New York State, Inc. v. Pataki, 388 F. Supp. 2d 6 (N.D.N.Y. May 17, 2005), rev'd by 471 F.3d 87 (2d Cir. 2006).

analysis is the specific type of speech activity regulated. Instead, the Court's inquiry focused only on whether the employer's speech was limited in contravention of the free debate protected by the act (and the extent to which states have control over state funds not connected to any programmatic message).

### 2. Limited By Employers Covered

Another alternative to an AB 1889-type regulation would be restrictions on state funds targeted specifically at certain industries or economic sectors, affecting only a limited number of employers. Florida, for example, passed such a law in May 2002, restricting the use of state funds to promote or deter unionization only in nursing homes.[90] Rhode Island has passed a law with a similar aim, preventing Medicaid reimbursement funds from being used to influence an employee's decision to join a union.[91]

Some laws with a similar limited scope have been upheld prior to the Supreme Court's decision in *Chamber of Commerce v. Brown*. For example, the Seventh Circuit found that an Illinois statute requiring that entities wishing to receive a subsidy for the construction of certain renewable fuel plans have a labor agreement establishing wages and benefits and including a no-strike clause.[92] Although the court found that the state was not acting in a proprietary capacity, it nevertheless found that the statute was not preempted by the NLRA because Illinois did not seek to affect labor relations generally through this targeted statute and thus was not engaging in regulation.[93]

Although supporters of this type of legislation may point to *Lavin* as blessing limitations targeted to a specific group of employers, such an argument may suffer from several weaknesses. First, the statute at issue in *Lavin* was exceptionally narrow. Neither the Florida nor the Rhode Island statutes affect such a narrow group of employers. Second, and more importantly, the Supreme Court explained in *Chamber of Commerce v. Brown*, that targeted statutes

[90] See Fla. Stat. 400.334.

[91] See R.I. Gen. Laws, § 40-8.2-23.

[92] Northern Illinois Chapter of Assoc. Builders & Contractors, Inc. v. Lavin, 431 F.3d 1004 (7th Cir. 2005).

[93] *Id.* at 1006.

(much like the federal limitations in programs such as Head Start) may fall within the prerogative of Congress, but "[u]nlike the States, Congress has the authority to create tailored exceptions to otherwise applicable federal policies, and (also unlike the States) it can do so in a manner that preserves national uniformity without opening the door to a 50-state patchwork of inconsistent labor policies."[94] Such a statement seems to foreclose the ability of states to implement restrictions on employer speech targeted to affect only certain groups of employers.

Such targeted restrictions are more likely to survive the NLRA's preemptive force if those restrictions can be drafted to fall within the market-participant exception to preemption.[95] One drawback to structuring laws in this manner is that certain industries simply may not be susceptible to influence exercised in this manner, particularly health care and other non-construction service industries where it is difficult to allocate state funds on a per-project basis.[96] The draw-back to structuring laws in this manner, however, is that a state's participation in the market is by its very nature not meant to broadly regulate. Any restriction falling within the market-participant exception to preemption will likely have nothing more than a negligible effect on labor relations more generally.

### 3. Neutrality Agreements/Labor Peace Legislation

Some states and localities have taken greater strides towards limiting employer speech by requiring employers to enter into agreements with unions as a condition of receiving certain state funds or contracts.[97] Although certain of these regulations have been upheld

---

[94] Chamber v. Brown, 128 S. Ct. at 2418.

[95] See Bldg. & Constr. Trades Counsel of the Metro. Dist. v. Associated Builders & Contractors of Mass/R.I., Inc., 507 U.S. 218, 229–30 (1993); see also Wisconsin Dept. of Industry v. Gould Inc., 475 U.S. 282, 291 (1986) (explaining that a state may act as a market participant when the enactment is "specifically tailored to one particular job" or a "legitimate response to state procurement constraints or to local economic needs").

[96] See Brian R. Garrison & Joseph C. Pettygrove, Yes, No, and Maybe: The Implications of a Federal Circuit Court Split Over Union-Friendly State And Local Neutrality Laws, 23 *Labor Lawyer* 121, 150 (2007).

[97] See Benjamin I. Sachs, *supra* note 81, at 388.

in the past,[98] other regulations have been held to be preempted by the NLRA.[99] The Supreme Court's statement in *Chamber of Commerce v. Brown* that "[a]lthough a State may choose to fund a program dedicated to advance certain permissible goals, it is not permissible for a State to use its spending power to advance an interest that—even if legitimate in the absence of the NLRA—frustrates the comprehensive federal scheme established by that Act"[100] seems to suggest that legislation requiring such labor peace agreements may be preempted by the NLRA. And even if regulations of this type are not found to be preempted by the NLRA, they may be subject to an independent claim that they violate the First Amendment by imposing impermissible speech-based restrictions on the provision of government benefits.[101]

## C. Federal Legislation Restricting Employer Speech

If the Supreme Court's decision in *Chamber of Commerce v. Brown* increases the risk that state and local legislation will be found to be preempted by the NLRA, unions and their supporters may refocus their attention on Congress. The general substance of the federal law governing the labor-management relationship has remained largely unchanged for decades. Critics—primarily unions and their supporters—complain that employers have prevented reform at the expense of declining unionization. But these same critics fail to convincingly argue that restricting the free debate on unionization will necessarily lead to a better represented workforce.

Indeed, certain members of Congress have recognized a need to turn attention away from legislation that seeks to fundamentally alter the balance struck by the NLRA. For example, Senator Arlen

[98] See, e.g., Hotel Employees & Rest. Employees Union, Local 57 v. Sage Hospitality Res., 390 F.3d 206 (3d Cir. 2004) (upholding Pittsburgh regulation on the grounds of market-participant exception).

[99] See, e.g., Metro. Milwaukee Ass'n of Commerce v. Milwaukee County, 431 F.3d 277 (7th Cir. 2005) (finding Milwaukee regulation to be preempted because the county's spending power could not be used as a pretext to regulate labor relations).

[100] Chamber v. Brown, 128 S. Ct. at 2417.

[101] See, e.g., Perry v. Sindermann, 408 U.S. 593, 597 (1972) (the government "may not deny a benefit to a person on a basis that infringes his constitutionally protected speech"); see also Brief of the Cato Institute as Amicus Curiae in Support of Petitioners, Chamber of Commerce v. Brown, U.S. Supreme Court, No. 06-939, at 13.

Specter advocates instead that Congress focus on increasing the effectiveness of the NLRB: "Congress must hold hearings on how to reduce the window of time during which both sides could cheat and how to increase remedies when cheating does occur. Second, it must pass legislation that focuses on securing employees' freedom of choice in the workplace, rather than on serving the interests of unions or employers."[102] And, as Senator Specter recognizes, "[l]egislating on the assumption that all organizers have pure motives would be a mistake."[103] To be fair, the same caution applies to employers' motives, and for that very reason, legislation that seeks to change processes, rather than to limit the exchange of information, is a more prudent course.

Whether unions ultimately support proposals that strengthen the NLRB's enforcement powers, it is safe to assume that they will continue to press their long-term agenda to limit employer opportunities for speech against unionization. In the wake of *Chamber of Commerce v. Brown*, unions may consider two approaches to legislating speech restrictions nationally.

### 1. Limited Restrictions

Throughout the AB 1889 litigation, the parties argued over the meaning of several targeted federal statutes that prevented recipients of certain federal funds from using those funds to "assist, promote, or deter union organizing."[104] Nobody questioned the validity of these restrictions, and the Court determined that the federal government may enact targeted restrictions on the spending of federal dollars without affecting the preemptive power of NLRA.[105] Unions

---

[102] Arlen Specter & Eric S. Nguyen, Representation Without Intimidation: Securing Workers' Right to Choose Under the National Labor Relations Act, 45 Harv. J. on Legis. 311, 319 (2008).

[103] *Id.* at 321.

[104] See 29 U.S.C. § 2931(b)(7) ("Each recipient of funds under [the Workforce Investment Act] shall provide to the Secretary assurance that none of such funds will be used to assist, promote, or deter union organizing"); 42 U.S.C. § 9839(e) ("Funds appropriated to carry out [the Head Start Programs Act] shall not be used to assist, promote, or deter union organizing"); 42 U.S.C. § 12634(b)(1) ("Assistance provided under [the National Community Service Act] shall not be used by program participants and program staff to . . . assist, promote, or deter union organizing").

[105] Chamber v. Brown, 128 S. Ct. at 2417–18.

may pursue the enactment of funding restrictions to limit employer speech on unionization in particular contexts. The effect of such restrictions would vary based on the funds targeted, but restrictions attached to, say, Medicare funding, could have a substantial impact on the health care industry as a whole, where unions have already concentrated their efforts.

A collateral effect of the passage of such targeted restrictions might be the weakening of the NLRA's preemptive effect. Such an effect may be extrapolated from the Court's observation that the "three federal statutes relied on by the Court of Appeals neither conflict with the NLRA nor otherwise establish that Congress 'decided to tolerate a substantial measure of diversity' in the regulation of employer speech."[106] If a "patchwork" of targeted restrictions is enacted, however, the effect over time may be exactly the tolerance of such diversity.

### 2. Broader Restrictions

A more ambitious undertaking would be to amend the NLRA itself, and faced with the Court's decision, unions might seek to directly undermine the protections of free debate provided by section 8(c) that the Court recognized as preempting AB 1889. Ignoring the political challenges inherent in passing such legislation, restricting employer speech in such a manner may raise First Amendment concerns. Although section 8(c) has been understood to "merely implement[] the First Amendment,"[107] section 8(c) itself manifests a particular "congressional intent to encourage free debate on issues dividing labor and management,"[108] and is therefore not simply an embodiment of First Amendment protections.

The Supreme Court has recognized employers' First Amendment right to engage in noncoercive speech about unionization that exists independent of section 8(c).[109] The contours of this speech right have not been fully developed, in large part because of the NLRA's separate guarantee of the right. But unlimited noncoercive advocacy

[106] Id. at 2418.

[107] NLRB v. Gissell Packing Co., 395 U.S. 575, 617 (1969).

[108] Linn v. Plant Guard Workers, 383 U.S. 53, 62 (1966).

[109] Thomas v. Collins, 323 U.S. 516, 537–38 (1945); NLRB v. Virginia Elec. & Power Co., 314 U.S. 469, 477 (1941).

serves to better inform the employee and is consistent with the general First Amendment speech protections.

## D. *Efforts to Diminish the Importance of Employer Speech*

Given the difficulties that arise with regard to actually limiting employer speech, the more politically feasible (and perhaps more legally defensible) option available to unions and their supporters may be to attempt to diminish the importance of employer speech in an employee's decisionmaking process. Unions assert that employer speech has an inordinate effect on unionization, in large part because employers' speech is "likely to reflect their perceptions about the speaker's basic power over their work lives rather than the persuasive content of the words themselves."[110] In other words, unions are less effective in convincing employees when employers speak not because the employer provides useful or persuasive information when speaking, but simply because the employer speaks.

But the reality of declining rates of unionization is far more complicated. In addition to a shifting economy, declining union membership may be attributable to workers enjoying the fruits of union efforts without having to pay union dues. Union efforts to increase worker pay, benefits, and working conditions generally may themselves play a large role in declining unionization.[111] Moreover, in the modern economy, it simply may not be true—as some union supporters advocate—that "[l]abor needs more power for the U.S. economy to prosper."[112]

One method has already begun to gain momentum: Requiring employers to recognize unions based on card checks—employees signing authorization forms—instead of secret-ballot elections. The advantage to unions in card check procedures is two-fold. First, signing a union authorization card requires less effort, and is often done with less forethought, than participation in an election. Second, unions are able to exert more influence over individual employees

---

[110] James J. Brudney, Neutrality Agreements And Card Check Recognition: Prospects For Changing Paradigms, 90 Iowa L. Rev. 821, 832 (2005).

[111] See Eugene Scalia, Ending Our Anti-Union Federal Employment Policy, 24 Harv. J.L. & Pub. Pol'y 489, 491 (2001).

[112] Avrum D. Lank, Obama Adviser pushes for more labor power: He says aiding unions helps the economy, Milwaukee Journal Sentinel (June 26, 2008) (quoting Jared Bernstein, an economic adviser to Democratic presidential nominee Barack Obama).

in card signature drives than the union would be able to assert in an election.[113] Both of these factors make the employer more of a remote player in the unionization process, thus diminishing the importance of employer speech to an employee's decision.

Certain states, such as California, have already passed limited "card check recognition" laws for sectors not covered by the NLRA.[114] And unions have made inroads by negotiating permissible voluntary recognition agreements with employers, usually as part of negotiated neutrality agreements.[115]

But the cornerstone to the card check proposals is federal legislation requiring the NLRB to allow card checks instead of secret ballot elections when union representation is disputed. Legislation is currently pending in Congress that would accomplish this. The current incarnation of the Employer Free Choice Act has passed the House of Representatives, but failed to receive enough votes to invoke cloture in the Senate.[116]

Although union support for such a measure predates the *Chamber of Commerce v. Brown* decision, the Court's articulated limits on the ability of unions to seek state and local restrictions on employer speech may further rally support for federal card check legislation. For example, Stephen Berzon recently stated that *Brown* "highlights the importance of labor-backed legislation—passed by the House, but stalled in the Senate—that would require an employer to recognize a union if a majority of employees signed affiliation cards."[117]

Support for card check recognition is also a key issue in the 2008 presidential campaign.[118] AFL-CIO leaders have made the Employee

---

[113] For example, a local union organizer may be able to more easily pressure individual employees with threats or mislead employees about the purpose of signing an authorization card. See, e.g., Specter & Nguyen, *supra* note 102, at 320–21 (describing testimony from February 2007 House Subcommittee on Labor, Education and Pensions hearing "Strengthening America's Middle Class through the Employee Free Choice Act" regarding union abuses in connection with union organization drives and authorization cards).

[114] See Cal. AB 1281 (2001) (requiring employers to recognize unions for public employees when a majority of employees sign authorization cards).

[115] See Brudney, *supra* note 110, at 828–830.

[116] See H.R. 800 and S. 1014 (110th Cong. 2007).

[117] See Egelko, *supra* note 85.

[118] See, e.g, Ann Zimmerman & Kris Maher, Wal-Mart Warns of Democratic Win, Wall Street Journal, A1 (August 1, 2008).

Free Choice Act central to their platforms,[119] and advisors to Democratic nominee Barack Obama have championed his support for the measure.[120]

## Conclusion

The Supreme Court's decision in *Chamber of Commerce v. Brown* has reinforced the NLRA's protection of free debate in the unionization context. As unions adjust their policy objectives in the wake of this decision, it is likely that limiting employer speech or its effects will remain a priority on their legislative agendas. Enacting legislation to further these policy objectives, however, would be a mistake: The NLRA's speech protections are not limited to employer speech, but extend to the other voices in the unionization debate. Allowing opinions to be aired is consistent with the First Amendment's protections and, moreover, is consistent with informed decisionmaking by all participants in the labor market.

[119] See AFL-CIO Secretary Treasurer Richard Trumka, Speech to United Steelworkers Annual Convention (July 2, 2008), reprinted in John Nichols, AFL's Trumka: Labor Must Battle Racism To Elect Obama, Capital Times (Madison, WI) (July 3, 2008) ("Union companies are no less competitive, the fact is they're more competitive.... Brothers and sisters, labor market flexibility is about one thing only: it isn't helping companies be more competitive, it's about making unions weaker. And, I'll tell you one other thing: that stops the day the Employee Free Choice Act is signed!").

[120] Lank, *supra* note 112 ("Foremost among them is allowing unions to be certified without an election if a majority of workers want one, he said. The prospects for such legislation are not good with the current Congress, Bernstein said. However, he said Obama, a senator from Illinois, supports such a measure, as does organized labor.... However, the laws are now tilted too far in the direction of management, with companies using numerous legal tactics to delay an election after a majority of workers ask for one.").

# Stoneridge Investment Partners v. Scientific-Atlanta:
# The Political Economy of Securities Class Action Reform

*A. C. Pritchard**

## I. Introduction

*Stoneridge Investment Partners, LLC v. Scientific-Atlanta, Inc.*[1] is the latest in a series of recent Supreme Court decisions restricting securities class actions. The Court's holding in *Stoneridge*—rejecting scheme liability that would have roped in third party defendants—is of a piece with the Court's recent skepticism toward securities class actions. The Court's recent decisions reflect a retrenchment from a two-decade-old decision by the Court, *Basic, Inc. v. Levinson,*[2] which was the high-water mark for the implied cause of action the courts have found in the Securities Exchange Act § 10(b) and its implementing Rule 10b-5.[3] *Basic* opened the doors wide to securities fraud class actions under Rule 10b-5 by creating a presumption of reliance for lawsuits involving securities traded in the secondary public markets—the fraud on the market theory (FOTM). The result of the *Basic* decision was an upsurge in securities class actions.

That upsurge was met by a predictable backlash from the targets of those suits: public companies and their officers and directors, accountants, and investment bankers. Those potential defendants complained that companies were unfairly targeted by securities class actions based on no more than a drop in the stock price, with the plaintiffs' bar looking to extort settlements based on frivolous suits.

*Professor, University of Michigan Law School. Thanks to Alicia Davis Evans, Nico Howson, and Bob Thompson for helpful comments and suggestions.

[1] 552 U.S. ____ , 128 S.Ct. 761 (2008).

[2] 485 U.S. 224 (1988).

[3] 15 U.S.C. § 78j and 17 C.F.R. § 240.10b-5.

And their complaints were heard by Congress and the Court, both of which have taken steps to rein in securities class actions. Congress enacted the Private Securities Litigation Reform Act,[4] which imposes a series of procedural barriers for securities fraud class actions, and the Securities Litigation Uniform Standards Act,[5] which checks efforts to evade the PSLRA's barriers by resort to state court.[6] The Court's interpretations of those statutes have generally been considered defendant-friendly.[7]

*Stoneridge* is certainly defendant-friendly; the Court put itself through serious intellectual contortions to get to its goal of exculpating secondary actors. *Stoneridge*'s interpretation of the reliance element, however, suggests that while the Court will resist expansion of the Rule 10b-5 cause of action, we cannot expect more fundamental reform from that quarter. In this essay, I compare the institutions and actors that might change how securities class actions work: the Court, Congress, the SEC, and shareholders.

I begin in Part II by explaining the wrong turn that the Court took in *Basic*. The *Basic* Court misunderstood the function of the reliance element and its relation to the question of damages. As a result, the securities class action regime established in *Basic* threatens draconian sanctions with limited deterrent benefit. Part III then summarizes the cases leading up to *Stoneridge* and analyzes the Court's reasoning in that case. In *Stoneridge*, like the decisions interpreting the reliance requirement of Rule 10b-5 that came before it, the Court emphasized policy implications. Sometimes policy implications are invoked to broaden the reach of the Rule 10b-5 cause of action. More recently, policy implications have been invoked to narrow its reach. Part IV explores the policy choices made by Congress in the express private

---

[4] Pub. L. No. 104-67, 109 Stat. 737 (1995) (codified in part at 15 U.S.C. §§ 77z-1, 78u-4).

[5] Pub. L. No. 105-353, 112 Stat. 3227 (1998) (codified at 15 U.S.C. §77p, 78bb(f)).

[6] See David M. Levine and Adam C. Pritchard, The Securities Litigation Uniform Standards Act of 1998: The Sun Sets on California's Blue Sky Laws, 54 Bus. Law. 1 (1998).

[7] See, e.g., Tellabs, Inc. v. Makor Issues & Rights, Ltd., 127 S. Ct. 2499 (2007); Merrill Lynch, Perce, Fenner & Smith, Inc. v. Dabit, 547 U.S. 71 (2006); Dura Pharmaceuticals, Inc. v. Broudo, 544 U.S. 336 (2005). My own view is that *Tellabs* was as generous to plaintiffs as the text of the PSLRA would allow. The opinion did, however, reverse a more generous, but implausible, interpretation from the Seventh Circuit.

causes of action in the securities laws, and the implications of those choices for securities fraud class actions under Rule 10b-5. The choices reflected in those explicit causes of action suggest that the *Basic* Court erred by failing to calibrate the damages measure in Rule 10b-5 class actions to accord with the attenuated version of reliance that it adopted. In secondary-market class actions, I argue, damages should be measured by disgorgement of unlawful gains rather than compensation of defrauded shareholders. Doing so would bring damages closer in line with social costs; more importantly, such a reform promises to make securities fraud class actions a more cost-effective mechanism for deterring fraud.

I then turn in Part V to the question of *who* can reform securities class actions. Which institution—the Court, Congress, the SEC, or shareholders—is most likely to bring about the needed changes to the damages measure? The available evidence suggests that the three government actors in this list are largely paralyzed from overhauling securities class actions in a meaningful way. I argue that shareholders, the parties who bear the costs of the current regime, must take matters into their own hands. I briefly outline the path by which shareholders could opt out of the current dysfunctional class action regime, replacing it with a more precisely targeted deterrent scheme focused on disgorgement. Part VI concludes.

## II. The *Basic* Mistake

Congress did not create a private right of action when it enacted the anti-fraud provision in Exchange Act § 10(b). The courts, left to their own imagination in implying a cause of action under Rule 10b-5, have relied heavily on the requirements of the common law action for deceit.[8] Reliance under the common law required the plaintiffs to allege that they had relied on the misstatement and that it affected their decision to purchase. Applying that model to the Rule 10b-5 cause of action, plaintiffs were required to allege that they read the misstatements that they claimed were distorting the price of a company's stock before purchasing or selling that security.

---

[8] Dura Pharmaceuticals, 544 U.S. at 341 (2005) (private right of action under § 10(b) "resembles, but is not identical to, common-law tort actions for deceit and misrepresentation.").

The Supreme Court, in a 4-2 vote with Justice Harry Blackmun writing for the majority, adopted a "fraud on the market" presumption of reliance in *Basic*.[9] In *Basic*, the defendant company repeatedly denied that it was in merger negotiations. When the company eventually announced a merger at a substantial premium to its prevailing market price, disappointed shareholders who had sold during the time that the company was denying the merger negotiations brought suit. The Court (in another opinion by Justice Blackmun) had excused the reliance requirement in an earlier case, *Affiliated Ute Citizens of Utah v. United States*, in which the gravamen of the fraud had been deceptive nondisclosure in breach of a fiduciary duty.[10] In that case, it was obviously impossible for the plaintiffs to plead actual reliance because the violation was a failure to speak, rather than a misstatement, so the Court concluded that materiality of the omission would "establish the requisite element of causation in fact."[11] The Court treated reliance as simply a subset of the tort concept of proximate causation (that is, whether the defendant's conduct is sufficiently close to the plaintiff's harm).

*Affiliated Ute*'s presumption of reliance did not extend, however, to affirmative misstatements. The reliance requirement for misstatements posed two obstacles to certifying a class of securities purchasers under Rule 10b-5, one rooted in the law and the other rooted in investor behavior. The legal obstacle lies in the standards for certifying a class action. If each member of the plaintiff class were required to allege that he had read and relied on the misstatement in making her decision to purchase, it would defeat the commonality requirement for class actions.[12] The obstacle posed by investor behavior is that most purchasers of the company's stock would not have read or heard the alleged misstatement, which would substantially limit

---

[9] Anthony Kennedy had not yet taken his seat as Lewis Powell's replacement; Chief Justice William Rehnquist and Antonin Scalia recused themselves. Given their votes in other securities cases, it seems likely that the result would have been reversed if Kennedy, Rehnquist, and Scalia had participated.

[10] 406 U.S. 128 (1972) (fraudulent non-disclosure of certain conditions attaching to the transfer of commercial paper related to tribal trust assets).

[11] *Id.* at 154.

[12] Fed.R.Civ.P. 23(b)(3) (class action maintainable if "the court finds that the questions of law or fact common to the members of the class predominate over any questions affecting individual class members").

the size of the class. The FOTM presumption allows plaintiffs to skip the step of alleging personal reliance on the misstatement, instead allowing them to allege that the *market* relied on the misrepresentation in valuing the security. The plaintiffs in turn are deemed to have relied upon the distorted price produced by a deceived market. The empirical premise underlying the FOTM presumption is the efficient capital market hypothesis, which holds that efficient markets rapidly incorporate information—true or false—into the market price of a security. Thus, the price paid by the plaintiffs would have been inflated by the fraud, rendering the misstatement the cause in fact of the fraudulently induced purchase. The FOTM presumption assumes that purchasers would not have paid the prevailing market price if they knew the truth.[13]

The FOTM presumption avoids the evidentiary difficulties of showing actual reliance and, as a by-product, greatly expands the size of the class, thus increasing the potential amount of damages. Herein lies the problem: Once the FOTM presumption is in play, the potential damages available under Rule 10b-5 become enormous. Every investor who purchased during the time that a misrepresentation was affecting the company's stock price—and did not sell it before the truth was revealed—has a cause of action and potential remedies under Rule 10b-5.[14] As a result, the question of damages takes on vital importance.

Blackmun and the Supreme Court punted on this question in *Basic*, brushing the point off in a footnote. Blackmun ducked the issue of damages at the insistence of Justice John Paul Stevens, who wanted it left for another day.[15] This is perhaps fortunate, because Blackmun might well have made things worse. He was focused solely on compensation; there is no evidence that he even considered disgorgement.[16] The elements of reliance and damages, however,

[13] The presumption also applies if the misstatement has depressed the price of the stock, although this scenario is much less common.

[14] Shareholders who purchased before the fraud are excluded by the "purchase or sale" requirement announced in Blue Chip Stamps v. Manor Drug Stores, 421 U.S. 723 (1975).

[15] Harry Blackmun, Conference Notes, Basic v. Levinson, No. 86-279 (November 4, 1987) (Harry A. Blackmun Collection, Library of Congress).

[16] Letter from Harry A. Blackmun to William J. Brennan, Jr., No. 86-279, *Basic v. Levinson* (January 15, 1988) (Thurgood Marshall Collection, Library of Congress) ("there are at least two theories of damages that a plaintiff could propose, and this opinion does not lend particular support to either. . . . [T]he plaintiff could argue that

are not so easily severed. In adopting the FOTM presumption, Blackmun followed his earlier opinion in *Affiliated Ute*, which Blackmun characterized as holding that reliance was satisfied as long as "the necessary nexus between the plaintiff's injury and the defendant's wrongful conduct had been established."[17]

In *Affiliated Ute*, the connection between reliance and damages was self evident. The fraudulent transaction at issue fit neatly into the tort action for deceit. The plaintiffs' losses corresponded to the defendants' gains; the defendants had withheld material information about the value of the securities that they were purchasing from the plaintiffs. The ordinary "out of pocket" measure of tort damages— the difference between the price paid to the victim and the security's "true" value—makes sense in this context. In this scenario, requiring that the defendant compensate the plaintiff for her losses corrects the distortions caused by fraud in two ways. First, requiring compensation to the victim discourages the defendant from committing fraud. Second, compensation discourages investors from spending resources trying to avoid fraud.[18]

Expenditures on committing fraud and avoiding fraud are the real social costs that the anti-fraud cause of action is trying to prevent, and they underlie the reliance element of the tort action for deceit. Expenditures by both the perpetrator and the victim due to fraud are a social waste, so discouraging those expenditures by requiring compensation makes sense when the corporation is benefiting from the fraud. Indeed, fraud may influence how investors direct their capital. Firms selling securities in the primary market disclose more information in an effort to attract investors. If those disclosures are fraudulent, investors will pay an inflated price for those securities and companies will invest in projects that are not cost-justified. That risk of fraud will lead investors to discount the value of securities,

he would not have sold had he known about the merger discussion, and thus that he should receive the difference between the price at which he sold ($18) and the eventual merger price ($42). Alternatively, one could argue that a plaintiff should recover the difference between the price he sold ($18) and what the price would have been had defendants not misrepresented the facts ($20).").

[17] Basic, 485 U.S. at 243.

[18] Paul G. Mahoney, Precaution Costs and the Law of Fraud in Impersonal Markets, 78 Va. L. Rev. 623, 630 (1992) ("If fraud is not deterred, market participants will take expensive precautions to uncover fraud so as to avoid entering into bargains they would not have concluded in an honest market.").

thus raising the cost of capital for publicly traded firms. Fraud is worth deterring when the defendant is a party to the securities transaction, and requiring compensation ensures that fraud does not pay.

*Basic's* FOTM presumption, however, does not require that the defendant have purchased or sold the security whose price was allegedly affected by the misstatement. In fact, in the overwhelming majority of securities fraud class actions, plaintiffs' attorneys sue the corporation and its officers for misrepresenting the company's operations, financial performance, or future prospects that inflate the price of the company's stock in secondary trading markets. Because the corporation has not sold securities (and thereby trans- ferred wealth to itself), it has no institutional incentive to spend real resources in executing the fraud—and thus no reason to encourage investor reliance.

On the other side of the equation, secondary-market fraud does not create a net wealth transfer away from investors, at least in the aggregate. For every shareholder who *bought* at a fraudulently inflated price, another shareholder has *sold*: The buyer's individual loss is offset by the seller's gain.[19] If we assume all traders are ignorant of the fraud, we can expect them to win as often as lose from fraudulently distorted prices.[20] With no expected loss from fraud on the market, shareholders do not need to take precautions against the fraud. Thus, secondary-market fraud fits awkwardly in the confines of a tort action for deceit, which is premised on misrepresentation in a face-to-face transaction. In face-to-face trans- actions, parties naturally take precautions to manage the risk of fraud.

Oddly enough, the status of many shareholders as passive price takers in the secondary market was one of the rationales offered by the *Basic* Court for adopting the FOTM presumption. The Court has it exactly backwards: Because these shareholders are passive, they are not relying in the economically relevant sense, which is to say, they are not making a choice to forego verification. Verification is not an option for the passive investor; checking the accuracy of a

---

[19] Frank Easterbrook & Daniel Fischel, Optimal Damages in Securities Cases, 62 U. Chi. L. Rev. 607, 611 (1985).

[20] Alicia Davis Evans, Are Investors' Gains and Losses from Securities Fraud Equal Over Time? Some Preliminary Evidence, Working Paper, University of Michigan (2008) (demonstrating that diversified traders' gains and losses from securities fraud average out to essentially zero).

corporation's statements is a task that can be taken on only by an investment professional, and even these sophisticated actors are unlikely to succeed in uncovering fraud. Passive investors can protect themselves against fraud much more cheaply through diversification. Fraud, like other business reversals, is a firm-specific risk, so assembling a broad portfolio of companies essentially eliminates its effect on an investor's portfolio. The few bad apples will be offset by the gains from the honest companies. The irony of the FOTM presumption, intended to protect passive investors, is that the ultimate passive investors—holders of index funds—have already protected themselves against fraud in the secondary market, and at a very low cost.

Notwithstanding the ability of shareholders to protect themselves through diversification, the FOTM presumption, when coupled with the "out of pocket" tort measure of damages, puts the corporation on the hook to compensate investors who come out on the losing end of a trade at a price distorted by misrepresentation.[21] The current rule applied by the lower courts holds corporations responsible for the entire loss of all of the shareholders who paid too much for their shares as a result of fraudulent misrepresentations. Critically, the "out of pocket" measure of damages provides no offset for the windfall gain on the other side of the trade. The investors lucky enough to have been selling during the period of the fraud do not have to give their profits back. Given the trading volume in secondary markets, the potential recoverable damages in securities class actions can be a substantial percentage of the corporation's total capitalization, easily reaching hundreds of millions of dollars, and sometimes billions. With potential damages in this range, class actions are a big stick to wield against fraud. More importantly, the "out of pocket" measure exaggerates the social harm caused by FOTM because it fails to account for the windfall gains of equally innocent shareholders who sold at the inflated price. Absent insider trading, the losses and gains will be a wash for shareholders in the aggregate, even though some individual shareholders will have suffered substantial losses.

---

[21] For a thorough discussion of damages issues under Rule 10b-5, see Robert B. Thompson, "Simplicity and Certainty" in the Measure of Recovery Under Rule 10b-5, 51 Bus. Law. 1177 (1996).

The case for deterring fraud with enormous damages is weaker when the corporation does not benefit from the fraud. The standard argument for vicarious liability in this context is that it will encourage the company to take precautions to prevent the fraud. A similar argument applies to third parties, such as accountants and investment banks. This argument, however, assumes that fraud sanctions are being imposed accurately. Securities fraud class actions are inevitably scattershot. Distinguishing fraud from mere business reversals is difficult. The external observer may not know whether a drop in a company's stock price is attributable to a prior intentional misstatement about its prospects (i.e., fraud) or a result of risky business decisions that did not pan out (i.e., misjudgment or bad luck). Unable to distinguish the two, plaintiffs' lawyers must rely on limited publicly available indicia (SEC filings, press releases from the company, evidence of insider trading by the managers alleged to be responsible for the fraud, the rare instance of a public revelation by a whistleblower, etc.) when deciding whom to sue. Thus, a substantial drop in stock price following news that contradicts a previous optimistic statement may well produce a lawsuit.

That leaves courts with the difficult task of sorting the meritorious cases from those with weak evidence of fraud (so-called strike suits). Courts and jurors, with hindsight, may have difficulty distinguishing false statements (which were known to be false at the time) from unfortunate business decisions. Both create a risk of liability and thus provide a basis for filing suit. If plaintiffs can withstand a motion to dismiss, defendants generally will find settlement more attractive than litigating to a jury verdict, even if the defendants believe that a jury would share their view of the facts. From the company's perspective, the enormous potential damages make the merits of the suit a secondary consideration in the decision of whether or not to settle. The math is straightforward: A 10 percent chance of a \$250 million judgment means that a settlement for \$24.9 million makes sense.[22] For many companies facing a securities fraud class action, the choice is settle or risk the very real possibility of a jury verdict that threatens bankruptcy.

---

[22] *See* Janet Cooper Alexander, Rethinking Damages in Securities Class Actions, 48 Stan. L. Rev. 1487, 1511 (1996) ("The class-based compensatory damages regime in theory imposes remedies that are so catastrophically large that defendants are unwilling to go to trial even if they believe the chance of being found liable is small.").

If the threat of bankruptcy-inducing damages were not enough, any case plausible enough to get past a judge may be worth settling just to avoid the costs of discovery and attorneys' fees, which can be enormous in these cases. Securities fraud class actions are expensive to defend because the focus of litigation will often be scienter: What did the defendants know, and when did they know it? The most helpful source for uncovering those facts will be the documents in the company's possession. Producing all documents relevant to the knowledge of senior executives over many months or even years—for example, all email sent or received by the top management team—can be a massive undertaking for a corporate defendant. Having produced the documents, the company can then anticipate a seemingly endless series of depositions, as plaintiffs' counsel investigates whether the executives' recollections square with the documents. Beyond the cost in executives' time, the mere existence of the class action may disrupt relationships with suppliers and customers, who will be understandably leery of dealing with a business accused of fraud.[23]

The recent experience of JDS Uniphase is illustrative.[24] After five years of litigation, the company was eventually exonerated by a jury after a trial—one of only four securities class actions to go to verdict out of 2,105 suits filed since 1995. The company knew that it was risking bankruptcy if it lost, but was unable to come to terms with the plaintiffs. JDS gambled and won—but only after paying a reported $50 million in legal fees. Even if JDS had been *certain* that it would prevail at trial, it would have been economically rational to settle the case when it was filed for $49 million. Combine this calculus with one other data point: The median settlement in securities fraud class actions was $6.4 million from 2002 to 2007.[25] Given JDS's experience, it is difficult to argue that any suit likely to be

---

[23] See, e.g., Blue Chip Stamps v. Manor Drug Stores, 421 U.S. 723, 742–43 (1975). The cost of discovery has been ameliorated somewhat by the PSLRA, which limits discovery while a motion to dismiss is pending. 15 U.S.C. § 78u-4(b)(3)(B).

[24] Ashby Jones, JDS Wins Investor Lawsuit, Bucking a Trend, Wall Street Journal, June 2, 2008, at B4.

[25] NERA Economic Consulting, Recent Trends in Shareholder Class Action Litigation: Filings Stay Low and Average Settlements Stay High—But Are These Trends Reversing? (September 2007). The average settlement was $23.2 million during that period.

filed that gets past a motion to dismiss can be defended for less than $6.4 million. This means that *at least* half of the suits that produce a settlement are settling for essentially nuisance value.

In sum, the combination of the potential for enormous judgments and the cost of litigating securities class actions means that even weak cases may produce a settlement if they are not dismissed at the complaint stage. The deterrent effect of class actions is thus diluted, because both wrongful and innocent conduct is punished. This possibility of extracting multimillion dollar settlements from strike suits has driven post-*Basic* efforts to rein in securities class actions. I turn now to the Court's part in those efforts.

## III. *Stoneridge*

As noted above, *Stoneridge* is the latest salvo in the Court's efforts to combat strike suits. The Court's most controversial post-*Basic* effort to curtail securities class actions also happens to be the precursor to *Stoneridge*: *Central Bank of Denver v. First Interstate Bank of Denver*.[26] *Central Bank*, like *Stoneridge*, was written by Justice Anthony Kennedy. The issue presented in *Central Bank* was whether private civil liability under § 10(b) (the authorizing statute for Rule 10b-5) extends to aiders and abettors of the violation.[27] The issuer of the securities in the case was the Public Building Authority, which raised $26 million in bonds to finance public improvements at planned residential/commercial development in Colorado. Central Bank acted as indenture trustee for the bonds. The bonds were secured by liens on real property, with a covenant requiring that the assessed value of that land must be at least 160 percent of the bonds' outstanding principal and interest. Additional covenants required AmWest Development—the developer—to give annual reports showing that the 160 percent test was being met.

Before an issue of the bonds in 1988 (but after a previous issue in 1986), AmWest gave Central Bank an updated appraisal showing no change in value of land from 1986. But the senior underwriter of the 1986 bond issue sent Central Bank notice questioning the 1986 valuation because property values had dropped in the region.

---

[26] 511 U.S. 164 (1994).

[27] See Ernst & Ernst v. Hochfelder, 425 U.S. 185, 214 (1976) (holding that Rule 10b-5's "scope cannot exceed the power granted the Commission by Congress under § 10(b)").

Central Bank asked its in-house appraiser to review the 1988 appraisal, who concluded that it was too optimistic. Instead of insisting on a new independent appraisal, Central Bank agreed to delay the outside full appraisal until after the 1988 bond offering. The building authority later defaulted and the bondholders filed suit against Central Bank, alleging that the bank had aided and abetted the Building Authority's Rule 10b-5 violation.

Blackmun assigned the opinion to Kennedy, who had voted at conference to uphold the aiding and abetting cause of action.[28] After further review, however, Kennedy switched his vote.[29] The open-ended nature of aiding and abetting liability clearly raised concerns about strike suits for Kennedy. He warned that uncertainty over the scope of liability could induce secondary actors to settle "to avoid the expense and risk of going to trial."[30] The risk of having to pay such settlements could cause professionals, such as accountants, to avoid newer and smaller companies, and "the increased costs incurred by professionals because of the litigation and settlement costs under 10b-5 may be passed on to their client companies, and in turn incurred by the company's investors, the intended beneficiaries of the statute."[31]

In an effort to increase Rule 10b-5's predictability, Kennedy's opinion adopted a two-part framework for addressing the scope of the private right of action under § 10(b), a significant departure from the free-wheeling approach of *Basic*.[32] In the first step of the inquiry,

---

[28] See Harry A. Blackmun, Conference Notes, No. 92-854, Central Bank of Denver v. First Interstate Bank (Dec. 3, 1993) Harry A. Blackmun Papers, Library of Congress (noting Kennedy's vote); Letter from Harry A. Blackmun to Chief Justice Rehnquist, No. 92-854, Central Bank of Denver v. First Interst. Bank, (Dec. 7, 1993) Harry A. Blackmun Papers, Library of Congress (informing the Chief that Kennedy would write for the majority).

[29] Letter from Anthony M. Kennedy to Harry A. Blackmun, Re: Central Bank v. First Interstate, No. 92-854 (February 17, 1994) Harry A. Blackmun Papers, Library of Congress. ("After working through the cases, particularly *Blue Chip Stamps*, *Ernst & Ernst*, *Pinter*, and *Musick*, I came to the conclusion that our precedents require us to confine the 10b-5 cause of action to primary violators, without extension to aiders and abettors.").

[30] Central Bank, 511 U.S. at 189.

[31] *Id.*

[32] I apply the two-step inquiry of *Central Bank* to the relationship between reliance and damages below.

228

Kennedy examined the text of § 10(b) to determine the scope of the conduct prohibited by the provision. He had little difficulty determining that the text of § 10(b) "prohibits only the making of a material misstatement (or omission) or the commission of a manipulative act."[33] This, in Kennedy's view, was sufficient to resolve the question: aiding and abetting was not prohibited by § 10(b).

Nonetheless, Kennedy set forth a second-step to the inquiry:

> When the text of § 10(b) does not resolve a particular issue, we attempt to infer how the 1934 Congress would have addressed the issue had the 10b-5 action been included as an express provision in the 1934 Act. For that inquiry, we use the express causes of action in the securities Acts as the primary model for the § 10(b) action. The reason is evident: Had the 73d Congress enacted a private § 10(b) right of action, it likely would have designed it in a manner similar to the other private rights of action in the securities Acts. . . .[34]

The plaintiffs' argument also failed under this second step, because the explicit causes of action afforded by Congress in the Securities Act and the Exchange Act were similarly silent on the question of aiding and abetting.[35]

In passing, Kennedy noted one additional problem with the plaintiffs' argument, which would have important consequences in *Stoneridge*: "Were we to allow the aiding and abetting action proposed in this case, the defendant could be liable without any showing that the plaintiff relied upon the aider and abettor's statements or

---

[33] Central Bank, 511 U.S. at 177.

[34] *Id.* at 178 (citations and internal quotation marks omitted). The Court has used the approach of looking to express causes of action to infer appropriate elements under the implied cause of action under Rule 10b-5 in other cases. Lampf, Pleva, Lipkind, Purpis & Petigrow v. Gilbertson, 501 U.S. 350 (1991) (applying statute of limitations from Securities Act claims to Rule 10b-5 claim); Musick, Peeler & Garrett v. Employers Ins. of Wausau, 508 U.S. 286, 297 (1993) (finding an implied right of contribution under Rule 10b-5 based on express right of contribution under explicit causes of action in the Exchange Act).

[35] Whether the question is resolved under the first or the second step of this inquiry has potentially significant consequences. When the Court interprets § 10(b), it is defining not only the limits of the private cause of action, but also the reach of the SEC's authority. When it constructs the hypothetical cause of action in the second step, only the private cause of action is implicated.

actions."[36] The Court left the door open for some liability for secondary participants, such as accountants, investment bankers, and lawyers, but only if they have exposed themselves to that risk by acting in a way that induces investor reliance. The bottom line after *Central Bank* is that a defendant must make a misstatement (or omission) on which a purchaser or seller of a security relies. Kennedy did not explain further the connection between reliance and the scope of Rule 10b-5; that issue would reemerge in *Stoneridge*.

If *Central Bank* was intended to enhance predictability, Kennedy's effort failed. What did it mean to "make" a misstatement? What sort of reliance was required? Not surprisingly, the lower courts arrived at different answers to these questions. The Ninth Circuit found that substantial participation in the making of a misstatement would suffice, even without public attribution of that statement to the defendant.[37] The Second Circuit adopted a narrower approach, finding participation in the making of a statement insufficient; public attribution of the statement to the defendant was required.[38]

This split over the interpretation of *Central Bank*'s holding brought the question of the scope of a primary violation of Rule 10b-5 back to the Court in *Stoneridge*. The *Stoneridge* plaintiffs attempted an end run around *Central Bank*: Instead of alleging that the secondary defendants had made or participated in the making of a misstatement, the plaintiffs alleged that the secondary defendants were part of a "scheme to defraud," thus invoking a separate provision of Rule 10b-5's anti-fraud prohibition.[39]

The scheme alleged by the plaintiffs in *Stoneridge* involved two suppliers of the cable company Charter Communications. The plaintiffs' complaint alleged that Charter engaged in a massive accounting fraud that inflated Charter's reported operating revenues and cash flow. The plaintiffs also named as defendants two equipment suppliers who provided cable set-top boxes to Charter, Scientific-Atlanta, and Motorola. The plaintiffs alleged that Charter paid the suppliers $20 extra for each set-top box in return for the supplier's agreement

---

[36] Central Bank, 511 U.S. at 180.

[37] In re Software Toolworks Inc. Sec. Litig., 50 F.3d 615, 628–629 (9th Cir. 1994).

[38] Wright v. Ernst & Young, LLP, 152 F.3d 169, 175 (2d Cir. 1998).

[39] Exchange Act Rule 10b-5(a).

to make additional payments back to Charter in the form of advertising fees. Charter then capitalized the $20 extra expense (shifting the accounting cost into the future) while treating the advertising fees as current income, artificially boosting Charter's current accounting revenues at the expense of future income. The suppliers had no direct role in preparing or disseminating the fraudulent accounting information, nor did they approve Charter's financial statements. The plaintiffs alleged, however, that the vendors facilitated Charter's deceptions by preparing false documentation and backdating contracts. The district court granted the suppliers' motion to dismiss, relying on *Central Bank* to hold that the vendors were not primary violators for Rule 10b-5 purposes. The court of appeals affirmed, concluding that the suppliers had not engaged in any deception because they had made no misstatements, had no duty to disclose to Charter's investors, and had not engaged in manipulation of Charter's shares.[40]

The Supreme Court, by a vote of 5–3 (with Justice Stephen Breyer recused), affirmed. Justice Kennedy, writing for the Court, rejected the appellate court's holding that there was no deception, noting that "[c]onduct itself can be deceptive."[41] He instead hung the affirmance on the other doctrinal point from his *Central Bank* decision, the incompatibility of aiding and abetting liability with the "essential element" of reliance.[42] He concluded that Blackmun's presumptions of reliance from *Affiliated Ute* and *Basic* did not apply because the suppliers had no fiduciary duty to Charter's shareholders and the suppliers' statements were not disseminated to the public. In this case, investors relied on Charter for its financial statements, not the cable set-top box transactions underlying those financial statements. Why did Kennedy focus on the defendants' conduct, rather than the plaintiffs, when assessing reliance? According to Kennedy, "reliance is tied to causation, leading to the inquiry whether [suppliers'] acts were immediate or remote to the injury."[43] Kennedy, following Blackmun's lead, was treating the reliance inquiry as a species of the tort concept of proximate cause.

---

[40] In re Charter Communications, Inc. Sec. Litig., 443 F.3d 987, 990–93 (8th Cir. 2006).

[41] Stoneridge, 128 S.Ct. at 769.

[42] *Id.*

[43] *Id.* at 770.

Like *Central Bank*, Kennedy's principal concern was the specter
of unlimited liability. According to Kennedy, "[w]ere this concept
of reliance to be adopted, the implied cause of action would reach the
whole marketplace in which the issuing company does business."[44] If
accepted, the plaintiff's theory threatened to inject the § 10(b) cause
of action into "the realm of ordinary business operations."[45]

Kennedy's rationale for limiting the concept of reliance could have
more naturally been put into the "in connection with the purchase
or sale of any security" language from § 10(b). Kennedy pointed to
that language, but said that it did not control in this case because
the "in connection with" requirement goes to the "statute's coverage
rather than causation."[46] Another reason for not putting the limit into
that doctrinal category is that the Court had only recently affirmed a
very broad scope for that requirement.[47] A more substantial reason
is that cabining Rule 10b-5 through the "in connection with the
purchase or sale" requirement would limit not only private plaintiffs
but, potentially, the SEC, whose enforcement authority is limited by
the reach of the statute. Kennedy conceded that the SEC's enforcement authority might reach commercial transactions such as those
between Charter and its suppliers, but he was reluctant to grant the
same freedom to the plaintiffs' bar.[48]

Given the need to cabin the plaintiffs' bar, but maintain the SEC's
discretion, the reliance requirement was an attractive tool. The reliance requirement, despite being an "essential element," has no basis
in the language of § 10(b), but is instead derived from the common
law of deceit.[49] More importantly for Kennedy's purposes, reliance
does not apply in enforcement actions brought by the SEC, or criminal prosecutions brought by the Justice Department.[50] Putting the

[44] *Id.*

[45] *Id.*

[46] *Id.*

[47] SEC v. Zandford, 535 U.S. 813 (2002).

[48] Stoneridge, 128 S.Ct. at 770–771 ("Were the implied cause of action to be extended
to the practices described here . . . there would be a risk that the federal power would
be used to invite litigation beyond the immediate sphere of securities litigation and
in areas already governed by functioning and effective state-law guarantees.").

[49] See, e.g., List v. Fashion Park, Inc. 340 F.2d 457 (2d Cir. 1965).

[50] Geman v. SEC, 334 F.3d 1183, 1191 (10th Cir. 2003) ("The SEC is not required to
prove reliance or injury in enforcement cases."); United States v. Haddy, 134 F.3d
542, 549–51 (3d Cir. 1998) (government need not prove reliance in criminal case).

limit on secondary party liability in the reliance element allowed the Court to have its cake—unfettered government enforcement—and eat it too—constrain the scope of private actions.

The importance of the SEC's enforcement efforts had been reinforced by Congress's response to *Central Bank*. Rebuffing calls to restore aiding-and-abetting liability, Congress instead gave that authority only to the SEC.[51] Accepting the plaintiff's argument in *Stoneridge*, Kennedy reasoned, would thus "undermine Congress' determination that this class of defendants should be pursued by the SEC and not by private litigants."[52] The Court's rationale for the need to constrain private litigants echoed and amplified the policy concerns of *Central Bank*. Expanding liability would undermine the United States' international competitiveness and raise the cost of capital because companies would be reluctant to do business with American issuers. Issuers might list their shares elsewhere to avoid these burdens.[53]

Most telling was the Court's treatment of the basic question of the existence of the implied private right of action. Kennedy made it clear that the initial implication of a private cause of action had been a mistake; under current doctrine, private causes of action are based only on explicit instruction from Congress.[54] Having now recognized the mistake, the Court was not going to compound the error: "Concerns with the judicial creation of a private cause of action caution against its expansion. The decision to extend the cause of action is for Congress, not for us. Though it remains the law, the § 10(b) private right should not be extended beyond its present boundaries."[55] Thus, *Stoneridge* stands for the proposition that the

---

[51] PSLRA § 104, 109 Stat. 757 (codified at 15 U.S.C. § 78t(e)).

[52] Stoneridge, 128 S.Ct. at 771.

[53] *Id.* at 772.

[54] *Id.* ("Though the rule once may have been otherwise, it is settled that there is an implied cause of action only if the underlying statute can be interpreted to disclose the intent to create one.") (citations omitted). See also *Id.* at 779 (Stevens, J., dissenting) ("A theme that underlies the Court's analysis is its mistaken hostility towards the § 10(b) private cause of action. The Court's current view of implied causes of actions is that they are merely a relic of our prior heady days.") (citations and internal quotation marks omitted).

[55] *Id.* at 773.

Rule 10b-5 cause of action is now frozen, at least when it comes to the expansion of liability.[56]

## IV. Fixing the Mistake

How do we fix the problem created by *Basic*? One way of getting at this question is through revisionist history. How would the reliance question in *Basic* have come out if we applied the two-step inquiry from *Central Bank*? Step 1: What does the statutory text tell us? Nothing; Congress did not mention reliance in § 10(b), hardly a surprise given that it did not intend to create a private cause of action. That silence sends us to the second step, which attempts to glean Congress's intent with respect to the implied cause of action under Rule 10b-5 by looking to the explicit private causes of action in the securities laws. What do those explicit causes of action tell us about the appropriate relation between damages and reliance under Rule 10b-5? They tell us that the Court has made a mistake in thinking about the implied right of action under Rule 10b-5 as a species of the tort action for deceit. The focus should be deterrence; a more apt model for the FOTM action would be unjust enrichment.[57]

There are six explicit causes of action relevant to our inquiry.[58] The first two come from the Securities Act of 1933. How do these causes of action treat reliance? Section 11 of that law allows the plaintiff to sue a corporate issuer, along with its officers and directors, for damages if the company has a material misstatement in its registration statement for a public offering.[59] Section 11 has no reliance requirement. Plaintiffs do not need to have read the registration statement that is alleged to be misleading. Damages, however, are

---

[56] See *Id.* ("when [the aiding and abetting provision of the PSLRA] was enacted, Congress accepted the § 10(b) private cause of action as then defined but chose to extend it no further.").

[57] On the unjust enrichment measure under Rule 10b-5, see Thompson, *supra* note 21.

[58] Two other provisions, § 15 of the Securities Act, 15 U.S.C. § 77o, and § 20 of the Exchange Act, 15 U.S.C. § 78t, extend liability to control persons of violators of those laws. It seems reasonable to conclude, however, that the control person benefitted from the wrongdoing of its affiliate if the affiliate benefitted. Even then liability is excused if the control person can show that it acted in good faith and was not complicit in the wrongdoing.

[59] 15 U.S.C. § 77k.

limited to the offering price.[60] The corporate issuer's liability exposure cannot be greater than its benefit from the fraud. Section 12(a)(2)
provides a parallel cause of action for material misstatements in a
prospectus or an oral statement made in connection with a public
offering.[61] Section 12(a)(2) also does not require reliance, but its
remedy is rescission—plaintiffs who prevail are entitled to put their
shares back to the seller in exchange for their purchase price (or
rescissory damages, if the plaintiff has sold before bringing suit).
Under either formula, damages are limited to the amount that the
seller received from the investor.[62] This parallels the unjust enrichment measure, not the out-of-pocket measure from tort.

Turning to the Exchange Act private causes of action, § 28 preserves existing rights and remedies, but bars plaintiffs from recovering "a total amount in excess of his actual damages on account of
the act complained of."[63] This provision clearly bars double recovery,
but has also been construed to bar punitive damages.[64] It tells us
nothing, however, about the relation between reliance and damages.

Section 9(e) allows for recovery in cases of market manipulation.[65]
Section 9 does not require reliance, and it is silent on the measure
of damages. There is little doubt, however, that the defendant in a
manipulation case is benefiting from the fraud. Manipulation
requires a showing of intent, and it is hard to conjure up incentives
for market manipulation other than extracting profits from that market. Although reliance is not required, § 9 does impose a challenging
standard requiring the plaintiff to show that his transaction "price
. . . was affected by" the manipulation, a difficult task in the face of
the myriad influences that can affect the price of a security. The
requirement that plaintiff tie his losses to the manipulation inevitably
means that there will be some correspondence between the plaintiff's
losses and the defendant's gains.[66]

[60] *Id.* at § 77k(g).

[61] *Id.* at § 77l(a)(2).

[62] Under certain circumstances, § 12(a) allows for recovery from persons who have
solicited on behalf of the seller. See Pinter v. Dahl, 486 U.S. 622 (1988).

[63] 15 U.S.C. § 78bb.

[64] See, e.g., Green v. Wolf Corp., 406 F.2d 291, 302–303 (2d Cir. 1968).

[65] 15 U.S.C. § 78i(e).

[66] There is little case law on this subject, as § 9(e) "has been virtually a dead letter
so far as producing recoveries is concerned." Louis Loss & Joel Seligman, Securities
Regulation 4279 (3rd Ed. 2004).

More illuminating are the two explicit causes of action allowing for recovery from insider traders. Neither cause of action requires reliance, but both limit damages to the benefit that the insider trader obtained from his violation. They are therefore modeled on unjust enrichment, and not the tort model of deceit. First, § 16(b) allows shareholders to bring derivative suits on behalf of the corporation to recover "short swing" gains made by insiders trading in the company's shares (that is, profits gained, or losses avoided, for "round trip" transactions—buy/sell or sell/buy—within six months of each other).[67] The remedy is limited to the defendant's benefit from the violation, in this case the profits the insider gained (or the losses he avoided) within the six-month period that defines the offense. Second, § 20A creates a private cause of action for insider trading, this time for conduct that violates § 10(b) because the insider has breached a duty of disclosure.[68] The provision allows investors who have traded contemporaneously with insiders to recover damages from those insider traders. Reliance is excused in such cases by *Affiliated Ute*, but damages once again are limited to "the profit gained or loss avoided in the transaction."[69] Moreover, even that measure is reduced by any disgorgement obtained by the SEC based on the same violations. Thus, where the Exchange Act excuses reliance, recovery is limited to the defendant's gain, not the plaintiff's loss.

Completing our survey of the explicit causes of action in the principal securities laws, § 18 of the Exchange Act comes closest to the Rule 10b-5 FOTM class action. Section 18 allows investors who have relied on a corporation's filings with the SEC to recover damages for misstatements in those filings.[70] Section 18 does not limit damages, thus standing in sharp contrast to the other causes of action. It is also unique in requiring that a plaintiff demonstrate that he purchased or sold "in reliance upon" the misstatement in

[67] 15 U.S.C. § 78p(b).

[68] 15 U.S.C. § 78t-1. This provision was added to the Exchange Act as an amendment in 1988. Insider Trading and Securities Fraud Enforcement Act of 1988, Pub.L. No. 100-704, § 5 (1988).

[69] 15 U.S.C. § 78t-1(b)(1).

[70] *Id.* § 78r.

the company's filings with the SEC.[71] Damages are limited to the "damages caused by such reliance," an implicit recognition by the 1934 Congress of the connection between reliance and the social costs of fraud. Section 18 is best understood as a statutory expansion of the tort cause of action for deceit, premised on the assumption that SEC filings are in reality communications directed toward shareholders. Shareholders who rely on them have invested in information and should be compensated if the communications are false or misleading.

The basic principle that emerges from these explicit causes of action is that damages should be limited to some measure of the defendant's benefit (the disgorgement measure of unjust enrichment), unless the plaintiff can show actual reliance on the misstatement, in which case the out-of-pocket measure from the action for deceit is appropriate.[72] The choices made by Congress in these explicit causes of action are consistent with my argument in Part II that the damages measure currently used in FOTM actions is simply too large because the damages available do not track the social costs of secondary-market fraud. If we limit § 10(b) damages in the way the explicit securities causes of action do, only those plaintiffs who can show actual reliance would be entitled to recover the "out of pocket," compensatory measure of losses, assuming that they can show that the losses were proximately caused by the defendant's misstatement. This follows the pattern of § 18, but that does not render the Rule 10b-5 cause of action redundant. Rather than being limited to misstatements in SEC filings, plaintiffs could also recover if they relied on press releases or statements by company officers. Such plaintiffs are investing in information; if we believe that their investments are worthwhile, we need to compensate those plaintiffs when their reliance has been fraudulently manipulated.[73]

---

[71] *Id.* § 78r(a). Section 18 further stands out in allowing the court to assess reasonable attorneys' fees against the losing party, which no doubt goes a long way toward explaining the provision's disuse.

[72] The Court noted the actual reliance requirement of § 18 in *Basic*, 485 U.S. at 243, but essentially ignored it.

[73] Mahoney, *supra* note 18, at 632 (arguing that wealth transfer can serve as a proxy for investment in lying, precaution costs and allocative losses where fraud results in transfer from victim to fraudster).

For plaintiffs who cannot make a showing of actual reliance (the passive price takers), a disgorgement rule would bring about a substantial departure from current practice.[74] Under the current "out of pocket" rule, corporations are liable for all losses resulting from public misstatements by their agents. If we limited the remedy for Rule 10b-5 to a benefits rule when the plaintiffs could not demonstrate actual reliance, we would force defendants to disgorge their gains (or possibly expected gains, for those who fail in their scheme) from the fraud. So if a corporation were issuing securities while distorting the market price of its stock, it would be required to disgorge to investors the amount by which it inflated the price of the securities.

In most FOTM cases, however, the corporation has not benefited from the misrepresentation that is the basis of the class action. Indeed, the corporation is usually the victim of the fraud. The corporation is victimized when executives are awarded a bonus that is undeserved because they create the appearance of having met the target stock price. The corporation is also victimized when CEOs keep their job for a bit longer than they should because they create the appearance of adequate performance.[75] The proper remedy in such cases is for the executives to return the bonus or salary earned from the fraud. And if the executives benefit from the fraud by cashing out stock options at an inflated price, those profits also can be disgorged.

Reformulating damages under Rule 10b-5 to focus on disgorgement will sharpen the deterrent effect of securities class actions. The "out of pocket" measure of damages currently used encourages plaintiffs' lawyers to pursue the wrong party—the corporation. The current regime for secondary-market class actions largely produces an exercise in "pocket shifting."[76]

---

[74] I have previously proposed such a move in Should Congress Repeal Securities Class Action Reform? Cato Policy Analysis No. 471 (2003), reprinted in After Enron: Lessons for Public Policy (William A. Niskanen, ed., 2004).

[75] Jennifer H. Arlen & William J. Carney, Vicarious Liability for Fraud on Securities Markets: Theory and Evidence, 1992 U. Ill. L. Rev. 691.

[76] Janet Cooper Alexander, Rethinking Damages in Securities Class Actions, 48 Stan. L. Rev. 1487, 1503 (1996) ("Payments by the corporation to settle a class action amount to transferring money from one pocket to the other, with about half of it dropping on the floor for lawyers to pick up.").

Traditionally, class action settlements have not included a contribution from corporate officers individually. Plaintiffs' lawyers forgo that source of recovery because they can reach a settlement much more quickly if they do not insist on a contribution from the individual defendants. The only reason that officers and directors are named is to improve the plaintiffs' lawyers' bargaining position. The big money for plaintiffs' attorneys is in pursuing the corporation and its insurers, and the officers and directors are happy to buy peace for themselves with the corporation's money. The dirty secret of securities class actions is that companies and their insurers pay the costs of settlement, which effectively means that shareholders are paying the costs of settlements to shareholders.[77] Settlement payments and insurance premiums reduce the cash flow available for dividends and share repurchases.

A disgorgement measure of damages would take away the corporation's exposure when it did not benefit from the fraud, thereby increasing the attorneys' incentive to pursue the executives responsible for the fraud. Instead of relying on the corporation's coffers for their payday, plaintiffs' lawyers would have to extract settlements from executives' bonuses and stock options. Deterrence is maximized by sanctioning the person who is most at fault for the fraud, so turning the sights of the class action bar on the culpable individuals would give us substantially more deterrent bang for our class action buck. And reducing the potential dollar figures involved would eliminate the ability of plaintiffs' lawyers to extract nuisance settlements in weak cases. If defendants believe they can prevail at trial, a small probability of losing an enormous judgment will no longer tip the balance in favor of settlement. We can expect more cases would be tried to a jury, which would give us a much better picture of what Rule 10b-5 actually prohibits. As it stands now, we are mainly making informed guesses based on judicial resolution of motions to dismiss, which apply a standard much more generous to the plaintiffs.

---

[77] See Arlen & Carney, *supra* note 75, at 719 ("Although compensating victims may be a laudable goal, enterprise liability does not serve the goal of just compensation because it simply replaces one group of innocent victims with another: those who were shareholders when the fraud was revealed. Moreover, enterprise liability does not even effect a one-to-one transfer between innocent victims: a large percentage of the plaintiffs' recovery goes to their lawyers.").

## V. The Political Economy of Securities Class Action Reform

The answer to the problem created by *Basic* is straightforward—fix the damages measure. Getting to that answer in the real world, however, is considerably more complicated. How can we shift from deceit to unjust enrichment, thereby recalibrating the damages rule for § 10(b) suits to focus on deterrence? Which body—the Supreme Court, Congress, the SEC, or shareholders acting collectively—is most likely to bring about the needed reform?[78]

### A. The Supreme Court?

The Court does not hear a lot of securities cases, averaging about one case per year. The Court's wariness here is not surprising, given the dearth of prior experience that the current justices have in the field. The members of the Court are all former government officials, academics, appellate advocates, etc. Simply put, they are not equipped to confront the highly technical field of securities law. It has been more than 20 years since the last justice with substantial experience as a corporate lawyer—Lewis F. Powell, Jr.—retired from the Court.[79]

Unfortunately, Powell retired before *Basic* was decided (though one of his last votes to grant certiorari in a securities case was *Basic Inc.* v. *Levinson*). The Court's efforts since his departure do not instill confidence; its forays into this area have been occasionally impenetrable[80] and sometimes bizarre.[81] The Court is at its most coherent when it simply regurgitates the SEC's party line.[82] In sum, the Court

---

[78] I have previously made a similar proposal for reforming securities fraud enforcement, suggesting that it could be implemented through the exchanges. See A. C. Pritchard, Markets as Monitors: A Proposal to Replace Class Actions with Exchanges as Securities Fraud Enforcers, 85 Va. L. Rev. 925 (1999). The exchanges have not taken me up on the suggestion.

[79] The full story of Powell's influence is detailed in my article, Justice Lewis F. Powell, Jr. and the Counter-Revolution in the Federal Securities Laws, 52 DUKE L.J. 841 (2003).

[80] See Virginia Bankshares, Inc. v. Sandberg, 501 U.S. 1083, 1109 (1991) (Scalia, J., concurring) (describing the Court's opinion as a "psychic thicket").

[81] See, e.g., Gustafson v. Alloyd Co., 513 U.S. 561 (1995); see also Hillary A. Sale, Disappearing Without a Trace: Sections 11 and 12(a)(2) of the 1933 Securities Act, 75 Wash. L. Rev. 429, 456 (2000) (criticizing *Gustafson*).

[82] See, e.g., Dura Pharmaceuticals, Inc. v. Broudo, 544 U.S. 336 (2005).

is essentially rudderless when it ventures into the deep waters of securities regulation.[83]

Looking at the question of reliance, it is difficult to extract any consistent guiding principle from *Affiliated Ute*, *Basic*, *Central Bank*, and *Stoneridge*. Justice Stevens, dissenting in *Stoneridge* (as he had in *Central Bank*), hammered on this point:

> *Basic* is surely a sufficient response to the argument that a complaint alleging that deceptive acts which had a material effect on the price of a listed stock should be dismissed because the plaintiffs were not subjectively aware of the deception at the time of the securities' purchase or sale. This Court has not held that investors must be aware of the specific deceptive act which violates § 10(b) to demonstrate reliance. . . .
>
> The fraud-on-the-market presumption helps investors who cannot demonstrate that they, themselves, relied on fraud that reached the market. But that presumption says nothing about causation from the other side: what an individual or corporation must do in order to have "caused" the misleading information that reached the market. The Court thus has it backwards when it first addresses the fraud-on-the-market presumption, rather than the causation required.[84]

It is fair to say that Justice Blackmun, who wrote *Affiliated Ute* and *Basic*, would have reached a different outcome in *Stoneridge*. As Blackmun noted in his memo to the file after reviewing the *Affiliated Ute* briefs, "I feel we should plump for a high standard in this area, and that this is in line with the intent of Congress in enacting the legislation."[85] Blackmun set a "high standard" in *Affiliated Ute* and *Basic*; Kennedy ratcheted it down in *Central Bank* and *Stoneridge*.

The point is not that one side or the other is correct in their divining of congressional intent. That quest seems futile. Rule 10b-5's reliance element is nowhere to be found in the language of § 10(b)

---

[83] See Donald C. Langevoort, Words from on High About Rule 10b-5: *Chiarella's* History, *Central Bank's* Future, 20 Del. J. Corp. L. 865, 868 (1995) ("[S]cholars and learned practitioners are giving the Court's securities law opinions low grades for logic, clarity, and usefulness in future cases.").

[84] Stoneridge, 128 S.Ct. at 776 (Stevens, J., dissenting).

[85] Harry A. Blackmun, Memo, No. 70-78—Affiliated Ute Citizens v. United States (10/18/71), Harry A. Blackmun Papers, Library of Congress.

or Rule 10b-5; the Court borrowed it from the common law of deceit. But the Court does not refer to the common law when it is interpreting the reliance requirement for the Rule 10b-5 private cause of action. In *Stoneridge*, Kennedy brusquely rejected the argument that the plaintiffs had adequately pled reliance under common law standards: "Even if the assumption is correct, it is not controlling. Section 10(b) does not incorporate common-law fraud into federal law."[86] It would seem more accurate to say that the incorporation is selective: The Court borrows the common law element of reliance, without really explaining why, but then disregards it when inconvenient, as it did in adopting the FOTM theory in *Basic* and Kennedy's rejection of common law standards in *Stoneridge*. The Court treats the reliance element as a do-it-all tool to implement its policy choices of the moment, without fully understanding the implications of those choices. It is charting its own common law course but its interventions are episodic; the Court takes an insufficient number of securities cases to develop this "common law" in any meaningful manner.

The interpretive approach of *Central Bank* purports to depart from the common law interpretation that typified Rule 10b-5 for many years. Cases like *Affiliated Ute* and *Basic* focused on assuring recovery for the plaintiffs, with little regard for the costs created by private litigation. Generally, the Court used a common law, policy-oriented approach when it was expanding Rule 10b-5, viewing the private cause of action as an "essential supplement" to the SEC's enforcement efforts.[87] *Central Bank* promised a textual, formalist approach when the Court turned to reining in the reach of the private cause of action. *Stoneridge*, with its return to a fuzzy "requisite causal connection" notion of reliance,[88] fails to deliver on that promise, instead returning to an essentially common law mode of decision-making. The opinion does little more than tell us that the defendants' conduct was "too remote" for plaintiffs to rely on.[89] The bottom line is that both factions of the Court manipulate the reliance element to achieve their preferred scope for the securities fraud cause of action.

---

[86] Stoneridge, 128 S.Ct. at 771.

[87] Tellabs, Inc. v. Makor Issues & Rights, Ltd., 127 S. Ct. 2499, 2504 (2007).

[88] Stoneridge, 128 S.Ct. at 769 (quoting Basic, 485 U.S. at 243).

[89] *Id.* at 770.

Moreover, the Court has offered scant guidance on Rule 10b-5 damages, addressing the issue only twice. The first time was in *Affiliated Ute*, which applied the out-of-pocket measure in the context of a face-to-face transaction involving fraudulent nondisclosure in breach of fiduciary duty. The Court said this about damages:

> In our view, the correct measure of damages under § 28 of the Act is the difference between the fair value of all that the . . . seller received and the fair value of what he would have received had there been no fraudulent conduct, except for the situation where the defendant received more than the seller's actual loss. In the latter case, damages are the amount of the defendant's profit.[90]

In this face-to-face transaction, the Court invokes both the out-of-pocket measure and unjust enrichment. The Court's only opportunity to consider the appropriate measure of damages in a case in which the defendant did not benefit because it was not a party to the transaction (the standard scenario in FOTM class actions) was *Basic* itself, and there, as I have noted, the Court passed on the question.[91] And the Court is unlikely to ever have an opportunity to consider the damages question because companies almost invariably settle rather than risk bankruptcy.

In Part IV I argued that what was required was a fundamental rethinking of the relationship between reliance and damages. We do not know what the Court thinks about damages in FOTM cases, but it appears oblivious to the connection between precaution costs and reliance. The Court's other recent forays into securities fraud class actions have been reactions to Congress's activity in the area, generally involving interpretive questions arising under the PSLRA.[92] The Court has made it clear that it intends to defer to Congress in this area: "It is the federal lawmaker's prerogative . . . to allow, disallow, or shape the contours of—including the pleading and proof requirements for—§ 10(b) private actions."[93] Thus, we

---

[90] Affiliated Ute, 406 U.S. at 155.

[91] See *supra*, note 15 and accompanying text. The Court's other foray into Rule 10b-5 damages focuses on the need to deprive the defendant of his benefit from the fraud. Randall v. Loftsgaarden, 478 U.S. 647 (1986).

[92] See, e.g., Dura Pharmaceuticals, 544 U.S. 336; Tellabs, 127 S. Ct. 2499.

[93] Tellabs, 127 S. Ct. at 2512.

should not expect the Court to be anything more than a passive observer here, looking to Congress to take any bold step toward reform.

## B. Congress?

Is it realistic to expect Congress to take such a step? Probably not. Congress had its opportunity to tackle the relation between reliance and damages at a moment in time when there was tremendous momentum for reform of securities class actions—and it ducked.

In 1995, Congress reacted to the flood of securities class actions that *Basic* spawned. Accountants and the high-tech sector clamored for relief from the "stock price drop" suits that were besetting them; money flowed into campaign coffers from these proponents, as well as from the opposition (plaintiffs' lawyers). High on the wish list of reforms was a reversal of *Basic*. The House of Representatives considered sweeping changes to securities class actions in the Common Sense Legal Reforms Act of 1995.[94] As originally introduced, that bill would have eliminated the FOTM presumption. The SEC opposed the provision,[95] however, and it was abandoned in favor of a codification of the doctrine that would have set forth more clearly when the presumption would apply.[96] By the time the bill came out of conference as the PSLRA, even this codification of the FOTM presumption had been abandoned.[97]

Instead of changing the FOTM presumption and out-of-pocket damages formula that create the economic incentive to bring strike suits, Congress chose to erect a series of procedural barriers to make them harder to pursue.[98] The effect of these restrictions has been to

[94] H.R. 10, 104th Cong., 1st Sess. (1995). A complete account of the legislative history of the PSLRA can be found in John W. Avery, Securities Litigation Reform: The Long and Winding Road to the Private Securities Litigation Reform Act of 1995, 51 Bus. Law. 335 (1996).

[95] Testimony of Chairman Arthur Levitt Concerning Litigation Reform Proposals Before the House Subcommittee on Telecommunications and Finance, Committee on Commerce, February 10, 1995 (available at http://www.sec.gov/news/testimony/testarchive/1995/spch025.txt).

[96] H.R. 10, 104th Cong., 1st Sess. (1995), reprinted in H.R. Rep. No. 104-50, 104th Cong., 1st Sess., pt. 1, at 2 (1995).

[97] H.R. Rep. No. 104-369, 104th Cong., 1st Sess. (1995).

[98] For a discussion of these provisions, see Marilyn F. Johnson, Karen K. Nelson, & A.C. Pritchard, Do the Merits Matter More? The Impact of the Private Securities Litigation Reform Act, 23 J. L. Econ. & Org. 627 (2007).

force plaintiffs to focus on objective evidence—such as restatements, insider trading, and SEC enforcement actions—as the basis for bringing suit.[99] This means that securities class actions are now brought when the evidence of fraud is relatively obvious. And not surprisingly, cases continue to be brought when the damages calculation is greatest, with large stock price drops and heavy trading.[100] This means that the companies punished hardest by the market are also the ones that are most likely to face a class action. If securities class actions are a "necessary supplement" to SEC enforcement,[101] Congress's reforms have ensured that the supplement is directed where it is least needed.

Why did Congress back away from undoing *Basic*'s FOTM presumption? One answer is that the original House bill offered nothing in its place. Requiring plaintiffs to plead actual reliance largely eliminates class actions, leaving fraud deterrence exclusively in the hands of the SEC and the Justice Department. Another reason may be that eliminating compensation is a political non-starter. The "pocket shifting" element of secondary-market class actions has been well known for a long time, but it does not seem to have influenced legislative thinking. Congress's latest contribution on the subject came in the Sarbanes-Oxley Act in 2002, which includes a provision requiring the SEC to use recoveries from its enforcement actions to compensate investors.[102] Providing compensation to widows and orphans sells well on the campaign trail, even if the widows and orphans can protect themselves against the risk of fraud through portfolio diversification. Compensating defrauded investors takes some of the sting out of putting all of their eggs in one basket, hardly the investment strategy that our public policy should promote. Never let it be said that Congress does not look out for the financially reckless!

[99] Stephen J. Choi, Karen K. Nelson, & A.C. Pritchard, The Screening Effect of the Private Securities Litigation Reform Act, 6 J. Empirical. Leg. Stud. _____ _____ (forthcoming, 2009).

[100] Johnson et al., *supra* note 98.

[101] Bateman Eichler, Hill Richards, Inc. v. Berner, 472 U.S. 299, 310 (1985).

[102] 15 U.S.C. § 7246(a). Under that provision, the SEC has collected at least $8 billion for distribution to harmed investors since 2002. See 2006 Performance and Accountability Report, U.S. Securities and Exchange Commission (available at http://www.sec.gov/about/secpar/secpar2006.pdf).

## C. The SEC?

As noted above, the SEC opposed eliminating the FOTM presumption when Congress considered that move back in 1995. Is there any reason to think that the SEC's views have changed in the intervening years? Not really. The SEC consistently sides with the plaintiffs' bar in its amicus role,[103] and even minor deviations from that role bring a firestorm of criticism from the plaintiffs' bar and its allies.[104] The SEC's support for the plaintiffs' bar in part reflects its own institutional interests. The agency favors broad interpretations of its governing statutes; as we saw in *Stoneridge*, a narrow interpretation of § 10(b) could reduce the SEC's enforcement discretion. The SEC's commitment to the plaintiffs' bar goes beyond that interest, however, because it sides with the plaintiffs' bar even on issues that relate purely to the terms of the implied Rule 10b-5 cause of action, such as the reliance issue in *Basic*. This commitment can be ascribed only to ideology, as the agency staff views its investor protection role broadly and sees plaintiffs' lawyers as allies in that fight.

The staff's affinity for the plaintiffs' bar only rarely meets any resistance from the commissioners. The SEC has consistently supported the FOTM presumption, beginning in *Basic* and continuing to the present day.[105] The majority of the commissioners wanted to file a brief siding with the plaintiffs in *Stoneridge*,[106] but the agency

[103] And has for a long time. See Pritchard, *supra* note 78 at 923 (quoting Lewis Powell complaining that "SEC usually favors *all* π. I can't recall a case in which this was not so.")

[104] See, e.g., Stephen Labaton, S.E.C. Seeks to Curtail Investor Suits, N.Y. Times, Feb. 13, 2007, at C1; Stephen Labaton, Is the S.E.C. Changing Course? N.Y. Times, March 1, 2007, at C1. Labaton is the son of a prominent plaintiffs' lawyer, Ed Labaton.

[105] Brief of the Securities and Exchange Commission, Amicus Curiae, In re Worldcom Securities Litigation, 2nd Cir. 03-9350 (April 2004) (available at http://www.sec.gov/litigation/briefs/wchevesi_amicus.htm#summaflowry) (noting SEC's support for FOTM presumption in *Basic* and arguing for application of presumption to reports by securities analysts). See also Donald C. Langevoort, *Basic* at Twenty: Rethinking Fraud-on-the-Market, Working Paper, Georgetown University Law Center (2008) ("[T]he *Basic* opinion was for all practical purposes authored by the SEC and the Solicitor General's Office. The key arguments, analysis, quotes and citations that one finds in the Courts' holdings on both materiality and reliance come directly out of the *amicus curiae* brief filed on behalf of the SEC.").

[106] The vote was 3-2. See Paul Atkins, Just Say 'No'' to the Trial Lawyers, Wall St. J., Oct. 9, 2007, at A17. Chairman Christopher Cox voted with the majority, despite having introduced the bill that in 1995 that would have reversed *Basic*. Joel Seligman, The Transformation of Wall Street 663–64 (3d Ed. 2003). The SEC had filed a brief

was overruled by the Solicitor General, who sided with the defendants.[107] The SEC has the authority to make the necessary changes to Rule 10b-5,[108] but it is unrealistic to expect reform to come from that quarter.

## D. Shareholders?

That brings us to our last, best hope for reforming securities fraud class actions: shareholders. Shareholders have the right incentives for evaluating reforms because they are forced to internalize both the benefits and the costs of securities class actions. Shareholders benefit from securities class actions if those suits generate deterrence. Deterrence promotes accurate share prices and thereby reduces the cost of participation in the securities markets. These benefits flow to corporations as well because they translate into a lower cost of capital. Shareholders (at least some of them) are also the beneficiaries of the compensation paid out in securities class actions, modest though it may be. On the other side of the equation, all shareholders ultimately bear the costs of securities fraud class actions, which include the payment of attorneys' fees on both sides of the litigation, the cost of experts, and the distraction costs to executives arising from defending the lawsuit. Directors and officers (D&O) insurance will cover some of these costs, but the premiums to secure that insurance are ultimately paid by the shareholders. Less tangible, but perhaps more substantial, are costs firms incur to avoid being sued: more money spent on lawyers' fees for flyspecking disclosure documents, higher auditors' fees, new projects that are rejected because of the risk of suit, and less forthcoming disclosure. These costs are

---

in a Ninth Circuit case raising similar issues arguing that ""[t]he reliance requirement is satisfied where a plaintiff relies on a material deception flowing from a defendant's deceptive act, even though the conduct of other participants in the fraudulent scheme may have been a subsequent link in the causal chain leading to the plaintiff's securities transaction." SEC Reply Br. at 12, Simpson v. AOL Time Warner, Inc., No. 04-55665 (Feb. 7, 2005) (available at http://www.sec.gov/litigation/briefs/homestore_020405.pdf).

[107] Brief for the United States as Amicus Curiae Supporting Affirmance, 2007 WL 2327639 (August 15, 2007). The government's argument was essentially adopted by the Court, as it frequently has been in securities cases since Powell retired.

[108] 15 U.S.C. § 78mm (granting the SEC broad exemptive authority); Joseph Grundfest, Disimplying Private Rights of Action under the Federal Securities Laws: The Commission's Authority, 107 Harv. L. Rev. 961 (1994); John C. Coffee, Jr., Reforming the Securities Class Action: An Essay on Deterrence and its Implementation, 106 Columbia L. Rev. 1534, 1582–83 (2006).

not covered by insurance. How does the balance tip between these benefits and costs? Perhaps shareholders should be allowed to weigh for themselves.[109]

My suggestion is that shareholders change the damage measure in Rule 10b-5 securities fraud class actions involving the company, its officers, and directors, to focus on deterrence rather than compensation. Specifically, shareholders could adopt an unjust enrichment model by making a partial waiver of the FOTM presumption of reliance in the corporation's articles of incorporation.[110] The waiver would stipulate to a disgorgement measure of damages, requiring violators to give up the benefits of the fraud, if the FOTM presumption were invoked in a securities class action. This partial waiver would not limit shareholder-plaintiffs who could plead actual reliance on a misstatement; they could still seek the tort out-of-pocket measure of damages. Thus, in an FOTM suit, the company itself would be liable only when making an offering or repurchasing shares. It would be liable only for out-of-pocket compensation to plaintiffs who actually relied to their detriment.[111] Executives who violated Rule 10b-5 would be liable to repay their compensation tied to the stock price (bonuses, stock, and options) during the time that price was fraudulently manipulated; here the FOTM presumption could be invoked.[112]

---

[109] See Marilyn F. Johnson, Karen K. Nelson, & A.C. Pritchard, *In re Silicon Graphics Inc.*: Shareholder Wealth Effects Resulting from the Interpretation of the Private Securities Litigation Reform Act's Pleading Standard, 73 S. Cal. L. Rev. 773 (2000) (arguing that shareholder wealth effects are relevant to design of securities class action regime).

[110] Cf. Myriam Gilles, Opting Out of Liability: The Forthcoming, Near-Total Demise of the Modern Class Action, 104 Mich. L. Rev. 373, 424 (2005) (suggesting that companies might opt out of securities class actions through their corporate charters).

[111] Cf. Donald C. Langevoort, On Leaving Corporate Executives "Naked, Homeless and Without Wheels": Corporate Fraud, Equitable Reemdies, and Debate Over Entity Versus Individual Liability, 42 Wake Forest L. Rev. 627, 656–657 (2007) (offering similar suggestion).

[112] Such cases would likely implicate the executives' duty of loyalty under state corporate law. Under state corporate law, the cause of action would be derivative, rather than direct, so the recovery would properly go to the corporation, rather than the shareholder members of the class. It is clear, however, that the federal cause of action would be direct under Rule 10b-5 because plaintiffs must have been a purchaser or seller to have standing per *Blue Chip Stamps v. Manor Drug Stores*, 421 U.S. 723 (1975), so the disgorgement could be paid to the shareholders who purchased during the class period. For an argument that Rule 10b-5 actions should be treated as deriva-

Obviously, the damages paid under a disgorgement measure are unlikely to afford full compensation, but settlements currently compensate for only a small percentage of investor losses. More fundamentally, compensation is not the cure for securities fraud in the secondary market; diversification is. The goal of securities fraud class actions should be that of unjust enrichment: deterrence. The purpose of the FOTM version of the Rule 10b-5 cause of action should be to deprive wrongdoers of the benefits they obtained by violating Rule 10b-5.

This goal is well served by my proposal, which focuses sanctions on actual wrongdoers, unlike the current regime. In addition, the requirements for invoking the FOTM presumption could be relaxed. If we are focused on defendants' gains from the fraud, rather than shareholders' losses, the informational efficiency of the market for the security is unimportant. Under the current regime, smaller companies largely get a free pass from securities class actions because the market for their shares is not efficient enough to invoke the FOTM presumption. Relaxing the FOTM standards would widen the range of companies that could be sued in a Rule 10b-5 action— a clear gain for deterrence.

The main objection to this proposal is that it reduces the incentive to bring suit. The argument would be that if plaintiffs' lawyers cannot expect a payday in the hundreds of millions of dollars, they cannot be expected to sue. Deterrence would suffer as a result. One answer to this objection is that the average settlement is not the billion dollar payday that attracts big publicity, but much smaller, and suits nonetheless get filed. According to a leading economic consulting firm, the average settlement was $13.5 million from 1996 to 2001 and $23.6 million from 2002 to 2007.[113] More modest still are median settlements; the median settlement was $4.7 million from 1996 to 2001 and $6.4 million from 2002 to 2007.[114] These figures suggest that the lure of relatively modest settlements is sufficient incentive to bring suit in a substantial number of cases. Moreover,

tive suits, see Richard A. Booth, The End of the Securities Fraud Class Action as We Know It, 4 Berkeley Bus. L.J. 1 (2007).

[113] NERA Economic Consulting, "Recent Trends in Shareholder Class Action Litigation: Filings Stay Low and Average Settlements Stay High—But Are These Trends Reversing?" (September 2007).

[114] *Id.*

they are not grossly out of line with typical compensation packages for CEOs these days.[115] And litigation would be less expensive if the remedy sought were disgorgement because some very expert-intensive issues, such as loss causation, would drop out, and others, such as damages, would become much simpler to calculate.

Remember, too, that out-of-pocket damages would be available to plaintiffs who could show actual reliance. Those plaintiffs are likely to be institutional investors, who may have substantial losses in a given security that is affected by fraud. Those individual actions could be consolidated with the main proceeding for disgorgement, thus economizing on discovery costs and streamlining adjudication.

The incentive to bring suit can be bolstered, however, if shareholders deem it necessary. Rather than simply having the court award attorneys' fees based on a percentage of recovery (the "common fund" doctrine currently employed), the corporation could commit to paying an hourly fee to attorneys who succeed in bringing securities claims against the corporation, its officers, or directors. The fee could be subject to a review for reasonableness by a judge or arbitrator, and perhaps include a multiplier to reflect the risk of suit. This one-way fee shifting would effectively allow the corporation to pay the plaintiffs' bar to monitor for fraud. It is surely within the corporation's power to pay for that valuable service, and those attorneys' fees could be covered by the company's D&O insurance.

Any judgments obtained by the plaintiffs' lawyers, however, are unlikely to be covered by the company's D&O policy because such policies typically exclude coverage when there has been a finding of fraud or self-dealing. A Rule 10b-5 suit seeking disgorgement involves both. Indemnification by the corporation would also be barred in the event of a judgment because indemnification requires a finding of "good faith,"[116] which is hard to square with the finding of fraudulent intent needed to establish liability under § 10(b).[117]

---

[115] This relatively low median has two obvious implications for the current regime: First, most suits are settling for a small percentage of investor losses; and second, half of the suits are settling for essentially nuisance value. If a suit has gotten past a motion to dismiss, it is unlikely that it could be defended for less than $6.4 million dollars.

[116] Del. Gen. Corp. L. § 145(a).

[117] Ernst & Ernst v. Hochfelder, 425 U.S. 185, 193 (1976). See also Coffee, *supra* note 108, at 1567–68 (collecting cases holding that securities law liabilities cannot be indemnified).

A settlement avoids an adjudication that the officer or director acted with fraudulent intent, but it would not entitle the officer or director to automatic indemnification; the board of the company would still need to make a finding of good faith.[118] If the settlement were not covered by D&O insurance, a requirement of a finding of good faith would require a close look from the company's board of directors if it chose to indemnify an officer. Under the current regime, the corporation is typically a party to the lawsuit, so it is easy to justify a settlement as avoiding the risk of catastrophic liability to the corporation. Under a disgorgement regime, plaintiffs' lawyers will be less likely to sue the corporation because of the difficulty of showing the requisite benefit to the corporation from the fraud.

Can shareholders do this? Do legal barriers prevent shareholder-led reform of securities fraud class actions? We can test this.[119] Under Exchange Act Rule 14a-8, shareholders can make proposals to be included in the company's proxy statement, including suggestions that the directors amend the articles of incorporation.[120] The rule allows companies to exclude shareholder proposals for a variety of reasons, but they must submit their rationale for exclusion to the SEC for review.[121] If the SEC agrees with the company, the agency issues a "no action" letter allowing the proposal to be excluded. A proposal recommending that the directors amend the articles would be excludable only if it "would, if implemented, cause the company to violate any state, federal, or foreign law to which it is subject."[122]

Does the proposal violate state law? Unlikely. Delaware affords corporations broad latitude to include provisions in their articles of

---

[118] See Waltuch v. Conticommodity Services, Inc., 88 F.3d 87 (2d Cir. 1995) (construing Del. Gen. Corp. L. § 145(c) to require automatic indemnification only when the officer or director has avoided making a settlement payment). Jack Coffee has proposed requiring the corporation to disclose how they arrived at the determination that an officer should be indemnified. See Coffee, *supra* note 108, at 1576.

[119] The suggestion here applies to companies that are already public. Companies that are not yet public could include such a provision in their charter before making their initial public offering.

[120] Exchange Act Rule 14a-8. Any amendment approved by the board would also have to be approved by the shareholders. Del. G. Corp. L. § 241.

[121] Exchange Act Rule 14a-8(j).

[122] Exchange Act Rule 14a-8(i)(2). Rule 14a-8 provides other bases for exclusion, but none apply to the proposal here.

incorporation "creating, defining, limiting and regulating the powers of the corporation, the directors, and the stockholders . . . if such provisions are not contrary to the laws of this State."[123] This language has been read to authorize provisions unless they can be said to "clash[] with fundamental policy priorities that clearly emerge from the Delaware General Corporation Law or our common law of corporations."[124] No such priorities are apparent in Delaware corporate law.[125] Delaware generally views anti-reliance clauses as enforceable as a matter of contract law.[126] Corporations adopting the proposal will need to highlight the provision in their periodic SEC filings to maximize the likelihood that a court will apply the reliance waiver. If they do so, state law is unlikely to block the adoption of the disgorgement proposal.

The more substantial argument would be that the proposal violates federal law because it runs foul of § 29 of the Exchange Act, which voids "[a]ny condition, stipulation, or provision binding any person to waive compliance with any provision of this title or of any rule or regulation thereunder." Read broadly, § 29 would bar any provision affecting a right created by the Exchange Act. And written broadly, an anti-reliance provision could arguably waive compliance with § 10(b) (although SEC and criminal enforcement would still be available).[127] The Supreme Court has not addressed

---

[123] Del. Gen. Corp. L. § 102(b)(1).

[124] Jones Apparel Group, Inc. v. Maxwell Shoe Co., Inc., 883 A.2d 837, 843 (Del. Ch. 2004).

[125] Del. Gen. Corp. L. § 102(b)(7), which allows corporations to exempt their directors from paying money damages for breaches of the duty of care, would not apply to the disgorgement proposal because the provision is limited to breaches of fiduciary duty.

[126] See MBIA Insurance Corp. v. Royal Indemnity Co., 426 F.3d 204, 218 (3rd Cir. 2005) ("When sophisticated parties include a broad but unambiguous anti-reliance clause in their agreement, the Delaware Supreme Court will likely indulge the assumption that they said what they meant and meant what they said."). Cf. In re Appraisal of Ford Holdings, Inc. Preferred Stock, 698 A.2d 973, 974 (Del. Ch. 1997) (certificate can stipulate fair value of preferred stock for appraisal under § 262).

[127] Reliance waivers have received mixed treatment in the courts. Compare AES Corp. v. The Dow Chemical Co., 325 F.3d 174, 182 (2003) ("[T]o hold that a buyer is barred from relief under Rule 10b-5 solely by virtue of his contractual commitment not to rely would be fundamentally inconsistent with Section 29(a)."); Caiola v. Citibank, N.A., 295 F.3d 312, 330 (2d Cir. 2002) ("A disclaimer [of reliance] is generally enforceable only if it tracks the substance of the alleged misrepresentation.") (citations and internal quotations omitted); Rogen v. Ilikon Corp., 361 F.2d 260, 268 (1st Cir. 1966) ("Were we to hold that the existence of this provision constituted the basis (or

waiver of reliance clauses; it has only interpreted § 29 in connection with mandatory arbitration clauses. After initially concluding that arbitration provisions conflicted with the anti-waiver provisions in the securities law,[128] the Court reversed course, concluding that forum selection clauses[129] and arbitration provisions[130] were enforceable.

In response to the claim that arbitration amounted to a waiver of the Exchange Act's conferral of "exclusive jurisdiction" to the federal courts in § 27, the Court declined to read § 29 so broadly:

> § 29(a) forbids . . . enforcement of agreements to waive "compliance" with the provision of the statute. But § 27 itself does not impose any duty with which persons trading in securities must "comply." By its terms, § 29(a) only prohibits waiver of the substantive obligations imposed by the Exchange Act. Because § 27 does not impose any statutory duties, its waiver does not constitute a waiver of "compliance with any provision" of the Exchange Act under § 29(a).[131]

The proposed amendment to the articles of incorporation does not excuse compliance with the anti-fraud provision—it simply alters the remedy available under certain circumstances. Indeed, by focusing on deterring the most culpable actors, the disgorgement proposal promises *greater* compliance with Rule 10b-5 without waiving claims based on actual reliance. Finally, it is difficult to see the FOTM presumption as a "substantive obligation[] imposed by the Exchange

---

a substantial part of the basis) for finding non-reliance as a matter of law, we would have gone far toward eviscerating Section 29(a)."); with Rissman v. Rissman, 213 F.3d 381, 384 (7th Cir. 2000) ("[A] written anti-reliance clause precludes any claim of deceit by prior representations."); Harsco Corp. v. Segui, 91 F.3d 337, 343–344 (2nd Cir. 1996) (upholding no reliance clause in contract between sophisticated commercial parties); One-O-One Enterprises, Inc., v. Caruso, 848 F.2d 1283 (D.C. Cir. 1988) (same).

[128] Wilko v. Swan, 346 U.S. 427 (1953) (construing § 14 of the Securities Act to bar arbitration).

[129] Scherk v. Alberto-Culver Co., 417 U.S. 506 (1974) (upholding arbitration clause in international contract between sophisticated parties).

[130] Shearson/American Express, Inc. v. McMahon, 482 U.S. 220 (1987) (Exchange Act claims arbitrable); Rodriguez de Quijas v. Shearson/American Express, Inc., 490 U.S. 477 (U.S. 1989) (overturning *Wilko* and holding arbitration clauses enforceable in Securities Act disputes).

[131] Shearson/American Express, 482 U.S. at 228.

Act." It is a procedural device, created by the courts, not Congress, intended to facilitate class actions.

Will shareholders vote for such a proposal? Interests will vary. All investors have an interest in deterrence; the proposed regime compares favorably with the current system on that ground. Interests will diverge, however, in compensation, which would be reduced under the proposed regime. The relatively low rate of participation in securities class action settlements suggests that shareholders as a class do not value compensation all that highly. Shareholders who are holders, trading infrequently, are likely to favor the proposal because they are typically on the paying end of litigation and settlement. Investors who index, whether individual or institutional, are likely to see things the same way as holders. Indexers have protected themselves against the firm-specific risk of fraud; they are unlikely to favor paying large premiums to lawyers for additional insurance that they do not need. The votes of institutional investors who actively pick stocks are harder to handicap. On the one hand, they are more likely to have been trading during a fraud period, so they are more likely to be members of an FOTM class.[132] On the other, the proposed regime would still allow such investors to pursue an individual or joint action if they have relied on a misstatement.

We will get prompt feedback if investors make the wrong assessment with their vote. If waiving the FOTM presumption of reliance undermines deterrence (or signals a management likely to commit fraud), we would expect to see a stock price drop for the firm that has adopted the amendment. That will be powerful evidence for opponents who think that the proposal is misguided, which they will no doubt raise if another company proposes such an amendment. My instinct is that the market reaction will be positive for companies that opt out. My greater worry is that managers will be reluctant to opt into a disgorgement regime because it arguably increases their personal exposure. Optimistically, one could argue that refusing to adopt the disgorgement regime here would signal that a management team felt it had something to hide. Implementing the regime may require the efforts of institutional investors to press this case

---

[132] Of course, these investors are also more likely to have gotten a windfall gain from the fraud if they sold during the period that the stock price was inflated. This would be true regardless of the regime, however, so it is unlikely to influence their votes on the proposal raised here.

and push outside directors to adopt the proposal over the managers' objections.

## VI. Conclusion

The Supreme Court has now been struggling for 20 years with the wrong turn it took in *Basic*. *Stoneridge*, like the Court's earlier reliance decisions in *Affiliated Ute*, *Basic*, and *Central Bank*, uses the reliance element to expand or contract the private cause of action under Rule 10b-5 based on no discernible principle. The FOTM regime established in *Basic* shifts money from one shareholder pocket to another at enormous expense. *Stoneridge* limits the adverse consequences of that regime, which does provide some benefit to shareholders. The decision is a step in the right direction, but it fails to grapple with the fundamental problem: Out-of-pocket damages should be tied to actual reliance. The appropriate model for reform is found in the explicit causes of action provided by Congress, which limit plaintiffs to rescission or disgorgement if they cannot plead reliance.

The disgorgement amendment to the articles of incorporation proposed here promises greater deterrence at a lower cost. The Court, Congress, and the SEC have all had the opportunity to fix the problem created by *Basic*, but none of these institutions has risen to the occasion. Shareholders bear the costs of the FOTM regime, and shareholders fortunately have the power to fix it. Will shareholders clean up the mess that the Supreme Court has created with securities class actions? Stay tuned.

# Federal Preemption at the Supreme Court

*Daniel E. Troy and Rebecca K. Wood**

## Introduction

It has been a striking time for federal preemption at the Supreme Court. This past term, the Court heard six preemption cases, deciding four in favor of federal preemption by large margins, one against preemption, and coming to a draw in the sixth case in which Chief Justice John Roberts did not participate.[1] In the coming term, the Court is poised to hear two additional significant preemption cases.[2]

*Daniel E. Troy is senior vice president and general counsel of GlaxoSmithKline. Until recently he was a partner in the Life Sciences and Appellate practices at Sidley Austin LLP, and before that was chief counsel of the Food and Drug Administration. Rebecca K. Wood is a partner in the Appellate and Products Liability practices at Sidley Austin LLP. The authors have represented the party or amicus curiae in each of the three cases involving federal preemption in the prescription drug and medical device contexts at the Supreme Court in the last year: *Warner-Lambert v. Kent*, *Riegel v. Medtronic, Inc.*, and *Wyeth v. Levine*. Sidley Austin LLP also filed amicus briefs in two other cases discussed in this article, *Exxon Shipping Co. v. Baker*, and *Rowe v. N.H. Motor Trans. Ass'n*. The authors would like to thank Carter G. Phillips and Eamon P. Joyce, their colleagues at Sidley Austin LLP, and Will Adams, a 2008 summer associate at Sidley Austin LLP and law student at Harvard Law School, for contributing to this article. The views expressed here are solely their own. A version of this article also will appear in *Engage: The Journal of the Federalist Society's Practice Groups*.

[1] See Table, *infra*. The pro-preemption decisions are: Chamber of Commerce v. Brown, 554 U.S. ___, 128 S. Ct. 2408 (2008); Preston v. Ferrer, 552 U.S. ___, 128 S. Ct. 978 (2008); Riegel v. Medtronic, Inc., 552 U.S. ___, 128 S. Ct. 999 (2008); and Rowe v. N.H. Motor Trans. Ass'n, 552 U.S. ___, 128 S. Ct. 989 (2008). The Court rejected preemption (in a somewhat different sense) in Exxon Shipping Co. v. Baker, 554 U.S. ___, 128 S. Ct. 2605 (2008), see note 68, *infra*, and divided 4-4 in Warner-Lambert v. Kent, 552 U.S. ___, 128 S. Ct. 1168 (2008) (per curiam), with the Chief Justice recusing. See note 72, *infra*.

[2] See Wyeth v. Levine, No. 06-1249 (filed Mar. 12, 2007) (addressing preemption of state-law challenges to prescription drug warnings approved by the FDA) (to be argued Nov. 3, 2008); Altria Group v. Good, No. 07-562 (filed Oct. 26, 2007) (addressing preemption of state-law challenges to statements in cigarette advertising authorized by the Federal Trade Commission) (to be argued Oct. 6, 2008).

Although the number of preemption cases considered by the Court this term is actually somewhat below the historical average, the Court does appear to be deciding in favor of preemption somewhat more often than usual, and by greater margins.[3] This term's preemption decisions tended to reflect broad agreement, with a series of nine-, eight-, and seven-justice majorities—often joining together some of the Court's most liberal and conservative members. The table on the following page illustrates the point.

Critics from a variety of perspectives contend that the Court has "display[ed] a troubling trend" in favor of federal preemption that is inconsistent with the Court's supposedly traditional presumption against preemption.[4] We unpack this charge and offer several observations that may help explain where the Court is coming from and where it is going.

From the outset, it is worth pausing to review some preemption fundamentals. Simply stated, preemption is the power of federal law to trump state law in certain circumstances. Of course, preemption is nothing new. It is rooted in the Supremacy Clause of the Constitution, which establishes that the federal "Constitution, and the Laws of the United States . . . shall be the supreme Law of the Land; and the Judges in every State shall be bound thereby, any Thing in the Constitution or Laws of any State to the Contrary notwithstanding."[5] Under well-known standards, federal preemption may be "expressed or implied" in the pertinent federal regime.[6] Express preemption involves discerning the meaning of an explicit preemption provision. There are "at least two types of implied pre-emption:

[3] From 1983 to 2003, the Court decided on average more than 6.3 preemption cases per term, and upheld federal preemption in about half of them. See Note, New Evidence On The Presumption Against Preemption: An Empirical Study of Congressional Responses To Supreme Court Preemption Decisions, 120 Harv. L. Rev. 1604, 1613 (2007). Last term, the Court upheld federal preemption in four of six cases. See Table, *infra*.

[4] See, e.g., Erwin Chemerinsky, Troubling Trend in Preemption Rulings, 44 Trial 62 (May 2008) ("One would expect that a conservative Court, committed to protecting states' rights, would narrow the scope of federal preemption. After all, a good way to empower state governments is to restrict the federal government's reach. Restricting pre-emption gives state governments more autonomy. But there is every indication that the Roberts Court, although unquestionably conservative, will interpret preemption doctrines broadly when businesses challenge state and local laws.").

[5] U.S. Const. art. VI, cl. 2.

[6] E.g., Gade v. Nat'l Solid Wastes Mgmt. Ass'n, 505 U.S. 88, 98 (1992).

| OCTOBER TERM 2007: CASES INVOLVING FEDERAL PREEMPTION | | | | | |
|---|---|---|---|---|---|
| *Case* | *Vote* | | | *Pre-emption Upheld* | *Express Pre-emption* |
| | Majority (* wrote) | Concur | Dissent | | |
| *Rowe v. N.H. Motor Trans. Ass'n* | 9 Breyer,* Roberts, Stevens, Kennedy, Souter, Thomas Ginsburg, Alito, Scalia (in part) | 2 Ginsburg, Scalia (in part) | 0 | Yes | Yes |
| *Riegel v. Medtronic* | 8 Scalia,* Roberts, Kennedy, Souter, Thomas, Breyer, Alito, Stevens (in part) | 1 Stevens (in part and in judgment) | 1 Ginsburg | Yes | Yes |
| *Preston v. Ferrer* | 8 Ginsburg,* Roberts, Stevens, Scalia, Kennedy, Souter, Breyer, Alito | 0 | 1 Thomas | Yes | Func-tionally (see dis-cussion) |
| *Exxon Shipping Co. v. Baker* | 8 (On this point) Souter,* Roberts, Scalia, Kennedy, Thomas, Stevens, Ginsburg, Breyer (Alito took no part) | 2 Scalia, Thomas | 0 | No | Yes |
| *Chamber of Commerce v. Brown* | 7 Stevens,* Roberts, Scalia, Kennedy, Souter, Thomas, Alito | 0 | 2 Breyer, Ginsburg | Yes | Func-tionally (see dis-cussion) |
| *Warner-Lambert v. Kent* | 4 Unreported (Roberts took no part) | 0 | 4 Un-reported | No opinion | No |

field pre-emption . . . and conflict pre-emption."[7] Field preemption recognizes limited, but exclusive, areas of federal domain even in the absence of an explicit preemption provision from Congress.[8] Conflict preemption tends to paint with a narrower brush and applies to particular issues "where it is impossible for a private party to comply with both state and federal law,"[9] or where state law "'stands as an obstacle to the accomplishment and execution of the full purposes and objectives of Congress'" or of a federal agency acting within the scope of its congressionally delegated authority.[10]

Preemption debates can make for odd coalitions that appear to defy conventional left/right, liberal/conservative analysis.[11] On the one hand, plaintiffs' counsel, consumer groups, and state officials may contend that federal preemption improperly displaces the states' traditional police power to protect their citizens, particularly in matters involving public health and safety. On the other hand, federal agencies and entities regulated by those agencies may urge that preemption is a necessary bulwark "against unwarranted and inconsistent state interferences with the national economy and against aggressive trial lawyers and attorneys general who upset carefully crafted regulatory compromises."[12] Even advocates of federalism, within its proper sphere, may recognize a profound need to protect regulated entities from contrary state-law liabilities when conduct is closely regulated and mandated by federal government action. Indeed, although their voting records are still emerging, it

---

[7] Id.

[8] See, e.g., Cipollone v. Liggett Group, Inc., 505 U.S. 504, 516 (1992) (plurality opinion).

[9] Crosby v. Nat'l Foreign Trade Council, 530 U.S. 363, 372–73 (2000); see also, e.g., Int'l Paper Co. v. Ouellette, 479 U.S. 481, 494 (1987) (state law preempted if it interferes with the methods by which a federal law is implemented and its purposes realized); Florida Lime and Avocado Growers, Inc. v. Paul, 373 U.S. 132, 142–43 (1963) (finding conflict preemption where "compliance with both federal and state [law] is a physical impossibility").

[10] Hillsborough County, Fla. v. Automated Med. Labs., Inc., 471 U.S. 707, 713 (1985) (citation omitted); Capital Cities Cable, Inc. v. Crisp, 467 U.S. 691, 698–99 (1984) (citation omitted).

[11] See, e.g., Richard A. Epstein & Michael S. Greve, Introduction: Preemption in Context 1–21, in Federal Preemption: States' Powers, National Interests (Epstein & Greve, eds., 2007).

[12] Id. at 1.

may well be that notwithstanding a general sympathy toward federalism (at least where the federal government is intervening in areas beyond its proper domain), Chief Justice Roberts and Justice Alito—both of whom were federal executive and judiciary branch officials for years before being elevated to the Court—are comfortable with upholding the exercise of federal power, at least when it occurs within its properly delegated realm. Indeed, they both joined the pro-preemption majority in each of the four preemption decisions they both participated in this term.

The tendency toward lopsided majorities that emerged in this term's preemption cases may be part of a more general and self-conscious effort by the Court to produce less fractured decisions, and may also reflect several features about those cases. We make three general observations about the Court's current preemption cases:

*First,* there is a significant focus on statutory interpretation, rather than grand constitutional conflicts, such as federalism. Although not completely silent, the lurking federalism debate was largely quiet this term, especially where Congress had spoken in an express preemption provision or federal policy was otherwise clear. Indeed, a majority of the Court's cases involved express preemption—which requires discerning the meaning of an express statutory provision, rather than divining Congress's intent through the application of implied conflict preemption principles—or some functionally similar form of federal statutory analysis. This is not to suggest that implied preemption arguments are weaker as a doctrinal matter,[13] but the absence of text as a focal point may lead to a tendency to fracture and open the door to more controversial aspects of a preemption analysis. Unless one posits that the statutes at issue this term were simply unusually clear—a point that seems questionable given that the Court accepted review to answer disputes in the lower courts about their meaning—there seems to be something else going on. One answer is that the cases reflect a concerted and self-conscious effort, under the guidance of the new chief justice, to build consensus, even if it means issuing narrower rulings.

---

[13] See generally Buckman Co. v. Plaintiffs' Legal Comm., 531 U.S. 341, 352 (2001) ("[N]either an express preemption provision nor a savings clause '[b]ars the ordinary working of conflict pre[]emption principles.'") (quoting Geier v. American Honda Motor Co., 529 U.S. 861, 869 (2000)).

At his confirmation hearing, Chief Justice Roberts expressed a commitment to working toward increased clarity and uniformity in decisions: "[O]ne of the things that the Chief Justice should have as a top priority is to try to bring about a greater degree of coherence and consensus in the opinions of the court" because "we're not benefited by having six different opinions in a case."[14] In keeping with this goal, there has been some apparent movement toward narrower opinions that avoid hot-button, controversial issues in favor of a narrower position more justices can join. While it is too soon to tell whether this will be a hallmark of the Roberts Court— and there have been too few cases annually to know whether it is an aberration—a noticeable feature overall this term has been a decrease in 5–4 decisions. Overall, only 11 of the 67 signed opinions (16.4 percent) were decided 5–4; last term, in contrast, there were 24 split decisions in 69 signed opinions (34.8 percent).[15] In addition, the Court's business cases appeared to produce a higher level of agreement than non-business cases: Though these cases accounted for less than 30 percent of the overall caseload, nearly half were decided by 9–0 or 8–1 margins.[16] For those living under these decisions, of course, this development may be something of a two-edged sword. On the one hand, increased clarity and certainty of legal rules as embodied in a single majority opinion may make it easier to appreciate and plan for risk—at least in fact patterns that closely resemble the case the Court decided. On the other hand, extremely narrow consensus opinions that hew closely to the circumstances in the given case may offer scant guidance beyond the four corners of the circumstances presented. Paradoxically, this may actually

[14] Confirmation Hearing on the Nomination of John G. Roberts, Jr. to be Chief Justice of the United States: Hearing Before the S. Comm. on the Judiciary, 109th Cong. (2005), available at 2005 WL 2237049.

[15] See generally Jason Harrow, Measuring "Divisiveness" in OT06, SCOTUS blog.com, http://www.scotusblog.com/wp/measuring-divisiveness-in-ot06/ (July 2, 2007, 9:48 a.m.); Charles Lane, Narrow Victories Move Roberts Court to Right, Wash. Post, June 29, 2007, at A4.

[16] See generally Harrow, supra note 15; Lane, supra note 15, at A4. Overall, the number of unanimous decisions was 17.9 percent in the 2007 Term, down from 37.7 percent in the 2005 Term and 23.9 percent in the 2006 Term. See generally Rupal Doshi, Georgetown Univ. Law Ctr. Sup. Ct. Inst., Supreme Court of the United States October Term 2006 Overview 4 (2007).

leave parties with less certainty and necessitate more litigation to unpack the outer boundaries of the Court's decision.

*Second*, other things being equal, the Court appears more inclined towards preemption where a case involved matters of special national interest or where an expert federal agency has issued a calibrated judgment that is threatened by contrary state action. The Court seems receptive to the plight of regulated entities that, absent preemption, would be subjected to a patchwork of dueling state and federal burdens. Of course, as detailed below, the perspective from which one begins this analysis—that of the regulating federal agency or the state—may influence where one ends up.

*Third*, a related point: The Court appears to take some comfort in the reality of a federal agency's having applied its expert judgment within the scope of its delegated power and urging that there be preemption. It generally did so, however, without expressly wading into a formal—and sometimes divisive—analysis of the nature or degree of deference due to the agency.

## I. Focus on Statutory Interpretation

A significant feature of this term's preemption cases is that rather than explicitly turning on sweeping philosophical debates about the merits of federal power versus federalism (sometimes embodied in presumptions about preemption)[17] or wading into administrative law battles about the degree of deference due federal agencies, many opinions hewed closely to the text of the federal statute, with a practical nod to the federal interests at stake in the overall federal scheme relating to that subject matter. Critics of judicial overreaching

---

[17] The notion of a presumption *against* preemption arose in the context of field preemption. See generally Rice v. Santa Fe Elevator Corp., 331 U.S. 218, 230 (1947) (discussing the "assumption" that the "historic police powers of the States" are not superseded where "Congress legislate[s] . . . in [a] field which the States have traditionally occupied" unless Congress makes its intent to do so "clear and manifest"). Although the Court's decisions have not always been consistent, there is a strong argument that no such presumption applies in the face of an express preemption provision. Indeed, in *Riegel*, the notion of a presumption against preemption garnered only a single dissenting vote. See 128 S. Ct. at 1006–07, 1013–14; see also Sprietsma v. Mercury Marine, 537 U.S. 51, 62–63 (2002) (concluding that the Court's "task of statutory construction must in the first instance focus on the plain wording of the [express preemption] clause, which necessarily contains the best evidence of Congress' pre-emptive intent"); CSX Transp., Inc. v. Easterwood, 507 U.S. 658, 664 (1993) (same).

can take some comfort in this approach for interpretations that more closely follow the statutory text tend to give the political branches greater control.

Perhaps as a result of this tailored approach, this term's cases tended to produce significant pro-preemption majorities. Indeed, on the same day in February 2008, the Court issued a trio of preemption decisions in which it spoke in nearly one voice:[18] *Rowe v. New Hampshire Motor Transportation Association* was unanimous on the core holding (with two justices also writing separate concurrences); *Riegel v. Medtronic, Inc.* and *Preston v. Ferrer* each had only one dissenter (with one justice in *Riegel* also separately concurring in part with the majority). As detailed below, each of these cases turned on a federal statute with an express preemption provision—or at least a federal provision that operated very much as such. The Court embraced a textual approach, conscious of the overall statutory setting in which the provision arose, rather than engaging in a broader inquiry into any potential congressional purpose less readily reflected in the statutory language itself. Put another way, even if "[t]he purpose of Congress is the [Court's] ultimate touchstone" in judging preemption,[19] where that purpose can be discerned from text and statutory context, the justices appear to have been able to assemble larger coalitions in favor of preemption, without delving into perhaps more controversial discussions of legislative intent or other hot-button methods for decisionmaking.

Indeed, in both *Rowe* and *Riegel*, the Court's interpretation of the statutes' preemption clauses stayed close to the language of the express preemption provision—even though a minority of justices expressed doubt about whether Congress actually intended the preemption that resulted from this reading. For example, as Justice Stevens put it in his separate concurrence in *Riegel*, even though the "significance" of the express preemption provision perhaps "was not fully appreciated until many years after it was enacted" and "[i]t is an example of a statute whose text and general objective cover territory not actually envisioned by its authors," nevertheless,

---

[18] See Tony Mauro, The Majority Flexes Its Muscles, Legal Times, Feb. 25, 2008 (quoting Robin Conrad, U.S. Chamber of Commerce, referencing February 20, 2008 as "quite a hat trick" when the Court issued these three pro-preemption decisions in one day); table, *supra*.

[19] Cipollone, 505 U.S. at 516 (internal quotation omitted, first alteration original).

"'it is ultimately the provisions of our laws rather than the principal concerns of our legislators by which we are governed.'"[20] Thus, although Stevens "agree[d]" with the "description of the actual history and principal purpose of the pre-emption provision at issue in this case" articulated in Justice Ginsburg's dissent, he—like the remaining seven justices—was "persuaded that its text *does* preempt."[21]

It is worth noting that the Court's emphasis on statutory text in the last term may have been foreshadowed two terms ago in *Watters v. Wachovia Bank, N.A.*[22] In that case, Michigan attempted to enforce a series of state disclosure laws against a subsidiary of Wachovia Bank. Wachovia resisted, citing the National Bank Act (NBA), which preempts state authority to examine and inspect the records of national banks, but is silent about regulation of such banks' subsidiaries.[23] Upholding preemption, the Court concluded that Congress intended the NBA's preemption clause to cover activities associated with banks—the "business of banking"—and not look narrowly to the banks' corporate form.[24] Justice Ginsburg, writing for a five-justice majority, read the NBA to preempt state law that "significantly impair[ed] the exercise of [federal] authority, enumerated or incidental" where the state-federal conflict implicated the "general purposes of the NBA."[25]

## A. *Rowe v. New Hampshire Motor Transport Association*

In *Rowe*, the Court rejected a state's intent-based policy arguments about what the pertinent federal regime meant. Instead, the Court

---

[20] Riegel, 128 S. Ct. at 1011 (Stevens, J., concurring) (quoting Oncale v. Sundowner Offshore Servs., 523 U.S. 75, 79–80 (1998)).

[21] *Id.* (emphasis added).

[22] 550 U.S. \_\_\_\_ , 127 S. Ct. 1559 (2007).

[23] *Id.* at 1568 (citing 12 U.S.C. § 484(a)).

[24] *Id.* at 1570–71.

[25] *Id.* at 1566–7. Not every justice, however, found the express preemption provision so clear. An odd coalition—Justice Stevens, joined by Chief Justice Roberts and Justice Scalia—dissented, arguing that the fact Congress had extensively regulated national banks without explicitly extending state law preemption to banks' subsidiaries actually demonstrated the opposite, an intent to permit state regulation of those subsidiaries. *Id.* at 1578–79 (Stevens, J., dissenting). The dissent reasoned that Congress had ample opportunity in the preemption clause's 140 year history to extend it to cover subsidiaries without the Court expanding the provision's reach. *Id.* Justice Thomas did not participate in the decision.

parsed the express preemption clause and focused on precedent interpreting similar statutory language. At issue was an express preemption provision of the Federal Aviation Administration Authorization Act of 1994 (FAAAA) that prohibits states from enacting "any law 'related to' a motor carrier 'price, route, or service.'"[26] In the face of this provision, Maine enacted a law requiring companies shipping tobacco products into the state to use a delivery service that assured recipients were at least 18 years old.[27] Invoking its earlier interpretation of similar preemption language in the Airline Deregulation Act of 1978, the Court began its analysis with the general principle of statutory interpretation that "'when judicial interpretations have settled the meaning of an existing statutory provision, repetition of the same language in a new statute indicates, as a general matter, the intent to incorporate its judicial interpretations as well.'"[28] Although the Court acknowledged that the Maine provision, in referencing "shippers" rather than "carriers," "is less 'direct' than it might be," the effect is the same and the state law is therefore preempted: "[C]arriers will have to offer tobacco delivery services that differ significantly from those that, in the absence of [state] regulation, the market might dictate."[29]

Maine urged that there should be an implied public health exception to the express preemption provision because its law "help[s] it prevent minors from obtaining cigarettes" and "federal law does not pre-empt a State's efforts to protect its citizens' public health, particularly when those laws regulate so dangerous an activity as underage smoking."[30] The state contended that an implied public health exception could be discerned based on legislative history and a separate federal enactment denying federal funds to states that refuse to forbid tobacco sales to minors.[31] Criticizing Maine's proposed exception as amorphous and without apparent limits, the Court made quick work of rejecting these arguments. Surveying

[26] Rowe, 128 S. Ct. at 993 (quoting 49 U.S.C. § 14501(c)(1)).

[27] Id. at 993–94.

[28] Id. at 994 (quoting Merrill Lynch, Pierce, Fenner & Smith, Inc. v. Dabit, 547 U.S. 71, 85 (2006)).

[29] Id. at 996.

[30] Id.

[31] Id. at 996–97.

the statute's list of express exceptions to the express preemption provision, it determined that none resembled the state's theory and refused to read into the statute exceptions that were not made explicit.[32] The Court likewise readily concluded that neither the legislative history nor a separate federal enactment answered the question presented.[33]

More broadly, the Court emphasized that a state's traditional interest in public health does not solve the preemption question here because "'[p]ublic health' does not define itself" and may depend on the "kind and degree" of the applicable risk.[34] Here, if all states could individually regulate carrier services, national uniformity would be undermined:

> Given the number of States through which carriers travel, the number of products, the variety of potential adverse public health effects, the many different kinds of regulatory rules potentially available, and the difficulty of finding a legal criterion for separating permissible from impermissible public-health-oriented regulations, Congress is unlikely to have intended an implicit general "public health" exception.[35]

Justice Ginsburg, who might be expected to be more receptive to arguments that sound in Congress's ultimate purpose, concurred in the result, even though she wrote separately to note that Congress probably did not intend a preemption outcome.[36] Noting that at the time of the FAAAA's passage there was a strong federal policy in favor of restricting minors' access to tobacco, she encouraged Congress to fill the "perhaps overlooked" regulatory gap FAAAA created.[37]

## B. Riegel v. Medtronic

The Court continued its focus on the text of an express preemption provision in *Riegel*. There, the Court held that the express preemption provision of the Medical Device Amendments of 1976 (MDA) to the

[32] *Id.*

[33] *Id.*

[34] *Id.* at 997.

[35] *Id.*

[36] *Id.* at 998–99 (Ginsburg, J., concurring).

[37] *Id.* at 999.

Federal Food, Drug, and Cosmetic Act (FDCA) barred certain state-law claims regarding the 1 percent of medical devices to which the FDA had extended pre-market approval (PMA). The PMA process is FDA's most rigorous level of review, in which it determines the safety and effectiveness of a specific medical device after many hundreds or thousands of hours of agency review, and imposes parameters on every aspect of the device, including design and labeling.[38] The MDA prohibits states from enforcing any "require-ment" for medical devices that is "different from, or in addition to, any [federal] requirement applicable . . . to the device."[39]

Riegel followed from the logic of Medtronic, Inc. v. Lohr,[40] in which FDA's generally less vigorous oversight of so-called 510(k) medical devices was held insufficient to impose federal "requirements" within the meaning of the express preemption provision. In so doing, Lohr juxtaposed the 510(k) process against the "rigorous" PMA pro-cess, observing that the "[t]he § 510(k) notification process is by no means comparable to the PMA process."[41] It concluded that 510(k) review was "quite unlike a case in which the Federal Government has weighed the competing interests relevant to the particular requirement in question, reached an unambiguous conclusion about how those competing considerations should be resolved in a particu-lar case or set of cases, and implemented that conclusion via a specific mandate on manufacturers or producers."[42] In the wake of Lohr, the vast majority of lower courts had recognized preemption in the PMA context.[43]

Riegel echoed this analysis.[44] After concluding that PMA review imposed federal "requirements," the Court relied on a line of prece-dent[45] to hold that state law claims—including common law claims

---

[38] Riegel, 128 S. Ct. at 1004.

[39] Id. at 1003 (quoting 21 U.S.C. § 360k(a)).

[40] 518 U.S. 470 (1996).

[41] Id. at 477–79.

[42] Id. at 501.

[43] See, e.g., McMullen v. Medtronic, Inc., 421 F.3d 482 (7th Cir. 2005), cert. denied, 547 U.S. 1003 (2006); Cupek v. Medtronic, Inc., 405 F.3d 421 (6th Cir.), cert. denied sub nom., Knisley v. Medtronic, 546 U.S. 935 (2005); Horn v. Thoratec Corp., 376 F.3d 163 (3d Cir. 2004); Brooks v. Howmedica, Inc., 273 F.3d 785 (8th Cir. 2001) (en banc); Martin v. Medtronic, Inc., 254 F.3d 573 (5th Cir. 2001); but see Goodlin v. Medtronic, Inc., 167 F.3d 1367 (11th Cir. 1999).

[44] Riegel, 128 S. Ct. at 1006–07; see also Section III, infra.

[45] See Bates v. Dow Agrosciences LLC, 544 U.S. 431, 443 (2005) (concluding that a state-law "requirement" under the express preemption provision of the Federal

and jury verdicts—constitute state "requirements" under the provision.[46] Because the state requirements plaintiff sought to enforce were different from the federal requirements, they were preempted under the terms of the express preemption provision.

The sole *Riegel* dissenter, Justice Ginsburg, failed to persuade any other justice to withhold preemption based on a reading of what Congress may have intended when it enacted the MDA. Indeed, Justice Scalia—writing for the eight-justice majority—emphasized that the Court's decision turned on the plain text of the statute and that it "is not our job to speculate upon congressional motives."[47] In contrast, Justice Ginsburg's dissent recounted the history surrounding the legislation's enactment, emphasizing that Congress passed the MDA around the time of the Dalkon Shield litigation, which had resulted in hundreds of lawsuits.[48] Given this context, she opined that Congress was familiar with common law suits over medical devices and would have preempted common law claims more clearly if it had intended to do so.[49] As noted, this view failed to sway even one other justice, notwithstanding a nod from Justice Stevens to Justice Ginsburg's historical examination, in the face of the statutory enactment.

## C. Preston v. Ferrer

Although there is some debate about whether it involves an express preemption provision as such, *Preston* provides another

---

Insecticide, Fungicide, and Rodenticide Act (FIFRA) "reaches beyond [state-law] positive enactments, such as statutes and regulations, to embrace common-law duties"); Cipollone, 505 U.S. at 521–22 (observing that "requirement" "sweeps broadly and suggests no distinction between positive enactments and common law" in provision of the Public Health Cigarette Smoking Act of 1969); *id.* at 548–49 (Scalia, J., and Thomas, J.) (creating majority on this point); see also Geier v. American Honda Motor Co., 529 U.S. 861, 867, 896–97 (2000) (acknowledging that *Lohr* concluded that the term "requirement" in the MDA express preemption provision encompasses state-law damages claims); Lohr, 518 U.S. at 512 (opinion of O'Connor, J., joined by Rehnquist, C.J., and Scalia and Thomas, JJ.) (common law actions constitute state-law "requirements" under MDA); *id.* at 503–04 (opinion of Breyer, J.) (fifth justice joining majority).

[46] Riegel, 128 S. Ct. at 1007–08.

[47] *Id.* at 1009.

[48] *Id.* at 1014–15 (Ginsburg, J., dissenting).

[49] *Id.* Interestingly, this line of argument echoes the dissent in *Watters* the term before, a case in which Ginsburg not only did not join the dissent, but authored the majority opinion. See note 25, *supra*.

example of a large majority of justices coalescing around the text of a federal provision that expressly privileges arbitration elected by private contract over court-based adjudication.[50] As all but one justice agreed, the Federal Arbitration Act "declares a national policy favoring arbitration of claims that parties contract to settle in that manner" that "forecloses state legislative attempts to undercut the enforceability of arbitration agreements."[51] Indeed, "[t]he FAA's displacement of conflicting state law is now well-established and has been repeatedly affirmed."[52]

This case involved a contract between a television personality (Judge Alex) and his talent agent that required the parties to arbitrate "'any dispute . . . relating to the terms of [the contract] or the breach, validity, or legality thereof . . . in accordance with the rules [of the American Arbitration Association].'"[53] Judge Alex challenged the validity of the contract, urging that such matters must be heard by the state labor commissioner.[54] Justice Ginsburg, writing for an 8–1 majority, observed that the "best way to harmonize" the competing provisions was for the arbitrator, not the state labor commissioner, to decide the contract's validity under state law.[55] Even though the state eventually would have allowed arbitration to occur following the labor commissioner's review, such a delay in final resolution would be contrary to the FAA's purpose, to speed dispute resolution.[56] Alone in dissent, Justice Thomas did not expressly critique

---

[50] The pertinent Federal Arbitration Act language states that "'a written provision in any . . . contract evidencing a transaction involving commerce to settle by arbitration a controversy thereafter arising out of such contract or transaction . . . *shall be valid, irrevocable, and enforceable,* save upon such grounds as exist at law or in equity for the revocation of any contract'" as a matter of general applicability. Preston, 128 S. Ct. at 983 (quoting 9 U.S.C. § 2) (emphasis added). To be sure, the Court previously observed that the FAA "contains no express pre-emptive provision," instead treating the statute as involving implied conflict preemption. Volt Info. Scis., Inc. v. Board of Trs. of Leland Stanford Junior Univ., 489 U.S. 468, 477 (1989). But Preston did not embrace this analysis, and otherwise held that reliance on *Volt* "is misplaced." Preston, 128 S. Ct. at 998.

[51] *Id.* at 983 (internal quotation and alterations omitted).

[52] *Id.* (internal quotation omitted).

[53] *Id.* at 982 (quoting contract) (alterations and omissions in the original).

[54] *Id.*

[55] *Id.* at 989.

[56] *Id.* at 986.

the majority's interpretation of the FAA, but wrote briefly to adhere to his position that the FAA does not apply to state proceedings.[57]

## D. *Chamber of Commerce v. Brown*

Although the National Labor Relations Act contains no express preemption provision as such, a seven-justice majority seized on language in a recent NLRA amendment, concluding that it "forcefully buttresses the pre-emption analysis," rendering preemption "both implicit and explicit" and making this case even "easier" than prior NLRA cases on point.[58]

At issue in *Brown* were provisions of California law that forbid employers that received state funds from using those funds to "assist, promote, or deter union organizing."[59] The Court held that Congress "implicitly mandated" preemption of certain matters "necessary to implement federal labor policy," including that "certain zones of labor activity be unregulated."[60] Although the NLRA prohibits employers from "interfer[ing] with, restrain[ing], or coerc[ing]" employees in their decisions whether to organize,[61] a later amendment clarified that an employer's "express[ion] of any views, argument, or opinion" about organizing that contains no threat of reprisal or a promise of benefit is not prohibited.[62] The Court focused on this amendment, calling it "explicit direction from Congress"[63] that employers and employees both should be allowed to enter a "free debate" about unionization.[64] Because the California statute curtailed this debate, the NLRA preempted it.

In dissent, Justices Breyer and Ginsburg urged that the case for preemption in the NLRA's text was not nearly as clear as the majority suggested. For one thing, the state statute did not explicitly regulate employers' speech. Employers that received state funds still could

---

[57] *Id.* at 989 (Thomas, J., dissenting).

[58] Brown, 128 S. Ct. at 2414.

[59] *Id.* at 2410–11 (quoting Cal. Gov't Code §§ 16645–16649 (West Supp. 2008)).

[60] *Id.* at 2411–12.

[61] *Id.* at 2413 (quoting 29 U.S.C. § 158(a)(1)).

[62] *Id.* (quoting 29 U.S.C. § 158(c)).

[63] *Id.* at 2414.

[64] *Id.* at 2413.

have expressed their opinion about union organizing; the state statute only said not to "do so on [the state's] dime."[65] The dissent charged that the majority's reliance on the state statute's preamble implicitly recognized this deficiency given that it was the preamble, rather than the statute's text, that detailed the state's policy "not to interfere with an employee's choice" about whether to unionize.[66] A reading of the statute more sympathetic to the state's position would have been that the state was merely trying to control how its money was spent and wanted to disengage from aiding one side in a labor dispute, in harmony with federal labor policy. But the presence of express language from Congress appeared to tip the balance for the majority.[67]

*E. Exxon Shipping Co. v. Baker*

Although the focus of the *Exxon* case was punitive damages, the Court also had occasion to address briefly whether an express preemption provision of the Clean Water Act preempts the availability of maritime punitive damages under federal common law.[68] The pertinent statutory provision protects "navigable waters . . . adjoining shorelines . . . [and] natural resources," of the United States, subject to a savings clause that reserves "obligations . . . under any provision of law for damages to any publicly owned or privately owned property resulting from a discharge of any oil."[69] Although the Court struggled to discern the company's precise preemption theory, all eight justices participating in the decision found it "too hard to conclude that a statute expressly geared to protecting 'water,' 'shorelines,' and 'natural resources' was intended to eliminate *sub*

[65] *Id.* at 2420 (Breyer, J., dissenting).

[66] *Id.* at 2411, 2415.

[67] For more on this case, see William J. Kilberg and Jennifer J. Schulp, Chamber of Commerce v. Brown: Protecting Free Debate on Unionization, 2007–2008 Cato Sup. Ct. R. 189 (2008).

[68] 128 S. Ct. 2605, 2616–20 (2008). It should be noted that *Exxon* involved "preemption" in a somewhat different sense than that described above, in that the issue was whether an express statutory provision of federal law could preempt *federal* maritime common law claims.

[69] *Id.* at 2618 (citing 33 U.S.C. § 1321(b) & (o)) (alteration and second omission in original).

*silentio* oil companies' common law duties to refrain from injuring the bodies and livelihoods of private individuals."[70]

The Court also held "untenable" the argument that the Clean Water Act "somehow preempts punitive damages" but not compensatory damages.[71] Although the Court's preemption analysis is minimal, this appears to join the general trend of large majorities of justices coalescing around a specific statutory provision—this time all agreeing there was no preemption under the text.

### F. *Warner-Lambert v. Kent*

In *Kent*—the sole exclusively implied preemption case the Court heard last term—the vote fractured 4–4.[72] Although there is no opinion from which reliably to discern what animated the different votes, in contrast to the super-majorities witnessed in the five decisions in which the Court relied on an express (or pseudo-express) preemption provision, the absence of an express provision may have made consensus more difficult. This is not to suggest that the case for implied preemption is necessarily weaker in a given case than in the express preemption context—as detailed below, there was a strong case for implied preemption in *Kent*—but only that the absence of an express statute may open the door to additional doctrinal issues that make it harder for the Court to reach broad agreement. We address some of those currents below.

### II. Federal and State Interests

Although the presence of express preemption provisions in a majority of the Court's cases allowed it to avoid focusing—or fracturing—on federal versus state power issues, there still appears to be a tendency to uphold preemption where the issue at hand was thought to be fundamentally federal. Indeed, although the Court sometimes has recognized a presumption *against* preemption in matters traditionally "reserved" to the states,[73] the rationale for any such

---

[70] *Id.* at 2619.

[71] *Id.*

[72] The Chief Justice recused himself. Consistent with its practice, the Court issued a per curiam order affirming the judgment below by an equally divided court without releasing a substantive opinion or identifying how any justice voted. Such dispositions effectively leave the legal landscape where the Court found it and are "not entitled to precedential weight." Rutledge v. United States, 517 U.S. 292, 304 (1996).

[73] See note 17, *supra*.

thumb-on-the-scale evaporates when the federal government acts in an area in which it has "exclusive, or at least plenary, authority to regulate"[74]—or where there is a conflict between federal and state law—because "one can assume that Congress or an agency ordinarily would not intend to permit a significant conflict" between federal and state law.[75]

Looking at the history of one area of federal law, the Court has been particularly willing to preempt state laws that touch on foreign affairs. In *Crosby v. National Foreign Trade Council*, for instance, Massachusetts passed a law that restricted the authority of state agencies to purchase goods or services from companies doing business with Burma, in light of that country's despotic regime.[76] Like the state law provision in *Brown*, the Massachusetts statute was framed as a restriction on using state funds for undesirable activities that arguably furthered national policy on the matter.[77] Yet *Crosby* found the state law preempted because Congress had "calibrated [foreign] policy [in] a deliberate effort to steer a middle path"—a path that left no place for competing state action.[78]

This approach is echoed in other federal contexts in which Congress, or an expert federal agency to which Congress delegated decisionmaking authority, already has balanced and resolved competing policy objectives.[79] Indeed, despite the overall focus on statutory analysis, this theme played out this term in cases in which the Court noted established national policies governing motor carrier

[74] Thomas W. Merrill, Agency Preemption: Speak Softly, But Carry a Big Stick?, 11 Chap. L. Rev. 363, 387 (2008) (arguing for a presumption in *favor* of preemption in matters within exclusive or plenary federal control); see also United States v. Locke, 529 U.S. 89, 108 (2000) (where a matter has long been subject to federal control, "there is no beginning assumption that concurrent regulation by the State is a valid exercise of its police powers").

[75] Geier, 529 U.S. at 885; see Felder v. Casey, 487 U.S. 131, 138 (1988) ("Under the Supremacy Clause of the Federal Constitution, '[t]he relative importance to the State of its own law is not material when there is a conflict with a valid federal law,' for 'any state law, however clearly within a State's acknowledged power, which interferes with or is contrary to federal law, must yield.'") (citations omitted).

[76] 530 U.S. 363, 366 (2000); see also American Ins. Ass'n v. Garamendi, 539 U.S. 396 (2003).

[77] Id. at 367.

[78] Id. at 377–78 (internal quotation omitted).

[79] See, e.g., Geier, 529 U.S. 861; see also Section III, *infra*.

transportation (*Rowe*),[80] regulation of complex medical devices (*Riegel*),[81] arbitration of private disputes (*Preston*),[82] and labor law (*Brown*)[83] that the state laws at issue would undermine.

There was also a strong argument for the uniquely federal nature of the question at issue in *Kent*. That case involved a product liability suit filed against a pharmaceutical company alleging personal injuries caused by taking a prescription medication. Michigan, where the patients filed the suit, provides a statutory defense to suits against manufacturers of prescription drugs that were approved by the FDA and in compliance with FDA requirements.[84] The state statute creates an exception to this defense, however, which requires the state factfinder to speculate whether (1) the manufacturer intentionally withheld or misrepresented information to the FDA that was required to be submitted under various provisions of federal law (2) that would have materially affected the FDA's decision to approve the drug for nationwide marketing or withdraw it.[85] Although the plaintiffs asserted that this exception applied, the FDA itself never found any violation of its federal disclosure requirements or took any action to withdraw the product because of fraud on the agency.[86] The solicitor general and the company contended that determining whether there had been proper disclosures to a federal agency and how an agency would respond to any fraud on it was a matter exclusively reserved to the agency itself.[87] Indeed, the Court previously had held in *Buckman Company v. Plaintiffs' Legal Committee* that "[s]tate-law fraud-on-the-FDA claims inevitably conflict with

---

[80] 128 S. Ct. 989.

[81] 128 S. Ct. 999.

[82] 128 S. Ct. 978.

[83] 128 S. Ct. 2408.

[84] See Mich. Comp. Laws § 600.2946(5).

[85] See Mich. Comp. Laws § 600.2946(5)(a).

[86] See Brief for the United States as Amicus Curiae Supporting of Petitioners at 5, 21, Warner-Lambert Co. v. Kent, No. 06-1498 (Nov. 28, 2008), 2007 WL 421889 ("U.S. Kent Br."); Desiano v. Warner-Lambert & Co., 467 F.3d 85, 87 (2d Cir. 2006), aff'd by an equally divided court sub nom., Warner-Lambert v. Kent, 128 S. Ct. 1168 (2008).

[87] See, e.g., U.S. Kent Br. at 6–7 ("Michigan law is preempted to the extent it requires courts to determine whether a manufacturer defrauded FDA and whether FDA would have denied or withdrawn approval of a drug but for the fraud."); Garcia v. Wyeth-Ayerst Labs., 385 F.3d 961 (6th Cir. 2004) (same).

the FDA's responsibility to police fraud consistently with the Administration's judgment and objectives" and are therefore preempted.[88]

The Second Circuit below had procedurally distinguished the claims in *Kent* from *Buckman*, ruling that the claims here were not for fraud-on-the-FDA per se, but "sound[ed] in traditional state tort law."[89] As the solicitor general and the company pointed out, however, this is a distinction without a difference. Consistent with *Buckman*, "the relationship between a federal agency and the entity it regulates is inherently federal in character because the relationship originates from, is governed by, and terminates according to federal law" and "[p]olicing fraud against federal agencies is hardly a field which the States have traditionally occupied."[90] The Court's divide in *Kent* may stem from a difference of opinion in whether to view the question presented as sounding in traditional state tort law or in federal law. Where you start may be where you end up.

Whether the Court begins from the perspective of the federal or state interest may partly explain the outcome in the other preemption cases as well. In *Brown*, for example, the state argued for its prerogatives in controlling how its own state treasury funds were used. But the Court viewed *Brown* as primarily implicating federal labor policy instead of a state's control over its funds. Nor was the Court receptive to arguments that the state statute actually was consistent with and furthered federal labor policy. Indeed, the *Brown* dissent argued that Congress had even used language identical to the state statute to prevent employers from using federal funds to interfere with union organizing.[91] What was good for the federal goose, California argued, was good for the state gander. Nevertheless, the Court reasoned that the state statute improperly implicated "federal labor policy" because Congress intended to strike a balance on employer speech that neither violated the employers' First Amendment rights nor coerced employees.[92] That balance prevented states such as California from "opening the door to a 50-state patchwork of inconsistent labor policies."[93]

[88] 531 U.S. at 350.

[89] Desiano, 467 F.3d at 94.

[90] Buckman, 531 U.S. at 347 (internal quotation omitted); see U.S. Kent Br. at 9–10.

[91] See Brown, 128 S. Ct. at 2420 (Breyer, J., dissenting).

[92] *Id.* at 2412.

[93] *Id.* at 2418.

The Court used similar language to describe the nature of the federal interest in *Riegel* and *Buckman*. In *Riegel*, the Court noted that state tort law threatens the federal agency's cost-benefit analysis.[94] In *Buckman*, a state tort law finding that the manufacturer had made false statements to the FDA was preempted because of the "delicate balance" the FDA must strike in evaluating submissions from regulated entities and the need to prevent a "deluge of information" from being submitted to the agency during the approval process out of nothing more than a self-protective desire to avoid potential state tort liability rather than for a legitimate federal regulatory purpose.[95]

The Court's apparent difficulty with finding predictable criteria to determine whether a claim implicates federal or state power is not new, but can be seen in two of the Court's earlier preemption cases, *Hillsborough County v. Automated Medical Laboratories, Inc.*[96] and *Lorillard Tobacco Co. v. Reilly*.[97] In *Hillsborough*, the Court unanimously held that federal law did not preempt local regulation of blood plasma collection that required blood plasma centers to pay the county a registration fee, to register blood donors, and to make sure that donors passed certain health tests before donating.[98] The FDA had promulgated its own regulations requiring physicians to determine the suitability of blood donors and inform donors of the procedure's risks, and it imposed various procedural and labeling requirements.[99] A chain of blood plasma centers challenged the local regulations, arguing that they were preempted due to the extent of the FDA's regulations and the importance of the federal government's interest in ensuring the quality of the national blood supply.[100] The Court disagreed, based largely on its characterization of the claim as a traditional "health and safety matter[]."[101] The Court's argument began (and perhaps ended) with the presumption that

---

[94] Riegel, 128 S. Ct. at 1008; Section III, *infra*.

[95] Buckman, 531 U.S. at 348, 350–51.

[96] 471 U.S. 707 (1985).

[97] 533 U.S. 525 (2001).

[98] Hillsborough, 471 U.S. at 710, 723.

[99] *Id*.

[100] *Id*. at 714.

[101] *Id*. at 719.

laws touching on "the historic police powers of the States" will not be preempted unless Congress expresses a "clear and manifest purpose" to do so.[102] In so doing, the Court contrasted the health and safety subject area with foreign affairs, where the federal interest "is made clear by the Constitution" and "intertwined with responsibilities of the national government."[103]

But the *Hillsborough* consensus on "health and safety" broke apart in *Reilly* where state regulations restricted the sale and advertising of tobacco products with an eye toward preventing underage tobacco use. A group of tobacco companies challenged the state regulations under the Federal Cigarette Labeling and Advertising Act,[104] which expressly preempted any state "requirement or prohibition based on smoking and health . . . with respect to the advertising or promotion of cigarettes. . . ."[105] Despite this express preemption provision, the state argued that Congress did not intend to preempt state authority to address youth smoking through advertising regulations, nor did Congress intend to preempt state regulation of the location of the advertisements (as opposed to their content).[106] Although the Court recognized the serious danger of underage smoking and the federal policy against it, the Court concluded that "Congress enacted a comprehensive scheme to address cigarette smoking . . . even with respect to youth," and therefore the state regulations were preempted.[107] Justice Stevens, writing for four justices in dissent, argued that the majority mischaracterized the central issue, urging that disposition against preemption was "straightforward" given the Court's strong presumption against preemption when a state's historic police powers are implicated.[108] The dissent noted two traditional state powers at issue: "the power to regulate land usage" and "the power to protect health and safety."[109] Yet the majority saw it as principally a federal issue.

[102] *Id.* at 715 (internal quotation omitted).

[103] *Id.* at 719 (internal quotation omitted).

[104] 15 U.S.C. § 1331 et seq.

[105] Reilly, 533 U.S. at 541 (quoting 15 U.S.C. § 1334).

[106] *Id.* at 550–51.

[107] *Id.* at 571.

[108] *Id.* at 590–91 (Stevens, J., concurring in the judgment in part and dissenting in part).

[109] *Id.*

Thus, even though the justices may be more apt to fracture in the absence of an express preemption provision, a properly defined federal interest may still bode well for preemption.

## III. Federal Agency Expertise and Review

The rise of the administrative state has brought with it heavy federal regulation. Compliance costs can burden regulated entities, particularly as they endeavor to meet local, state, federal, and international demands. This can put regulated entities in inconvenient or even untenable positions as they cope with regulations that may impose competing and even mutually exclusive requirements. These realities have resulted in an apparent increase in *actual* deference to the federal agency in at least two senses.

*First*, although the Court has not been enthusiastic about undertaking formal administrative deference analyses—and detailing what degree of deference various agency interpretations of the statutes, regulations, or other matters they author or administer are entitled to under the well-known but often divisive frameworks of *Chevron*, *Auer*, and *Skidmore*[110]—in practice, the Court nonetheless has tended to follow the agency's position on whether there should be preemption. For example, as one commentator has observed, in all but one of the recent preemption cases involving product liability issues, the Court has followed the federal agency's preemption position (be it pro or con in a given case) even though it generally did not engage in a formal agency deference analysis.[111]

---

[110] See Chevron USA, Inc. v. Natural Res. Def. Council, Inc., 467 U.S. 837, 844 (1984) (recognizing the legally binding effect of non-arbitrary interpretations of ambiguous statutory provisions by the agency charged with administering those provisions.); Auer v. Robbins, 519 U.S. 452, 461 (1997) (recognizing that an agency's interpretation of its own ambiguous regulation is "controlling unless plainly erroneous or inconsistent with the regulation") (internal quotation omitted); Skidmore v. Swift & Co., 323 U.S. 134, 140 (1944) (recognizing some lesser degree of deference in other circumstances "depend[ing] upon the thoroughness evident in [the agency's] consideration, the validity of its reasoning, its consistency with earlier and later pronouncements, and all those factors which give it power to persuade").

[111] See Catherine M. Sharkey, Products Liability Preemption: An Institutional Approach, 76 Geo. Wash. L. Rev. 449, 477 (Apr. 2008) ("Out of the preemption muddle, then, a glimmer of clarity emerges at least with respect to the products liability cases—the Court's final decisions line up with the positions urged by the agency."). Those cases are Lohr, 518 U.S. 470; Geier, 529 U.S. 861; Buckman, 531 U.S. 341; Sprietsma, 537 U.S. 51; and Riegel, 128 S. Ct. 999. The one outlier is Bates, 544 U.S. 431, in which the Court rejected the agency's pro-preemption position. In *Kent*, the agency also favored the pro-preemption position, but the Court did not issue a

In *Lohr*, for instance, the Court simply stated that the agency's interpretation—against preemption for the less heavily regulated medical devices at issue in that case—"substantially informed" its reading of the express preemption statute.[112] Similarly this term, Justice Scalia, writing for the majority in *Riegel*, again picked up on this "substantially informed" language with respect to the agency's position that the more heavily regulated devices at issue in that case implicated federal "requirements" within the meaning of the preemption provision; but the Court did not explicitly cite agency deference doctrine or provide further explanation.[113] Indeed, on another point, the Court sidestepped deciding the case on administrative law grounds even though they may have supported the majority's view. The plaintiffs had pointed to an FDA regulation that limited the pertinent statute's preemptive scope where "state or local requirements [were] of general applicability" to argue against preemption.[114] The FDA interpreted its own regulation only to withhold preemption from general duties such as fire codes or rules about trade practices, not the tort duties at issue in *Riegel*.[115] There is a strong argument that the agency's reading of its own regulation was entitled to substantial deference under *Auer*. Yet Justice Scalia "[n]either accept[ed] nor reject[ed]" the FDA's interpretation, avoiding the matter and concluding that the regulation was unnecessary to the outcome of the case.[116]

---

precedential opinion addressing the issue. See *supra*. Perhaps the lesson learned from these cases is that without the federal agency's support, preemption may be difficult; with it, preemption is likely but not guaranteed.

[112] Lohr, 518 U.S. at 495–96 (observing that the FDA "is uniquely qualified to determine whether a particular form of state law stands as an obstacle to the accomplishment and execution of the full purposes and objectives of Congress, and, therefore, whether it should be pre-empted") (internal quotation omitted); see *id.* at 506 (noting the FDA's "special understanding of the likely impact of both state and federal requirements, as well as an understanding of whether (or the extent to which) state requirements may interfere with federal objectives") (Breyer, J., concurring). The *Lohr* majority perhaps did not go so far, however, as to "admit to deferring to [the FDA's] regulations," and, to the dissent's mind at least, it was an open question whether "an agency regulation determining the pre-emptive effect of *any* federal statute [was] entitled to deference." *Id.* at 512 (O'Connor, J., concurring in part and dissenting in part).

[113] Riegel, 128 S. Ct. at 1006.

[114] *Id.* at 1010 (quoting 21 C.F.R. § 808.1(d)(1)) (alteration omitted).

[115] *Id.*

[116] 128 S. Ct. at 1011.

This apparent trend also was evident in *Watters*, a significant preemption case from the term before last. *Watters* was expected by many to be a landmark administrative law case but, in the end, the Court avoided the issue. The primary question administrative law academics hoped would be answered was whether an agency that does not have express authority to preempt state laws nonetheless can preempt them by regulation under its general rulemaking authority.[117] Focusing on the text of the statute, the Court did not reach what it called this "academic question" because the regulation at issue "merely clarifie[d] and confirm[ed]" the statute's clear meaning.[118] The Court instead read the text of the preemption provision in its overall context.[119]

*Second*, as noted above, the Court has a history of crediting federal agency balancing of complicated policy issues when contrary state law threatens to disrupt that balance. Where an expert federal agency has considered an issue within the proper bounds of its authority, the Court appears to give significant deference to the agency about the proper solution. One possibility is that the Court may extend actual deference to an agency's view where the Court is convinced about the rigor of the process Congress or the agency has devised for reviewing a particular policy issue. This review of the regulator may be born of a growing recognition of the agencies' comparative competency to make decisions in highly technical areas.

In *Riegel*, for example, the Court assessed the comparative advantage of having an expert agency make technical public health judgments about the safety and effectiveness of complex medical devices, instead of a jury. The majority opinion, while disclaiming reliance on anything but the controlling statutory text, took care to detail the FDA's extensive process for determining whether certain medical devices are safe and effective. The opinion devoted numerous pages of discussion to the FDA's "rigorous regime of premarket approval" in which "[t]he FDA spends an average of 1,200 hours reviewing each application" and reviews a "multivolume application" that includes "a full description of the methods used" in manufacturing and processing the device."[120]

---

[117] See, e.g., Merrill, *supra* note 74, at 376.

[118] Watters, 127 S. Ct. at 1572.

[119] See section I.A, *supra*.

[120] Riegel, 128 S. Ct, at 1003–05 (internal quotation omitted).

As between a jury and the FDA, the former is likely to be less competent at determining trade-offs between a device's safety and effectiveness because the jury "sees only the cost of a more dangerous design, and is not concerned with its benefits; the patients who reaped those benefits are not represented in court."[121] It would "make little sense" for Congress to have intended dual FDA and jury determinations of medical device safety, the opinion concluded, because where those determinations conflict they would expose device manufacturers to contradictory obligations.[122] Consistent with this approach, in the earlier *Lohr* case, the Court also had looked to the rigor of the federal agency review to aid in deciding whether state actions were preempted. Observing that the review at issue in *Lohr* merely judged a device's *"equivalence* [to other devices], not safety" and did "not in any way denote official FDA approval of [the] device," the Court came to the opposite conclusion, that no preemption was warranted for the different category of devices at issue in *Lohr.*[123]

In October Term 2008, the *Wyeth* prescription drug preemption case provides the Court with an opportunity to revisit its actual deference to agency expertise and an agency's call for preemption.[124] In *Wyeth*, although Congress charged the FDA with determining the appropriate warnings for prescription drugs marketed in the United States—and even though the agency was "fully aware of the risk" ultimately visited on the plaintiff and approved calibrated warning

---

[121] *Id.* at 1008.

[122] See *id.*

[123] Lohr, 518 U.S. at 493 (emphasis in original).

[124] We will not repeat here the full case for FDA preemption in many prescription drug contexts, which has been developed extensively elsewhere. See, e.g., Brief for the United States as Amicus Curiae Supporting Petitioner, Wyeth v. Levine, No. 06-1249 (June 2, 2008), 2008 WL 2308908 ("U.S. Levine Br.") (arguing that the Federal Food, Drug and Cosmetic Act preempts state tort claims that would impose liability for the use of labeling that the FDA approved after being informed of the relevant risk); Brief of DRI—The Voice of the Defense Bar as Amicus Curiae in Support of Petitioner at 3, Wyeth v. Levine, No. 06-1249 (June 3, 2008) 2008 WL 2355772 ("DRI Levine Br.") (arguing that "[p]ermitting States—and lay fact-finders—to serve as quasi-regulators able to require additional warnings inconsistent with FDA's own judgments creates irreconcilable conflicts with federal law and thwarts the attainment of important [federal] public health objectives"); Daniel E. Troy, The Case for FDA Preemption 81–112, in Federal Preemption, *supra* (preemption is needed "to protect the FDA's mission and objectives, as defined by Congress, against independent threats emanating from state tort law").

language alerting prescribers to that potential risk[125]—plaintiff challenged the warning as inadequate and told the jury "we don't rely on the FDA to . . . make the safe[ty] decision" or determine "the extent to which [a company] should have warned" because the "FDA doesn't make the decision, you do."[126]

The plaintiff's argument ignores the federal regulatory process for approving prescription drugs for marketing on the nationwide market—an issue reserved to the FDA and its statutory predecessors for over a century[127]—and may become a focus of the analysis if the Court adheres to the interpretive methods discussed above. The United States and other amici detail the FDA's extensive labeling review process.[128] In striking parallel to the PMA process at issue in *Riegel*, the FDA's review process for prescription drugs is "expert" and "rigorous," "scrutiniz[ing] everything about the drug," and the goal of which is to "strike a balance" between notifying prescribing physicians and their patients about a drug's potential dangers and overwarning (which may lead to prescribing physicians' avoiding treatments whose potential benefits would outweigh their potential risks for a particular patient out of unsubstantiated fears).[129] Indeed, this balance is peculiarly difficult in the context of prescription drugs because the potential for harm is often inseparable from the potential for benefit.[130]

Justice Breyer appeared to foreshadow this core issue in *Wyeth* when questioning plaintiffs' counsel at the *Kent* oral argument:

> You came up and began and said this drug has side effects that hurt people. And that's a risk when you have a drug, and it's a terrible thing if the drug hurts people. There's a risk on the other side. There are people who are dying or seriously sick, and if you don't get the drug to them they die. So there's a problem. You've got to get drugs to people

[125] U.S. Levine Br. at 1–7.

[126] Joint Appendix at 211–12, 217, Wyeth v. Levine, No. 06-1249 (May 27, 2008), 2008 WL 2309484.

[127] See, e.g., Pure Food and Drug Act of 1906, Pub. L. No. 59-384, 34 Stat. 768 (1906); United States v. Walsh, 331 U.S. 432, 434 (1947) ("The [FDCA] rests upon the constitutional power resident in Congress to regulate interstate commerce" and Congress has regulated drugs "[t]o the end that the public health and safety might be advanced.").

[128] See, e.g., U.S. Levine Br. at 1–4, 11–15; DRI Levine Br. at 4–16.

[129] U.S. Levine Br. at 11, 13, 17.

[130] See, e.g., *id.* at 8–9, 16–17; Troy, *supra* note 124, at 84.

and at the same time the drug can't hurt them. Now, who would you rather have make the decision as to whether this drug is, on balance, going to save people or, on balance, going to hurt people? An expert agency, on the one hand, or 12 people pulled randomly for a jury rol[l] who see before them only the people whom the drug hurt and don't see those people who need the drug to cure them?[131]

Thus, even where there is no express preemption provision, there is a powerful argument to defer to federal expertise at least where a matter is one of proper federal concern and the agency is acting well within the proper scope of its congressionally delegated power. The alternative is to disregard congressional design and place regulated entities between the rock of federal mandates and the hard place of trying to comply with a patchwork of different and competing state law standards.

## Conclusion

Perhaps in keeping with the new Chief Justice's expressed goal of forging consensus opinions, there was considerable uniformity in the justices' votes in this term's preemption cases. The Court's text-based approach to interpreting express preemption provisions provided a pivot point for securing broad consensus and avoiding perhaps more controversial issues of federalism and agency deference. Although reluctant to wade into formal federalism debates, the Court seemed particularly sympathetic to preemption where the matter at hand was significantly federal. With the exception of foreign affairs, however, it may be difficult to predict with certainty whether a given matter that may have both federal and state law features will be viewed principally from a state or federal vantage point. Finally, the Court has tended to preempt state laws when federal agencies make considered, often technical judgments with respect to highly regulated matters within their congressionally delegated expertise. In according *actual* deference to the procedural and substantive judgments of expert agencies, though, the Court generally avoided wading into formal, and often divisive, administrative law analysis.

---

[131] Oral Argument Transcript at 30, Warner-Lambert Co. v. Kent, No. 06-1498 (Feb. 25, 2008), 2008 WL 495030.

# A Deal Is Still a Deal:
# *Morgan Stanley Capital Group*
# *v. Public Utility District No. 1*

*Richard P. Bress, Michael J. Gergen, and Stephanie S. Lim**

A deal is a deal. This concept is firmly entrenched in American culture and law,[1] and is widely viewed as an essential cornerstone of economic development and stability.[2] It has thus long been understood in our nation that it is not the role of the government to relieve contracting parties of "hard bargains" resulting from their "indiscretions and bad judgments"; rather, the Constitution "with

---

* Richard P. Bress and Michael J. Gergen are partners, and Stephanie S. Lim is an associate, at Latham & Watkins LLP. The authors represented various sellers in the proceedings addressed in this article. The authors would like to thank Barry J. Blonien, also an associate at Latham & Watkins LLP, and David G. Tewksbury, a partner at Kirkland & Ellis LLP, for their assistance in preparing this article.

[1] See, e.g., Charles Fried, Contract as Promise: A Theory of Contractual Obligation (Harvard University Press 1981) (characterizing American contract law as being rooted in a moral obligation to enforce a promise).

[2] Economists have long recognized the critical importance of contracts as a source of economic growth. See, e.g., Adam Smith, The Wealth of Nations bk. I, ch. IX, at 133 (Edwin Cannan ed., Bantam Dell 2003) (1776) ("When the law does not enforce the performance of contracts, it puts all borrowers nearly upon the same footing with bankrupts."); Ross Levine, The Legal Environment, Banks and Long-Run Economic Growth, 30 J. Money, Credit and Banking 596 (1998) (contract enforceability facilitates the development of efficient banking systems and financial markets, which, in turn, support economic growth); Daniel Kaufman, et al., Governance Matters, World Bank Policy Research Working Paper No. 2196 (1999) (contract enforceability a key component of the "rule of law," which is critical to economic development). More recently, economists have stressed the importance of contract enforcement in promoting development, especially with respect to economic regulation of capital-intensive industries, such as the electric and natural gas industries. See, e.g., Mark A. Jamison, et al., Measuring and Mitigating Regulatory Risk in Private Infrastructure Investment, 18 Electricity J. 36 (July 2005); Mario Bergara, et al., Political Institutions and Electric Utility Performance: A Cross Nation Analysis, 40 Cal. Mgmt. Rev. 18 (1998); Pablo Spiller, A Positive Political Theory of Regulatory Instruments: Contracts, Administrative Law or Regulatory Specificity, 69 S. Cal. L. Rev. 477 (1996).

its conservative energy . . . requires contracts, not illegal in their character, to be enforced as made by the parties, even against any State interference with their terms."[3]

This historical respect for the integrity of contracts was tested and strongly reaffirmed this term in *Morgan Stanley Capital Group Inc. v. Public Utility District No. 1 of Snohomish County.*[4] *Morgan Stanley* presented the Supreme Court with the question whether the Federal Energy Regulatory Commission (FERC or the Commission)[5] could or should exercise its authority under the Federal Power Act (FPA) to abrogate or modify contracts for the purchase and sale of large amounts of electricity entered into in the western energy crisis of 2000–2001.[6]

During the western energy crisis, many large sophisticated parties faced with volatile spot markets signed long-term contracts to meet their electricity needs. While the contract rates were undeniably high relative to historic forward market prices, they were generally lower than contemporaneous spot prices and insulated the buyers from any further price increases in the spot and forward markets. The buyers initially expressed satisfaction with the deals they struck, and some resold portions of their allotments for huge profits in the spot markets. But the buyers' satisfaction was short-lived. By the summer of 2001, prices in the spot markets had declined significantly, and the contract rates no longer appeared favorable. The buyers cried foul and filed complaints asking FERC to relieve them

---

[3] Wilmington & W.R. Co. v. King, 91 U.S. 3, 5 (1875) (also recognizing that governmental intrusion into contractual relations simply to relieve parties of their "hard bargains" would "create an insecurity in business transactions which would be intolerable").

[4] 555 U.S. ___, 128 S. Ct. 2733 (2008).

[5] Throughout this article, we also use the terms "FERC" or the "Commission" to refer to the Federal Power Commission, FERC's predecessor.

[6] The scheme of regulation under the FPA, which applies to the interstate transmission and sale at wholesale of electricity, is "substantially identical" to that under the Natural Gas Act (NGA), which applies to the interstate transport and wholesale sale of natural gas, and decisions addressing the FPA and NGA are therefore cited "interchangeably." Ark. La. Gas Co. v. Hall, 453 U.S. 571, 578 n.7 (1981) (citation omitted). Accordingly, while *Morgan Stanley*, and thus this article, is specifically focused on the regulation of electricity contracts under the FPA, the case's holdings and implications are equally applicable to the regulation of natural gas contracts under the NGA.

of their contractual obligations, now claiming that the prices they had lauded were "unjust and unreasonable." FERC rejected these complaints, finding that contract modification was not required simply because the contracts had "become[ ] uneconomic over time."[7]

The buyers found a more sympathetic ear in the Ninth Circuit. In a decision that trampled the law's traditional deference to contracts, the court of appeals reversed the Commission's ruling. In the Ninth Circuit's view, an electricity or natural gas contract cannot be enforced as written unless FERC first has the opportunity to decide whether the contract is "just and reasonable" and ensures that no exogenous factors affected the "propriety of the contract's formation."[8] And even then, if the party challenging the contract is the buyer claiming the price is too high, FERC, as the federal agency charged with protecting consumer welfare, must lower the rate to marginal cost—regardless of the effect of such interference on the long-term supply and cost of power.

The Supreme Court flatly rejected the Ninth Circuit's decision and its conception of the FPA as an all-encompassing regulatory scheme with pervasive governmental oversight of contractual relations. Drawing on the language of the statute and decades of precedent, the Court reaffirmed that government interference with contracts is permitted only in rare circumstances of overwhelming public necessity. In so holding, the Court recognized the presumptive reasonableness of voluntary agreements and the long-term harm to consumers that would result from casual governmental interference with contractual bargains. By firmly reinforcing the limits of permissible government interference with private energy contracts, even in the face of a historic energy crisis that produced unprecedented high prices and volatility, the Court's decision in *Morgan Stanley* makes it clear that, at least with respect to FERC-regulated electricity and natural gas contracts, a deal is still a deal.

## I. Regulatory Background

Congress enacted Part II of the FPA in 1935 to regulate the interstate transmission and sale at wholesale of electricity "in the public

[7] Nev. Power Co. v. Enron Power Mktg., Inc., 103 F.E.R.C. ¶ 61,353, at 62,384 (2003) ("Nevada Power Initial Order"), reh'g denied, 105 F.E.R.C. ¶ 61,185 (2003) ("Nevada Power Rehearing Order").

[8] Pub. Util. Dist. No. 1 of Snohomish County, Washington v. FERC, 471 F.3d 1053, 1077 (9th Cir. 2006) ("Snohomish").

interest"[9] because it was concerned that the market was dominated by vertically integrated utilities with the ability to use their monopoly power to raise prices.[10] At the same time, Congress recognized that electricity sales might not be well-suited for the traditional model of regulation in which utilities are required to file generally applicable rate tariffs. As with natural gas, the sale or transmission of electricity "typically require[s] substantial investment in capacity and facilities for the service of a particular distributor," and therefore required "individualized arrangements" that would not conform to broadly applicable tariff schedules.[11] Further, "[i]n wholesale markets, the part[ies] . . . were often sophisticated businesses enjoying presumptively equal bargaining power, who could be expected to negotiate a 'just and reasonable' rate as between the two of them."[12]

Under the FPA's regulatory scheme, FERC is directed to ensure that all rates for electricity are "just and reasonable."[13] But this does not mean that the Commission must take an active role in setting rates. The FPA "departed from the scheme of purely tariff-based regulation" and "acknowledged that contracts between commercial buyers and sellers could be used in ratesetting."[14] Whether contractual or tariff-based, the rates filed with the Commission automatically become effective "[u]nless the Commission otherwise orders."[15] At the same time, the Commission is required to correct any rate that it finds to be "unjust, unreasonable, unduly discriminatory or preferential."[16]

## II. The *Mobile-Sierra* Doctrine

By allowing parties to enter into and set rates through contract and yet also requiring the Commission to ensure that all rates are just

[9] 16 U.S.C. § 824(a).

[10] See FPC v. Texaco Inc., 417 U.S. 380, 397–98 (1974).

[11] United Gas Pipe Line Co. v. Mobile Gas Servs. Corp., 350 U.S. 332, 339 (1956).

[12] Verizon Commc'ns, Inc. v. FCC, 535 U.S. 467, 479 (2002).

[13] 16 U.S.C. § 824d(a).

[14] Verizon, 535 U.S. at 479; see also 16 U.S.C. § 824d(c) (requiring contracts to be filed with the Commission).

[15] 16 U.S.C. § 824d(d).

[16] 16 U.S.C. § 824e(a). The Commission's authority to modify rates, however, is not limitless—rather, rate changes ordered by the Commission have only prospective effect. See id.; see also 16 U.S.C. § 824e(b) (the Commission may only order refunds for sales occurring after a "refund effective date" that is established, at the earliest, upon the filing of a complaint).

and reasonable, Congress enacted a regulatory scheme that requires balance between the freedom and obligations of contract and governmental ratemaking responsibility. The Court first addressed this balance in two companion cases decided in 1956.

In the first case, *United Gas Pipe Line Co. v. Mobile Gas Services Corp.*,[17] United Gas Pipe Line Company agreed to sell natural gas under a long-term contract at a rate substantially lower than its normal price. The buyer, in turn, entered into a separate contract to resell the gas at a rate just slightly higher than that set in its contract with United. During the term of the contract, however, United asked the Commission to set a new and higher rate that would be consistent with United's other rates. The Commission approved the new rate over the buyer's objections.

The Supreme Court reversed. The Court distinguished common carrier regimes such as "the Interstate Commerce Act, which in effect precludes private rate agreements by its requirement that the rates to all shippers be uniform."[18] The Natural Gas Act, in contrast, "permits the relations between the parties to be established initially by contract,"[19] and "evinces no purpose to abrogate private rate contracts as such."[20] Because the NGA "purports neither to grant nor to define the initial rate-setting powers of natural gas companies,"[21] the Court found "that, except as specifically limited by the Act, the rate-making powers of . . . companies were to be no different from those they would possess in the absence of the Act," including the power "to fix by contract, and change only by mutual agreement, the rate agreed upon with a particular customer."[22] Under this scheme, the Commission simply has no authority to permit a party to renege on its contractual bargain. The Court observed that, "[b]y preserving the integrity of contracts, [the Act] permits the stability of supply arrangements which all agree is essential to the health of the natural gas industry."[23] At the same time, "the contracts remain

---

[17] 350 U.S. 332 (1956) ("Mobile").
[18] *Id.* at 338.
[19] *Id.* at 339.
[20] *Id.* at 338.
[21] *Id.* at 341.
[22] *Id.* at 343.
[23] *Id.* at 344.

fully subject to the paramount power of the Commission to modify them when necessary in the public interest."[24] By retaining this governmental oversight, the statute "affords a reasonable accommodation between the conflicting interests of contract stability on the one hand and public regulation on the other."[25]

The very same day, the Court issued *FPC v. Sierra Pacific Power Co.*,[26] which addressed similar issues in the context of the FPA. In *Sierra*, a seller, Pacific Gas and Electric Company (PG&E), had voluntarily agreed to make long-term sales at a "special low rate"[27] to dissuade one of its customers from seeking out alternative supply sources. As in *Mobile*, the seller later asked the Commission to raise the contract rate to bring it in line with the seller's other rates. However, there was one notable difference: Before accepting the new rate, the Commission found the existing contract rate to be "'unreasonably low and therefore unlawful.'"[28] Nonetheless, applying the reasoning of *Mobile*, the Supreme Court reversed. The Court held that proof of an "unreasonably low" rate does not, by itself, permit the agency to modify a contract. It explained that,

> while it may be that the Commission may not normally impose upon a public utility a rate which would produce less than a fair return, it does not follow that the public utility may not itself agree by contract to a rate affording less than a fair return or that, if it does so, it is entitled to be relieved of its improvident bargain.[29]

"In such circumstances," the Court held, "the sole concern of the Commission would seem to be whether the rate is so low as to adversely affect the public interest—as where it might impair the financial ability of the public utility to continue its service, cast upon other consumers an excessive burden, or be unduly discriminatory."[30]

[24] *Id.*
[25] *Id.*
[26] 350 U.S. 348 (1956).
[27] *Id.* at 352.
[28] *Id.* at 354.
[29] *Id.* at 355.
[30] *Id.*

Together, these two decisions gave rise to what has become known as the *"Mobile-Sierra* doctrine," under which the Commission may modify contracts "only in circumstances of unequivocal public necessity."[31] Based on the Court's references to the "public interest" in *Mobile* and *Sierra*, the courts and the Commission began to refer to this strict standard (somewhat confusingly, as we discuss later) as the "public interest standard." Proposed contract modifications will be reviewed under the public interest standard unless the contract contains explicit language indicating that the parties intended otherwise.[32] Where a contract does explicitly disclaim application of the public interest standard, the Commission will review proposed changes under the same standard it uses for non-contract rates, which is commonly referred to as the "just and reasonable standard."[33] While the Commission has considerable discretion in determining the boundaries of the two standards, the courts have made it clear that the public interest standard is far more deferential to parties' contractual bargains.[34] In fact, one court of appeals has gone so far as to characterize the burden imposed by the public interest standard as "practically insurmountable."[35]

[31] In re Permian Basin Area Rate Cases, 390 U.S. 747, 822 (1968); see also Ark. La. Gas Co. v. Hall, 453 U.S. 571, 582 (1981) (contract modification permitted only in "extraordinary circumstances").

[32] See United Gas Pipe Line Co. v. Memphis Light, Gas & Water Div., 358 U.S. 103, 110–13 (1958) ("Memphis") (finding *Mobile* and *Sierra* not to be applicable in the case of a contract that explicitly contemplated the contract price to be subject to modification by the seller); Morgan Stanley Cap. Group Inc. v. Pub. Util. Dist. No. 1 of Snohomish County, 128 S. Ct. 2733, 2739 (2008). Since the Supreme Court's decision in *Memphis*, the courts have generally held that the *Mobile-Sierra* doctrine applies unless the contract explicitly provides otherwise in a *"Memphis* clause." See, e.g., Texaco Inc. v. FERC, 148 F.3d 1091, 1096 (D.C. Cir. 1998); Boston Edison Co. v. FERC, 233 F.3d 60, 67 (1st Cir. 2000); La. Power & Light Co. v. FERC, 587 F.2d 671, 675 (5th Cir. 1979).

[33] See Morgan Stanley, 128 S. Ct. at 2740.

[34] See, e.g., Atlantic City Elec. Co. v. FERC, 295 F.3d 1, 14 (D.C. Cir. 2002) (public interest standard "is much more restrictive than the just and reasonable standard"); Ne. Utils. Serv. Co. v. FERC, 55 F.3d 686, 691 (1st Cir. 1995) ("[T]he 'public interest' standard [is] 'a more difficult standard for the Commission to meet than the statutory "unjust and unreasonable" standard.'" (citation omitted)).

[35] Potomac Elec. Power Co. v. FERC, 210 F.3d 403, 407 (D.C. Cir. 2000); see also Papago Tribal Util. Auth. v. FERC, 723 F.2d 950, 954 (D.C. Cir. 1983). Despite this hyperbole, the courts have in several instances affirmed FERC's authority to modify electricity and natural gas agreements when it has found that necessary in the public interest. See, e.g., Ariz. Corp. Comm'n v. FERC, 397 F.3d 952, 953–95 (D.C. Cir. 2005)

*Mobile* and *Sierra* have been described as two of the "best-known public utility decisions by the Supreme Court in [the 20th] century,"[36] and buyers and sellers of electricity and natural gas have understood for decades that they bargain "in the shadow of the [*Mobile-Sierra*] doctrine."[37] Although the Commission has often chafed at the limitations on its authority imposed by *Mobile-Sierra*,[38] the courts have repeatedly reaffirmed the protection the doctrine affords freedom of contract.[39]

## III. FERC Applies *Mobile-Sierra* to Reject Buyers' Challenges to the Long-Term Contracts They Signed During the Western Energy Crisis

The western energy crisis has been characterized as "the worst electricity-market crisis in American history."[40] From the summer of 2000 through the spring of 2001, prices in the California spot electricity markets "jumped dramatically—more than fifteenfold," and those high prices "spilled over into other Western States."[41] The causes of those high prices have been the subject of much litigation, which we do not address in detail here, except to note that FERC has attributed the price increases to a "confluence of factors," including:

> flawed market rules; inadequate addition of generating facilities in the preceding years; a drop in available hydropower due to drought conditions; a rupture of a major pipeline supplying natural gas into California; strong growth in the economy and in electricity demand; unusually high temperatures; an increase in unplanned outages of extremely old generating facilities; and market manipulation. This was not

(affirming modification of contracts that would have jeopardized the service provided to third parties); Transmission Access Policy Study Group v. FERC, 225 F.3d 667, 709–12 (D.C. Cir. 2000) (modification of contracts justified in light of industry restructuring), aff'd sub nom. New York v. FERC, 535 U.S. 1 (2002).

[36] Boston Edison Co., 233 F.3d at 66.

[37] *Id.*

[38] See *id.* at 69 (noting FERC's hostility to the *Mobile-Sierra* doctrine).

[39] See, e.g., Potomac Elec. Power Co., 210 F.3d at 409; Texaco, Inc. v. FERC, 148 F.3d 1091, 1096–97 (D.C. Cir. 1998); Ne. Utils. Serv. Co. v. FERC, 993 F.2d 937, 960 (1st Cir. 1993).

[40] Brief for the Federal Energy Regulatory Commission in Opposition at 12, Sempra Generation v. Pub. Util. Comm'n of Cal., Nos. 06-1454, et al. (U.S. Aug. 2007).

[41] Morgan Stanley, 128 S. Ct. at 2742, 2743.

a situation in which one or a few factors stressed the market; rather, it was an unprecedented situation in which numerous adverse events occurred simultaneously to place California and the entire West in an electricity crisis that had never before been experienced.[42]

These problems placed utilities with an obligation to serve retail customers in the unenviable position of having to choose between purchasing high-priced electricity in the volatile spot markets or entering into long-term contracts at fixed rates that were "very high by historical standards"[43] but would protect them against future price increases and provide a stable source of future energy. Anticipating continued spot market instability, many utilities chose the long-term contract option. In binding themselves to fixed rates over the long term, both the buyers and the sellers took substantial, calculated risks—buyers risked that spot prices would fall below the fixed forward prices they had agreed to pay; sellers risked that spot prices would continue to rise, increasing supply costs and the opportunity cost of forward contracts.[44] Less than a year into the contracts, spot prices in fact declined significantly, and the forward contract prices therefore became substantially higher than the prices the buyers could obtain in the spot markets. Instead of assuming the responsibility to pay those higher prices to which they had expressly agreed, many buyers rushed to file complaints at FERC alleging that their contract rates were "unjust and unreasonable" under the FPA, and should be abrogated or modified.[45]

Notably, the backdrop of the western energy crisis provided the buyers and their supporters with substantial ammunition. Beyond the sheer magnitude of the price increases in the spot markets during

---

[42] CAlifornians for Renewable Energy, Inc. v. Cal. Pub. Utils. Comm'n, 119 F.E.R.C. ¶ 61,058, at 61,246 (2007). See also James L. Sweeney, The California Electricity Crisis (Hoover Press 2002) (discussing the factors contributing to the energy crisis).

[43] Morgan Stanley, 128 S. Ct. at 2743.

[44] In addition, some of the sellers in *Morgan Stanley* purchased power to meet their contract obligations at prices that were comparable to the contract rates. See Nevada Power Initial Order, 103 F.E.R.C. ¶ 61,353, at 62,393.

[45] *Morgan Stanley* itself resulted from complaints filed with FERC by Public Utility District No. 1 of Snohomish County, Washington, Nevada Power Company, Sierra Pacific Power Company, and Southern California Water Company seeking to abrogate or modify their respective contracts.

the energy crisis, FERC found certain of the spot markets in California to have been "dysfunctional."[46] And it was later discovered that Enron and other sellers had attempted to manipulate those spot markets.[47] The buyers argued that the dysfunction in the spot markets tainted the forward contract offers they received, because long-term contracts are priced at the rates parties anticipate for future spot market sales. And that intuition was bolstered by a report prepared by FERC staff (though not officially adopted by the agency), which concluded that there was a statistical correlation between spot and forward prices.[48] The buyers also argued that the "dysfunctional" California spot markets left them no practical alternative but to enter into the challenged contracts to serve their retail customers, who would ultimately bear the burden of the high contract rates.[49]

After an evidentiary hearing, FERC rejected the complaints.[50] At the threshold, the Commission concluded that the public interest

[46] See, e.g., San Diego Gas & Elec. Co. v. Sellers of Energy & Ancillary Servs., 93 F.E.R.C. ¶ 61,121, at 61,349 (2000) (finding centralized auction markets administered by the California Independent System Operator and California Power Exchange to have been "dysfunctional").

[47] See Pub. Utils. Comm'n of Cal. v. FERC, 462 F.3d 1027, 1039–40 (9th Cir. 2006); Enron Power Mktg., Inc., 103 F.E.R.C. ¶ 61,343 (2003) (finding Enron to have engaged in market manipulation and imposing penalties), reh'g denied, 106 F.E.R.C. ¶ 61,024 (2004).

[48] See Staff of the Federal Energy Regulatory Commission, Final Report on Price Manipulation in Western Markets, Fact-Finding Investigation of Potential Manipulation of Electric and Natural Gas Prices, Docket No. PA02-2-000, at Chapter V (Mar. 26, 2003).

[49] Even though states retain their jurisdiction over retail sales and may require public utilities subject to their jurisdiction to enter only into prudent purchases, they may not prevent a public utility from passing through to its retail customers the wholesale rates approved by FERC. See, e.g., Entergy La., Inc. v. La. Pub. Serv. Comm'n, 539 U.S. 39, 41–42 (2003) ("FERC-approved cost allocations . . . may not be subjected to reevaluation in state ratemaking proceedings."); Nantahala Power & Light Co. v. Thornburg, 476 U.S. 953, 962 (1986) ("[I]nterstate power rates filed with FERC or fixed by FERC must be given binding effect by state utility commissions determining intrastate rates.").

[50] See Nevada Power Initial Order, 103 F.E.R.C. ¶ 61,353, reh'g denied, Nevada Power Rehearing Order, 105 F.E.R.C. ¶ 61,185. See also Pub. Utils. Comm'n of Cal. v. Sellers of Long Term Contracts to the Cal. Dep't. of Water Resources, 103 F.E.R.C. ¶ 61,354 (2003) (rejecting complaints by the California Public Utilities Commission and the California Electricity Oversight Board seeking to abrogate or modify contracts entered into by the California Department of Water Resources), reh'g denied, 105

standard applies to all the challenged contracts and rejected many of the buyers' attempts to distinguish the case from *Mobile* and *Sierra*. For example, the buyers had argued that, unlike *Mobile* and *Sierra*, which involved attempts by sellers to raise rates for their own benefit, they were attempting to lower prices for the ultimate benefit of retail customers. Along the same lines, some intervenors had argued that their challenges should not be treated as if they were parties who had agreed to the contracts, because they were state representatives acting to protect the interests of the consuming public. The Commission held that under *Mobile-Sierra* it "is no more at liberty to alter a contract 'to the prejudice of the producers than to do so in their favor,'"[51] and that no "precedent . . . supports a finding that a non-signatory party may challenge a *Mobile-Sierra* contract under the 'just and reasonable' standard of review, as opposed to the 'public interest' standard of review."[52]

In one important respect, however, the Commission apparently agreed with the buyers. As a result of various technological advancements and regulatory initiatives, the electric industry has moved from one dominated by a small number of large, vertically integrated utilities to one with numerous independent electric generators and in which all market participants have the ability to obtain transmission rights on a non-discriminatory basis.[53] In line with these developments, FERC has moved away from a scheme of cost-based ratemaking (where a seller must justify its price as a recovery of costs plus a reasonable rate of return) to a market-based rate regime (where sellers who demonstrate they lack market power are granted blanket authority to make sales at negotiated rates). Although market-based rate sellers are still subject to certain ongoing reporting requirements to ensure that they cannot exert market dominance, their individual contracts do not have to be filed with or reviewed by FERC before

F.E.R.C. ¶ 61,182 (2003); Pacificorp v. Reliant Energy Servs., Inc., 103 F.E.R.C. ¶ 61,355 (2003) (rejecting complaints by Pacificorp against five sellers).

[51] Nevada Power Rehearing Order, 105 F.E.R.C. ¶ 61,185, at 61,985 (quoting Pub. Serv. Comm'n of New York v. FPC, 543 F.2d 757, 798 (D.C. Cir. 1974)).

[52] Nevada Power Initial Order, 103 F.E.R.C. ¶ 61,353, at 62,389 (citations omitted).

[53] See Morgan Stanley, 128 S. Ct. at 2740–41 (describing competitive advances in the industry); Promoting Wholesale Competition Through Open-Access Non-Discriminatory Transmission Servs. by Pub. Utils., 61 Fed. Reg. 21,540 (May 10, 1996) (FERC rulemaking requiring transmission to be provided on a non-discriminatory basis).

becoming effective.[54] Because the challenged western energy crisis contracts were all market-based, they had not been filed with FERC. These contracts were therefore distinguishable, the buyers argued, from the contracts in *Mobile* and *Sierra*, which had been filed with and accepted by the Commission. How, the buyers essentially asked, can FERC be expected to satisfy its regulatory responsibilities under the FPA to ensure that all rates are "just and reasonable" if contracts that are not reviewed at all before becoming effective are later essentially immune to challenge as a result of *Mobile-Sierra*'s "practically insurmountable" public interest standard?

FERC did not contest that the public interest standard only applies to contracts that have been filed with and subject to review by the Commission. In FERC's view, however, any prior-review requirement was satisfied through its market-based regime. Specifically, FERC asserted that "[t]he need for prior Commission review ... was met when, after determining that the [sellers] lacked market power or had taken steps to mitigate it, the Commission authorized all of the [sellers] in this proceeding to make sales of power at market-based rates."[55] FERC explained that it "is not required specifically to review each agreement since the Commission, when it grants umbrella market-based rate authorization, pre-determines that rates under future contracts entered into pursuant to the market-based rate authorization will be just and reasonable."[56]

Having found the public interest standard applicable, the Commission concluded that the buyers failed to show that contract modification was required by the public interest. Pointing to the factors identified in *Sierra*, the Commission found "no credible record evidence that the contracts at issue are placing the [buyers] in financial distress so as to threaten their ability to continue service," that "other customers will bear an excessive burden as a result of upholding the challenged contracts," or that "the contracts terms are unduly discriminatory."[57] In addition, after examining the "totality of circumstances preceding and following the execution of the contracts

[54] See Morgan Stanley, 128 S. Ct. at 2741–42 (describing FERC's market-based regime).

[55] Nevada Power Initial Order, 103 F.E.R.C. ¶ 61,353, at 62,388 (footnotes and citation omitted).

[56] *Id.* at 62,389.

[57] *Id.* at 62,397.

at issue,"[58] the Commission concluded that the contracts "were the result of choices voluntarily made by the [buyers] and to the extent the [buyers] left themselves open to unnecessary risks, it was also their choice."[59] Allowing a party that "suddenly finds that its deal has become uneconomical" to undo its voluntary bargains is forbidden under the *Mobile-Sierra* doctrine and would create "uncertainty in the market"[60] that, in turn, would "erode investor confidence and willingness to invest in merchant energy projects, which . . . could have an adverse effect on infrastructure development, especially at a time when western markets need new generation and transmission."[61] Rejecting the complaints was "in the public interest because it balances effective rate regulation with respect for the sanctity of contracts, as dictated by the U.S. Supreme Court under the *Mobile-Sierra* doctrine."[62]

## IV. The Ninth Circuit Limits *Mobile-Sierra* and Imposes Layers of Agency Regulation on Private Contracts

The Ninth Circuit rejected FERC's conclusions.[63] The court of appeals characterized *Mobile* and *Sierra* as creating a presumption that a negotiated contract is "just and reasonable" only if FERC had an opportunity to review the contract for justness and reasonableness before it went into effect. The Ninth Circuit did not believe that condition was satisfied here because FERC's market-based regime does not provide for Commission review of individual contracts and only requires periodic reporting to ensure that sellers lack market power. In the Ninth Circuit's view, FERC's market-based rate regime is insufficient to ensure just and reasonable rates because it "precludes timely consideration of sudden market changes and offers no protection to purchasers victimized by the abuses of sellers

---

[58] *Id.* at 62,398.

[59] *Id.* at 62,399.

[60] Nevada Power Rehearing Order, 105 F.E.R.C. ¶ 61,185, at 61,982–83.

[61] Nevada Power Initial Order, 103 F.E.R.C. ¶ 61,353, at 62,393 (describing findings of the Administrative Law Judge).

[62] *Id.* at 62,384.

[63] See Snohomish, 471 F.3d at 1077; see also Pub. Utils. Comm'n of Cal. v. FERC, 474 F.3d 587 (9th Cir. 2006) (granting petitions for review of FERC's orders rejecting complaints by California state agencies based on the reasoning in *Snohomish*).

or dysfunctional market conditions that FERC itself only notices in hindsight."[64]

Although the Ninth Circuit's decision did not bind FERC to cost-based ratemaking, it effectively stripped market-based contract rates of any protection against future challenges. The court held that, in the context of market-based contracts, the *Mobile-Sierra* presumption would only apply in "limited circumstances" where three "prerequisites" were satisfied: (1) the contract, by its terms, cannot preclude the application of the *Mobile-Sierra* public interest standard; (2) "the regulatory scheme in which the contracts are formed must provide FERC with an opportunity for initial review of the contracted rate";[65] and (3) "the scope of that review must permit consideration of the factors relevant to the propriety of the contract's formation"[66]— retroactively, if necessary. The court's first prerequisite simply reflected the preexisting understanding that contracting parties may choose to opt-out of the public interest standard.[67] The second and third prerequisites, however, would have resulted in a radical expansion of FERC's regulatory authority over private contracts. In effect, these prerequisites would have negated *any* "presumption" of justness and reasonableness by requiring de novo substantive FERC review of the justness and reasonableness of every contract, including a full investigation of whether any exogenous factors had affected the parties' bargain. The court reasoned that, unless the second and third prerequisites were met, "FERC's reliance on the [*Mobile-Sierra*] presumption would amount to a complete abdication of its statutory responsibility under the FPA."[68]

In addition, even if *Mobile-Sierra* were found to be applicable to the buyers' claims, the Ninth Circuit found that FERC had applied "an erroneous standard for determining whether the challenged contracts affect the public interest."[69] The court held that the Commission erred in giving these contracts the same deference they would have been owed if challenged by a seller seeking to raise

---

[64] Snohomish, 471 F.3d at 1085.

[65] *Id.* at 1076.

[66] *Id.* at 1077.

[67] See *supra* note 32.

[68] Snohomish, 471 F.3d at 1075.

[69] *Id.* at 1087.

the rates. Because the Commission's primary responsibility is the protection of consumers, the court ruled that contract rates should receive no significant deference when challenged by a buyer seeking lower rates that would be passed on to its retail customers. The court instructed the Commission that "if a challenged contract imposes any significant cost on ultimate customers because of a wholesale rate too high to be within a zone of reasonableness, that contract affects the public interest."[70] And the court specified that rates will generally be within the "zone of reasonableness" only if they approximate marginal costs.[71]

The sellers sought Supreme Court review. Their efforts were supported by leading industry groups and economists who believed that, unless reversed, the Ninth Circuit's decision would endanger the nation's stable and efficient supply of electricity and inflict substantial harm on the electric and natural gas industries, and the economy in general. The Commission opposed Supreme Court review—which is hardly surprising because the Ninth Circuit's decision would have vastly expanded its regulatory authority to second-guess and modify contracts. Once certiorari was granted, however, FERC stepped up to defend its orders.

## V. *Morgan Stanley*: The Supreme Court Reaffirms the Application of Traditional Contract Principles

The Supreme Court squarely repudiated the Ninth Circuit's limitations on *Mobile-Sierra* and, for the authors and others who have been involved in contract disputes before FERC, the Court's decision in *Morgan Stanley* heralds a welcome return to the basic concept that a deal is a deal. The Court's opinion reaffirms two principles crucial to contract stability: First, that rates agreed to in freely negotiated contracts should be presumed just and reasonable, and second, that regardless of whether they are challenged as too low or too high, *Mobile-Sierra* contract rates are immune from regulatory interference by FERC except in extraordinary circumstances.

---

[70] *Id.* at 1089 (citation omitted). See also Pub. Utils. Comm'n of Cal. v. FERC, 474 F.3d at 596 (finding the public interest to be affected "[e]ven if rates did not increase . . . [if] the retail rates charged consumers because of these contracts might have been higher than they would have been had the wholesale contract rates been lower").

[71] Snohomish, 471 F.3d at 1089.

At the outset, Justice Scalia, writing for the Court, squarely rejected the notion that the *Mobile-Sierra* doctrine is itself unlawful. As previously explained, the Commission and various courts have stated that *Mobile-Sierra* contract rates can only be modified if the "public interest standard" is satisfied, while characterizing other rates as subject to modification under a less demanding "just and reasonable standard." Capitalizing on this confusing nomenclature, some buyers insisted that *Mobile* and *Sierra* erred in ignoring the statutory requirement that all rates must be "just and reasonable." The Court agreed with the buyers that "[t]here is only one statutory standard for assessing wholesale electricity rates, whether set by contract or tariff—the just and reasonable standard"[72]—but explained that *Mobile-Sierra* merely "provide[s] a definition of what it means for a rate to satisfy the just-and-reasonable standard in the contract context."[73]

The Court also rejected the Ninth Circuit's attempt to premise the application of *Mobile-Sierra* on FERC having initially determined upon a contract's filing that its rates are just and reasonable, as though the doctrine were merely a form of regulatory estoppel. The Court made clear that, regardless of *when* the Commission is asked to review a contract,[74] FERC must "presume that the rate set out in a freely negotiated wholesale-energy contract meets the 'just and reasonable' requirement imposed by law,"[75] and that this presumption "may be overcome only if FERC concludes that the contract seriously harms the public interest."[76]

These holdings are neither new law nor new limitations on the Commission's authority. They spring naturally from the Court's earlier recognition that the FPA and NGA were not intended to circumscribe a party's fundamental right to "establish *ex parte*, and change at will, the rates offered to prospective customers; or to fix by contract, and change only by mutual agreement, the rate

---

[72] Morgan Stanley, 128 S. Ct. at 2745.

[73] *Id.* at 2746.

[74] *Id.* at 2745.

[75] *Id.* at 2737.

[76] *Id.*

agreed upon with a particular customer."[77] In this respect, the FPA and NGA are dramatically different from schemes, like the now-overhauled Interstate Commerce Act,[78] that were intended to regulate the relationships between a dominant service provider and the public at large and therefore required a one-size-fits-all tariffing approach. By contrast, the wholesale power business regulated by FERC has always been characterized by "sophisticated businesses enjoying presumptively equal bargaining power, who can be expected to negotiate a 'just and reasonable' rate as between the two of them."[79]

Thus, the Court found it hardly surprising that Congress would have "departed from the scheme of purely tariff-based regulation and acknowledged that contracts between commercial buyers and sellers could be used in rate setting."[80] In a regulatory scheme grounded on the ability of "sophisticated businesses" to manage their own affairs and protect their own interests, there is no need for FERC to have an initial opportunity for plenary review before presuming that contract rates are just and reasonable. By concluding that contract rates should be presumed to be just and reasonable regardless of the opportunity for prior agency review, the Court's decision rightly prohibits the Commission from adopting a paternalistic approach that would constrain parties to agreements that are based on a traditional cost-based approach. *Morgan Stanley* upholds contracting freedoms by recognizing that the voluntary agreement of parties can substitute for the cost analysis that is generally used to initially assess the justness and reasonableness of unilateral rates.

---

[77] United Gas Pipe Line Co. v. Mobile Gas Servs. Corp., 350 U.S. 332, 343 (1956); see also In re Permian Basin Area Rate Cases, 390 U.S. 747, 822 (1968) ("The regulatory system created by the Act is premised on contractual agreements voluntarily devised by the regulated companies.").

[78] Interestingly, in rewriting the scheme for regulation of rail transportation under the Interstate Commerce Act, Congress expressly permitted parties to enter into contracts for rail transportation services and removed such contracts from agency supervision. See 49 U.S.C. § 10709(c).

[79] Verizon Commc'ns, Inc. v. FCC, 535 U.S. 467, 479 (2002). In contrast, limitations on the right to contract have often been upheld based on the need to protect contracting parties that are disadvantaged or in inferior bargaining positions. See, e.g., West Coast Hotel Co. v. Parrish, 300 U.S. 379 (1937) (upholding minimum wage laws intended to protect workers that lack bargaining power).

[80] Verizon, 535 U.S. at 479.

At the same time, the Court appreciated that prices set in wholesale electricity contracts may adversely affect the consumers who will ultimately be asked to bear those rates, and acknowledged that the FPA is intended, in part, "to protect power consumers against excessive prices"[81] and "against exploitation at the hands of" sellers.[82] Navigating between the market and regulatory paradigms, *Morgan Stanley* confirms FERC's power to "abrogate a valid contract . . . if it harms the public interest."[83] In this way, the Court's decision simply reflects the long-held understanding that "freedom of contract is the general rule and restraint the exception. The exercise of legislative authority to abridge it can be justified only by the existence of *exceptional circumstances.*"[84]

Although the Court thus strongly reaffirmed the continued viability of the *Mobile-Sierra* doctrine, it nonetheless remanded the case to FERC for further consideration because it found FERC's analysis of the public interest lacking in two respects. First, the Court found that FERC had failed adequately to consider "whether the contracts imposed an excessive burden on consumers 'down the line,' relative to the rates they could have obtained (but for the contracts) after elimination of the dysfunctional market."[85] Second, the Court directed FERC to consider whether "one party to a contract engaged in such extensive unlawful market manipulation" that the contract would not be presumed to be "just and reasonable,"[86] but made it clear that contract modification for that reason would only be

[81] Pennsylvania Water & Power Co. v. FPC, 343 U.S. 414, 418 (1952).

[82] FPC v. Hope Natural Gas Co., 320 U.S. 591, 610 (1944).

[83] Morgan Stanley, 128 S. Ct. at 2747. *Morgan Stanley* also leaves untouched basic contract principles by explicitly recognizing that the *Mobile-Sierra* presumption would not apply "where there is unfair dealing at the contract formation stage—for instance, if [there are] traditional grounds for the abrogation of the contract such as fraud or duress." *Id.*

[84] Advance-Rumely Thresher Co. v. Jackson, 287 U.S. 283, 288 (1932) (emphasis added) (citations omitted). See also Steele v. Drummond, 275 U.S. 199, 205 (1927) ("It is only because of the dominant public interest that one, who has had the benefit of performance by the other party, is permitted to avoid his own obligation on the plea that the agreement is illegal. And it is a matter of great public concern that freedom of contract not be lightly interfered with." (citations omitted)).

[85] Morgan Stanley, 128 S. Ct. at 2749–50.

[86] Id. at 2750.

warranted if there was "a causal connection between unlawful activity and the contract rate."[87]

In remanding for an analysis of those issues, however, the Court made it clear that the Commission's public interest analysis must give heavy weight to the integrity of contracts that is necessary to ensure a stable and sufficient supply of electricity. It squarely rejected the Ninth Circuit's view that FERC should be less deferential to a contract when the contract rate is being challenged by the buyer as too high. The Court explained that, by requiring FERC to assess the public impact of contract rates with reference to marginal cost, the Ninth Circuit had negated *Mobile-Sierra*'s presumption of validity and "reinstitut[ed] cost-based rather than contract-based regulation."[88] In order to "accord an adequate level of protection to contracts," the Court made it clear that "[t]he standard for a buyer's rate-increase challenge must be the same . . . as the standard for a seller's challenge: The contract rate must seriously harm the public interest."[89]

As mentioned before, the justness and reasonableness of tariff rates are traditionally assessed by reference to cost, with the seller permitted only to recover its cost plus a regulated rate of return. By contrast, under *Mobile-Sierra*, contract rates are presumptively just and reasonable and do not harm the public interest simply because they exceed cost. The Court emphasized in *Morgan Stanley* that the public interest standard is a "high one" which requires a showing of "something more than a small dent in the consumer's pocket."[90] There is nothing radical about the concept that "the ordinary mode for evaluating contractually set rates is to look to whether the rates seriously harm the public interest, not to whether they are unfair to one of the parties that voluntarily assented to the contract."[91] The law has long recognized that the exercise of the right to contract

---

[87] *Id.* at 2751.

[88] *Id.* at 2748.

[89] *Id.* at 2747. Unlike the Ninth Circuit, the D.C. Circuit has also refused to distinguish between buyers and sellers, holding the *Mobile-Sierra* doctrine to be equally applicable in challenges brought by buyers as well as by sellers. See, e.g., Potomac Elec. Power Co. v. FERC, 210 F.3d 403 (D.C. Cir. 2000); San Diego Gas & Elec. Co. v. FERC, 904 F.2d 727 (D.C. Cir. 1990).

[90] Morgan Stanley, 128 S. Ct. at 2749 n.6.

[91] *Id.* at 2746 (citation omitted).

will always "in some respect, however slight, affect the public,"[92] and "the mere declaration by a Legislature that a business is affected with a public interest is not conclusive of the question whether its attempted regulation on that ground is justified."[93] Indeed, the Court recognized long before *Mobile* and *Sierra* that "[t]he power to fix rates, when exerted, is for the public welfare, to which private contracts must yield; but it is not an independent legislative function to vary or set aside such contracts, however unwise and unprofitable they may be. Indeed, the exertion of legislative power solely to that end is precluded by the contract impairment clause of the Constitution."[94]

Instead of the marginal cost-based, "zone of reasonableness" analysis contemplated by the Ninth Circuit, which focuses solely on short-term concerns, the Court directed the Commission to adopt a long-term view and consider whether the contracts imposed an excessive burden on consumers "'down the line.'"[95] The dissent complained that this directive improperly interfered with the Commission's discretion to "balanc[e] the short-term and long-term interests of consumers."[96] The Court's holding, however, seems—at least to us—to be a natural consequence of Congress's express contemplation of private contracts in the FPA and NGA. After all, requiring contract modification any time the contract rate exceeds or falls below cost would, in essence, represent "a reinstitution of cost-based rather than contract-based regulation."[97] If there is to be any room under the FPA and NGA for contracts, there must be times when it is acceptable for "short-term rates for a subset of the public [to] be high by historical standards."[98] Indeed, because costs will invariably change over time, FERC has traditionally assessed "the justness and

[92] Nebbia v. State of New York, 291 U.S. 502, 524–25 (1934).

[93] Chas. Wolff Packing Co. v. Court of Industrial Relations of Kansas, 262 U.S. 522, 536 (1923).

[94] Ark. Natural Gas Co. v. Ark. R.R. Comm'n, 261 U.S. 379, 383 (1923).

[95] Morgan Stanley, 128 S. Ct. at 2750.

[96] Id. at 2756 (Stevens, J., dissenting).

[97] Id. at 2748 (majority opinion). As the Court observed, a cost-based standard for assessing contracts would also subject the Commission to the "onerous new burden" of having to conduct detailed analyses any time it was alleged that costs had risen or fallen. See id. at 2749.

[98] Id.

reasonableness of long-term contracts and their rates over the 'life-of-the-contract' rather than on a 'snapshot-in-time' basis, looking at the benefits and burdens over the full-term of the contract.'"[99]

Further, the long-term approach adopted by the Court is necessary for any rational view of the public interest. The Court correctly recognized that "contract stability ultimately benefits consumers,"[100] and that the shortsighted standard the Ninth Circuit sought to impose would undermine "the important role of contracts in the FPA, as reflected in . . . *Sierra*, and would threaten to inject more volatility into the electricity market by undermining a key source of stability."[101] Although consumers and their representatives will often seek the lowest current rates possible, imposing a regulatory cost-based cap on contracts would "'have a chilling effect on investments and a seller's willingness to enter into long-term contracts and this, in turn, can harm customers in the long run.'"[102]

The particular characteristics of the electric industry render contractual stability especially important to the public—and consumer—welfare. As prominent economists explained in an amicus brief in support of the sellers in *Morgan Stanley*,[103] electricity is a commodity that cannot be stored, making it particularly susceptible to price swings due to changes in demand or in prices of inputs to generation (such as natural gas). The ability to enter into long-term electricity contracts therefore provides parties with a critically needed tool to hedge against future market fluctuations. And, of course, these contracts can fulfill their stabilizing and risk-management functions only if they are enforceable. In addition, the electric industry is highly capital intensive, requiring large infusions of investment in order to meet growing demand as well as to replace aging infrastructure. In light of the move to competitive wholesale markets, however, power generators and marketers have no regulatory guarantees that they will be provided a reasonable opportunity

---

[99] N. Va. Elec. Coop., Inc. v. Old Dominion Elec. Coop., 116 F.E.R.C. ¶ 61,173, at 61,741 (2006) (citation omitted).

[100] Morgan Stanley, 128 S. Ct. at 2749.

[101] *Id.*

[102] *Id.* (citation omitted).

[103] See Brief of William J. Baumol, et al., as Amici Curiae in Support of Petitioners, Morgan Stanley, 128 S. Ct. 2733 (Nov. 2007) (Nos. 06-1457, 06-1462), 2007 WL 4232926 ("Economists' Brief").

to recover their costs. Enforceable long-term contracts provide an assured revenue source that helps ensure investments for the long-term benefit of the public. As FERC itself recognized in its underlying order, "[c]ompetitive power markets simply cannot attract the capital needed to build adequate generating infrastructure without regulatory certainty, including certainty that the Commission will not modify market-based contracts unless there are extraordinary circumstances."[104]

The Court also properly refused to exempt these cases from the strictures of *Mobile-Sierra* because of the extraordinary market upheavals caused by the western energy crisis. The Court held that "the mere fact that a market is imperfect, or even chaotic, is no reason to undermine the stabilizing force of contracts that the FPA embraced."[105] The Court emphasized that contracts are an important stabilizing force, particularly during times of market volatility, and that "[i]t would be a perverse rule that rendered contracts less likely to be enforced when there is volatility in the market."[106] The Court recognized, moreover, that markets are, by their nature, not "perfect,"[107] and that a party entering into a contract will never have a full understanding of all the factors affecting current prices or how these may change during the life of the contract. Indeed, many of these factors—for example, supply, demand, and the price of inputs—will be beyond the contracting parties' control. But it is for precisely these reasons that contracts are needed as a risk-allocation mechanism. By contrast, the Ninth Circuit's concept of regulation premised on a hindsight review of all factors potentially relevant to "the propriety of the contract's formation"[108] would undermine parties' attempts to allocate market risks among themselves.

[104] Nev. Power Co. v. Duke Energy Trading & Mtkg., L.L.C., 99 F.E.R.C. ¶ 61,047, at 61,190 (2002).

[105] Morgan Stanley, 128 S. Ct. at 2747.

[106] *Id.* at 2746.

[107] *Id.*

[108] Snohomish, 471 F.3d at 1061.

The Court also appropriately recognized that "evaluating market 'dysfunction' is a very difficult and highly speculative task."[109] In the western energy crisis, for example, it is not (and likely never will be) clear the extent to which forward price increases may have been caused by spot market manipulation as compared with other "legitimate" factors, such as increased demand and constrained supply.[110] Moreover, there are instances where even acknowledged "dysfunction" would not justify contract modification. For example, and as the Economists' Brief pointed out to the Court, "OPEC routinely engages in anticompetitive conduct that would violate U.S. antitrust laws, and that indisputably distorts energy markets."[111] Yet OPEC's monopoly power over oil prices would hardly provide a valid reason for overturning energy contracts. After all, the owner of an oil-fired generating facility would equally be the "victim" of oil prices as the buyer of the power. But under the Ninth Circuit's directive, FERC would have to decide that such "factors exogenous to the forward market"[112] constitute a valid basis for contract modification. *Morgan Stanley* avoids this murky and open-ended inquiry by applying traditional contract principles: The Commission is only required to determine if there was "unfair dealing at the contract formation stage"—that is, wrongdoing by a contracting party that directly affected the contract.[113]

---

[109] Morgan Stanley, 128 S. Ct. at 2747. Notably, even in the context of cost-based rates, it is acknowledged that FERC is not able or required to arrive at "perfect" rates. See, e.g., Cities of Batavia v. FERC, 672 F.2d 64, 84 (D.C. Cir. 1982) ("[T]he billing design need only be reasonable, not theoretically perfect."); Town of Norwood v. FERC, 53 F.3d 377, 380 (D.C. Cir. 1995) ("Long-range estimates are an integral feature of ratemaking and financial analysis in general, and we have regularly approved reliance on admittedly imperfect future cost estimates."); Tenneco Oil Co. v. FERC, 571 F.2d 834, 841 (5th Cir. 1978) ("Administrative expedience, the pursuit of the achievable rather than the perfect, provides a reasoned basis for the Commission's judgment").

[110] Compare Scott M. Harvey & William W. Hogan, Market Power and Market Simulations (2002) (available at http://www.hks.harvard.edu/hepg/Papers/Hogan_Harvey_Market_Power&Simulations_071602.pdf), with Paul L. Joskow & Edward Kahn, A Quantitative Analysis of Pricing Behavior in California's Wholesale Electricity Market During Summer 2000, 23 Energy J. 1 (2002).

[111] Economists' Brief, *supra* note 103, at 27.

[112] Snohomish, 471 F.3d at 1086.

[113] As discussed, pursuant to this analysis, the Court directed FERC, on remand, to consider whether market manipulation by any of the sellers had adversely affected the contract rates. Morgan Stanley, 128 S. Ct. at 2747, 2750–51.

## VI. Implications of *Morgan Stanley* for FERC's Future Regulation of Electricity and Natural Gas Contracts

*A.* Morgan Stanley *Requires Use of the Public Interest Standard for Third-Party Challenges*

In its underlying order, in which it rejected intervenors' arguments that *Mobile-Sierra* does not apply to third-party challenges, FERC explained that there was no precedent exempting non-contracting parties from the public interest standard.[114] That is consistent with numerous cases in which courts have required the Commission to use the public interest standard even where it is acting *sua sponte*, rather than at the behest of one of the contracting parties.[115] But in *Maine Public Utilities Commission v. FERC*,[116] issued just before *Morgan Stanley* was decided, a panel of the D.C. Circuit departed from that precedent. *Maine PUC* held that the Commission cannot approve an agreement "that applies the highly-deferential 'public interest' standard to rate challenges brought by non-contracting third parties."[117] The D.C. Circuit read the *Mobile-Sierra* doctrine as only applying "when 'one party to a rate contract on file with FERC attempts to effect a unilateral rate change by asking FERC to relieve its obligations under a contract whose terms are no longer favorable to that party.'"[118] Thus, the court reasoned, the doctrine cannot "deprive [third parties] of their statutory right to challenge rates under the 'just and reasonable' standard."[119]

Based on *Maine PUC*, FERC issued a string of orders adopting the view that contracting parties cannot bind third parties to the stringent public interest standard under *Mobile-Sierra*, and that the Commission has the authority to outright reject contract language

---

[114] See Nevada Power Initial Order, 103 F.E.R.C. ¶ 61,353, at 62,389.

[115] See, e.g., Ne. Utils. Serv. Co. v. FERC, 993 F.2d 937 (1st Cir. 1993); Boston Edison Co. v. FERC, 233 F.3d 60 (1st Cir. 2000).

[116] 520 F.3d 464 (D.C. Cir. 2008).

[117] *Id.* at 477.

[118] *Id.* at 478 (quoting Me. Pub. Util. Comm'n v. FERC, 454 F.3d 278, 284 (D.C. Cir. 2006)).

[119] *Id.* at 476.

purporting to do so.[120] In light of *Morgan Stanley*, however, FERC now has apparently reversed course, and it recently sought rehearing of *Maine PUC*'s third-party exemption[121] over the vociferous objections of certain FERC commissioners.[122] In our view, FERC now has it right, as the reasoning in *Morgan Stanley* squarely precludes the notion that third parties are exempt from *Mobile-Sierra*.

The Supreme Court made it clear in *Morgan Stanley*, when rejecting the Ninth Circuit's initial-review "prerequisite," that FERC is required to apply the public interest standard whenever it reviews contracts, even in the first instance, because rates freely negotiated by contracting parties are presumed to be just and reasonable under the FPA.[123] As the Court explained, the *Mobile-Sierra* doctrine is "grounded in the commonsense notion that '[i]n wholesale markets, the party charging the rates and the party charged [are] often sophisticated businesses enjoying presumptively equal bargaining power, who could be expected to negotiate a "just and reasonable" rate as between the two of them.'"[124] "Therefore," the Court explained, "only when the mutually agreed-upon contract rate seriously harms the consuming public may the Commission declare it not to be just and reasonable."[125] The Court's explanation of why *Mobile-Sierra*

---

[120] See, e.g., Entergy Servs., Inc., 124 F.E.R.C. ¶ 61,100, at ¶ 3 (2008); PJM Interconnection, L.L.C., 124 F.E.R.C. ¶ 61,105, at ¶ 21 (2008); Westar Energy, Inc., 123 F.E.R.C. ¶ 61,252, at ¶ 21 (2008); Duke Energy Carolinas, LLC, 123 F.E.R.C. ¶ 61,201, at 62,290 n.10 (2008).

[121] See Petition of Respondent Federal Energy Regulatory Commission for Panel Rehearing and Suggestion for Rehearing En Banc, Me. Pub. Utils. Comm'n v. FERC, Nos. 06-1403 and 07-1193 (D.C. Cir. Aug. 8, 2008).

[122] Commissioners Kelly and Wellinghoff dissented from FERC's decision to seek rehearing of *Maine PUC*. Dissenting opinion available at http://www.ferc.gov/about/com-mem/kelly/8-08-08-maine-PUC.pdf. In the wake of *Morgan Stanley*, Commissioners Kelly and Wellinghoff concede that the public interest test applies to voluntary bilateral agreements but continue to believe that in some circumstances—in *Maine PUC* itself, an agreement in settlement of a rate dispute—the less deferential just and reasonable standard should apply to any contract modifications sought by non-signatories. See *id.*; see also, e.g., Entergy Servs., Inc., 124 F.E.R.C. ¶ 61,100, at 61,562 (2008) (Wellinghoff and Kelly, Commissioners, dissenting); PJM Interconnection, L.L.C., 124 F.E.R.C. ¶ 61,105, at 61,607 (2008) (Wellinghoff and Kelly, Commissioners, dissenting); Consumers Energy Co., 124 F.E.R.C. ¶ 61,093, at 61,519-20 (2008) (Wellinghoff and Kelly, Commissioners, dissenting).

[123] Morgan Stanley, 128 S. Ct. at 2745.

[124] *Id.* (quoting Verizon, 535 U.S. at 479 (alterations in original)).

[125] *Id.*

applies regardless of *when* a contract rate is challenged equally explains why the doctrine applies regardless of *by whom* a contract rate is challenged. A rate that is presumed just and reasonable because it was freely negotiated does not lose that quality when challenged by non-contracting third parties.

Applying the *Mobile-Sierra* presumption to third-party challenges is also the only sensible rule in the circumstances. Because the FPA governs the interstate transmission and sale of electric energy at wholesale,[126] every contract reviewed by FERC will affect third party retail customers down the line, and there will accordingly always be some nonparty who would be willing to act as a surrogate for the buyer. *Mobile-Sierra* would therefore provide no real protection for contracts if the public interest test were not applicable to such indirect challenges. At the same time, because the public interest analysis mandated by *Mobile, Sierra,* and *Morgan Stanley* by definition takes into consideration the effect of a contract on others, there is no basis for asserting that the uniform application of the doctrine disenfranchises third parties. Applying the *Mobile-Sierra* doctrine in no way curtails the Commission's ability to act for "the protection of the public interest, as distinguished from the private interests of the utilities."[127]

*B. The Justness and Reasonableness of Freely Negotiated Contract Rates Is Not Dependent on Filing and an Opportunity for FERC Review*

In *Mobile,* the Supreme Court recognized that the NGA "requir[es] contracts to be filed with the Commission."[128] Nonetheless, the First and D.C. Circuits have required the Commission to apply the *Mobile-Sierra* doctrine even where the contract had not been previously filed with FERC.[129] In our view, *Morgan Stanley* confirms that approach. As discussed, it squarely rejects the notion that *Mobile-Sierra* acts

---

[126] 16 U.S.C. § 824(a).

[127] FPC v. Sierra Pacific Power Co. 350 U.S. 348, 355 (1956).

[128] United Gas Pipe Line Co. v. Mobile Gas Servs. Corp., 350 U.S. 332, 338 (1956); see also Ark. La. Gas Co. v. Hall, 453 U.S. 571, 582 (1981) ("[T]he clear purpose of the congressional scheme" is to "gran[t] the Commission an opportunity in every case to judge the reasonableness of the rate."); 16 U.S.C. § 824d(c) (requiring that rates be filed).

[129] See Ne. Utils. Serv. Co., 993 F.2d at 960–62; Sam Rayburn Dam Elec. Coop. v. FPC, 515 F.2d 998, 1008 (D.C. Cir. 1975); Borough of Lansdale v. FPC, 494 F.2d 1104, 1113 (D.C. Cir. 1974).

"'as the equivalent of an estoppel doctrine,' whereby filing and an initial Commission opportunity for review prevents the Commission from modifying the rates absent serious future harm to the public interest."[130] By concluding that the Commission must apply the *Mobile-Sierra* presumption to a contract regardless of *"when* [the] contract rate is challenged,"[131] the Court eliminated any basis for suggesting that a party's failure to satisfy the statutory filing requirement or FERC's failure to provide itself an opportunity for initial review would permit the Commission to modify the contract under the lesser standard applicable to non-contract rates.

The requirement that rates be on file still serves an important role by putting third parties, including the Commission, on notice so they may, if necessary, challenge the contract rate under the public interest standard of *Mobile-Sierra*.[132] And *Morgan Stanley* does not—by any stretch of the imagination—render the Commission powerless to enforce this or any other valid notice requirement, as a seller that fails to make a requisite filing may be subject to enforcement action or substantial penalties under the FPA.[133]

Reading the filing requirement under the FPA as a notice requirement rather than a substantive prerequisite to making a contract rate effective, however, does have significant implications for the treatment of contracts under FERC's market-based rate regime,

---

[130] Morgan Stanley, 128 S. Ct. at 2746 (quoting David G. Tewksbury & Stephanie S. Lim, Applying the Mobile-Sierra Doctrine to Market-Based Rate Contracts, 26 Energy L.J. 437, 457–458 (2005)).

[131] *Id.* at 2745 (emphasis in original).

[132] While *Mobile* pointed to the filing requirement imposed under the FPA (350 U.S. at 338), it did not suggest that some different standard would be applicable to contracts that were being filed with and reviewed by FERC for the first time. Instead, *Mobile* also appeared to view the filing requirement as simply providing an opportunity for Commission action. See *id.* at 339 (The act "permits the relations between the parties to be established initially by contract, the protection of the public interest being afforded by supervision of the individual contracts, which to that end must be filed with the Commission and made public.").

[133] See 16 U.S.C. § 825h (granting the Commission the authority "to perform any and all acts . . . as it may find necessary or appropriate to carry out the provisions of this Act"); 16 U.S.C. § 825o (providing for fines of up to $1,000,000 or five years imprisonment, or both, for a violation of the FPA, and for fines of up to $25,000 for each day for violating a Commission rule); 16 U.S.C. § 825o-1 (providing for a civil penalty of up to $1,000,000 per day for a violation of Part II of the FPA or any rule or order thereunder).

despite the Court's disclaimer in *Morgan Stanley* that it was not directly considering "the lawfulness of FERC's market-based-rates scheme."[134] It is well established that the Commission cannot completely delegate to the market's invisible hand its responsibility to ensure that prices are just and reasonable.[135] The Commission believes its market-based scheme satisfies that responsibility because the commission only authorizes sellers to charge market-based rates if they can demonstrate that they lack market power and continue to abide by reporting requirements.[136] We agree. But the respect accorded market-based rate contracts should not depend on whether that view is vindicated.

Although the Court recognized in *Morgan Stanley* that the market-based regime implemented by FERC "has its critics[,]"[137] the Court held unequivocally that *Mobile-Sierra* requires FERC to presume that all contracts are just and reasonable, and it made clear that "any needed revision in [FERC's market-based scheme] is properly addressed in a challenge to the scheme itself, not through a disfigurement of the venerable *Mobile-Sierra* doctrine."[138] This strongly suggests that, regardless of the lawfulness of FERC's market-based regime generally or of any party's compliance with that regime's requirements, its contract rate would be presumed just and reasonable and could only be undone if it were found to be contrary to the public interest. Of course, any seller that enters into a market-based contract without obtaining market-based rate authorization

[134] Morgan Stanley, 128 S. Ct. at 2747.

[135] See FPC v. Texaco Inc., 417 U.S. 380, 397–98 (1974). The Ninth Circuit has held, based on *Texaco*, that FERC's market-based regime is lawful only if, through its reporting requirements, FERC continues to exercise oversight over sellers with market-based rate authority. See Cal., ex rel. Lockyer v. FERC, 383 F.3d 1006 (9th Cir. 2004).

[136] See State of Cal., ex rel. Lockyer v. British Columbia Power Exchange Corp., 99 F.E.R.C. ¶ 61,247, at 62,061–65 (2002); see also generally Michael J. Gergen et al., Market-Based Ratemaking and the Western Energy Crisis of 2000 and 2001, 24 Energy L. J. 321 (2003).

[137] Morgan Stanley, 128 S. Ct. at 2747.

[138] *Id.* At the same time, the Court acknowledged that both the D.C. Circuit and the Ninth Circuit have generally approved FERC's market-based scheme and recognized "that when a seller files a market-based tariff, purchasers no longer have the option of buying electricity at a rate set by tariff and contracts no longer need to be filed with FERC (and subjected to its investigatory power) before going into effect." *Id.* at 2741–42.

or adhering to FERC's reporting requirements could be deemed to be in violation of the Commission's rules, and therefore be subject to enforcement action or penalties.[139] Under *Morgan Stanley*, however, this possibility would not appear to impact the enforceability of the contract rate itself. That is in our view also the correct policy result, because it permits market reliance on valid contracts while not excusing parties from filing obligations or depriving third parties and the Commission of the chance to assess the effect of contracts on the public interest.

## VII. Conclusion

In holding that FERC must presume contracts to be just and reasonable, the Supreme Court reaffirmed the contemplated role of private contracts in the electric and natural gas industries and the long-term benefits conferred by contracts in terms of stability and investments. Under *Morgan Stanley*, a deal is a deal, absent extraordinary and demonstrable harm to the public interest.

---

[139] See *supra* note 133.

# Quanta v. LG Electronics: Frustrating Patent Deals by Taking Contracting Options off the Table?

### F. Scott Kieff*

The Supreme Court's unanimous decision in *Quanta v. LG Electronics*[1] may make it significantly more difficult to structure transactions involving patents. While this decision does make a group of players into winners in the immediate term for existing patent deals (this group includes any customer who, like Quanta, buys patented parts without buying a patent license), almost everyone is likely to come out a loser going forward.

The Court in *Quanta* decided that a patent license that LG Electronics sold only to Intel—and explicitly limited to exclude Intel's customers, like Quanta, and priced to reflect these modest ambitions—would be treated by the Court as extending permission under the patent to those Intel customers. The legal "hook" on which the Court hung its decision is the patent law doctrine called "first sale" or "exhaustion."[2]

The *Quanta* decision is likely to have a serious negative effect on the nuts and bolts of patent licensing agreements. On one reading, it stands for little more than the unremarkable proposition that the actual patent license contract at issue was just badly written. But that would be a simple matter of applying state contract law to the

---

*Kieff is Professor of Law at Washington University in St. Louis and Research Fellow at Stanford University's Hoover Institution where he runs the Hoover Project on Commercializing Innovation, which studies the law, economics, and politics of innovation, and which can be found on the web at www.innovation.hoover.org. Together with Troy A. Paredes and R. Polk Wagner, and on behalf of various law professors, he filed an amicus brief in *Quanta*, on which this essay is largely based and for which such contribution is gratefully appreciated. Comments are welcome and may be sent to fskieff.91@alum.mit.edu.

[1] Quanta Computer, Inc. v. LG Elec., Inc., 555 U.S. _____ , 128 S. Ct. 2109 (2008).

[2] *Id.*, 128 S. Ct. at 2118, 21–22.

underlying facts of the contract—not the type of issue that typically gains the Supreme Court's attention. So the real motivating force behind the Court's decision to take the case is probably something else. The extensive briefing and commentary, as well as the opinion's colorful dicta, all suggest that the true import of the case is the way it speaks about what patent contracting can be done—as a matter of Court-created policy for federal patent law.

If this view of *Quanta* is correct, then the decision may be remarkably important in several respects. It may greatly frustrate the ability of commercial parties to strike deals over patents. It may also stand as an example of a seemingly conservative Court acting in direct contravention of clear congressional action.

## I. Business Background

While patent law, like many areas of law, is a specialized field with its own jargon, the underlying business impact of the *Quanta* decision is accessible to an audience with no special understanding of patent law or practice. The business deal at issue in *Quanta* can be seen as an ordinary sales transaction between a sophisticated seller and a sophisticated buyer, with subsequent downstream sales from the initial buyer to additional sophisticated buyers (where all relevant parties well understood the express terms of the relevant contract). Put differently, this is not a case that invokes the standard state contract law and policy problems of unfairly sharp bargaining across a huge differential in bargaining power (such as the infamous rent-to-own businesses operated in underprivileged neighborhoods), or of a mistake in signing onto hidden terms, and so on.

In this deal, all parties knew the contract was for the proverbial slice of bread (a limited patent license to one) not the whole loaf (a license to all). Nevertheless, and contrary to the contract's wording and the parties' intent, the Court decided that this deal transferred the whole loaf.

To the extent the Court's decision is merely one of contract interpretation, suggesting that a better-written contract would have been respected by the Court, then the case is largely unremarkable. But what if the effect of the Court's decision is to render void any contract for a mere slice?

Sometimes a buyer and a seller want to strike a deal with each other for a slice of bread at a modest price, not a whole loaf at a much higher price. When the law makes such modest deals unenforceable, several bad outcomes are likely:

1. Neither side of a potential deal may get what it wants because it has to buy or sell more than it would like;

2. The deal may not get done because the parties can't muster the resources needed to match the high price;

3. The costs of structuring the deal may increase significantly as the parties attempt side agreements and other work-around deal structures to achieve their desired results while obscuring their true goal from the courts;

4. With the knowledge that their assets can simply be taken away by such a powerful legal rule, potential sellers may invest much less in those assets; or

5. The potential seller may engage in protective mechanisms that are both privately and socially costly but are designed to avoid leaving the asset vulnerable to free transfer.

The Court may not have intended these negative consequences— or to influence contract or patent law altogether—but they are the likely results of the high probability that clever lawyers and shrewd business people will try to exploit such an expansive reading in particular cases.

## II. Legal Background

In this case, LG Electronics, the patentee, entered into a written contract with Intel, a large, sophisticated party, to settle a set of disputes about patent infringement by giving Intel a limited license to the patents. The contract expressly limited the settlement's effect on third parties and was reached at a price that reflected these modest ambitions. It made sense for Intel to seek such a blanket settlement of intellectual property cases to buy freedom from suit for itself—but only itself—because the company might otherwise have been found guilty of inducing third parties to infringe when it sold its products.

Quanta and the other alleged infringers in this case are also large sophisticated commercial entities. They bought products from Intel with notice of the limited terms of Intel's license and the opportunity to negotiate a price in their sales contracts that reflected this limited reach of Intel's license. They paid for products they knew were not licensed in their hands and ended up receiving, through the Court's decision, a full license for free.

The crux of the infringers' argument, and the Court's opinion, is the patent law doctrine that goes by two names: "patent exhaustion" and "first sale." The doctrine has the effect of recognizing certain terms—such as a license under a patent to use a purchased product—that may reasonably be implied into a contract for sale of a patented article from the patentee.

In the case of a patentee's unrestricted sale of a patented product, the buyer presumably has paid the patentee not only for title to the physical product (a sale of product), but also for permission to use the product for its intended purpose (a license under the patent). In transactions like this, the first sale doctrine operates as a default rule, to recognize certain terms (such as a license under a patent to use a purchased product) that may reasonably be implied into a contract for sale of the patented article from the patentee.

Under well-established principles of law and equity, there are several routes to arriving at a conclusion about implied terms of a contract. Implied-in-fact terms may be found as a matter of interpretation from evidence of the parties' intent. Implied-in-law terms are imposed in the interest of fairness to ensure that both parties receive the rights for which they bargained. But, as courts have long recognized, the implied-in-law doctrine only provides a default rule, and differing terms in a sale—such as a sale accompanied by a promise to make only a single use of the patented article—will be enforceable as long as they do not violate some other rule of positive law. The logic of this view is straightforward: absent a direct conflict with positive law, there is no room for the law to imply terms when the parties themselves have provided their own agreed-to terms as a matter of their express and properly formed contract.

The Court's decision in *Quanta* seems to apply the doctrine more expansively and rigidly than it has long been applied. This expansive approach converts a deal involving express contracting over a limited license to one party into a blanket license to a host of other commercial parties, regardless of the efforts by all parties to contract for a more modest result at a lower price.

The central criticism of this essay is in no way directed at all efforts to explore arguments that might achieve the basic business result of patent license that was reached in this case. The essay would embrace any such arguments that are supported by the facts when made in accordance with long-recognized categories of legal doctrines, such as express license, implied-in-fact license (including by first sale), or license implied by equitable or legal estoppel. The central criticism of the essay is with the Court's decision to essentially convert the long-standing first sale doctrine into an *über*-immutable rule that an expressly limited license to one party will be deemed by the courts to also be a license to all those who are downstream in the market.

### III. Some Key Legal Errors

Applying a seemingly common sense approach, much of the Court's opinion pays close attention to the question of whether the products at issue are substantially covered by each of the relevant patents. The Court decides that there is a close enough tie between each product and each patent that the first sale doctrine is triggered. The Court concludes that because the doctrine is triggered when the product is infringing, it also is triggered when the product is likely to be used by the end customer in a way that will substantially infringe. Out of fear that patentees might otherwise engage in strategic claim-drafting to include both product and process claims in each patent, the Court also concludes that because the doctrine is triggered for product patents it is also triggered for process patents. This all sounds reasonable, at first blush.

By following this approach, the Court is essentially guessing about how questions of patent infringement might have played out in a hypothetical case in the past, and which transactions the parties would have made with each other against the backdrop of a final and non-appealable judgment in such a case. The Court does so using post hoc factual knowledge and with the certainty that it is the court of last resort.

When real parties have that degree of confidence in specific facts and legal outcomes, they can—and sometimes do—strike sales and patent license agreements that expressly or implicitly speak in terms of specific patent numbers and product model numbers or product lines. But what is well-known by any attorney involved in patent licensing, settlement negotiations around ongoing or potential patent litigation, or mediation of a patent dispute, is that what the potential infringer often wants is mere peace from future litigation risk (often called "freedom to operate").

Sometimes the potential infringer has such sufficient ties to its customers or input-providers that it wants to buy freedom for them as well—and is willing to pay a sufficient price. But sometimes, as in *Quanta*, the patentee and the potential infringer elect to strike a contract that buys peace only for that potential infringer, at a much lower price, leaving others to fend for themselves when and how they see fit. And while it might well be the case that key supplier companies such as Intel could act as de facto coordinators by passing along license costs to customers, the goal of the first sale doctrine has never been—and should never be—to mandate particular business models. One size rarely fits all, especially in rapidly changing markets like those involving innovation. While the law should allow parties the option to do such all-up-front deals if they so desire, it should also leave them the option to strike more dynamic deals, such as those that let each customer get exactly the terms it prefers at the time it develops that preference.

Not only does the Court's focus on issues relating to the substantiality of infringement miss the parties' key business interests, but it also leads the Court to write broad pronouncements about patent law that are analytically problematic in several respects. In so doing, the Court overlooks the basics of the U.S. patent regime, historical experience with such subjective approaches, express congressional action to jettison the problems created by that historical case law, and a host of practical problems created by the Court's ex cathedra rulings.

By using the term "patent exhaustion" instead of "first sale," the Court overlooks the very basics of the patent right itself. As Judge Giles S. Rich pointed out:

> "Patent exhaustion" is a misnomer. To think clearly about this fact, one must consider two things: (1) the meaning of "exhaustion"; and (2) the nature of the patent right. "Exhaustion" means the state of having been drained or used up completely. It assumes there was something there to begin with that could be used up. The patent right, as recognized by the Supreme Court in *Bloomer v. McQuewan*, 55 U.S. (14 How.) 539 (1852), and as more recently defined in 35 U.S.C. § 154, is the right to exclude others from making, using,

> offering for sale, or selling the patented invention. When a
> patentee of a patented article sells the article, how is he in
> any way exercising his patent right to exclude others from
> doing so? Clearly he is not. If he is, therefore, not using it
> at all—let alone using it up—how can he be exhausting it?[3]

The distinction between these two terms is not merely a matter of
which label is more descriptive. The terms steer the analysis in
different directions. By treating the patent right as having been used
up, the term "exhaustion" suggests an immutable state of affairs,
leaving no opt-out possible. In contrast, the contractual nature of
the first sale doctrine focuses attention on the actual terms of the
initial sale that is said to give rise to the license. This encourages
observers to determine whether the parties to that sale opted out of
the default terms otherwise implied into such deals.

By focusing on how near a product is to a patent claim, the Court
overlooks the long and bad experience we had in the United States
during the first half of the 20th century, and the express response
Congress enacted to correct that mess. During the early 1900s, courts
routinely focused on which element of a patent claim was "key" or
at the "heart of the invention" to determine questions of contributory
infringement, induced infringement, patent misuse, and antitrust.
The inquiry was so subjective that it became the plaything of the
judiciary, with most courts in the early part of that period routinely
ruling in favor of patentees on each issue, while most courts in the
later part of the period routinely ruling against patentees. One of
the two central motivating factors behind the congressional decision
to promulgate the 1952 Patent Act—essentially our present patent
statute—was to statutorily jettison this entire line of cases and create
an objective framework for determining patent infringement and
valid patent licenses.[4]

By imposing a strong mandatory rule, the *Quanta* Court interferes
with the freedom of large commercial parties to strike the deals that
are essential to avoiding and resolving disputes, and that help them

---

[3] Judge Giles S. Rich, Address at Sixth Annual Conference on International Intellectual Property Law & Policy, Fordham University (April 16, 1998) (as quoted in F. Scott Kieff et al., Principles of Patent Law 1144 (4th ed. 2008)).

[4] For a more detailed discussion see F. Scott Kieff & Troy A. Paredes, The Basics Matter: At the Periphery of Intellectual Property, 73 Geo. Wash. L. Rev. 174 (2004).

better invest in new products and services. Such deals may now not materialize because the high price can't be paid, or will have to be structured in costly, confusing, and convoluted ways to avoid the blunt impact of such an immutable legal rule. For example, parties interested in contracting for a limited patent license may have to first initiate litigation and then strike deals labeled as settlement agreements instead of patent licenses, in the hopes of having courts see their contracts more as matters of state contract law and general federal policy in favor of settling litigation rather than matters of federal patent policy as potentially controlled by *Quanta*.

The Court also may be endeavoring to force free transfers of portions of overall intellectual property value from owners who would like to have been able to sell or even give more limited licenses. If this is the case, then these parties may invest too little in such assets (that they now know can be taken away). They may also have to engage in protective mechanisms that are both privately and socially costly but are designed to avoid leaving the asset vulnerable to free transfer. The risk is not imaginary. Soon after *Quanta* came down, a district court in California held that sales on eBay were allowed for limited-distribution promotional CDs that were loaned, for free, to a small set of industry insiders for pre-release review and clearly marked with express restrictions against sale or further distribution.[5]

## IV. Some Red Herrings

The recent fashion among commentators—which seems to be popular with the Court as well—is to see the Court of Appeals for the Federal Circuit as creating new law rather than following Supreme Court precedent. But at least for the first sale doctrine, the Federal Circuit case law is required by the Supreme Court's jurisprudence, in addition to statute.

The Federal Circuit's first sale doctrine closely follows the longstanding precedents of the Court stemming as far back as *Adams v. Burke*, which held that "when the patentee . . . sells a machine or instrument whose sole value is in its use, he receives the consideration for its use and he parts with the right to restrict that use."[6]

---

[5] UMG Recordings, Inc. v. Augusto, No. CV 07-03106 (AJWx), 2008 U.S. Dist. LEXIS 48689 (C.D. Cal. June 10, 2008) (court allows sale under first sale doctrine).

[6] 84 U.S. 453, 456 (1873).

Even the early cases in the Court's first sale jurisprudence made clear that the doctrine arises from the interaction between patent and contract law. For example, the Court focused on determining that the particular restrictions at issue in the *Adams* case were "not contemplated by the statute nor within the reason of the contract."[7] Similarly, in *Mitchell v. Hawley* the Court acknowledged the importance of the freedom of contract, re-emphasizing the ability to restrict contractually the otherwise implied-in-fact patent license at issue in that case.[8] The Court stated, "Sales of the kind may be made by the patentee with or without conditions, as in other cases."[9] In effect, the Court treated the first sale doctrine as a default rule that parties could opt out of contractually.

The power to contract around the default first sale rule was clearly demonstrated in numerous cases over the ensuing years.[10] The view was also reaffirmed after the 1952 Patent Act in cases like *Aro Mfg. Co. v. Convertible Top Replacement Co.*, which pointed out that "it is fundamental that sale of a patented article by the patentee or under his authority carries with it an 'implied license to use.'"[11] The Federal Circuit has closely followed these precedents of the Court. For example, in *Mallinckrodt v. Medipart*, the court upheld a single-use restriction in a label license as long as the terms were not objectionable on grounds applicable to contracts in general—for example, if they violate a rule of positive contract law such as by being adhesionary or unconscionable.[12] Explaining a bit further, the court in *B. Braun Med., Inc. v. Abbott Labs.*, stated that the first sale doctrine

> does not apply to an expressly conditional sale or license. In such a transaction, it is more reasonable to infer that the parties negotiated a price that reflects only the value of the

---

[7] *Id.*

[8] 83 U.S. 544 (1872).

[9] *Id.* at 548.

[10] See, e.g., Waterman v. Mackenzie, 138 U.S. 252, 255 (1891); Keeler v. Standard Folding-Bed Co., 157 U.S. 659, 662–63 (1895); Gen. Talking Pictures Corp. v. W. Elec. Co., 304 U.S. 175 (1938).

[11] 377 U.S. 476, 484 (1964) (quoting Adams v. Burke, 84 U.S. 453, 456 (1873)).

[12] 976 F.2d 700 (Fed. Cir. 1992). The Federal Circuit's view is also shared by prominent decisions in sister circuits. See, e.g., ProCD, Inc. v. Zeidenberg, 86 F.3d 1447 (7th Cir.1996) (Easterbrook, J.) (non-commercial use restriction in shrink-wrap copyright license for computer program held valid and enforceable as a contractual limit on use).

"use" rights conferred by the patentee. As a result, express conditions accompanying the sale or license of a patented product are generally upheld.[13]

The *Quanta* Court focuses a great deal on the decision in *United States v. Univis Lens Co.*[14] But that case simply does not support the broad sweep the *Quanta* opinion gives it. To the contrary, the most that *Univis* can be fairly understood to have accomplished is a slight expansion of the first sale doctrine to apply regardless of whether "the patented article [is sold] in its completed form or . . . before completion for the purpose of enabling the buyer to finish and sell it."[15] In addition, *Univis* must be understood as what it expressly purports to be: a government enforcement case brought under the Sherman Act to enjoin the enforcement of contract requirements to maintain certain resale prices that were determined to be illegal under then-prevailing views of antitrust (and the related doctrine of patent misuse). Unlike in *Univis*, the contract terms at issue in *Quanta* have not been held to be illegal, and would not be today because prevailing antitrust jurisprudence now treats such vertical pricing restraints under the more permissive rule of reason analysis, instead of under the old per se illegality analysis.[16]

Indeed, as mentioned previously, the contract-based view of doctrines like first sale was a central animating principle behind the 1952 Patent Act, which remains the applicable set of patent statutes. As the Court has itself carefully recounted in the lengthy 1980 *Dawson* opinion reviewing this history, the '52 Act expressly revived contributory infringement by substantially narrowing patent misuse and statutorily overruled cases doctrinally related to *Univis*.[17] For many years before the '52 Act, patentees were severely limited in the exercise of the rights to sue or license those who induced or contributed to infringement by the too-often-applied doctrine of patent misuse, which stemmed largely from then-existing antitrust principles. Section 271 set forth express provisions for direct, induced, and contributory infringement, as well as an express provision that

[13] 124 F.3d 1419, 1426 (Fed. Cir. 1997).

[14] 316 U.S. 241 (1942).

[15] *Id.* at 252.

[16] See State Oil v. Khan, 522 U.S. 3 (1997); Leegin Creative Leather Prods., Inc., v. PSKS, Inc., 555 U.S. _____ , 127 S. Ct. 2705 (2007).

[17] See Dawson Chem. v. Rohm & Haas, 448 U.S. 176 (1980).

effectively allowed a patentee to sue, license, or even restrictively license anyone otherwise guilty of direct or indirect infringement without committing patent misuse.[18]

Ironically, the *Quanta* opinion's broad anti-contract reading of *Univis* is in conflict with the principles embodied in the '52 Act, as reaffirmed and extensively reviewed by the Court in *Dawson*. As a result, this approach more closely resembles those of the Warren Court in decisions like *Brulotte v. Thys Co.*,[19] than it does the reasoning of the Burger Court in decisions like *Dawson* and *Aronson v. Quick Point Pencil Co.*[20]

It also is fashionable to see cases like *Quanta* as highlighting the tension between two somewhat conflicting legal principles: one generally in favor of freedom of contract, and one generally in favor of freedom from unknown servitudes running with chattels. While the law is rightly skeptical toward restrictive servitudes, especially those that might run with the sale of ordinary chattels,[21] this policy it not so strong and far-reaching as to prevent the commonplace contractual restrictions at issue in limited patent licenses, which, it should be noted, are not even sales of chattels.

There is no need to overturn as an undue imposition on the freedom from servitudes, the long-standing first sale doctrine—which recognizes the enforceability of limited licenses because a number of existing companion doctrines already exist to protect legitimate interests of innocent third parties. As a result, it is possible for all parties to potential transactions to identify sensible categories of cases to which established principles of law or equity apply without resorting to case-by-case judgments of the social desirability of patents where none of the traditional grounds for intervention are

---

[18] See 35 U.S.C. § 271(d). See also Ill. Tool Works Inc. v. Indep. Ink, Inc., 547 U.S. 28 (2006) (holding that a patent does not support a presumption of market power and abrogating Morton Salt Co. v. G.S. Suppiger Co., 314 U.S. 488 (1942), Int'l Salt Co. v. United States, 332 U.S. 392 (1947), United States v. Loew's Inc., 371 U.S. 38 (1962), and Jefferson Parish Hosp. Dist. No. 2 v. Hyde, 466 U.S. 2 (1984)).

[19] 379 U.S. 29 (1964) (Douglass, J.).

[20] 440 U.S. 257 (1979).

[21] See Thomas W. Merrill & Henry E. Smith, Optimal Standardization in the Law of Property: The Numerus Clausus Principle, 110 Yale L.J. 1, 18 & n.68 (2000) (pointing out that "American precedent is largely, if not quite exclusively, in accord" with the view that "one cannot create servitudes in personal property").

present. But of central importance is the ability of parties to determine, *ex ante*, whether their case meets or fails the requirements of the legal tests that trigger these other doctrines when applied on their own terms. Put differently, it would be unfair and inefficient to bestow the protections provided by such doctrines without requiring a showing that all elements of their legal tests have been met. A broad reading of the *Quanta* decision would obliterate the nuances of existing legal principles that already accommodate appropriate concerns.

The types of contractual restrictions that implement a limited patent license are not foreign to property or contract law generally, are commonly used throughout consumer society, and are even more common in transactions among large commercial parties. Consider, for example, a typical lease for the rental of real or personal property containing a restriction against subleasing: Even the general view favoring the ability to assign and delegate rights and obligations in intangible assets like contracts fully respects the power of restrictive terms in an underlying contract governing whether or how such third-party rights in it can be created.

At the same time, courts have long recognized a host of legal and equitable doctrines to protect purchasers of patented goods from unfair surprise and charges of infringement when patentees have led the purchasers reasonably to think that no patent infringement will lie. Examples of these doctrines include implied-in-fact and implied-in-law licenses, equitable and legal estoppel, and the first sale doctrine itself. Also relevant are contract law doctrines governing contract formation, such as mistake, fraud, misrepresentation, duress, and both procedural and substantive unconscionability, among others.

The law has long recognized that patent law does not include a good-faith purchaser rule. Even an innocent infringer, without knowledge of a patent, who makes something covered by a valid patent claim with her own hands from materials gathered from land she and her ancestors have owned free and clear since time immemorial, is nonetheless liable for patent infringement. The infringement can be of patents that were in existence at the time the product was made. Subsequent patents also may be infringed. Absent a fully paid judgment from a victorious infringement lawsuit against a competitor to convert infringing products into licensed products, even innocent buyers who buy from an infringer can be sued for patent infringement. The Court and Congress have both expressly recognized that patentees may therefore face the daunting task of having to sue for infringement all customers who bought from their competitor and stepped in to help patentees by making available causes of action for indirect infringement (like those that motivated the underlying license at issue in this case):

> The court permitted the patentee to enforce his rights against the competitor who brought about the infringement, rather than requiring the patentee to undertake the almost insuperable task of finding and suing all the innocent purchasers who technically were responsible for completing the infringement.[22]

Indeed, the risk of widespread infringement across commercial transactions is so well-known that it has been expressly allocated as a matter of most states' commercial law to merchants regularly dealing in goods of the kind (who are by default required to warranty their buyers against infringement), and to buyers (who are by default required to warranty their sellers) if they provide their sellers with specifications for the goods.[23]

But this does not leave third parties unduly exposed because the doctrines of implied license by equitable estoppel and legal estoppel appropriately step in to fill needed gaps. Although the clearest grant of permission to engage in activities otherwise constituting patent infringement generally is an express grant from the patentee in a contractual license,[24] or even a settlement agreement following a suit for patent infringement,[25] courts have long recognized that the grant need not be express. In addition to the doctrine of first sale as an implied-in-fact contract, at least two distinct additional legal grounds exist to create authority by less than express contractual grant: (1) the doctrine of implied license by legal estoppel triggered when

---

[22] Dawson, 448 U.S. at 188 (citing Wallace v. Holmes, 29 F. Cas. 74, 80 (C.C.D. Conn. 1871)).

[23] See U.C.C. § 2-312(c).

[24] See McCoy v. Mitsubishi Cutlery, Inc., 67 F.3d 917 (Fed. Cir. 1995) (license is a contract governed by ordinary principles of state contract law).

[25] See Gjerlov v. Schuyler Laboratories, Inc., 131 F.3d 1016 (Fed. Cir. 1997) (suit for breach of settlement agreement is matter of state contract law and treble damages under patent law are unavailable).

a patentee has licensed or assigned a right, received consideration, and then sought to derogate from the right granted; and (2) the doctrine of implied license by equitable estoppel triggered by a patentee's conduct that reasonably leads another to act in reliance in such a way that it would be unjust to allow the patentee to exclude the actions taken in reliance.

The doctrine of implied license by equitable estoppel illustrates the broad reach of these existing doctrines. Equitable estoppel arises in those cases in which the active conduct of a patentee leads some other party to reasonably believe that it has a right to practice the patented invention. For example, as the Federal Circuit wrote in *Wang Labs., Inc. v. Mitsubishi Electronics of America, Inc.*:

> The record shows that Wang tried to coax Mitsubishi into the SIMM [short for "Single In-line Memory Module"] market, that Wang provided designs, suggestions, and samples to Mitsubishi, and that Wang eventually purchased SIMMs from Mitsubishi, before accusing Mitsubishi years later of infringement. We hold, as a matter of law, that Mitsubishi properly inferred consent to its use of the invention of Wang's patents.[26]

The court noted that "[a]lthough judicially implied licenses are rare under any doctrine, Mitsubishi proved that the 'entire course of conduct' between the parties over a six-year period led Mitsubishi to infer consent to manufacture and sell the patented products."[27]

Importantly, the Federal Circuit has also made clear that the inference of license can be eroded by several factors including: (1) whether the price paid for the relevant product is more closely linked to alternative non-infringing uses than infringing uses, and (2) whether the party asserting the reasonable belief about the license was ever actually in contact with the patentee in a way that would suggest communications about a license had occurred.[28] At the same time, the court has admonished that efforts by patentees to ward off any impression that the grant of a license should be implied will

---

[26] 103 F.3d 1571, 1582 (Fed. Cir. 1997) (relying on De Forest Radio Tel. Co. v. United States, 273 U.S. 236, 241 (1927)).

[27] *Id.* at 1581–82.

[28] See Bandag, Inc. v. Al Bolser's Tire Stores, Inc., 750 F.2d 903 (Fed. Cir. 1984).

be ineffective if made after the purchase of the underlying products.[29] Thus, whereas evidence of actual reasonable reliance can be essential to a claim of license under this doctrine, evidence designed to defeat reliance must have arisen at the appropriate time to support a claim of no license.

At bottom, that implied license by estoppel situations may be rare is not a reason to doubt the sense of the legal rule from cases like *Wang Labs*. It is a reflection of the sensible fact that in most high-value deals, the parties will negotiate adequate legal agreements for the benefit of all. Yet *Wang Labs* shows that the principles of equity will work as an important barrier against sharp conduct.

As with cases of laches, the particular applications of these doctrines of equitable and legal estoppel are likely to be fact-intensive, and their proper resolution necessarily requires the use of judicial discretion of the sort that the Federal Circuit applied in *Wang Labs*. But three points are worthy of notice. First, the use of the principles of discretion does not necessarily require a full trial. Some cases are clear enough for judgments as a matter of law. Second, the application of estoppel principles in no way upsets the balance of strong property rights needed for commercialization, as the patentee has it always within its power to avoid the conduct that, depending on the scope of the estoppel, leads to the loss of past damages, injunctive relief, or both. Third, in some cases, the extent of the reliance and the nature of the course of dealing could justify protection against injunctive relief—an issue not explicitly addressed in *Wang Labs*. Indeed, relief by estoppel may even be prospective, as in real estate cases like *Holbrook v. Taylor*.[30]

## Conclusion

The long-standing first sale doctrine has been a gap-filling default rule. It merely implies into contracts for sale of patented products from the patentee that are otherwise silent as to license some terms that reflect the parties' actual intent giving the buyer license to use the purchased products. The *Quanta* decision appears to upset this efficient and long-established landscape by doing violence to the

---

[29] See Met-Coil Sys. Corp. v. Korners Unlimited, Inc., 803 F.2d 684 (Fed. Cir. 1986).
[30] 532 S.W.2d 763 (Ky. 1976).

expressed intent of even commercially sophisticated contracting parties—as reflected in their actual contract terms that are designed to create only a limited patent license. Such license restrictions should be enforceable as long as they comply with contract law and other applicable areas of law. This would help parties resolve and avoid litigation, thereby helping them bring new products and services to market. For all these reasons, let's all hope that *Quanta* will be limited to its facts—including the particular contract terms at issue—which the Court hopefully saw as having merely failed as a matter of contract law to achieve on their own terms the limited license that would ordinarily be enforced under the long-established first sale doctrine.

# October Term 2008

*Thomas C. Goldstein and Ben Winograd\**

## Introduction

As the Court approached the start of October Term 2007, it faced a severe docket crunch. The justices had agreed to decide only 26 cases, well below the number needed to fill the fall argument calendar. At the conclusion of the summer recess, the shortfall forced the Court to expedite briefing schedules in numerous cases granted to avoid canceling the January argument session outright. Over the course of the term, it never caught up. While the Court managed to fill its calendar for three of the final four argument sessions, in total the justices heard argument in only 70 cases, the lowest figure in more than 50 years.[1]

By contrast, the Court enters October Term 2008 having accepted a comparatively plentiful 43 cases for argument. Ordinarily, that total would be sufficient to fill the Court's argument calendar well into January or February. In a switch from past terms, however, the Court has scheduled three arguments (rather than two) on most days in the October and November sittings, and is expected to hear only one argument per day during the spring. By frontloading the calendar, Chief Justice John Roberts has said, the Court would have more time to finish opinions over the winter recess and thereby avoid its usual crunch at the end of the term.[2]

---

\*Thomas C. Goldstein is a partner at Akin Gump Strauss Hauer & Feld LLP and co-head of the firm's litigation and Supreme Court practice. Ben Winograd is a special assistant to Akin Gump's Supreme Court practice and a law student at Georgetown University Law Center. Goldstein is the founder of SCOTUSblog, to which Winograd also contributes. The authors wish to thank SCOTUSblog writers Kristina Moore, Brian Sagona, and Max Schwartz for their contributions to this article.

[1] Three granted cases were dismissed before argument by mutual consent of the parties: No. 06-1346, Ali v. Achim; No. 07-110, Arave v. Hoffman; and No. 07-480, Huber v. Wal-Mart.

[2] Tony Mauro, Next Term: A Fatter, Faster Calendar for Supreme Court, Legal Times, July 3, 2008.

The cases for the term, of course, span an array of substantive areas.

## Voting Rights

For decades, federal law has forbidden nine states and nearly six dozen counties[3] with histories of racial voting discrimination from making any change to their election laws without first receiving the approval of either the U.S. Department of Justice or a panel of three federal judges in Washington. For many of the covered jurisdictions, most of which are located in the South, this "preclearance requirement," contained in section 5 of the Voting Rights Act of 1965, has long served as a source of resentment. Indeed, opponents of the Act see the obligation as a modern-day scarlet letter—no longer primarily intended to ensure minority participation in the political process, but rather to prevent certain regions of the country from escaping their racist pasts.

Thus, after Congress in 2006 overwhelmingly extended the law for another 25 years, few were surprised that it came quickly under attack. Calling the requirement nothing more than a "badge of shame," a municipal district in Travis County, Texas, sought a declaratory judgment that its continued application was unconstitutional. But last May a panel of three federal judges in Washington, D.C., disagreed.[4] Citing numerous examples of voting changes to which the DOJ had objected over the previous two decades, the panel found Congress had ample justification under the Fourteenth or Fifteenth Amendments to continue to impose the preclearance requirement. Shortly thereafter, attorneys for the district filed a notice of a direct appeal to the Supreme Court—the vehicle for review of such cases—setting up what, if the Court notes probable jurisdiction, will perhaps be the biggest case of the term.

The plaintiff, Northwest Austin Municipal District Number 1, was formed in the late 1980s to provide infrastructure and services to a planned subdivision of some 3,000 residents. Though situated inside the boundaries of both Austin and Travis Counties, the district,

---

[3] The states are Alabama, Alaska, Arizona, Georgia, Louisiana, Mississippi, South Carolina, Texas, and Virginia. For the complete list of counties, see http://www. usdoj.gov/crt/voting/sec_5/covered.htm.

[4] Northwest Austin Mun. Utility Dist. No. One v. Mukasey, 2008 WL 2221034 (D.D.C. 2008) (hereinafter "NAMUDNO").

under state law, remains independent of both. Elections for the district's five-person board of directors are held every two years. Formed more than a decade after the DOJ first required Texas jurisdictions to meet the preclearance requirements, the district claimed the most recent extension to be both costly and unfair. It noted that, because section 5 covers any "change in practices or procedures affecting voting," even the most minor alterations must first be submitted to Washington for approval. As one example, the district said it had to seek preclearance to relocate a polling place from a residential garage to a public school.

More important, given the progression in voting rights over the passage of time, the district argued that Congress lacked any present justification to continue imposing the preclearance requirements. It contended that by relying on what it characterized as an "ancient formula" in reauthorizing section 5 obligations, Congress created a regime that is both over- and under-inclusive. "The district and its voters are being punished for conditions that existed thirty years ago but have long since been remedied," the district's complaint states, "while jurisdictions where similar conditions exist today are spared because the conditions did not exist thirty years ago."

Both parties moved for summary judgment. In a 121-page opinion, the panel ruled for the DOJ. After quickly disposing of the district's claim that it was eligible to seek a "bailout" from the preclearance requirements,[5] the panel embarked on a lengthy analysis that ultimately affirmed Congress's power to extend section 5—whether under the "rational basis" test set forth in *South Carolina v. Katzenbach*[6] for legislation passed under the Fifteenth Amendment, or under the stricter "congruent and proportional" test established in *City of Boerne v. Flores*[7] for legislation passed under the Fourteenth Amendment.

Key to the panel's analysis was its conclusion, supported in a 15-page appendix, that numerous covered jurisdictions continue to

---

[5] The panel held that only states and counties—or entities that themselves conducted voter registration—could take advantage of the provision of the Voting Rights Act enabling political subdivisions to end their preclearance requirements.

[6] 383 U.S. 301 (1966).

[7] 521 U.S. 507 (1997).

resist racial equality in voting, and that the legislative record compiled by Congress in considering the 2006 extension was far more extensive than those the Supreme Court found adequate in two cases upholding Congress's legislative power under the Fourteenth Amendment—*Nevada Dept. of Human Resources v. Hibbs*,[8] involving the states' record of gender discrimination, and *Tennessee v. Lane*,[9] involving the ability of the disabled to access state courts.[10]

In the closing pages of its opinion, the panel characterized the district's burden in meeting the preclearance requirement as "trivial."

> Throughout its two decades of existence, the District has filed only eight preclearance requests, and the cost of these submissions—$223 per year—is modest, especially when compared to the District's average annual budget of $548,338. As the Attorney General points out, moreover, the District has never received an objection letter or been targeted by a section 5 enforcement suit. Nor has the District identified a single voting change that it considered but chose not to pursue because of section 5. Finally, given that state law controls most features of the District's electoral system, it has limited autonomy to adopt voting changes in the first place. In light of this evidence—all uncontested by the District—we find it impossible to conclude that section 5 imposes any meaningful burden on the District, much less an unconstitutional one.[11]

The district's jurisdictional statement is due at the Court by September 8.

A second voting rights case, which the Court has already agreed to consider, involves minority influence districts. It presents the question whether a racial minority group constituting less than 50 percent of a proposed legislative district can state a "vote dilution" claim under section 2 of the Voting Rights Act. The case, *Bartlett v. Strickland*,[12] arises from a dispute over North Carolina's 2003 redistricting plan, which split the General Assembly's 18th District

[8] 538 U.S. 721 (2003).
[9] 541 U.S. 509 (2004).
[10] NAMUDNO, 2008 WL 2221034, at *48.
[11] NAMUDNO, 2008 WL 2221034, at *59.
[12] No. 07-689.

between parts of two counties to create a district whose minority voting population neared 40 percent. The Board of Commissioners of Pender County later sued the state, arguing the plan violated a provision in the state constitution that barred dividing counties between different legislative districts. State officials said the move was required under section 2 of the Voting Rights Act, but the state supreme court disagreed, holding that, under the U.S. Supreme Court's ruling in *Thornburg v. Gingles*,[13] the Voting Rights Act was not implicated since the district did not contain a majority black population.[14] The Court, which had expressly left open the question on five prior occasions, including its recent decision in *LULAC v. Perry*,[15] granted the state's petition for certiorari in March, and oral argument is scheduled for October 14.

**Post-September 11**

From Abu Ghraib to Guantanamo Bay to "black sites" in Eastern Europe, U.S. military and intelligence personnel all but certainly engaged in gross maltreatment—some would say, torture—of detainees in their custody. While the allegations are seemingly less well-known, members of the Federal Bureau of Prisons—as well as top officials in the DOJ—similarly stand accused of committing (or at least condoning) abuse of Arab and Muslim detainees swept up in the months following the attacks of September 11. These latter accusations, implicating no less than former Attorney General John Ashcroft and FBI Director Robert Mueller, are the focus of the upcoming case *Ashcroft v. Iqbal*.[16]

The plaintiff in the case, Javaid Iqbal, was one of hundreds of Muslim immigrants arrested shortly after September 11 and held at the Metropolitan Detention Center in Brooklyn.[17] Initially arrested for using a false Social Security card, Iqbal was soon classified as a detainee of "high interest" to the FBI's ongoing investigation of September 11. Officials subsequently placed him in solitary confinement in the center's "Administrative Maximum Special Housing

[13] 478 U.S. 30 (1986).

[14] Pender County v. Bartlett, 649 S.E.2d 364 (N.C. 2007).

[15] 548 U.S. 399 (2006).

[16] No. 07-1015.

[17] Iqbal originally filed the suit with a co-plaintiff, an Egyptian named Ehad Elmaghraby, who subsequently settled his claim for $300,000.

Unit." For the next six months, prison staffers allegedly subjected Iqbal to gross mistreatment. Among the more disturbing allegations, Iqbal claimed guards disabled his toilet, conducted daily body-cavity searches, left his cell light on 24 hours per day, repeatedly confiscated his Koran, blasted the air conditioning after leaving him in the rain, and subjected him to frequent and baseless beatings.

Iqbal, who lost 40 pounds while in custody, ultimately pled guilty to document fraud and was deported to his native Pakistan. In 2004 he filed a federal suit not only against the immediate perpetrators of the abuse but also against Ashcroft and Mueller. According to Iqbal's complaint, both officials personally approved a policy shortly after September 11 requiring all detainees arrested in connection with the FBI's ongoing investigation to be held under harsh conditions until investigators had cleared them of all wrongdoing, regardless of any suspected link to terrorism.[18] Iqbal alleged that, in the absence of individualized suspicion, he and other detainees were segregated from the general prison population unit solely on account of their race, religion, or national origin. In his *Bivens*[19] action, Iqbal sought damages on numerous constitutional grounds, including violations of the First and Fifth Amendments, and under the Religious Freedom Restoration Act and the federal statute allowing lawsuits claiming a conspiracy to interfere with civil rights.[20]

The following year, U.S. District Judge John Gleeson denied most of the defendants' motions to dismiss. While noting that mere assertions that high-ranking executive branch members crafted unconstitutional policies would not have been sufficient to state valid claims, Gleeson found that outside evidence lent credence to Iqbal's accusations.[21] In particular, he cited a 2003 report from the Justice Department's inspector general suggesting Ashcroft's and Mueller's personal involvement in crafting the "until cleared" policy.[22] In mid-2007, over strenuous objections from the government, a panel of the U.S. Court of Appeals for the Second Circuit affirmed.

[18] The complaint describes Ashcroft as a "principal architect" of the policy and alleges Mueller was "instrumental" in its adoption and implementation.

[19] Named after Bivens v. Six Unknown Named Agents of Federal Bureau of Narcotics, 403 U.S. 388 (1971).

[20] 42 U.S.C. § 1985.

[21] Judge Gleeson also rejected the administration's contention that "special factors" surrounding the post-September 11 environment precluded relief under *Bivens*.

[22] The report is available at http://www.usdoj.gov/oig/special/index.htm.

Writing for the panel, Judge Jon O. Newman first rejected Ashcroft and Mueller's claims of qualified immunity. Newman wrote that any "reasonably competent" officer would have known the alleged policies and conduct violated the Constitution.[23] Newman likewise rejected the government's claim that Iqbal failed to satisfactorily allege Ashcroft's and Mueller's personal involvement. Reasoning that officials in their position would have been likely to take part in crafting policies concerning individuals arrested in connection with the FBI's investigation, the panel found Iqbal's complaint satisfied the "plausibility standard" necessary to proceed to discovery.[24]

The Supreme Court granted the government's petition for certiorari in June, and the case will be argued in December or January.[25] As one of the final cases argued during the Bush presidency, it may occasion calls to hold high-ranking members of the administration accountable for a range of post-9/11 detention practices that have garnered condemnation from the international community. By the time the decision comes down, the new president will have been sworn in. And whoever the new occupant of the White House happens to be, and regardless of what his supporters may wish, any president entering office presumably would not favor a ruling that makes suing his cabinet officers less difficult. The case also may allow the justices to clarify the standard for pleading requirements under their 2007 decision in *Bell Atlantic v. Twombly*,[26] which the government's petition characterized as requiring plaintiffs to do more than "create a suspicion of actionable wrongdoing."

Depending on the date on which the petition for certiorari is filed, the Court during the upcoming term may also agree to consider the president's authority to indefinitely detain a legal alien dubbed an "enemy combatant" inside the United States. In July, a fractured en banc panel of the Fourth Circuit held that the Authorization for Use of Military Force, passed in the wake of 9/11, gave the president authority to militarily detain any individual the government believes to be an enemy combatant, regardless of the location of capture or

---

[23] Iqbal v. Hasty, 490 F.3d 143, 174 (2d Cir. 2007).

[24] *Id.* at 175–176.

[25] It is possible, though probably unlikely, that the case will be scheduled for argument the day after the next president is sworn into office.

[26] 127 S. Ct. 195.

possession of U.S. citizenship.[27] Lawyers for the detainee, Ali Saleh Kahlan Al-Marri, a Qatari citizen studying at Bradley University and living with his family in Peoria, Illinois, at the time of his arrest, quickly indicated they planned to ask the justices to review the determination. If the petitioner does not seek an extension, the petition for certiorari would be due October 13, meaning the case could be heard and decided during the upcoming term. Meanwhile, a separate majority of the en banc court held that even assuming the president possessed authority to detain Al-Marri, Al-Marri had not received sufficient opportunity to challenge his enemy combatant designation. But in a statement[28] released after the decision, the DOJ indicated that it would not seek the Court's review of that holding.

### First Amendment and Related Issues

*Pleasant Grove City, Utah v. Summum*[29] arises out of a request by a little-known religious organization to erect a monument depicting the "Seven Aphorisms of Summum" in the city's Pioneer Park. Founded in 1975, the Summum believe, among other things, that the Old Testament's Ten Commandments are not a complete expression of nature's laws without inclusion of the seven principles on which their faith is based—the "Seven Aphorisms." Although Pioneer Park already houses multiple monuments donated by outside groups—including one depicting the Ten Commandments—the city denied the group's application. The city found that the proposed monument did not meet basic selection criteria; namely, that it neither related directly to the history of Pleasant Grove nor was donated by a group with long-standing ties to the community. The Summum promptly filed suit, claiming a violation of the organization's First Amendment right to free speech, and sought injunctive relief allowing immediate construction of the proposed monument. The district court rejected their claim.[30]

On review, the Tenth Circuit reversed the district court with instructions to grant the preliminary injunction.[31] The court first

[27] Al-Marri v. Pucciarelli, 2008 WL 2736787 (4th Cir. 2008).

[28] Available at http://www.scotusblog.com/wp/wp-content/uploads/2008/07/doj-statement-july-15.doc.

[29] No. 07-665.

[30] Summum v. Pleasant Grove City, 2006 WL 1794770 (D. Utah 2006).

[31] Summum v. Pleasant Grove City, 483 F.3d 1044 (10th Cir. 2007).

found that the speech at issue was private, not governmental. It thus rejected the city's argument that, after donation, the monument became government property and any associated speech was governmental in nature. Next, the court determined that the park was a traditional public forum, requiring any city restrictions on freedom of private expression to satisfy "strict scrutiny." Finding that the city would not likely survive such a standard of review, the Tenth Circuit ruled that when a government entity accepts and displays a monument donated by a private party, it must—absent a compelling interest—accept and display additional monuments from competing groups. The Tenth Circuit rejected Pleasant Grove's request for rehearing en banc by an equally divided six-to-six vote.

As it comes to the Supreme Court, the case presents two questions. First, is a monument donated to a municipality—and thereafter owned, controlled, and displayed by the municipality—considered government or private speech? Second, is a municipal park that displays monuments proposed by private parties a public forum? As framed by the petitioner, the decision really can be reduced to whether the First Amendment compels public parks to allow the construction of any and all monuments if they have previously accepted any privately donated monuments.[32] Argument has been scheduled for November 12.

Ever since the Court's 1978 decision in *FCC v. Pacifica Foundation*,[33] which upheld civil sanctions against the daytime radio broadcast of the late comedian George Carlin's monologue "Filthy Words," broadcasters have understood Federal Communications Commission policy to bar the use of repeated obscenities but otherwise to exempt the use of single or "fleeting" expletives. But the FCC changed that policy in 2004 in the wake of public and congressional displeasure over celebrities' use of expletives at various award shows.[34] The FCC levied no fines against the broadcasters carrying

[32] Petition for Writ of Certiorari at 3, Pleasant Grove City, Utah v. Summum (No. 07-665).

[33] 438 U.S. 726.

[34] In January 2003, U2 lead singer Bono declared his receipt of a Golden Globe Award to be "really, really fucking brilliant." The same year, Nicole Richie of Fox's television show *The Simple Life*, said during the Billboard Music Awards, "Have you ever tried to get cow shit out of a Prada purse? It's not so fucking simple."

the shows, but a host of networks brought suit against the commission for failing to provide a sufficient basis for the shift. A divided panel of the U.S. Court of Appeals for the Second Circuit agreed with the plaintiffs, dubbing the change "arbitrary and capricious" and hence invalid under the Administrative Procedure Act.[35] By remanding the case for further agency explanation, the panel did not reach the plaintiffs' First Amendment challenge to the new policy. In a long section expressly labeled as dicta, however, the panel "questioned whether the FCC's indecency test can survive First Amendment scrutiny."[36]

In its petition for certiorari, the FCC argued that the ruling forced it to choose between two per se rules: "allowing one free use of any expletive . . . or else adopting a (likely unconstitutional) across-the-board prohibition against expletives."[37] Acknowledging that the justices infrequently review rulings remanding cases to agencies, the FCC nonetheless argued that because it had already presented its best explanation for the new policy, it was "clear that the Commission is unlikely to be able to say anything on remand that the court would find satisfactory to justify that policy."[38] The case, *FCC v. Fox*,[39] will be argued November 4, election day.

Meanwhile, in July, the Third Circuit struck down the FCC's fine against the CBS network and its affiliates over Janet Jackson's infamous "wardrobe malfunction" during the halftime show of Super Bowl XXXVIII. In that ruling, the court likewise found arbitrary and capricious the FCC's change of policy to permit punishment for fleeting exposure of obscene visual (non-verbal) images. In so ruling, the court suggested that the FCC might lack the authority under federal law to treat words and images differently. If the FCC wishes to apply its authority broadly, "to reach all varieties of indecent content," the court said, this "requires that the FCC treat words and images interchangeably."[40]

---

[35] Fox TV Stations, Inc. v. FCC, 489 F.3d 444 (2d Cir. 2007).

[36] *Id.* at 465.

[37] Pet. Br., FCC v. Fox, No. 07-582.

[38] *Id.* at 26.

[39] No. 07-582.

[40] CBS v. FCC, 2008 WL 2789307, at *13, n.13 (3d Cir. July 21, 2008).

At the justices' opening conference in September, the Court will consider two other controversial First Amendment petitions. *Stanton, et al. v. Arizona Life Coalition, et al.*,[41] involves First Amendment free speech rights as applied to specialty license plate programs. Arizona Life Coalition, an anti-abortion group, applied in 2002 for a specialty plate displaying the organization's motto "Choose Life." Although the Arizona Department of Transportation certified the request as meeting statutory requirements, the state License Plate Commission denied the application. The commission did not provide a rationale for this decision, but earlier debate indicated concerns over whether the public would infer state endorsement of the pro-life message.

Arizona Life Coalition filed suit in district court, contending the commission violated its First Amendment right to free speech by arbitrarily denying the application. The district court granted summary judgment in favor of the government.[42] On appeal, the Ninth Circuit found that messaging conveyed through specialty plates, although possessing some aspects of governmental speech, represents primarily private speech.[43] Further, by establishing the specialty license plate program, Arizona created a "limited public forum" for all organizations meeting established statutory requirements. Because denial of the Arizona Life Coalition application was not grounded in those statutory requirements, the Ninth Circuit reversed the district court's decision, citing a violation of the coalition's constitutional rights to free speech.

The other pending petition, *Smith v. Al-Amin*,[44] asks whether the opening (but not reading) of a prison inmate's legal mail amounts to a free speech violation distinct from a Sixth Amendment access-to-courts claim. The prisoner, Jamil Al-Amin,[45] claimed that correctional facility personnel repeatedly opened his legal correspondence outside of his presence—specifically, mail from his wife, an attorney, that was clearly marked as attorney-client privileged. The district court ruled for Al-Amin and the Eleventh Circuit affirmed, reasoning

[41] No. 07-1366.

[42] Arizona Life Coal., Inc. v. Stanton, 2005 WL 2412811 (D. Ariz. 2005).

[43] Arizona Life Coal., Inc. v. Stanton, 515 F.3d 956 (9th Cir. 2008).

[44] No. 07-1485.

[45] Before converting to Islam, Al-Amin was formerly known as H. Rap Brown and was a high-ranking member of both the Student Nonviolent Coordinating Committee and the Black Panther Party in the mid-1960s.

that by repeatedly and knowingly opening the prisoner's privileged mail, the correctional facility inhibited and chilled Al-Amin's mail communications with his attorney,[46] which, though not causing actual injury, violated Al-Amin's First Amendment right to free speech.

## Separation of Powers

In *Winter, Secretary of the Navy v. Natural Resources Defense Council,*[47] the Supreme Court has agreed to determine whether the National Environmental Policy Act compels the U.S. Navy to limit its use of mid-frequency active (MFA) high-powered sonar, despite presidential intervention on the basis of national security.

The respondents, a coalition of environmental organizations, claim that the Navy's use of MFA sonar during pre-deployment joint exercises is harmful to marine mammals. Citing that risk, the Natural Resources Defense Council filed suit in federal court seeking to compel the Navy to complete an environmental impact statement (EIS). The district court found a likelihood that the exercises were harmful to marine life and that the Navy had failed to comply with NEPA by failing to complete an EIS in advance of the exercises. It enjoined the Navy's use of MFA sonar.[48] In the order, the district court severely restricted the Navy's use of the sonar when marine mammals were, or could be expected to be, within close proximity of the naval strike groups.

In short order, the chief of naval operations concluded that the injunction unacceptably risked training and readiness and thus the effectiveness and safety of naval units scheduled to deploy during a time of war. The president agreed, determined that use of MFA sonar during the exercises was "essential to National Security," and exempted the Navy from the governing provisions. Concurrently, the Council on Environmental Quality, applying a longstanding regulation, found "emergency circumstances" for permitting the Navy's compliance with NEPA without completion of the EIS. The actions of both the president and the CEQ would have allowed

---

[46] Al-Amin v. Smith, 511 F.3d 1317 (11th Cir. 2007).

[47] No. 07-1239.

[48] NRDC v. Winter, 2007 WL 2481037 (C.D. Cal. 2007).

the Navy to go ahead with the planned exercises off the coast of southern California.

In February 2008, a Ninth Circuit panel found that the CEQ lacked authority to provide a waiver of the EIS requirement and affirmed the preliminary injunction.[49] In so ruling, however, the court of appeals modified the order to allow the use of sonar during "critical points" of the exercise, albeit at lower levels when marine mammals are present.

At the administration's urging, the Supreme Court has agreed to review whether the CEQ permissibly construed its own regulation in finding "emergency circumstances" and allowing the presidential waiver, and whether the injunction is inconsistent with established equitable principles limiting discretionary injunctive relief. At the solicitor general's request, the Court moved the argument up to October 8 because of possible complications (including mootness) if heard later.

Among pending petitions, the justices will consider a major Appointments Clause challenge that threatens to scuttle years of rulings of the Patent and Trademark Office. The case, *Translogic Technology, Inc. v. Jonathan W. Dudas, Director, PTO,*[50] arises from legislation enacted in 2000 that delegated the power to appoint administrative patent judges to the director of the PTO. In this case, the petitioner—a party to recent litigation before the PTO's Board of Patent Appeals and Interferences—claims that one member of the board was appointed in violation of Article II of the Constitution, which allows Congress to "by law vest the Appointment of such inferior Officers, as they think proper, in the President alone, in the Courts of Law, or in the Heads of Departments."[51] The judge in question was appointed not by the head of the Department of Commerce, but by the PTO director.

## Business

Last term the Court considered four cases raising questions of federal preemption—and in all four it sided with Congress or federal

---

[49] NRDC v. Winter, 518 F.3d 658 (9th Cir. 2008).

[50] No. 07-1303.

[51] Art. II, § 2, cl. 2.

regulatory agencies over conflicting state laws.[52] For the upcoming term, the justices already have granted certiorari in two cases featuring large corporations seeking shelter under federal law against more consumer-friendly state statutes. *Altria Group v. Good*,[53] the first such case that will be argued next term, deals with the application of the Federal Cigarette Labeling and Advertising Act (Labeling Act) to "light" and "low tar" cigarettes. Altria Group, the parent company of Philip Morris, was sued under the state of Maine's Unfair Trade Practices Act. The plaintiffs alleged that Philip Morris violated the act by falsely claiming that light cigarettes were less harmful than regular cigarettes. On a motion for summary judgment, the defendants claimed the suit was explicitly preempted by the Labeling Act, which gives the Federal Trade Commission authority to regulate all cigarette labeling related to safety and health, and implicitly preempted by the FTC's 60-year policy of not challenging the "light" designation of certain cigarettes.

The district court granted the tobacco companies summary judgment but was reversed by the First Circuit. Applying the Supreme Court's decision in *Cipollone v. Liggett Group, Inc.*,[54] the panel found that because Maine's law imposed a duty "not to deceive customers," rather than a duty "based on smoking and health," the suit was not preempted.[55] It also found that because "the FTC has never issued a formal rule specifically defining which cigarette advertising practices violate the [FTC] Act and which do not," the Labeling Act did not expressly or impliedly preempt the Maine law.[56]

In a blow to Altria, the FTC has proposed nullifying the policy on which much of Altria's preemption argument rests. On July 12 the commission began soliciting public comment on revoking its

---

[52] Riegel v. Medtronic, Inc., 552 U.S.___, 128 S. Ct. 999 (2008); Preston v. Ferrer, 552 U.S. ___, 128 S. Ct. 978 (2008); Rowe v. New Hampshire Motor Transp. Assn., 552 U.S. ___, 128 S. Ct. 989 (2008); and Chamber of Commerce v. Brown, 553 U.S. ___, 128 S. Ct. 2408 (2008). A fifth case regarding preemption, Warner Lambert v. Kent, 552 U.S. ___, 128 S. Ct. 1168 (2008), was affirmed by an equally divided court (with Justice Kennedy recused). A sixth case, Exxon Shipping Co. v. Baker, 554 U.S. ___, 128 S. Ct. 2605 (2008), presented a preemption claim that was neither central to the outcome nor the reason the court granted cert.

[53] No. 07-562.

[54] 505 U.S. 504 (1992).

[55] Good v. Altria Group, Inc., 501 F.3d 29, 36 (1st Cir. 2007).

[56] *Id.* at 51.

general policy of not challenging cigarette descriptors like those at issue in the case. The decision followed the agency's filing of an amicus brief supporting the plaintiffs in which the commission argued that it "does not view respondents' lawsuit as undermining the FTC's policies in any way."[57]

The other preemption case before the Court, *Wyeth v. Levine*,[58] deals with Food and Drug Administration authority over the labeling of pharmaceuticals. The drug in question is called Phenergan, an anti-nausea drug produced and marketed by Wyeth. Phenergan, when in contact with arterial blood, can cause severe tissue damage; one method of injection, known as IV push, increases the likelihood of arterial exposure. Plaintiff Levine was injected with Phenergan using IV push to combat serious migraines. Due to arterial exposure, she developed gangrene and eventually was forced to have her arm amputated. In a suit filed in Vermont state court, the plaintiff argued that Wyeth's failure to ban IV push injection in its labeling of Phenergan constituted criminal negligence and also violated state failure-to-warn principles.

Wyeth argued the FDA's approval of its existing label—and rejection of a different label—barred all liability under state law. While conceding that Congress has not expressly preempted all state tort claims in the area, Wyeth claims that the FDA's rejection of a new label makes it impossible to simultaneously comply with both federal and state law. The Vermont Supreme Court rejected that argument, finding that the FDA's comment on rejection did not address the contested injection method and thus did not preempt more stringent labeling requirements under state law.[59] The case will be argued November 3.

For the third time in five years the Court will consider *Philip Morris USA v. Williams*,[60] a long-running dispute over a $79.5 million punitive damages award an Oregon jury granted to the widow of a longtime smoker. In 2003, after the Oregon Supreme Court initially

---

[57] Brief for FTC as Amicus Curiae Supporting Respondents at 14, Altria Group v. Good, No. 07-562 (cert. granted Jan. 18, 2008). See also Lyle Denniston, A second blow to tobacco appeal, SCOTUSblog.com, http://www.scotusblog.com/wp/a-second-blow-to-tobacco-appeal (July 9, 2008, 6:03 p.m.).

[58] No. 06-1249.

[59] Levine v. Wyeth, 944 A.2d 179 (Vt. 2006).

[60] No. 07-1216.

upheld the award, the Court vacated the judgment and remanded the case in light of its intervening decision in *State Farm Mutual Automobile Insurance Co. v. Campbell.*[61] In 2007, after the Oregon Supreme Court reaffirmed the judgment, the justices heard argument and once again overturned the award, finding that jurors may have sought to punish the tobacco company for harms to smokers not named in the case. According to the 5–4 majority, while harm to nonparties can help establish the degree of reprehensibility of a defendant's conduct, punitive damages cannot be used to directly inflict punishment for their alleged suffering.[62]

Earlier this year, the Oregon supreme court upheld the award once again—this time on the ground that Philip Morris had submitted a flawed jury instruction at the original trial that misstated state law. Having determined that the instruction in question was faulty, the Oregon court found that Philip Morris had procedurally defaulted its right to challenge the judgment. In its petition for certiorari, Philip Morris characterized the ruling as "nothing more than a pretext for the Oregon Supreme Court's refusal to protect Philip Morris's due process rights." The U.S. Supreme Court agreed to review that issue but declined to revisit the constitutionality of the award itself, which was many times larger than the $800,000 in compensatory damages the jury awarded.

Another major business case before the Court deals with the "predatory pricing" scheme known as "dumping"—when a manufacturer in one country exports a product to another country at a price either below the cost of the product or below what it charges domestically. *United States v. Eurodif*[63] concerns a specific step in the creation of uranium rods used in nuclear power plants. According to the United States, Eurodif, a French uranium processing company, took raw uranium imported from the United States, converted it into another product called low enriched uranium (LEU), and then "dumped" it on the U.S. market at illegally low prices. Pursuant to that determination, the Commerce Department levied a 20 percent tariff on those LEU products. The Court of International Trade nullified the tariff and the Federal Circuit affirmed, reasoning that the

---

[61] 540 U.S. 801 (2003).

[62] Philip Morris USA v. Williams, 549 U.S. 346 (2007).

[63] No. 07-1059, consolidated for argument with USEC v. Eurodif, No. 07-1078.

conversion of raw uranium into a more useful form "constitute[s] a provision of services, rather than a sale of goods."[64]

In its petition for certiorari, the government argued that the Federal Circuit had not shown proper deference to the Commerce Department and had "opened a potentially gaping loophole in the Nation's trade laws that will encourage domestic buyers and foreign producers to structure their transactions as contracts for 'services'"[65] rather than for goods. The case will be argued on November 4, election day.

### Criminal Law

The leading Fourth Amendment case next term, *Herring v. United States*,[66] asks whether the exclusionary rule should apply to evidence obtained incident to a warrantless arrest conducted due to the negligence of another law enforcement agency. In July 2004, Bennie Dean Herring was at the Coffee County, Alabama, Sheriff's Department to retrieve possessions from an impounded car. While Herring was at the station, Investigator Mark Anderson—who had a contentious history with the petitioner—arrived for work and, on a hunch, asked a records clerk to check a computer database to determine whether Herring had any outstanding warrants for his arrest. When no warrants were found in Coffee County, Anderson asked the clerk to check neighboring Dale County. Over the phone, a Dale County clerk said its database showed Herring had an outstanding warrant for failure to appear on a felony charge. As the Dale County clerk sought to retrieve a hard copy of the warrant, Anderson and another investigator left in pursuit of Herring, who by that point had driven away. After pulling him over and placing him under arrest, Anderson conducted a search and discovered methamphetamine on his person and an unloaded gun under the front seat.

Meanwhile, in searching for a hard copy of the warrant, the Dale County clerk discovered that Herring's arrest warrant had been recalled five months earlier but mistakenly had not been deleted from the database. The clerk called Coffee County to report the error, but the mistake was discovered too late. Herring was charged

---

[64] Eurodif S.A. v. United States, 411 F.3d 1355, 1357 (Fed. Cir. 2005).

[65] Pet. Br. at 16, United States v. Eurodif, No. 07-1059.

[66] No. 07-513.

on counts of drug and weapons possession and was sentenced to 27 months in prison. On appeal, he contended the district court erred by denying his motion to suppress the evidence obtained during the search. The Eleventh Circuit affirmed.[67]

*Herring* represents a follow-up to *Arizona v. Evans*[68] in which an error by a court clerk, rather than a law enforcement officer, resulted in an arrest. Seven justices held that the evidence seized incident to the arrest nonetheless should be admitted because "the exclusionary rule was historically designed as a means of deterring police misconduct, not mistakes by court employees."[69] In a footnote, however, three justices specifically declined to decide whether the same rationale would apply to mistakes made by law enforcement personnel.[70] *Herring* argues that negligent record keeping by law enforcement officers, especially in an era of police work reliant on computer databases, will be deterred by a strong reading of the exclusionary rule.[71] Oral argument is set for October 7.

The other granted Fourth Amendment cases are *Arizona v. Gant*,[72] which will address whether police officers must demonstrate a threat to their safety or a need to preserve evidence to justify a search under *New York v. Belton*[73]; *Arizona v. Johnson*,[74] regarding officers' abilities to conduct pat-down searches of car passengers not suspected of any crime; and *Pearson v. Callahan*,[75] involving qualified immunity for officers conducting a warrantless search based on a drug dealer's consent to an informant entering his home.[76] Finally, the pending petition in *Owens v. Kentucky*[77] asks whether the so-called "automatic companion" rule, under which police may frisk

---

[67] United States v. Herring, 492 F.3d 1212 (11th Cir. 2007).

[68] 514 U.S. 1 (1995).

[69] *Id.* at 14.

[70] *Id.* at 15.

[71] Petition for Writ of Certiorari at 18, Herring v. United States, No. 07-513.

[72] No. 07-542.

[73] 453 U.S. 454 (1981).

[74] No. 07-1122.

[75] No. 07-751.

[76] In granting certiorari, the Court also asked the parties to address whether the decision in Saucier v. Katz, 533 U.S. 194 (2001), should be overruled.

[77] No. 07-1411.

an individual following the arrest of his companion, violates the Fourth Amendment.

In the Sixth Amendment arena, in *Melendez-Diaz v. Massachusetts*[78] the Court will consider whether to extend *Crawford v. Washington*'s testimonial evidence rule to lab reports of forensic analysts prepared for use in criminal prosecutions. The petitioner, Luis Melendez-Diaz, challenged his 2002 cocaine trafficking conviction on the ground that he was denied the right to cross-examine the forensic lab technician who determined the substance found in his possession to be illegal narcotics. The Appeals Court of Massachusetts permitted prosecutors to introduce such reports without placing their authors on the stand. The case has implications for the national debate over wrongful convictions. In an amicus brief, the Innocence Project argues that at least half of the 218 nationwide exonerations based on DNA testing followed convictions based on faulty forensic evidence, such as reliance on unscientific methodology or flawed procedures, mistakes in reporting, or overstating the value of test results because of a scientist's bias toward the prosecution.[79] Oral argument is November 10.

Another Sixth Amendment case, *Oregon v. Ice*,[80] involving the right to a jury trial, will address whether the Court's holdings in *Apprendi* and *Blakely* apply to the state's consecutive sentencing statute. The defendant, Thomas Ice, was sentenced to 340 months' imprisonment, with three of the sentences running concurrently, on two counts of first-degree burglary and four counts of first-degree sexual abuse. Ice contended that the trial judge violated the Sixth Amendment in finding facts in setting the sentence. Oral argument has been scheduled for October 15.

Interesting criminal petitions on the horizon include *Lucero v. Texas*[81] and *Lee v. Louisiana*.[82] In *Lucero*, a capital case, a juror brought a Bible into the deliberation room and, after a straw vote over imposing the death penalty, the foreman read scripture to persuade holdout jurors who favored a sentence of life in prison. The petitioner,

---

[78] No. 07-591.

[79] Brief of Amici Curiae National Association of Criminal Defense Lawyers, et al, in Support of Petitioner, No. 07-591, at 14.

[80] No. 07-901.

[81] No. 07-1429.

[82] No. 07-1523.

sentenced to death for three murders, contends that his Sixth Amendment rights were violated by this outside influence. The petition also questions whether the Texas Court of Criminal Appeals—which rejected Lucero's Sixth Amendment claim and confirmed the capital sentence—erred by relying on jurors' after-the-fact affidavits to determine that the introduction of the Bible to the jury room was a "harmless error."

*Lee* asks the Court to overrule its 1972 decision in *Apodaca v. Oregon*[83] in which the Court held, in a splintered decision, that the Sixth Amendment's unanimous jury requirement does not apply to the states. The petitioner, Derrick Todd Lee, was convicted of first-degree murder for one of several alleged serial killings that occurred in Baton Rouge. The state subsequently linked him to two other violent crimes on the basis of circumstantial evidence and DNA analysis that Lee later sought to suppress. The state amended the charge to second-degree murder—a non-capital crime that, under Louisiana law, requires only 10 of 12 jurors to convict. At present, Louisiana and Oregon are the only states in the country that allow a felony conviction by a less than unanimous jury. In his petition for certiorari, Lee contends that legal developments and academic studies have undercut the reasoning of the *Apodaca* plurality.

## Civil Rights Cases

In *Imbler v. Pachtman*, the Supreme Court unanimously held that prosecutors enjoy absolute immunity from suit under 42 U.S.C. § 1983 for activities "intimately associated with the judicial phase of the criminal process."[84] At the same time, the justices declined to consider whether the same rule would apply when prosecutors act not as an advocate but as an "administrator" or "investigative officer."[85] Now, more than three decades later, the Court will have the opportunity in *Van De Kamp v. Goldstein* to clarify how the line should be drawn.

The respondent, Thomas Lee Goldstein, was convicted in 1980 of killing his neighbor in a darkened alley near his home in Long Beach, California. The prosecution's star witness was a heroin addict named

[83] 406 U.S. 404 (1972).
[84] 424 U.S. 409, 430 (1976).
[85] *Id.* at 430–431.

Edward Fink, who testified that Goldstein confessed to the crime while the two shared a holding cell. As in the past, authorities had promised Fink, a longtime informant, a lighter sentence in a separate case in exchange for his testimony. But that information was never relayed to the district attorneys prosecuting the case—or, as a result, to Goldstein's own lawyer. In 2004, federal courts granted Goldstein's habeas petition and ordered his release from prison on the ground that he was innocent. The former marine then filed a civil rights suit against not only the city of Long Beach and its police department, but also the heads of the office responsible for his prosecution. Specifically, Goldstein alleged that John Van De Kamp, the Los Angeles County district attorney at the time of his conviction, and Curt Livesay, his chief deputy, violated his rights under *Brady v. Maryland*[86] and *Giglio v. United States*[87] by failing to create a system that allowed line attorneys to share the identities of police informants with one another.

Finding the alleged conduct to be "administrative" rather than prosecutorial in nature, a district court denied the defendants' motion to dismiss in March 2006. One year later, a Ninth Circuit panel unanimously affirmed. The court of appeals reasoned that the Supreme Court had never addressed whether prosecutors retained absolute immunity against claims regarding the "failure to train, failure to supervise, or failure to develop an office-wide policy regarding a constitutional obligation."[88] But the court drew analogies to opinions from the Second and Third Circuits, which denied prosecutorial immunity against allegations that municipalities failed to train line prosecutors on *Brady* issues[89] or prevent them from introducing testimony from perjurious eyewitnesses.[90] Ultimately, the panel concluded that Goldstein's allegations concerned only how Van De Kamp and Livesay managed the District Attorney's Office, and not whether or how they chose to prosecute particular cases.

---

[86] 373 U.S. 83 (1963) (holding the Due Process Clause requires prosecutors to disclose evidence favorable to the accused).

[87] 405 U.S. 150 (1972) (holding, under *Brady*, that prosecutors must disclose promises to witnesses of benefit or leniency).

[88] Goldstein v. City of Long Beach, 481 F.3d 1170, 1174 (9th Cir. 2007).

[89] Walker v. City of New York, 974 F.2d 293 (2d Cir. 1992).

[90] Carter v. City of Philadelphia, 181 F.3d 339 (3d Cir. 1999).

In his petition for certiorari, Van De Kamp argued the Ninth Circuit's decision both narrows the circumstances under which prosecutors may receive absolute immunity and allows almost any claim barred against a line prosecutor to simply be restated against one or more supervisors for failure to provide adequate training and supervision.[91] On the merits, Van De Kamp further argued that, in contrast with investigative or personnel decisions, identifying and disclosing exculpatory information constitutes the type of core prosecutorial function for which district attorneys have long received immunity. And given that elected district attorneys technically oversee all prosecutions under their watch, Van De Kamp argued that the court of appeals' ruling will produce a "flood of lawsuits" from aggrieved defendants. The justices granted certiorari in April. Argument is scheduled for November 5.

In two other civil rights cases granted for the upcoming term, the Court will consider whether Title IX's implied right of action precludes the filing of a section 1983 suit against federally funded schools for allegedly unconstitutional sex discrimination; and whether the Supremacy Clause prohibits states from barring private damage suits against prison employees in state court. The first case, *Fitzgerald v. Barnstable School Committee*,[92] should resolve a circuit split over whether Title IX—the 1972 law requiring equal educational opportunities for male and female students—provides the exclusive remedy for claims of sex discrimination. The plaintiffs in the case, the parents of a female kindergarten student in Hyannis, Massachusetts, allege that an eight-year-old boy sexually harassed their daughter on the bus to school.[93] Unsatisfied with the school district's response, the parents filed suit claiming, in part, that school officials were more responsive to complaints of bullying from male students in general and gave their daughter's alleged harasser more favorable treatment in particular. Affirming the dismissal of the Equal Protection claim (which was brought under section 1983), the First Circuit reasoned that Title IX established a comprehensive remedial scheme that Congress intended to be the exclusive remedy for federally

---

[91] Petition for Writ of Certiorari at 9, Van De Kamp v. Goldstein, No. 07-854.

[92] No. 07-1125.

[93] According to the allegations, the older student, a third grader, made the victim lift up her skirt and pull down her underpants while on the bus.

funded schools that allegedly fail to address claims of sexual harassment.[94]

The other case, *Haywood v. Drown*,[95] involves a challenge to an unusual New York State statute stripping state courts of jurisdiction over all damages claims against correction officers. The statute requires such suits to be brought in a special claims court and only against the state itself. The petitioner, prisoner Keith Haywood, alleged that the law violates the Supremacy Clause by preventing state courts from hearing claims brought under section 1983. After acknowledging that the statute's constitutionality appeared "questionable" at first glance, the Court of Appeals of New York nevertheless concluded that the Supreme Court's decision in *Howlett v. Rose* permitted states to enact a "neutral state rule regarding the administration of the courts."[96] In other words, so long as New York barred its judges from hearing specific claims brought under state *or* federal law, "there is no Supremacy Clause violation because there is no discrimination against the federal claim in favor of similar state claims."[97]

Among civil rights petitions on the horizon, *Cerqueira v. American Airlines*[98] asks whether, and under what circumstances, airlines can be held liable for alleged racial discrimination in ostensibly refusing to transport passengers for safety reasons. The petitioner, a U.S. citizen of Portuguese descent, was removed from an American Airlines flight leaving Boston in late 2003 along with two Israeli passengers the crew mistakenly believed were speaking Arabic. Police cleared the men of suspicion, but a ticket agent told Cerqueira the airline made a corporate decision to deny him service. Finding American made the decision based on race, a jury awarded the petitioner $400,000 in compensatory and punitive damages. The First Circuit reversed with instructions to enter judgment for the airline, ruling that no reasonable juror could find that the captain, who originally

---

[94] In Davis v. Monroe County Board of Education, 526 U.S. 629 (1999), the Court held 5-4 that Title IX authorized damages claims against school boards found to have acted with deliberate indifference to claims of student-on-student sexual harassment.

[95] No. 07-10374.

[96] 496 U.S. 356, 372 (1990).

[97] Haywood v. Drown, 9 N.Y.3d 481, 488 (2007).

[98] No. 07-1495.

ordered the men off the flight, or the corporate manager, acted with discriminatory animus.[99]

## Employment Discrimination

In its 1974 decision in *Alexander v. Gardner-Denver Co.*,[100] the Supreme Court unanimously held that employees' right to litigate discrimination claims in federal court could not be foreclosed by a prior arbitration ruling under a nondiscrimination clause of a collective bargaining agreement. Seventeen years later, in *Gilmer v. Interstate/Johnson Lane Corp.*,[101] the justices held that individuals *could* be required to arbitrate civil rights claims under employment contracts to which they themselves, as opposed to a union, had agreed. Although it subsequently recognized the tension between the two cases, the Court explicitly declined to determine whether a union can waive employees' rights to have statutory discrimination claims resolved in a judicial, rather than arbitral, forum.[102] That is the question now before the Court in *14 Penn Plaza, LCC v. Pyett*,[103] a case from the Second Circuit.

For years, the plaintiffs, members of Service Employees International Union, Local 32BJ, worked as night watchmen at the defendant's commercial office building near Madison Square Garden. In mid-2003, in response to "post-9/11 security concerns,"[104] the defendant instead hired a separate (unionized) contractor to provide trained security guards for the building. The plaintiffs, all over 50 years old, were reassigned to what they deemed less prestigious and more physically demanding jobs.

Under the collective bargaining agreement, binding arbitration served as the "sole and exclusive" remedy for all employment discrimination claims—including any arising under Title VII, the Americans with Disabilities Act, and the Age Discrimination in Employment Act. The union, which had consented to the hiring of the new security guards, filed a grievance over the reassignment.

[99] Cerqueira v. American Airlines, Inc., 520 F.3d 1 (1st Cir. 2008).

[100] 415 U.S. 36 (1974).

[101] 500 U.S. 20 (1991).

[102] See Wright v. Universal Maritime Service Corp., 525 U.S. 70, 76–77 (1998).

[103] No. 07-581.

[104] Pet. Br. at 8, 14 Penn Plaza LLC v. Pyett, No. 07-581.

But prior to arbitration it withdrew the portion of the complaint alleging age discrimination. As the arbitration was pending on other claims, the plaintiffs filed a charge with the Equal Employment Opportunity Commission, and, after the agency issued right-to-sue letters, brought suit under the ADEA in federal court. Pursuant to the terms of the collective bargaining agreement, the employer sought to compel arbitration on the age discrimination claim. But a district judge denied the defendant's motion, and the Second Circuit affirmed.[105] Applying earlier circuit precedent, the panel found *Gardner-Denver* straightforwardly barred employers and unions from waiving workers' rights to resolve statutory discrimination claims in court. As such, it determined, any such waivers remain unenforceable, regardless of their clarity.

In its brief on the merits, the petitioner calls *Gardner-Denver* "not on point," maintaining the decision held only that arbitrators cannot issue binding decisions on statutory discrimination claims that the parties had not agreed to submit to arbitration in the first place.[106] Instead, the petitioner contends, the Federal Arbitration Act renders all promises to arbitrate enforceable so long as they are "clear and unmistakable."[107] The respondents counter that the underlying concerns of *Gardner-Denver* still apply—namely, the potential for conflict between unions' collective interests and workers' individual rights—and that, in any event, the language of the collective bargaining agreement does not grant employees themselves the right to arbitrate. Supporting the latter contention in an amicus brief, the local union notes that under the arbitration clause, "all Union claims are brought by the Union alone."[108] The Court has not yet scheduled argument, but the case almost certainly will be heard in December.

In another employment case, *Crawford v. Metropolitan Government of Nashville*,[109] the Court will consider whether Title VII's anti-retaliation provision protects workers from termination for cooperating in

---

[105] Pyett v. Pennsylvania Bldg. Co., 498 F.3d 88 (2d Cir. 2007).

[106] Pet. Br. at 15, 14 Penn Plaza LLC v. Pyett (No. 07-581).

[107] According to the petitioner, the collective bargaining agreement was crafted to meet the requirement of Wright v. Universal Maritime Service Corp., 525 U.S. 70, 80 (1998), that any waiver of rights to adjudicate statutory discrimination claims be "clear and unmistakable." Merits Brief at 6.

[108] Brief of Amicus Curiae the Service Employees International Union in Support of Petitioner, No. 07-581, at 7.

[109] No. 06-1595.

an employer's internal sexual harassment investigation. The employee in the case, Vicky Crawford, a school district payroll coordinator for some 30 years, told investigators that a supervisor about whom other workers had complained had repeatedly engaged in inappropriate behavior, such as asking to see her breasts, grabbing his crotch in front of her, and in one instance forcefully pulling her head toward his groin. Officials declined to discipline the supervisor under investigation, but allegedly fired Crawford and other employees who testified against him. Crawford brought suit under Title VII's anti-retaliation provision, which bars employers from taking adverse action against employees who either oppose the types of discrimination prohibited by the statute[110] (the "opposition clause") or participate in any investigation arising thereunder (the "participation clause").

Upholding the district court's grant of summary judgment for the employer, the Sixth Circuit ruled, first, that the "opposition clause" only protects employees who themselves protest unlawful workplace discrimination—that is, by actively complaining to their employer or to the government, rather than answering questions during an investigation initiated by others—and, second, that the "participation clause" applies only to statements made in investigations that stem from the filing of a charge with the EEOC.[111] The U.S. solicitor general, by contrast, argues that the ruling creates an "inexplicable gap" in Title VII's anti-retaliation coverage[112] that would dissuade employees from cooperating in internal employer investigations. Argument has been scheduled for October 8.

Among pending employment petitions, *Ricci v. Destefano*[113] already has received wide attention. In December 2003, the New Haven, Connecticut, Fire Department administered tests—which included both written and oral portions—for promotions to captain and lieutenant. In total, 118 applicants took the exams—68 of whom were white, 27 black, and 23 Latino. But among those whose scores qualified them to be considered for promotion, 17 were white, 2 were

---

[110] Broadly speaking, Title VII bars employment discrimination on the basis of race, color, religion, sex, or national origin.

[111] Crawford v. Metropolitan Gov't of Nashville, 211 Fed. Appx. 373 (6th Cir. 2006).

[112] Brief of Amicus Curiae the Solicitor General, No. 06-1595, at 15.

[113] No. 07-1428.

Latino, and none was black. The city's corporation counsel warned that certifying the results could form the basis of a Title VII disparate impact claim and, after a series of contentious hearings, the city's civil service board failed to muster the majority required for certification.[114] The plaintiffs, who were no longer eligible for promotion as a result of the decision, brought suit under Title VII and the Equal Protection Clause, among other claims. In effect, they argue that the city's professed desire to comply with federal anti-discrimination law was simply a pretext to discriminate against white test-takers. The district court granted the city's motion for summary judgment on the federal claims, and the Second Circuit affirmed in a per curiam opinion adopting the reasoning of the judge below. The full court split 7–6 in denying rehearing en banc.

### Conclusion

The Court's docket for October Term 2008 as of the summer recess—before the "long conference" that heralds a spate of cert grants a week before the new term begins—presents a number of very interesting cases, although few of historic importance. The term may well be most interesting for what it teaches about the Court's future in the wake of the appointments of Chief Justice Roberts and Justice Samuel Alito.

---

[114] The board split 2–2 on whether to certify the results of each exam. Another member was recused because her brother was a candidate for promotions. Ricci v. DeStefano, 2006 WL 2828419, at *7 n.5 (D. Conn. Sept. 28, 2006).

# Contributors

**Richard P. Bress** is a partner in the Washington, D.C., office of Latham & Watkins LLP. He is a member of the firm's litigation department and practices in the areas of appellate and constitutional litigation. Bress has handled scores of cases in the Supreme Court and courts of appeals for a diverse client base, including the U.S. House of Representatives, AOL, DirecTV, E.I. DuPont de Nemours & Company, Inc., HCA, Mirant, Monsanto, PG&E, Sempra, the Calvary Chapel ministry and the Republic of Peru. He is also a frequent commentator on appellate advocacy issues. Bress has particular expertise litigating disputes over federal agency action, including challenges to rules and orders of the Agriculture and Commerce Departments, EPA, FERC, FCC, HUD, and HHS. Before joining Latham, he served as an Assistant to the Solicitor General of the United States. During his tenure in the Solicitor General's Office, he argued six cases before the Supreme Court, drafted more than 100 briefs and petitions for certiorari, and assisted the Solicitor General in developing the government's position on a broad range of constitutional and commercial issues. Before his work in the Solicitor General's Office, Bress spent several years in private practice, engaged primarily in general and appellate litigation. Before entering private practice, he clerked for the Honorable Antonin Scalia and D.C. Circuit Judge Stephen F. Williams.

**Judge Janice Rogers Brown** sits on the U.S. Court of Appeals for the D.C. Circuit, a position she has held since 2005. Before her federal appointment, she was an associate justice on the Third Circuit of the California Court of Appeals and then on the California Supreme Court. Judge Brown graduated from California State University and received her J.D. from University of California School of Law. In 2004, she received an LL.M. from the University of Virginia School of Law. Before coming to the bench, Judge Brown was deputy legislative counsel in California's Legislative Counsel Bureau, deputy attorney general for the State of California, and deputy secretary and general counsel for California's Business, Transportation and Housing Agency. In 1990, Judge Brown briefly worked in the private sector as senior associate at Nielsen, Merksamer, Parinello, Mueller and Naylor LLP before joining Governor Pete Wilson's office as Legal Affairs Secretary. She was also an adjunct professor at University of the Pacific's McGeorge School of Law.

**David D. Cole** is a professor of law at Georgetown University Law Center and co-director of the Center for Transnational Legal Studies in London. As an attorney with the Center for Constitutional Rights, he litigated a number of major First Amendment cases, including *Texas v. Johnson* and *United States v. Eichman*, which established that the First Amendment protects flag burning. He is the legal affairs correspondent for *The Nation*, a regular contributor to *The New York Review of Books*, and the author, most recently, of *Justice At War: The Men and Ideas That Shaped America's War on Terror* (New York Review Books, 2008), *Less Safe, Less Free: Why America Is Losing the War on Terror* (New Press, 2007) (with Jules Lobel), and *Enemy Aliens: Double Standards and Constitutional Freedoms in the War on Terrorism* (New Press, 2d ed. 2005).

**Michael J. Gergen** is a partner in the Washington, D.C., office of Latham & Watkins LLP. He practices in the firm's finance department and is a member of the energy regulatory and markets group and the project development and finance group. He has extensive experience developing practical applications of economic theory, corporate finance and regulatory law to assist clients in a number of network industries, including electric power, railroads, and the transportation of natural gas and water, to compete successfully in an environment of market-based, open-access competition. He represents entities involved in electric generation and transmission, gas and water transportation, electric and gas marketing and trading, and investment and commercial banking, as well as foreign governments and financial institutions, on a variety of energy-related matters. He has assisted clients with matters before the FERC, DOJ, FTC, SEC, CFTC, Surface Transportation Board, International Chamber of Commerce, various state regulatory commissions, and numerous federal and state courts concerning ratemaking, trade regulation, antitrust, market regulation and compliance, and general regulatory and commercial matters. He has also served as an economist for an investor-owned public utility in New England, as well as an economic consultant for the California Energy Commission. He has been cited as a leading energy attorney in the 2008, 2007 & 2006 Chambers USA Legal Guides. He is a member of the Federal Energy Bar Association and the American Bar Association, and has given a variety of speeches on energy regulatory and policy matters.

**Thomas C. Goldstein** is partner at Akin Gump Strauss Hauer and Feld LLP, where he serves as co-head of the firm's litigation and Supreme Court practices. He has argued 18 cases before the Supreme Court, including matters involving federal patent law, class action practice, labor and employment, and disability law. In addition to practicing law, Goldstein teaches Supreme Court Litigation at both Stanford and Harvard Law Schools. Before joining Akin Gump, Goldstein was a partner at Goldstein & Howe, the firm he founded in 1999. He previously practiced law at Boies & Schiller, LLP and at Jones Day Reavis & Pogue. Since 2003, Goldstein has been principally responsible for SCOTUSblog, which is devoted to coverage of the Supreme Court and is widely regarded as one of the nation's premier legal Internet sites. Goldstein has been repeatedly recognized as a leading member of the bar. He is listed in the most recent edition of *The National Law Journal's* list of the nation's 100 Most Influential Lawyers. In 2008, *Legal Times* recognized him as one of the "90 Greatest Washington Lawyers of the Last 30 Years," and praised him for "transforming the practice" of Supreme Court law in the last decade. Among other recognitions, *The American Lawyer* lauded him as one of the "Star Laterals of the Year," and *Legal Times* named him as one of the leading appellate lawyers in Washington. In 2006, *Lawyers USA* named him one of seven lawyers in America who have positioned themselves to make a significant impact on their profession; *The National Law Journal* named him as one of the nation's leading attorneys under the age of 40; *The American Lawyer* recognized him as one of the nation's top 45 attorneys under the age of 45; and *Washingtonian* magazine named him one of the leading constitutional lawyers and one of a half-dozen attorneys to watch in the 21st century. Goldstein serves on the board of trustees of the Lawyers' Committee for Civil Rights Under Law, on the Amicus Committee of the ABA Intellectual Property Section and on the board of advisors of the Georgetown University Supreme Court Institute. Goldstein received his B.A. from the University of North Carolina and his J.D. summa cum laude from American University's Washington College of Law, after which he clerked for the Honorable Patricia M. Wald of the U.S. Court of Appeals for the D.C. Circuit.

**Erik S. Jaffe** is a solo appellate attorney in Washington, D.C., whose practice emphasizes the First Amendment and other constitutional issues. He is a 1986 graduate of Dartmouth College and a 1990 graduate of Columbia Law School, where he was the articles editor of the *Columbia Law Review*. Following law school, he clerked for Judge Douglas H. Ginsburg on the U.S. Court of Appeals for the D.C. Circuit, practiced for five years at Williams & Connolly LLP in Washington, D.C., clerked for Justice Clarence Thomas on the U.S. Supreme Court during the 1996 term, and then began his solo private practice. Since 1999, Jaffe has been involved in 24 cases at the merits stage before the Supreme Court. He represented one of the successful respondents in the First Amendment case of *Bartnicki v. Vopper* and authored Cato's amicus briefs in *Wisconsin Right to Life v. FEC, Randall v. Sorrell, McConnell v. FEC,* and *New York State Board of Elections v. López Torres*. Jaffe has also authored amicus briefs in cases such as *Republican Party of Minnesota v. Kelly* (judicial speech), *Zelman v. Simmons Harris* (vouchers), *Watchtower Bible and Tract Society v. Village of Stratton* (anonymous speech), *Veneman v. Livestock Marketing Association* and *United States v. United Foods, Inc.* (compelled advertising), *Boy Scouts of America v. Dale* (freedom of expressive association), and *United States v. Morrison* (Commerce Clause). He is a member and former chairman of the Federalist Society's Free Speech and Election Law Practice Group.

**F. Scott Kieff** is a law professor at Washington University in St. Louis with a secondary appointment as a professor in the School of Medicine's Department of Neurological Surgery and a research fellow at Stanford's Hoover Institution. At Stanford he directs the Hoover Project on Commercializing Innovation, which studies the law, economics, and politics of innovation, including entrepreneurship, corporate governance, banking, finance, economic development, intellectual property, antitrust, and bankruptcy. He also serves as a faculty member of the Munich Intellectual Property Law Center in Germany and previously has been a visiting professor in the law schools at Northwestern, Chicago, and Stanford, as well as a faculty fellow in the Olin Program on Law and Economics at Harvard. His law school courses include contracts, patents, intellectual property, contracts and intellectual property, commercializing intellectual property, law and economics of patents, and biotechnology; and he co-authored a leading casebook and treatise, *Principles of Patent Law*, now in its fourth edition. Before attending law school at the University of Pennsylvania, Kieff studied molecular biology and microeconomics at MIT and conducted research in molecular genetics at the Whitehead Institute for Biomedical Research. Having practiced law for over six years as a trial and patent lawyer for Pennie & Edmonds LLP in New York and Jenner & Block LLP in Chicago and as law clerk to U.S. Circuit Judge Giles S. Rich, he regularly serves as a testifying and consulting expert, mediator, and arbitrator to law firms, businesses, government agencies and courts. He served for the first two years of the Federal Circuit's Appellate Mediation Panel and in December of 2007 he was appointed by Secretary of Commerce Carlos Gutierrez to a three-year term on the Patent Public Advisory Committee of the Patent and Trademark Office, advises the Under Secretary of Commerce for Intellectual Property and PTO Director on matters relating to the policies, goals, performance, budget, and user fees of the patent operation.

**William J. Kilberg** is a partner with Gibson, Dunn & Crutcher LLP. He is a member of both the Executive and Management Committees of the firm, is the senior partner in the Labor & Employment Law Group, and has served as Partner-in-Charge of the Washington office. Kilberg counsels clients in all aspects of employee relations, labor relations, and employee compensation and benefits. He has appeared numerous times in trial courts on behalf of employers in class and collective actions under the myriad of employment laws, including ERISA, Title VII of the Civil Rights Act, and the Fair Labor Standards Act. He has argued many matters before the U.S. Courts of Appeals and has successfully argued two cases before the Supreme Court, *Egelhoff v. Egelhoff*, and *Murphy v. UPS*. Kilberg's practice also includes advocacy before congressional committees, the Departments of Labor, Justice, and the Treasury, the EEOC, the IRS, the

NLRB, and the PBGC. In 1973, he was appointed by President Richard Nixon and confirmed by the Senate as the solicitor for the U.S. Department of Labor (the youngest person ever to be appointed to a sub-Cabinet post), a position he held until 1977. He also has served as associate solicitor of labor for Labor Relations and Civil Rights, general counsel of the Federal Mediation and Conciliation Service, and as a White House Fellow and special assistant to Secretary of Labor George P. Shultz. Kilberg was also president of the White House Fellows Association in 1982–83, and was appointed by President Reagan to the Commission on White House Fellowships. He is a member of the board of the College of Labor and Employment Lawyers, the advisory board of the American Employment Law Council, the Legal Advisory Council of the National Legal Center for the Public Interest, and of the ERISA Roundtable. He also serves as an officer of the Labor and Employment Committee of the Federalist Society. In 2008, Kilberg was named as one of the Top Ten Leaders of the Pack: Employment Litigators in the nation by *Human Resource Executive* and *Lawdragon*. He was identified as the Best Employment Litigator in the Washington-metropolitan area in 2005 by the *Washington Business Journal* and as one of 100 "Superlawyers" by the *Washington Post*. *Legal Times* has characterized him as one of the "Twelve Leading Labor & Employment Litigators in the D.C. Area" and *Chambers & Partners USA—America's Leading Lawyers for Business* has listed him in every one of its editions. *Lawdragon* magazine has also named Kilberg as one of the 500 leading lawyers in the nation, describing him as "the labor lawyer of choice for corporate America." He is co-author of the monograph *Saga of Reform: Regulation of Worker Overtime* (National Legal Center for the Public Interest, 2004) and is co-author of the books *Employer's Rights and Responsibilities: Legal Dilemmas in the Changing Workplace*, and *Pitfalls for Japanese Employers in the United States*. He is the recipient of a number of awards, among them the League of United Latin American Citizens Award for Outstanding Service to the Spanish-speaking community, the D.C. Chamber of Commerce Arthur Flemming Award for Exceptional Public Service, and the School of Industrial and Labor Relations at Cornell University Judge William B. Groat Alumni Award for Outstanding Contributions to the Field of Industrial & Labor Relations. In 2007, Kilberg delivered the inaugural Donald S. Shire Lecture at the United States Department of Labor. Kilberg graduated from Cornell University and received his law degree from Harvard Law School.

**Stephanie S. Lim** is an associate in the Washington, D.C., office of Latham & Watkins LLP. She practices in the firm's finance department and is a member of the energy regulatory and markets group and the project development and finance group. Lim regularly provides advice on federal and state regulatory issues and regional market developments that impact clients in the energy industry, including issues arising under the Federal Power Act, Natural Gas Act and various state energy industry restructuring statutes. She has been involved in representations before the FERC, federal and state courts and state public utility commissions on behalf of independent power producers, project developers, energy traders and financial institutions. These representations have involved a range of issues relating to electric market design, energy asset acquisitions and divestitures, negotiated energy purchase and sale contracts, litigated contract disputes and matters relating to project development and permitting. She holds a J.D. and M.A. from Duke University and a B.A. from Amherst College.

**Edward J. Loya Jr.** is, at the time this *Review* goes to press, due to assume a new position as a trial attorney in the Criminal Division at the U.S. Department of Justice. He is a graduate of the University of California, San Diego, and Stanford Law School. At Stanford, he served as editor-in-chief of the *Stanford Journal of Law, Business & Finance* and was selected by his classmates to serve as co-president of the graduating class. He has clerked for the Honorable Harris L Hartz of the U.S. Court of Appeals for the Tenth Circuit and the Honorable S. James Otero of the U.S. District Court for the Central District of California. He also taught law for a semester at California Western School of Law. Loya's scholarly interests focus on white-collar crime, ethics, and criminal law and procedure. His writing has appeared in the *Cumberland Law Review, Stanford Journal of Civil Rights & Civil Liberties,* and *Stanford Journal of Law, Business & Finance.* Since 2005 he has contributed Supreme Court commentary to the Los Angeles and San Francisco Daily Journals.

**Clark Neily** is a senior attorney at the Institute for Justice, where he litigates economic liberty, property rights, school choice, First Amendment and other constitutional cases in both federal and state courts. For example, he served as counsel in a successful challenge to

Nevada's limousine licensing practices, which effectively prevented small business-persons from operating their own limousine services in the Las Vegas area and he was the lead attorney in the Institute's successful defense of the Mackinac Center for Public Policy against a lawsuit by the Michigan Education Association challenging the Center's right to quote the MEA's president in fundraising literature. He is currently leading IJ's opposition to a nationwide effort to cartelize the interior design industry through unnecessary and unreasonable occupational licensing. Neily is also the leader of the Institute's school choice team. Before joining IJ, Neily spent four years as a litigator at the Dallas-based firm Thompson & Knight LLP, where he received first-chair trial experience and worked on a wide variety of matters, including professional malpractice, First Amendment and media-related matters, complex commercial cases and intellectual property litigation. Neily received his undergraduate and law degrees from the University of Texas, where he was the Chief Articles Editor of the *Texas Law Review*. After law school, he clerked for Judge Royce Lamberth on the U.S. District Court for the District of Columbia. Most recently, Neily was co-counsel for the respondent in the landmark Second Amendment case, *D.C. v. Heller*.

**Roger Pilon** is the vice president for legal affairs at the Cato Institute. He holds Cato's B. Kenneth Simon Chair in Constitutional Studies and is the founder and director of Cato's Center for Constitutional Studies. Established in 1989 to encourage limited constitutional government at home and abroad, the Center has become an important force in the national debate over constitutional interpretation and judicial philosophy. Pilon's work has appeared in the *New York Times, Washington Post, Wall Street Journal, Los Angeles Times, Legal Times, National Law Journal, Harvard Journal of Law & Public Policy, Notre Dame Law Review, Stanford Law & Policy Review, Texas Review of Law and Politics*, and elsewhere. He has appeared, among other places, on ABC's Nightline, CBS's 60 Minutes II, National Public Radio, Fox News Channel, CNN, MSNBC, and CNBC. He lectures and debates at universities and law schools across the country and testifies often before Congress. Before joining Cato, Pilon held five senior posts in the Reagan administration, including at the State and Justice Departments. He has taught philosophy and law and was a national fellow at Stanford's Hoover Institution. Pilon holds a B.A.

from Columbia University, an M.A. and a Ph.D. from the University of Chicago, and a J.D. from the George Washington University School of Law. In the 1989, the Bicentennial Commission presented him with the Benjamin Franklin Award for excellence in writing on the U.S. Constitution. In 2001, Columbia University's School of General Studies awarded him its Alumni Medal of Distinction.

**Eric A. Posner** is Kirkland and Ellis Professor of Law, University of Chicago. His books include *Law and Social Norms* (Harvard, 2000); *Chicago Lectures in Law and Economics* (Foundation, 2000) (editor); *Cost-Benefit Analysis: Legal, Economic, and Philosophical Perspectives* (University of Chicago, 2001) (editor, with Matthew Adler); *The Limits of International Law* (Oxford, 2005) (with Jack Goldsmith); *New Foundations of Cost-Benefit Analysis* (Harvard, 2006) (with Matthew Adler); and *Terror in the Balance: Security, Liberty, and the Courts* (Oxford 2007) (with Adrian Vermeule). He is also an editor of the *Journal of Legal Studies.* He has published articles on bankruptcy law, contract law, international law, cost-benefit analysis, constitutional law, and administrative law, and has taught courses on international law, foreign relations law, contracts, employment law, bankruptcy law, secured transactions, and game theory and the law. His current research focuses on international law, immigration law, and foreign relations law. He is a graduate of Yale College and Harvard Law School.

**A.C. Pritchard** teaches corporate and securities law at the University of Michigan Law School. He is the author of *Securities Regulation: Cases and Analysis* and *Securities Regulation: The Essentials* (both with Stephen J. Choi). His current research focuses on the role of class action litigation in controlling securities fraud and the history of the securities law in the Supreme Court. Pritchard holds B.A. and J.D. degrees from the University of Virginia, as well as an M.P.P. from the Harris School of Public Policy at the University of Chicago. Pritchard served as senior counsel in the Office of the General Counsel of the SEC, where he wrote appellate briefs and studied the effect of recent reforms in the areas of securities fraud litigation. Pritchard has been a visiting professor in the law schools at Northwestern, Georgetown, and the University of Iowa. He has also been a visiting scholar at the Securities and Exchange Commission and a visiting fellow in capital market studies at the Cato Institute. Pritchard is on the editorial board of the *Cato Supreme Court Review.*

**Jennifer J. Schulp** is an associate in the Washington, D.C., office of Gibson, Dunn & Crutcher LLP, where she practices in the firm's litigation department. Before joining the firm in 2005, Schulp served as a law clerk to the Honorable E. Grady Jolly of the U.S. Court of Appeals for the Fifth Circuit. She received her law degree in 2004 from the University of Chicago, where she received both the Llewellyn Cup and the Thomas R. Mulroy Prize for excellence in appellate advocacy for her participation in the Hinton Moot Court competition. Schulp received an A.B. with honors in political science from the University of Chicago in 2001.

**Ilya Shapiro** is a senior fellow in constitutional studies at the Cato Institute and editor-in-chief of the *Cato Supreme Court Review*. Before joining Cato, he was Special Assistant/Advisor to the Multi-National Force-Iraq on rule of law issues and practiced international, political, commercial, and antitrust litigation at Patton Boggs LLP and Cleary Gottlieb LLP. Shapiro has contributed to a variety of academic, popular, and professional publications, including the *L.A. Times*, *Washington Times*, *Weekly Standard*, *Roll Call*, *National Review Online*, and from 2004 to 2007 wrote the "Dispatches from Purple America" column for *TCS Daily.com*. He also regularly provides commentary on a host of legal and political issues for various TV and radio outlets, including Fox News, CBS, WGN, Voice of America, and American Public Media's "Marketplace." He is also an adjunct professor at The George Washington University Law School and lectures regularly on behalf of the Federalist Society, The Fund for American Studies, and other educational and professional groups. Before entering private practice, Shapiro clerked for Judge E. Grady Jolly of the U.S. Court of Appeals for the Fifth Circuit, while living in Mississippi and traveling around the Deep South. He holds an A.B. from Princeton University, an M.Sc. from the London School of Economics, and a J.D. from the University of Chicago Law School (where he became a Tony Patiño Fellow). Shapiro is a native speaker of English and Russian, is fluent in Spanish and French, and is proficient in Italian and Portuguese.

**Daniel E. Troy** is vice president and general counsel at GlaxoSmithKline. Before joining GSK in September 2008, he was a partner in Sidley Austin LLP's Life Sciences Practice, as well its Appellate

Litigation group. Troy is also the former chief counsel of the Food and Drug Administration. Troy, who headed the ABA's Section of Administrative Law and Regulatory Practice from 2006 until 2007, is also the former chief counsel of the FDA, and was President George W. Bush's first appointee to that agency. In that capacity, he reviewed and approved major regulations and important guidances issued during that time. He played a key role in the drafting of the rule modifying the process by which generic drugs come to market, and successfully argued two Hatch-Waxman cases for the FDA. He also oversaw the agency's warning and untitled letters, helped raise the agency's focus on First Amendment issues, and played a principal role in the FDA's generally successful assertion of preemption in selected product liability cases. Before joining the FDA, Troy regularly argued cases in federal and state courts of appeals, including a successful appearance before the Supreme Court in *Vera v. Bush* (14th Amendment challenge to race-based redistricting plan). He participated in the briefing on *Brown and Williamson v. FDA*, and presented the First Amendment argument for the tobacco and advertising industries at the district court level. He also played a key role in *Washington Legal Foundation v. FDA*. He has filed numerous amicus briefs before the Supreme Court on issues such as the appropriate scope of constitutional protection for commercial speech, abstention, preemption, and other issues. He has also argued many challenges to FCC decisions, including *RTNDA v. FCC*, (successfully contended that FCC's 15 year delay in failing to revoke the personal attack and political editorial rules was unlawful), and *COMSAT Corp. v. FCC* (successful challenge to FCC imposition of fees on COMSAT). Troy has testified before the Senate and House Judiciary Committees, the House Committee on Science, and many other state and local bodies. He has given more than 200 speeches, speaking on topics including Hatch-Waxman reform, preemption, a variety of First Amendment and other constitutional issues, telecommunications, the role of the courts, and administrative law. He has also served on the editorial advisory board of the *Food and Drug Law Journal*, and is currently on the legal policy board of the Washington Legal Foundation, and the editorial advisory board of the FDA Enforcement Manual. Troy was listed by *Chambers USA* as one of the "Leading Lawyers in the District of Columbia" and is "Recommended" in Healthcare. He was named by *Washingtonian Magazine* as one of the

"Top Lawyers in Washington." From 1996 to 2000, Troy was also an associate scholar at the American Enterprise Institute, for whom he published the book *Retroactive Legislation*. He has also written at least 13 law review articles and book chapters, is a contributor to the *Heritage Guide on the Constitution*, and has published more than 55 articles in publications such as the *Wall Street Journal*, *Los Angeles Times*, *Legal Times*, *The National Law Journal*, *Weekly Standard*, *Washington Times*, *Commentary*, and *Policy Review*. He served in the Justice Department's Office of Legal Counsel from 1987 until 1990 and clerked for D.C. Circuit Judge Robert H. Bork in 1983–84.

**Ben Winograd** is a law student at the Georgetown University Law Center, a special assistant to the Supreme Court practice at Akin Gump Strauss Hauer & Feld LLP, and a contributor to SCOTUSblog. He holds a B.S. from Northwestern University.

**Rebecca K. Wood** is a partner in the appellate and products liability practices in the Washington, D.C., office of Sidley Austin LLP. A significant focus of her practice is product liability and mass tort litigation, as well as representing corporations, religious institutions, and states in appellate matters. She has served as national counsel to several major pharmaceutical companies in product liability litigation. She has significant experience in federal preemption, multidistrict litigation and coordination, federal removal and jurisdiction issues, class actions and multi-plaintiff cases, *Frye* and *Daubert* issues, and the defense of product liability cases. She also has represented clients in major product liability cases at the trial level, primarily for the purpose of briefing key motions and preparing high-exposure cases for potential appeal. Her appellate work includes merits and amicus briefing to the U.S. Supreme Court in numerous matters, including *Warner-Lambert v. Kent*, *Riegel v. Medtronic, Inc.* and *Wyeth v. Levine*, cases involving issues of federal preemption in the drug and medical device contexts. She has given a number of speeches on preemption-related topics including a presentation last summer to the British Institute of International and Comparative Law. Before joining Sidley, Wood was a law clerk to the Honorable Pasco M. Bowman II of the U.S. Court of Appeals for the Eighth Circuit. She is a graduate of New York University School of Law, where she was an editor of the *Environmental Law Journal*, and a semi-finalist in the Marden Moot Court Competition, and of Yale University, where she graduated magna cum laude and Phi Beta Kappa.

## ABOUT THE CATO INSTITUTE

The Cato Institute is a public policy research foundation dedicated to the principles of limited government, individual liberty, free markets, and private property. It takes its name from *Cato's Letters,* popular libertarian pamphlets that helped to lay the philosophical foundation for the American Revolution.

Despite the Founders' libertarian values, today virtually no aspect of life is free from government encroachment. A pervasive intolerance for individual rights is shown by government's arbitrary intrusions into private economic transactions and its disregard for civil liberties.

To counter that trend, the Cato Institute undertakes an extensive publications program that addresses the complete spectrum of policy issues. It holds major conferences throughout the year, from which papers are published thrice yearly in the *Cato Journal,* and also publishes the quarterly magazine *Regulation* and the annual *Cato Supreme Court Review.*

The Cato Institute accepts no government funding. It relies instead on contributions from foundations, corporations, and individuals and revenue generated from the sale of publications. The Institute is a nonprofit, tax-exempt educational foundation under Section 501(c)(3) of the Internal Revenue Code.

## ABOUT THE CENTER FOR CONSTITUTIONAL STUDIES

Cato's Center for Constitutional Studies and its scholars take their inspiration from the struggle of America's founding generation to secure liberty through limited government and the rule of law. Under the direction of Roger Pilon, the center was established in 1989 to help revive the idea that the Constitution authorizes a government of delegated, enumerated, and thus limited powers, the exercise of which must be further restrained by our rights, both enumerated and unenumerated. Through books, monographs, conferences, forums, op-eds, speeches, congressional testimony, and TV and radio appearances, the center's scholars address a wide range of constitutional and legal issues—from judicial review to federalism, economic liberty, property rights, civil rights, criminal law and procedure, asset forfeiture, tort law, and term limits, to name just a few. The center is especially concerned to encourage the judiciary to be "the bulwark of our liberties," as James Madison put it, neither making nor ignoring the law but interpreting and applying it through the natural rights tradition we inherited from the founding generation.

CATO INSTITUTE
1000 Massachusetts Ave., N.W.
Washington, D.C. 20001